William Archer Butler, Thomas Woodward

Sermons

Doctrinal and practical. Sixth Edition

William Archer Butler, Thomas Woodward

Sermons
Doctrinal and practical. Sixth Edition

ISBN/EAN: 9783337116590

Printed in Europe, USA, Canada, Australia, Japan

Cover: Foto ©ninafisch / pixelio.de

More available books at **www.hansebooks.com**

SERMONS

DOCTRINAL AND PRACTICAL.

BY THE
REV. WILLIAM ARCHER BUTLER, M.A.

LATE PROFESSOR OF MORAL PHILOSOPHY IN
THE UNIVERSITY OF DUBLIN.

SECOND SERIES.

EDITED,
WITH A MEMOIR OF THE AUTHOR'S LIFE,
BY THE VERY REV. THOMAS WOODWARD, M.A.
DEAN OF DOWN.

NINTH EDITION

London:
MACMILLAN AND CO.
1873.

[*The Right of Reproduction and Translation is reserved.*]

LONDON:
R. CLAY, SONS, AND TAYLOR, PRINTERS,
BREAD STREET HILL.

ADVERTISEMENT.

The Editor of the Sermons contained in this Volume has confined himself to the simple task of presenting a faithful transcript of the original manuscript. He is aware that upon many of the points, which are directly treated or incidentally noticed, much difference of opinion must exist; and he is in no wise pledged to defend all the arguments and interpretations of Scripture adopted by the lamented Author. A posthumous work is necessarily imperfect, and discourses intended for oral delivery would doubtless have gained much in terseness of style and diction by a careful preparation for the press. But, even in their present form, these Sermons will be found to be of no ordinary merit. They are marked by the same originality and vigour of expression, the same richness of imagery and illustration, the same large views and catholic spirit, and the same depth and fervour of devotional feeling, which so remarkably distinguished the preceding Series, and which rendered it a most valuable accession to our theological literature.

CONTENTS.

SERMON I.
CHRIST THE SOURCE OF ALL BLESSINGS.

Of Him are ye in Christ Jesus, who of God is made unto us wisdom, and righteousness, and sanctification, and redemption.—1 Cor. i. 30 . . . 9

SERMON II.
LIVING AND DYING UNTO THE LORD.

For whether we live, we live unto the Lord; and whether we die, we die unto the Lord.—Rom. xiv. 8 25

SERMON III.
THE HOPE OF GLORY AND THE CHARITIES OF LIFE.

It doth not yet appear what we shall be: but we know that, when He shall appear, we shall be like Him; for we shall see Him as He is.—1 John iii. 2 34

SERMON IV.
THE HOLY TRINITY.

And He showed me a pure river of water of life, clear as crystal, proceeding out of the throne of God and of the Lamb.—Rev. xxii. 1 55

SERMON V.
THE SORROW THAT EXALTS AND SANCTIFIES.

Blessed are they that mourn, for they shall be comforted.—St. Matt. v. 4 . 67

SERMON VI.
THE PURIFYING POWER OF TRIBULATION.

What are these which are arrayed in white robes? and whence came they? . . . . These are they which came out of great tribulation.—Rev. vii. 13, 14 78

SERMON VII.
THE GROWTH OF THE DIVINE LIFE.

I write unto you, little children, because ye have known the Father.—
1 JOHN ii. 13 92

SERMON VIII.
LESSONS FROM A MONARCH'S DEATH.
(Preached on the Sunday after the death of William IV.)

Thus saith the Lord God; Remove the diadem, and take off the crown!
EZEK. xxi. 26 106

SERMON IX.
DYING TO SIN AND THE LAW.

Ye are become dead to the law by the body of Christ.—ROM. vii. 4 121

SERMON X.
THE RESTORER OF MANKIND.

I will restore health unto thee, and I will heal thee of thy wounds, saith the Lord.—JER. xxx. 17 138

SERMON XI.
THE TRUE FAST.
(Preached for the Mendicity Institution, at St. Stephen's Chapel, Dublin, Sunday Morning, July 23, 1837.)

Is not this the fast that I have chosen? . . . . Is it not to deal thy bread to the hungry, and that thou bring the poor that are cast out to thy house? When thou seest the naked, that thou cover him; and that thou hide not thyself from thine own flesh?—ISAIAH lviii. 6, 7 155

SERMON XII.
THE WAY TO DIVINE KNOWLEDGE.
(Preached for Peter's Schools, Peter's Church, Jan. 28, 1838.)

If any man will do His will, he shall know of the doctrine, whether it be of God.—ST. JOHN vii. 17 168

SERMON XIII.
THE ASCENSION.
(The Ascension Day.)

While they beheld, He was taken up; and a cloud received Him out of their sight.—ACTS i. 9 188

SERMON XIV.
THE FOLLY OF MORAL COWARDICE.
Be not thou, therefore, ashamed of the testimony of the Lord.—2 Tim. i. 8 . 199

SERMON XV.
THE WILL OF GOD TOWARDS HIS CHILDREN.
It is not the will of your Father which is in heaven, that one of these little ones should perish.—St. Matt. xviii. 14 214

SERMON XVI.
STRENGTH AND MISSION OF THE CHURCH.
(Preached at Leeds Parish Church, Nov. 21, 1841.)

The Lord hath founded Zion, and the poor of His people shall trust in it.—Isaiah xiv. 32 227

SERMON XVII.
THE INGRATITUDE OF THE JEWS.
(Preached at St. Stephen's Church, June 4, 1837.)

And, behold, the whole city came out to meet Jesus; and when they saw Him they besought Him that He would depart out of their coasts.—St. Matt. viii. 34 238

SERMON XVIII.
THE ADVENT EXALTS HUMAN RELATIONS.
(Preached for the Western Lying-In Hospital, Dublin, December 2, 1838. Advent Sunday.)

And she brought forth her firstborn son, and wrapped Him in swaddling clothes, and laid Him in a manger; because there was no room for them in the inn.—St. Luke ii. 7 254

SERMON XIX.
DANGER OF BACKSLIDING.
(Preached at St. Anne's Church, Dawson Street, July 2, 1837.)

Nevertheless I have somewhat against thee, because thou hast left thy first love.—Rev. ii. 4 271

SERMON XX.
THE WORD OF GOD.
(Preached at St. Stephen's, Mount Street, June 18, 1837.)

The people pressed upon Him to hear the Word of God.—St. Luke v. 1 . . 287

SERMON XXI.

THE CLAIMS OF SPIRITUAL DESTITUTION.

(Preached at St. Patrick's, Nov. 28, 1844, for the Additional Curates' Fund.)

... Having hope, when your faith is increased, that we shall be enlarged by you, according to our rule abundantly, to preach the Gospel in the regions beyond you, and not to boast in another man's line of things, made ready to our hand.—2 Cor. x. 15, 16 302

SERMON XXII.

THE BLESSEDNESS OF SUBMISSION.

(Preached at the Magdalen Asylum, May 28, 1837.)

For my yoke is easy, and my burden is light.—St. Matt. xi. 30 . . . 317

SERMON XXIII.

THE HOLY TRINITY.

(Trinity Sunday, May 21, 1837.)

And the Word was God.—St. John i. 1 328

SERMON XXIV.

WATCHMAN, WHAT OF THE NIGHT?

(College Chapel, Friday, May 31, 1839.)

He calleth to me out of Seir, Watchman, what of the night? Watchman, what of the night? The watchman said, The morning cometh, and also the night: if ye will inquire, inquire ye; return, come.—Isaiah xxi. 11, 12 . 339

SERMON XXV.

THE PRINCIPLES OF THE FINAL JUDGMENT.

(Preached in behalf of the Association for the Relief of Distressed Protestants, St. Peter's Church, Dublin, Sunday June 13, 1841.)

And the King shall answer, and say unto them, Verily I say unto you Inasmuch as ye have done it unto one of the least of these my brethren, ye have done it unto me.—St. Matt. xxv. 40 347

SERMON XXVI.

ETERNAL PUNISHMENT.

(First Sunday after Trinity.)

Between us and you there is a great gulf fixed: so that they which would pass from hence to you cannot; neither can they pass to us, that would come from thence.—St. Luke xvi. 26 369

SERMON I.

CHRIST THE SOURCE OF ALL BLESSINGS.

1 CORINTHIANS I. 30.

Of Him are ye in Christ Jesus, who of God is made unto us wisdom, and righteousness, and sanctification, and redemption.

THE relation of Christ Jesus to the Church at large by covenant, the relation of Christ Jesus specially to those within that Church, who, fulfilling the terms of the covenant, make the promised blessings their own,—is the most wondrous of all conceivable subjects of thought. In the view of the inspired teachers it seems to absorb everything into itself, to comprehend everything, to transform everything; it is the sun in the vast heaven of their contemplation, attracting all around it, and by whose light alone every object, to be visible at all, must be seen. It is as if they had suddenly received new organs adapted to a new and spiritual illumination, and become utterly blind to every other;—it is as if ordinary men were but as those who walk in sleep, who come forth in their dreaming state uttering strange fancies of unreal and shadowy worlds that each builds for himself and none can communicate to his fellow; but that *these* men were given to burst the slumber, to see the vast, solid, immutable, reality of things, the true unshaken world,—the same for every unsealed eye that beholds it,—and thence evermore cried aloud to the dreaming millions around them—" Awake, thou that sleepest! and CHRIST shall give thee light." And all this, which is the unrivalled character of the New Testament, without a particle of mysticism, of cold unpractical exaltation. When men desert the homely familiarities of life, it is easy to glide into ecstacies; persons of warm fancies are perpetually doing so; and we know how such perilous excitement is pleasurably maintained as long as the dull realities of daily existence are forgotten; but one harsh thought of the actual world destroys all the enthusiast's power, unnerves the wings of fancy; it is,—to use a mechanical metaphor,—*the jet of cold water* which at once condenses all the evaporation! But the Apostles, in their hours of brightest thought, are at home among the minutest concerns of common life, they accompany us into every recess of domestic duty, their "bread of life" is "*daily* bread;" and perhaps they are never more truly elevated than when they discourse of the humblest topics of the Christian's household. The lark when half hidden in the clouds can discern the minutest speck among the grass and flowers; the spirit of Paul and John could look forth from its place of repose in heaven to see only the more distinctly every affection and duty and relationship that belongs to the lowliest earthly estate.

And thus nothing is forgotten, but all is sanctified. Life is here; but life blended with the Life of heaven. The great characters of human existence are unchanged, its relationships,—father and child, monarch and subject, master and servant, husband and wife,—are as before; but there is a seal upon them stamped by the signet of God,—they are all "in Christ." "Children, obey your parents, *in the Lord*." "Pay ye tribute, for they *are God's ministers*." "Servants, be obedient,—as the *servants of Christ*,—for ye serve *the Lord*." "Husbands, love your wives, *even as Christ loved* the church." This new and celestial connexion with Christ became the ground and motive of everything. The Church was intended to be the world, but the world of Christ; it was to be "the City of God," a specimen of what, even on earth and before the redemption of the body, a polity might be through every region of which the living graces of Christ were circulating.

And thus all the chief features of human life were preserved, the lines of the portrait remained; but they were coloured with a Divine pencil, the hues of heaven were on them, "into that Image" were they "changed, from glory to glory, even as by the Spirit of the Lord!"

From birth, then, (for men, to live eternally, must be "born of the Spirit," which is "the Spirit of Christ") to death (for men, to live eternally, must "fall asleep in Christ") He is the one central glory of the Church. The covenant is "the covenant of God in Christ," it is "His promise in Christ;" His purpose was "to gather in one all things in Christ;" that all might be "one in Christ Jesus," all "one body in Christ." We need not wonder, then, that in the passage before us He is set forth as the channel of every spiritual blessing; that on Him all is made to depend which fits the trembling sinner's soul for glory. But shall we *not* wonder at those, who, reading such things of this wondrous Being, seeing in Him the golden link that binds the spirit of a man to the God who inhabiteth eternity, can yet conceive that the nature of man, or of angel, was adequate to accomplish what *He* accomplished? to be "the express image of the Father's person," and thence to be to us, "from Him" as Fountain, our wisdom, our righteousness, our sanctification, and our redemption?

The Apostle in the context is speaking of the rejection of Christ,—his rejection among Jews and Gentiles. He declares that this great object,—a crucified Saviour,—was "to the Jews a stumbling-block, to the Greeks foolishness." In truth, it was a trying office the Apostle had to discharge. He had to publish to the world as its only Hope, a man despised by his own nation through life, and dying as a malefactor at their hands. It was not merely to vindicate the innocence of this man, for in that the world could have been little concerned; it was to declare Him "the power of God and the wisdom of God," to force them to see, through all the degradation and the horrors of this man's death, the eternal purposes of heaven stretching into dim infinity beyond them. It appears to me, —yet I do not offer it as more than a conjecture,—that the expressions of the Apostle in the text are fitted with a very peculiar adaptation to the passage preceding it. In the 27th and 28th verses he mentions four classes of persons and things which are concerned in this great work of salvation through Christ, though in different ways: the foolish things of the world, the weak things of the world, the base things of the world, the things which are not,—the absolutely non-existent. These are (in the mysterious working of God) the commissioned army of Heaven, these are the instruments by which the stupendous purpose of Divine mercy is to be wrought out. The result he states in the 29th verse, "that no flesh should glory in His presence," that the power might be clearly seen to be that of God alone,—seen, alike by those who are to receive the benefit, and those who are to be the means of bestowing it. But in the Divine Martyr of the Cross, the Church was ever to find its image and model; and hence (as it seems) the Apostle proceeds to invest *Christ* with an attribute answering in each instance to the classes already mentioned of His "servants and followers." "The foolish things of the world" shall "confound the wise," for Christ is made unto us "wisdom;" "the weak things of the world" shall "confound the mighty," for Christ, in being made to us "righteousness" or "justification," has already, in the weakness of humble humanity, overcome principalities and powers; "the base and despised things of the world hath God chosen," for Christ is made unto us "sanctification,"—the *source*, and the earnest, and the beginning, to "him that humbleth himself," of eternal and ineffable glory; the "things that are not" shall "bring to nought things that are,"—shall supersede, eclipse, and transcend them,—for Christ is made to us "redemption," He rescues from bondage thousands who till His redemption "were not," did not exist in the empire of Divine mercy,—He *shall* achieve that still more wondrous "redemption *of the body*," which I think to be the "redemption" mainly intended here,—whereby a frame virtually non-existent shall be re-created to immortality and blessedness unknown in "the things that are,"—in the present creation. And thus are the gifts which Christ bestows, ordained to be the glorious supplements of the infirmities of His Church; His wisdom, of its ignorance; His justification, of its helplessness; His sanctification, of its debasement; His redemption, of its nothingness.

But whether this was the *peculiar* course of thought in the Apostle's mind or not when he framed this memorable sentence, the instruction it contains remains substantially the same, the consolation it tenders to the dependent Christian equally unaltered. Let us for a while reflect on it; it is a miniature of the Gospel portrait. Wondrous words indeed are these! So few, yet so rich with boundless meaning; level to the capacities of children, profound enough to exhaust the conceptions of angels.

It is my wish to speak, for the present, briefly and simply of them, avoiding the harsh and unpractical controversies that have peculiarly harassed this passage, as they have done every passage of Scripture in direct *proportion* to the fulness of its blessedness of consolation,—for these are as insects that ever select the *ripest* fruit in the Eden of God to fasten on and to corrode. My own object (I will confess it) has long been to strive after that great and single thought of which all these controversies as to the Work of Christ in relation to the soul of Man,—His righteousness imputed and His holiness imparted,—seem to present us but detached and therefore lifeless portions. These disputations give us truth indeed; but truth partial and imperfect: it is as if one should labour to reflect the whole amplitude of Heaven in each of the scattered fragments of a broken mirror. And when these poor fragments are bound together in the framework of a human system, the case is little mended; they are fragments still; the joinings and the fissures are too palpable,—they still cross and distort the image. What then is that great and fundamental thought which, if any other, involves in it the fulness of the Gospel; on which all the breadth and fulness of Divine glory rests reflected; which suffices to all who would be humbly happy, while it presents unfathomed mystery to all who would dare be more? What but this—that as the basis of all knowledge of God is contained in the revelation of His threefold unity;—so the root of all Christian Faith as to God's Work in Man is in the parallel and not less wondrous truth, that we are called to be One with Him. Mysterious as is the oneness of the Father and the Son, it is not one whit more mysterious than the oneness of the Regenerate Spirit of Man with the same God in Christ Jesus. It is the perfection of this union which all the rival dogmas attempt, after their fashion, to express;—it is the full conception of this union which ought to supersede all these contentions, by placing us on a height from which we can afford to look down upon them all!

And now let us see how the thought is worked out in the words before us. St. Paul seems to have had in his mind (for many are the relations that meet together in a single passage of the Holy Ghost's writing) a conception of the gradual growth of the Christian spirit under the hand of Christ, from its dawn of grace to its final fulfilment in glory. He seems to view Christ as the great dispenser of the Father's treasures, accumulating gifts upon the Believer's soul till it brightens into the very Image of Himself; to view it rising higher and higher, as it is drawn nearer and nearer to Him, till the crisis of the final redemption is come and it is lost from the eye, hidden beyond the clouds. I do not myself much sympathise with the spirit of precise and uniform measurement that some persons profess to be able to apply to the history of the Christian Course; yet in this place stages of progress seem certainly intimated, blessings that surpass each other; the words are as the ladder in the Patriarch's vision, "set up on the earth, and the top of it reached to heaven; and behold, the angels of God ascending and descending on it."

In God Himself,—the pure, essential Diety,—the whole is based. "Of God are ye in Christ;" and Christ is "made unto us" all these blessings "from God." God is the ultimate Source and Cause of the entire; Christ acts as the minister of His mercies; a Person divine and human is the appointed Mediator between the human and divine. "From *Him*" or "out of Him," the verse begins, "are ye in Christ Jesus;" born of God Himself by the instrumentality of Christ, and known for the children of God when wearing the signature of Christ. As there is no other channel to God but Christ Jesus, so there is no other beginning or termination to the work of Christ Jesus but God. The language of Scripture on this point is wonderful, unfathomable. It would appear that, as regards the work of grace, God sees nothing from His throne but Christ Jesus alone and altogether; as if all else was covered with clouds and darkness impenetrable to the eye of Divine love. It would seem as though the radiance that issues on all sides from the Divine nature were separable into distinct beams; that every ray of mercy gathered through this medium to the world, while all beside and beyond it burst forth only to scorch and to wither. The Church is His Body; and it is only as His Body that it is known or numbered, in the Councils of Heaven. The mercies, whatever they be, that stretch beyond the Church in the scheme of grace, are but the diffusive blessings that spread around His mystical Body, even as the hem of His garment had healing virtue of old; they are still given to glorify Him, and as appendages of His royalty. But, as all descends *through* Christ, so all descends *from* God. The Divine nature is still sovereign in this mysterious economy; the Christian would be but an idolater if he failed to recognise this. In adoring

Christ with all the fervour of utter worship, you must look beyond the man; the imagination must, indeed, fail to conceive Him, but the Reason must learn to acknowledge the co-eternal "Word of God," who, "with God," "*was* God;" and to know in that infallible Being, one with the Father and the Holy Spirit, the last source of every blessing the human Jesus gives. "*Of God* are ye in Christ Jesus."

How, then, is this mysterious union wrought, by which we are thus connected with the Godhead by being "in Christ Jesus?"

Brethren, there are two senses in which such a question as this may be understood; two senses which I heartily wish, for the peace of the Church, had been oftener carefully distinguished.

If a man ask me, what is the *very nature itself* of the union which takes place between a Christian and His God through Christ,—what is the actual process by which the work of Christ becomes appropriated to us and so gains us this blessing, —I reply, that I know not, and in this world never expect to know. The subject, in this view of it, lies utterly beyond all human conception. Whether wrought within us or without us,—whether indwelling or imputed,—the process itself is wholly inconceivable to a being formed as man is. Explain it to the utmost, and upon any system soever, we must come at length to something we *cannot* explain; and to see this clearly from the beginning, is the best security from fruitless, and irritating, and dangerous disputation. The connexion between Christ and the Soul is as really a mystery as the conjunction of God and Man in the Incarnation. Something there must be,—something there is,—as Scripture most amply attests—*done for us* when we are indeed "translated into the kingdom of God's dear Son," of a nature to us unimaginable, of which we cannot be directly conscious, which is known only to the Eternal Spirit that works it. We only know, that from being "born of the flesh," "earthly, sensual devilish,"—we become "born of the Spirit," introduced into the family and household of God;—we only know, that there is an interchange by which as Christ became man without ceasing to be God, so is the Regenerate, without ceasing to be man, identified with Christ, and righteousness, holiness, immortality, all things;—but *how* this is wrought, or can be wrought, no human theory has ever explained, no wise man will ever think of *attempting* to explain. We adore the mercy, we enlarge upon the blessing, but we comprehend it not! We live a natural life, but no man has yet discovered what is the *principle* of natural life. We *see*, and rejoice in the noontide light; but no man can tell *how* it is that light affects the optic nerve and wakes it into apprehending the thousand hues and shadows of loveliness with which God has invested His creation! Our very thoughts and their course are mysteries whose sources we cannot sound. It is hard, is it? to understand how we can be one with Christ in His privileges? let us first try can we understand how we are able to entertain the question, to *think* of that or of anything!

But if a man ask the wiser question,—what are the *circumstances* of this union whose basis is hid in fathomless mystery? what are the Scriptural characteristics of the connexion? we can then reply by stating the *results* perpetually dependent on this blessed participation; the gifts by which this hidden glory makes itself known. We can reply with the text, that it is by Christ's being "made to us wisdom, and righteousness, and sanctification, and redemption." We can express Him by His effects. He is made to us Wisdom by enlightening us, Righteousness by justifying us, Sanctification by purifying us, Redemption by purchasing us into immortality. Yet, while thus insisting upon the results, Christ—the ground and cause of the results—must ever be included as part of the blessing; if it be folly to think to explain the fact, it is far more deadly error to forget it. In every one of these particulars, He is alike the Giver, the Gift, and the Object of the

Gift; in every one of them He is (as is intimated in the expression "made unto us") identified with His people in the spiritual bonds of the same body and blood.

We have spoken of the passage as designating a *progress* of blessings; let us contemplate the Christian Soul making its first step upon this path of peace; and *then*, as possessing in Him who gave the power to make that step, all the fulness of grace it can lead to!

Wisdom—the apprehension of the true and Divine knowledge—is just this first stage; the clearing of the eye of reason for the prospect itself of eternity and of God. Christ who gives it,—Christ who of old was declared under the title of "Wisdom,"—He also is the Object most prominent in the foreground of the Picture which spiritual wisdom presents to the awakened soul of the convert. Christ, I must repeat, is here declared to be " to us made Wisdom," not so much because He is the giver of wisdom as because He is the ground and *object* of it; not so much because He declares to us the truth as because He *is* the truth. He gives us knowledge in giving us Himself. It is as Light is said to *show* us all things; while in reality all we see is still only light itself. The revealer is also the revelation. It is *hence* that St. Paul speaks of this " wisdom of God in a mystery " as that which Jew and Gentile alike spurned;—like the unhappy seceders of our own day, the wisdom of Christ's words they might allow, but the wisdom that saw in Himself the *object* of His own language, that turned the eye of the Soul on Him not merely for what He said but for what He *did*,—not as an inspired Preacher only, but as a Divine King and Priest and Sacrifice also,—this they could not receive. They could tolerate Christ on the Mount, but not Christ on the Cross. And hence they lost the blessing; to such Christ was not " made wisdom;" for round the Cross all the truest glories of Divine wisdom gather; and they who will not study heaven *there*, can never know it. But oh, the blessedness of that soul which, undisturbed by these vain suggestions, opens for the first time to the full appreciation of "the glory of God in the face of Jesus Christ," and feels the highest wisdom of earth grow pale in comparison! That bright infancy of grace, which has so much of the simplicity and devotedness of the infancy of nature! and to which on the other hand (let me add) the youth of Nature seems so peculiarly adapted. Think not, ye who are young in the life of this world, that the time is not yet come for this stage of the Christian course. The wisdom of Christ is the prerogative of no special age; but if its general spirit could claim any as peculiarly its own, would it not be among the young it would most naturally seek its disciples? Christ took *children* in His arms to bless them; you are baptized as infants, that there may be no delay in exercising its pledged graces and verifying its solemn vows. I speak for Christian education, which itself is built upon this principle; whose express object, wherever it is rightly conceived, is to assist this growth in grace, to sustain, guard, and cherish it by every human help. What, indeed, seems to combine more truly the loveliest and best of earth and heaven, than this simplicity of Divine wisdom in childhood and youth; this early surrender to God, which makes the life of nature and of grace begin almost together; which, by hallowing every innocent enjoyment with gratitude to its Giver, fits almost for heaven the mirth itself of this world, where mirth is so seldom wholly guiltless?

And now, before advancing farther, it is fit to mention to you (what our version very inaccurately conveys) that the first of these four important words is meant to embrace the rest. The "righteousness, sanctification, and redemption" are the ingredients of the "wisdom;" the exact translation of the original being,—" who is made unto us a wisdom from God (in contrast to the false wisdom which he had censured)—even righteousness, and sanctification, and redemption." Christ is our wisdom in being to us these things; that is—He is the prime object of all true wisdom, inasmuch as He is the source of all true blessedness.

This blessedness, we see, is threefold; and one word, Christ, expresses it all. I have no intention now of dilating on each of its members; we have no time to follow the course of each of these rivers of Paradise as they flow, and shall for ever flow, through the spirits of the elect of God; I pause rather by the Fountain; come and see how they issue from it.

I must again remind you to weigh well the force of the expression,—" is made unto us." Let no man persuade you that this can be satisfied by any remote or indirect connexion with Christ; it is intimate as life is; He Himself is made to us the thing He gives. As *one with Him*, we obtain the whole inheritance of Grace and Glory. The instant that we are incorporated into the mystical body of which He is the head; the instant in which we are made living stones of the temple of which He is corner-stone; the instant that we become branches of that celestial vine,—*that* instant we possess the seed of the entire, and all the life of the Christian,—yea, all his eternity is but the less or greater development of the Christ he bears within, around, and upon him. I have spoken of a progress of blessings; it *is* a progress to us; but not in the gift of Jesus Christ;—to receive Him is to receive the germ of every blessing that is written in the Book of God. One with Christ, we must have pardon; for how *could* God love the Head and hate the Members? One with Christ, we must have sanctification; for how *could* He that is boundlessly pure remain one with aught that is wilfully unholy? One with Christ, we must have the prospective redemption of the whole man to glory; for how *could* He abandon to the everlasting grave a portion of His own being, such as He has deigned to make us,—and think His happiness complete? Thus in blending Himself with us, " He hath done *all* things well;" He has in that one unfathomable mystery accomplished all mysteries. He is—not the declarer only, or the means only, or the instrument only,—He is "made unto us"—He hath Himself become—righteousness, sanctification, redemption. We have justification as we are seen in Him; we have sanctification as He is seen in us; we have increasing holiness, and mutual communion, and ultimate redemption, as both combine. "Abide in me and I in you...He that abideth in me and I in him, the same bringeth forth much fruit,"—there is our holiness. "*As* thou, Father, art in me, and I in thee, that they also may be *one in us*,"—there is our bond of mutual communion. "Ye are dead, and your life is hid with Christ in God; when Christ who is *our life* shall appear, then shall *ye also appear with Him in glory*,"—there is our ultimate redemption of body and spirit into the mansions of eternity. Christ reappears in all; for all the New Testament theology is but different perspective views of the one unchangeable object—the gift of Jesus Christ; seen in one direction it is Pardon, seen in another, it is Holiness, seen in another, it is Glory. He justifies as Christ crucified and risen without us; He sanctifies as Christ crucified and risen within us; He glorifies in virtue of both, as Christ enthroned in the fulness of consummate power, and at length "subduing *all* things unto Himself." Feel and know this as it ought to be felt and known; and you may leave the rest to the schools. These are days of harsh disputings, days when men are very bitter to each other for the love of God; I know not how others feel; but it seems to me as if,—could a man once thoroughly realize to himself the depth of this union with the infinite purity of Christ, could he once realize the heaven that is in him when Christ is there, could he gaze, not to question and criticise, but in humble adoring joy, upon the face of the risen Jesus, and there but once behold his own "acceptance in the Beloved;" all difficulties were dissolved in that blessed vision, every doubt would be forgotten in the fulness of its glory! Fix soul and spirit steadily upon the oneness of the Son of God with the forgiven and adopted sons of men, and all the littleness of proud restless disputation will disappear from the view, consumed in the blaze of that transcendent thought. "He is made unto us righteousness, sanctification, redemption;" what need of more? for all the practical purposes of comfort and holiness, what need of more? Why raise troublous and perplexing questions as to precise dates of pardon and purification? Receive the full blessing of Christ by faith, and in His ordinances; and these, and "all things," are yours; for "ye are washed, ye are sanctified, ye are justified, in the Name of the Lord Jesus, and by the Spirit of our God." Alas, that with something of the plain simple-hearted trust with which in the Church's first days these things were received, we could learn rather to realize the truth than to contend about its nature! We have a glorious inheritance; and instead of entering in and taking possession, we fritter away our short allowance of time in disputing about the wording of the title-deeds! Oh miserable, frivolous, faithless mockery! Conceive that, instead of receiving the sacramental token of remission, and hearing or reading the word of life, you stood in the very light of the vision of God; that you heard His own blessed voice pronounce the word of acceptance that translated you from the kingdom of darkness, and made you one with Him in His Divine Son; that thus assured and thus delighted, lost in inexpressible gratitude—with all the past of wretchedness, all the present and future of glory, pressing upon the soul;—conceive, I say, that in such an hour you were to turn to the blessed Revealer, and tell Him you could not be content to receive or enjoy His favours, unless He should explain with minuteness the precise mode in which this gift of Himself was to operate upon every separate faculty of your soul, and every particular relation between you and Him! The feeling and the cry of faith is— He gives us Christ, and in Him all things. Christ cannot be ours and any grace be absent; this King cannot enthrone Himself in our Spirit and not bring with Him His whole retinue of blessings. Blessings may—they *must* arise in succession to creatures that live in successive time; but the first instant that Christ is ours the seed of every blessing is ours, a life of sanctification is hidden in that moment, nay,—a long perspective of infinite glory is there,—death is conquered, Satan chained, and Heaven won; for He who accomplished all these things " is made unto *us* righteousness, and sanctification, and redemption." The gift is ours, let it expand as it will in our heart and life; Christ is here, and He, the " Son over His own house," will take care to rule it in wisdom; in having Him we have pardon, in having Him we have holiness, in having Him we have heaven itself,—" raised up together, and made to sit together in heavenly places in Christ Jesus."

All this is mysterious, indeed; of course it is; who is he that will believe God made one with man, and have the union wrought *without* mystery? Children of the living God! ye walk in mystery. Your spiritual birth is a mystery, your fellowship with Christ is a mystery, your daily graces are a mystery, your triumphant death is a mystery, your resurrection to glory will be but the consummation of mystery. Mystery there must be wherever an infinite Creator and his finite creature embrace; and it is, therefore, your glory that you are thus robed and shrouded in mystery. Trust no one who would draw you forth from it: it is the awful shadow which eternity casts across time. Believe no one who would give you a religion without much and solemn mystery;—and above all, when you think of God in Christ, of what He has done, and what He still does, and what He will do, be well assured that in all His dealings there must be much you can never expect to fathom; before which, therefore, you can but bow in prostrate humility of adoration; knowing—simply knowing —that all He will do He can do, such is His power; all He can rightly do He will, such is His love! These things are " known in part," and therefore, we can of them but " prophesy in part." But there is no one who knows not what ought to be the practical working of such a faith. He is all things to us, that we may be in all things His. He is to us "righteousness," that we may rejoice in His pardon with a joy of the Holy Ghost; He is to us "sanctification," that we may bear the fruits of His indwelling Spirit; He is to us "redemption," that we may walk in white as being "worthy,"—worthy to "follow Him whithersoever He goeth" hereafter in glory, as following Him whithersoever He goeth in sadness and suffering now. Go forth, then, ye ransomed ones, and remember that you bear through the world this day the image and superscription of Christ Jesus; in whatever company of men you stand, forget not that His signature is upon you;—and when men, thoughtless and ungodly, would win you from His service, tell them, that there is One in heaven with whom *you* are one, that you live as members of His spiritual frame, incorporated into Him, in and by Him righteous, sanctified, redeemed; and that being thus not your own but His, you are resolved, whatever the dreaming world may say, in Him to live that in Him you may die,—in Him to die that in Him you may live for ever!

SERMON II.

LIVING AND DYING UNTO THE LORD.

ROMANS XIV. 8.

For whether we live, we live unto the Lord ; and whether we die, we die unto the Lord.

THE Christian Church, my dearest brethren, is now advanced through many ages of its existence; but from its infancy to its maturity that natural human heart, on which its principles have had to operate, has continued the same. The being whom we find around us in the daily walks of life is the very being whom we meet in the pages of the New Testament:— the passions,—the hopes,—the fears,—the desires,—the prejudices,—which we find mirrored in *its* records, might,—except for the mere peculiarities of circumstance,—have been reflected from the human breast of this age, as well as from that of eighteen hundred years ago. It is this identity, indeed, which makes the little volume of the New Testament so invaluable and so perpetual a guide to the sincere disciple of Christ. In every sentence he recognises himself,—in every sentence he reads his own necessities, supplies, exhortations, censures, warnings:—the same corruptions which are *now* leading us astray are there enumerated and exposed; the same feebleness met and strengthened; the same temptations rebuked; the same Almighty Spirit promised; the same eternal reward suspended in the distance,—a reward of which it can only be said that its colours are *augmented* in brilliancy as the scene draws nearer,—for whatever be the time of the expected advent, it is at least certain that " now is our salvation nearer then when" *they* (our Christian forefathers) "believed." The New Testament is, then, to us and our successors the same precious inheritance its gospels, and epistles, and prophecies were to the first believers; with this only difference,—that as prophecy gathers to fulfilment, as the shadowy outlines of prediction begin to fill and flush with the vivid colours of *fact*, the story of Christ the Redeemer, and of the human heart as acted on *by* Christ,—the Bible-history of man,—becomes still more authentic and still more valuable. Truly,—" whatsoever things were written aforetime were written for *our* learning, that we, through patience and *comfort of the Scriptures*, might have hope" (Rom. xv. 4)! And hence,—when we hear men sighing for something above and beyond the Scriptures, when we hear them demanding " infallible" earthly guidance,—ecclesiastical oracles who are to be the sole commissioned delegates of the spirit of truth to mankind,—we may well censure,—not merely the presumptuousness of the request (involving a secret infidelity), but the unhappy misconception it betrays as to the whole purport of the Scripture revelation itself. Were it the purpose of God to make us the cold professors of a system of theology drawn out into long deductions and fortified at all points; were we to be (reversing the Apostle's language) " able ministers of the New Testament, *not* of the spirit but of the letter,"—such guidance from some permanent external authority might be requisite; for *such* guidance is certainly, in a very limited degree, to be found in the New Testament. But the object of the Scripture revelation of God is essentially a *practical* object; it seldom declares truths, except so far as they are necessary to found motives and directions for that new and spiritual life which is the great and ultimate end of the whole as a revelation of God to man. . . . Understood in this, its true light,—how admirably fitted is that little volume to be the perpetual directory of the Church! Over and above the preaching of Christ Himself, it gives us,—not merely doctrines of belief, nor merely precepts of conduct, but *ourselves* in all the difficulties of trial and temptation! It shows us, not what men *ought* to do solely, but what men *have* done and *may* do. It brings before us the wondrous picture of that infant Church, when as yet fresh from the hand of God it breathed of its origin,—when, among the thousands it already included through some of the most civilized regions of the earth, but one heart beat, one hope was felt, one heaven anticipated: and while thus it exhibits by example what a Christian should be,—in what Christians *have* been, teaches us to sigh,—would to God that it taught us to pray and to labour that we may be meet!—for the return of that golden age of our religion, in the return once more to earth of Him whose omnipotent Spirit produced it!

But I have said that, even in this blessed picture, the New Testament story exhibits the weakness of men as truly as their excellences. It does; and in this lies half the value of the record. The same natural tendency to pass from a high and inward and spiritual religion into the cold formalities of profession, which is now afflicting the Church (and for which some among ourselves have attempted so injudicious, so profitless, a remedy in external separation,—as if the work of " Christian separation" was to be wrought by the coarse machinery of external observances, and not by the " sword of the Spirit" rending asunder the ties that bind the world and the heart) — is found already menacing the earliest Churches (in which, I may add, no such remedy was ever prescribed); —the same occasional narrowness of mind which loses the substance in the form of godliness, and the same uncharitable estimation of minute differences in comparison with the great principles of faith and hope and love,—which so often chill the ardour and cordiality of Christian communion in our own days,—*these* are no novelties in the heart of man,—you find the same unhappy tendencies in the first records of the Church of Christ,—restrained and suppressed, indeed, by the overruling authority of the Apostles, by the recent and remembered lessons of the Saviour Himself, and perhaps, still *more*, by the pressure of external persecution which tightened the bonds of mutual affection among these exiles in the world;—*restrained*, I say, but still too clearly manifested in this *principle*, and too surely prepared for the Church of succeeding ages!

In the chapter from which the passage before us is extracted, we have a striking instance of these very tendencies, as well as of the spirit in which they were met and remedied by the inspired guides of the primitive Church.

I select the subject, and enlarge upon it; because it is specially applicable to those church-dissensions of our own times, in which an erroneous conscientiousness has driven from the field of our communion into a dreamy sectarianism, so many of the devoted children of God; and because, in extending the principle here developed, you will find the simplest example and guidance for the determination of your own course in similar cases. Observe then,—in reference to the chapter before us.—The first believers, gathered alike from the two Bible-divisions of the world,—from Jews and Gentiles,—brought into the new religion many of the prejudices of their preceding life. Eminently was this observable in the *Jew*, who, educated in the bondage of a strict and ceremonial creed, mistook the fetters of that bondage for the badges of freedom,—and could not endure to believe *that* system superseded which had made the boast and glory of his nation. Brought up in the shadowy twilight of preparatory forms and observances, the Christian Jew could not bear to resign these cherished privileges of his youth; and begged hard to be allowed to perpetuate these shadows, even under the now orient beams of the " Sun of righteousness" itself! Feelings whose very weakness was interesting contributed to the delusion. For ages the glory of Israel had been identified with its law; the Jew could scarcely feel as a patriot and consent to desert it; his hopes for the future, his remembrances of the past, were interwoven with his veneration for the ceremonies and sacrifices of the Mosaic code; to forsake *it* were to forsake the faith of his ancestors,—the faith ennobled by kings and consecrated by prophets,—nor this alone,—it were to desert the daughter of Zion in the hour of her *misfortune*, when the Pagan spoiler was already among her palaces! Judaism had become eminently a political religion,—it held the sign and countersign of those who loved the soil of Israel; to meet and whisper of the elder glories of Sinai and the mystic promises of prophecy, had become the favourite occupation of the despised and degraded Jew, whenever he could evade the vigilance of the detested foreigner whose foot polluted the vineyard of the Lord. These things bound him to the creed of his fathers,—but speaking in *Ireland*, need I *enlarge* upon the nature,—or the power,—or the prevalence,—or the *misfortune*, of such misdirected though not unamiable national affections in retarding the progress of free discussion,—of truth and of reason?

The consequence of all this, when the great revolution of Christianity took place, was natural and inevitable. The Christianized Jew,—though he surrendered (for it was of the very essence of Christianity to do so) his notion of the intended eternity of the Jewish Law of ceremonies,—though he admitted that "Christ is *the end* of the Law to every one that believeth," that in Him all the scattered rays of type and prophecy converge and are for ever lost,—yea rather are fixed and eternalized,—yet still could not resist his tendency to preserve some fragments of the old preparatory creed, and incorporate them into the spiritual religion of Christ. The abstinence from peculiar meats, the observance of peculiar days, and others of the formal traditions of the synagogue, he was loath altogether to resign, though he could not altogether justify ... Now what I wish you to observe is, the manner in which the Apostle deals with this critical question. Are Jew and Gentile to be severed for this difference?

Remark, then, that St. Paul feels and acknowledges the difference that separates the *fundamental* question of the faith of Christ from those of merely subordinate importance. Upon the former he will admit *no* compromise, *no* compensation, *no* second opinion. That Christ,—the commissioned Son of God, and himself " God manifest in the flesh,"—is the sole hope of the believer, exclusive of all reference to human *merit;* that if man will be just before the living God, it is only in and through Christ that he can be accepted as such; that His work is a complete work, to which man can add nothing, but *from* which man receives everything;—that this is the cardinal fact of the religion which God brought from heaven to earth, and that in this, as in a germ, is enfolded the whole glorious story of eternity,—St. Paul insists,—reiterates,—enforces. Whatever enfeebles this, is poison to the very vitals of the truth; and, therefore, with the questioner of this the Apostle will hold no parley. " Am I not an Apostle?" is the answer. " Though we, or an angel from heaven, preach any other Gospel unto you, than that which we have preached unto you, let him be accursed!" To disbelieve,—or to corrupt,—this doctrine,—would be to neutralize the whole blessed work of God to man; no error, then, can be overlooked which would reduce or qualify the Messiahship of Christ,—as Prophet, Priest, and King, to His people. Upon this he is peremptory; —upon this, in the very spirit and energy of Christian love, we must be peremptory likewise! God grant that no fear of man may ever unnerve the resolution with which His ministers shall preach,—serene among the contending errors of rival sects,—that consoling doctrine of the cross to the blood-bought people of the Redeemer!

But when from that doctrine, which is the corner-stone of salvation, the same Apostle descends to the harmless prejudices of the ignorant but conscientious Israelite,—the superfluous zeal of the feast-day and the fast;—when from the mighty theme of the dignity and the office of Christ, he comes, as in the chapter before us, to reconcile the prepossessions of Jew and Gentile about their favourite ceremonies,—we find him in another and even more attractive position. Of his own opinion, indeed, as to the value of such restrictions, there can be no doubt. The abstainer from peculiar meat is " weak in the faith." " There is nothing," says St. Paul, " unclean of itself." " The kingdom of God is not meat and drink ; but righteousness, and peace, and joy in the Holy Ghost." Yet— " Let not him that eateth despise him that eateth not!"— " *receive* him,—not to doubtful disputations!" And this *because* " to his own master he standeth or falleth." " We that are strong ought to bear the infirmities of the weak." Nay,—if our happier freedom insult or distress him, we ought to sacrifice our very freedom for his sake:—for (ver. 21) " it is good neither to eat flesh nor to drink wine, nor anything whereby thy brother stumbleth, or is offended, or is made weak." There is even a certain respect due to an unimportant error, when it takes place in the spirit of devotion to God ;—*that* common spirit sanctifies all,—" for none of us liveth to himself, and no man dieth to himself:—for whether we live, we live unto the Lord ; and whether we die, we die unto the Lord : whether we live, therefore, or die, we are the Lord's !" (ver. 7, 8.)

You have now a statement of the disposition with which the inspired Apostle regarded errors in the Church of Christ,— a spirit so widely differing from that which has dictated much of the wild enthusiastic separatism of the present day. Do I err when I would reduce it to the general maxim,— that in the cardinal points of the Christian faith, the evidence of inspiration should determine all; that in the minor differences of view, the principle of charity—wrought in us by that very belief of the main and fundamental truths—should be the guiding star, and everything gently dealt with, which, without impeaching the purity of the faith, is done in the spirit of devotion to that Christ who is " Lord both of the dead and living?"

We have seen *the occasion* of this maxim, in which St. Paul thus passes from outward forms to the inward and Spiritual Kingdom of God in the heart;—let us rest for a moment upon the maxim itself. " Whether we live, we live unto the Lord ; and whether we die, we die unto the Lord."

The " Lord" here spoken of is at once Christ and God ; as is manifest from the ninth verse, where Christ is identified with the " Lord of the dead and the living,"—from the tenth verse, where He is declared to be the supreme Judge of the world,—and finally from the eleventh, where the Apostle, to establish that title, directly applies to Christ that solemn declaration of the forty-fifth of Isaiah,—" I am God, and there is none else; unto Me every knee shall bow, every tongue shall swear!" The God, then, to whom this utter and unreserved surrender of the heart is required, is the God who was revealed in Christ Jesus; and who, by the mysterious union of the Divine and human natures, has consecrated the one by the other, and for ever reconciled both !

Unto Him, as Christians, we are called upon to live; He who is the principle of our spiritual life is also made the object of it; as the vapours of the ocean supply the rivers that return into the ocean itself. Unto Him, as Christians, we are called upon to die; He who died for us is made the object of our death likewise; that as " our life is hid with Christ in God," so " when He who is our life shall appear, then we also may appear with Him in glory." . . . No reserve, you hear, is admitted in the statement of our profession ; we live and die to Christ; our whole nature, in all its aspects and positions, is offered to Him, as one solemn and perpetual sacrifice ; " bought with a price," we are delivered to Him as His own spiritual property in this world; " we are Christ's, and Christ is God's,"—so that, as it were, through Him, as man, we pass into the very presence of the Supreme Divinity, enter within the verge of that ineffable Nature with which He connects us, and catch upon our weak and shivering humanity the beams of the everlasting light of God !

It would be superfluous to enter into explanation of the meaning of phrases too manifest for elucidation. "To live unto God" cannot but be understood by all who remember that, at every hour of life, they are in truth "living unto" some object or other, whether it be worthy or unworthy the affections of a human heart. To some object their nature is consecrated,—to some object the living sacrifice of the soul is perpetually presented. It is the very condition of our being, the most simple and the most universal of all; and hence it is that the Apostle employs, as the common character of the renovated heart, the quality of the object *it* embraces. In this very assembly the same sovereign test is applicable,—is even *now applied* by the all-perceiving Spirit of God. He can tell,— what I dare not pronounce,—whether, even in this hour of prayer and penitence, you have truly "lived unto God;" and how far the heaven of your secret hopes and supplications is that heaven which He has promised to His believing children, that heaven of which it is the highest and holiest character that " the life unto Him" is there immortal!

What, then, is it to " live unto God?" What is it but to return Him his own rights in the human heart; to concentrate on Him those affections which originally were formed for Him alone? What is it but to know and feel that even while this shadowy world encompasses us, there is around and above it a scene real, substantial, and eternal; a scene adequate,—and at this moment adequate,—to answer all the ardent longings of our bereaved souls,—a scene in which every holier affection, widowed and blighted here, is to be met and satisfied! . . . To live in this belief,—this hope; to read in the death of Christ death itself lost in immortality; to make the God of the New Testament the Friend, the Companion, the Consoler, of all earthly sorrow; to feel the brightest colours of ordinary life fade in " the glory that shall be revealed,"—this is to live the " life," that heralds the immortality, " unto God!"

The immortality *unto* **God!** For this is the heaven of the Christian. " Whether we live," says the Apostle — and heaven is the *eternal* life,—" we live unto God!" Brethren! beloved brethren! have we learned to desire an eternity such as this? I have endeavoured to speak to you plainly; I will make an effort to be yet more distinct. . . . Let us suppose that by some supernatural agent an offer were suddenly made to each of us, of at once being admitted into the immediate presence of God in Heaven! Remembering what the laws are by which that abode of blessedness is governed,—remembering the strict and undeviating purity which it is represented as exacting from all who are its residents,—remembering that a God who cannot endure iniquity is there more immediately present to his creatures, both in the person of the Lord Jesus and in the clearer revelation opened to the minds of the Blest with regard to God's character and dealings,—remembering that this kingdom of everlasting righteousness is only known to us by the plain intimation, that its whole tone of existence is opposed to all that is scripturally called " the World,"—and that a breath of unholiness cannot be suffered to taint its atmosphere of perfect peace,—holding all this in mind as the true portraiture of the Heaven of the New Testament,—I ask you, whether, with hearts whose every pulsation beats for worldly interests, with affections that not (on perhaps only too favourable a calculation) for one half-hour in the twenty-four are really lifted from the dust of the path on which we are together creeping to the grave,—with hopes that never were taught to stray beyond the clouds of this world's foul atmosphere,—with all your busy dreams about you (for we walk in visions), in none of which do Heaven or its God find a moment's place—Christians! I ask you, would you unhesitatingly rejoice in the offer? I do not ask you whether you would assent with your lips to the proposal; for, associating as we do Heaven with Happiness, perhaps no one would deliberately and verbally refuse it;—but I ask you, whether, with that spring and rapture of the heart which a great worldly prosperity brings, you would (bearing in mind the true nature of the change) grasp at the proposal, and call aloud for death to open the gate of the Kingdom of God? Would your *inmost Soul* accept the change? Would you agree to cast aside all the hopes and enjoyments of your state in this life, to be the calm and peaceful adorer of the world to come? Even to the afflicted I might ask—would they accept *peace* on such conditions as the peace of God imposes? Alas! few can sincerely answer that they would. The heaven of the gospel is no heaven to those who have not learned the holiness of the gospel. Is not the test, then, simple and decisive? Can we deem that we are "living unto God" in *this* world, if we shrink with dread from the notion of living unto Him in another, and living unto Him *for ever?*

What, indeed, is the Heaven of every man but the conceived realization of his own cherished wishes! As this ideal happiness varies, "Heaven" (which is but the expression of its ultimate completion) correspondingly varies. Accordingly, if you listen to the confidences of any man, you will infallibly detect in what quarter his Heaven is situated. It is a pole to which the magnet of his mind perpetually trembles. Thus it is that the world is filled with a thousand forgeries of heaven,— the illusion of that Deceiver who spreads out these phantoms of happiness to hide the yawning portals of ruin behind them! And hard indeed is the work of the servant of Christ, among all these gaudy visions of flushed and passionate pleasures, to secure even a glance at the cold outlines of the heaven *he* proposes. In the midst of a crowd of impassioned visionaries, he feels how unwelcome is his intrusion. When every mind is encompassed with its own favourite scenery, how can he, with his fond anticipations of spiritual enjoyments, expect even the refuse of men's thoughts? Will the walls of a church transform the souls and bodies of the listeners,—that those who are worldly and sensual up to its doors, shall enter them disengaged, and prepared to hear of eternal purity? We may crowd the temples of the Most High, but is it not too often as those whom the Prophet saw in the midst of the holy places; the visions of our idolatry accompany us even into the house of the living God; and though we kneel as in adoration, our busy hearts neglect to adore, and we are still,— "every man *in the chambers of his imagery!*" . . . God grant to us a strong desire to live the "life unto God,"—by patience and faith "to walk as seeing the Invisible,"—to yearn after that devotion of heart and soul unto Him, which, begun in this world, shall be perfected and consummated in the world of eternal peace!

To that world you know the passage. The Apostle has not neglected to state it. "Whether we *die*, we die unto the Lord."

When *he* wrote, there was a touching earnestness in the expression. Surrounded by persecution and distress, not certain but the next hour might bring the stake or the lions, the Apostle could indeed speak of death as a familiar theme. But he had been accustomed to look upon it with a welcoming eye. "To me to live is Christ, and to die is gain." He could declare himself desirous "to be absent from the body, and present with the Lord:"—" to be with Christ, which was far better." And oh! brethren,—to us also, who, with whatever preparation of heart, must pass through that tremendous hour, which no imagination can anticipate, and which none can return to tell of,—to us who must each in loneliness tread that valley of the shadow where the friend dearest and most devoted can no longer accompany us,—to us is it not also fitting to be preached that we should make it the lesson of life, "to die unto the Lord?" To the Christian who is worthy of the name, I need not tell you that that hour, which fancy invests with so fearful a gloom, is indeed radiant with a life from heaven, a light beseeming the birth-day of eternity! He "dies unto the Lord," because his earnest trust in a reconciled God has taught him to gladly yield his life where he had long yielded his heart and hopes. He "dies unto the Lord," because he feels that such a death is the crowning act of that sacrifice which it is his whole desire to make of himself to his eternal Master. He "dies unto the Lord," because he has long since *lived* unto the Lord, in dying unto the world! Above all,—he "dies unto the Lord,"—because he knows that death is but the passage into a wider scene of service, a more transcendent and more abiding scene for the exercise of his revived,—his thence for ever *undying* energies, in the cause, and to the glory, of God:—because he knows that no servant of Christ passes from this world into a heaven of lethargy and superannuation, but into a scene of busy happiness, where new faculties are given for new purposes,—where the spiritual mind is strengthened to will, and the spiritual frame is strengthened to act, with redoubled powers, in the service of the Creator,—and where, therefore, to "die unto the Lord" is to assume a new and better *life*,—to live unto the Lord, and through the Lord, and for the Lord, and *with* the Lord,—for ever and ever!

SERMON III.

THE HOPE OF GLORY AND THE CHARITIES OF LIFE.

1 John III. 2.

It doth not yet appear what we shall be; but we know that, when he shall appear, we shall be like him; for we shall see him as he is.

COMING before you this day, my brethren, to appeal to your Christian sympathies on behalf of poverty and orphanage, I know no other artifice of persuasion than to exhibit the simplicity of Christian motives. To advocate the claims of those who are thus compelled to be annual dependants on your benevolence, I have no magic of eloquence beyond that which speaks of your own free and unmerited prerogatives in a Saviour;—to plead the cause of poverty, I have no resource but to point to your wealth in "the riches of Christ;"—to plead for destitution, I can only speak of Him who has said to each confiding disciple,—" I will never leave thee nor forsake thee,"—to plead for orphanage, I can but echo that voice which whispered on the night of betrayal, " I will not leave *you* orphans;"—to plead for those,—young and untaught, —whose boon for eternity you may be instrumental in saving this day from being blighted for eternity, I have no better rhetoric than to speak of the splendours of that everlasting inheritance which the Victor of Calvary has won for them and for you, that Divine country to which you profess to be travellers, and the way to which you will surely not refuse to facilitate for these weaklings of the flock of Christ; that region of which all, or the highest that is directly revealed to us, is, —that its blessedness consists essentially in reflecting the image of a God of charity, and that, though it be not distinctly declared "what we shall be," it is yet a fixed and transcendent truth,—written beyond the stars,—that we shall resemble, because we shall see, in His genuine glory, the God of the New Testament, the God visible in Christ Jesus, whose title, and whose essence, is Love!

May God grant to us,—or confirm in us,—this morning, hearts that rejoice in such a hope; hearts that need, that exult in, such a consolation! If such be the blessed frame of those I address this day, few of the innocent stratagems of the pulpit will be necessary to insinuate benevolence, or surprise into charity. Such a confidence,—unlike the prosperity of this world, which hardens the heart,—will mould, and soften, and attemper it; such joy (mysterious interaction of the Christian graces!) is itself full of boundless sympathy with every form of sorrow; such anticipations, while they hang upon the far horizon of eternity and dwell upon its dawning light with rapture, lose from their view no one humble point of the intervening world, but can take into one loving glance the coming glory and the present grief,—yea, can illumine the one by the other, and see the sorrow better for the light beyond it, and know it more deeply for the glory it contrasts, and shed those very tears of joy which heaven calls forth, as tears of affliction, too, for the misery and the misfortunes of earth. Oh! if amid this multitude of eternal souls whom I now address, there be any,—I would fain hope there are not a few,—to whom these words are more than words,—who recognise this blessed connexion of our highest hopes in heaven with our tenderest charities in earthly life,—they at least will not disappoint my labours this day, when, pleading for helplessness and poverty, I would speak of that world where the "poor in spirit" are rich in glory;—when, calling on you to assist the ministers of God in deepening, under Christ, His image on His fallen creatures, I would discuss the nature or the process of that assimilation which is (as the text asserts) to transform us so wondrously hereafter;—when, telling you of your duties to these orphaned little ones of the Christian family, I would lift the lowly argument upon a higher basis, and take my stand upon the mount of God!

St. John, in the passage before us, is performing the work of a Consoler. He alludes,—and it is but passingly,—to the friendless position of his fellow-saints in this world. They were persecuted, it seems, because they were not understood. They spoke a dialect of motives and feelings which the world around them could not translate into any received phraseology; nay, the more intelligible language of their *lives* was little less misinterpreted. Their purity was called impure; their meekness was said to be the cloak of conspiracy and murder. They sighed under the pressure of these cruel calumnies. "The world knoweth us not," said St. John. But he adds the solution. He extends the ignorance, that he may acquit its objects. "The world knoweth us not, because it knew Him not." Marvel not if the world hate you. Forget not the words of the Master himself,—"If the world hate you, ye know that it hated me before it hated you."..."I have chosen you out of the world, *therefore* the world hateth you." Glory in these consecrated tribulations! You are identified with Him in *His* acceptance by the world, as you are identified with Him in *your* acceptance before the Father; this prophecy of your sufferings,—surely it was not a threat to dread, but a promise to welcome, since you share its terrors with *Him;* He, the Martyr-Conqueror of Sin, would have *you* also to take your Gethsemanes and your Calvaries on the road to glory!

But there is more than this. "We are now," adds the Apostle of love,—"we are now, beloved, *the Sons of God.*" United as we are with our Master in the world's contempt, the language of heaven has united us in title. As He was crucified *for* the world, so are we crucified *to* the world; while on the other hand, as He was the Son of God by that mysterious and eternal filiation which no created nature has ever held or can hold, so are we permitted from our dust to claim a shadowy image of that unfathomable relationship, and to recognise a Father in the Father of our Lord. "I go," said He, as He looked His last farewell upon His beloved—"I go to my Father and to *your* Father." And though no human nature could bear, unconsumed by its fires divine, the *love* with which the Father surrounds that Son who is "the brightness of His glory," yet even of this *we* receive our human transcript; nor was the Blessed One jealous of his own place in the bosom of the Parent God when He made it the dearest object of His parting supplication,—"that the world may know that thou hast loved *them* as thou hast loved me." . . . Well might the Apostle,—practised as he was in the story of celestial love,—exclaim in rapture and astonishment,—"Behold what manner of love the Father hath bestowed upon us, that we should be called the sons of God!"

"Beloved," proceeds the Apostle, "*now are we* the sons of God." We have no empty title unattended with real dignities and real privileges; we are not only "called" (as in the preceding verse) but we "are" the children of heaven. We are not merely invested with our rank by adopting favour, but we are in the exercise of our privileges by regenerating grace. This is even *now* the dignity freely accorded to the poor and persecuted disciple in the invisible empire of God. The title may be smiled at by the principalities of earth; but it is registered with honour in the archives of immortality.—Christian brethren, assembled this morning under the eye of God! do *you* indeed feel by an inward testimony which none can gainsay, that there is a copy of this entry written in your own hearts? Know you the blessedness of those first faint whispers of peace and hope, that tell how truly changed is the relation in which a spirit stands to the Father of spirits? that embolden you to draw nearer the throne than of old time, and to mingle your voices, no longer discordant, among the harmonies of heaven? Believe it,—this,—the tender, timid, yet confiding love of the forgiven child,—is the surest character and attestation of our adoption into the divine family—" Because ye are sons, God hath sent forth the Spirit of his Son into your hearts, crying, Abba, Father."

Such is the scenery of earth; but the Christian can look beyond even a redeemed and regenerated earthliness. The holy ambition of his love will not be contented with peace itself,—though it be a peace passing all understanding,—as long as a veil is hung between him and the presence of his God. But oh! may I not now say with my Master, to those whose scanty experience of the Christian life the faint representations I have offered overpass,—" If I have told you of earthly things and ye believe not, how shall ye believe, if I tell you of heavenly things?"

"It doth not yet appear," says St. John,—" it hath not yet been manifested,—what *we shall be*." This expression might, perhaps, be added as some contribution to the views of those who date our Epistle before the period of the Apocalypse; in the latter pages of which so transcendent (though figurative) a picture is sketched of at least the circumstances of this blessed state: and it might possibly be conjectured that the beloved Apostle had already received *some intimation* of the honour which was intended him as chosen interpreter of heaven, and at the time he addressed this precious letter to the churches was waiting in holy expectancy beside the gate of vision,—waiting till " in the spirit on the Lord's day" he should " hear behind him a great voice as of a trumpet,"—and " behold, a door opened in heaven," and one which said, " Come up hither, and I will show thee things which must be hereafter!" . . . " It hath *not yet* been manifested what we shall be."

But as this is at least but conjectural,—and as the accounts in the Book of Revelation are, after all, rather accounts of the external circumstances of blessedness, than (except occasionally) of its interior character;—let us for a moment pause upon the words of the prophet thus for a season disclaiming prophecy, and contemplate why it is that in its fulness of glory " it hath not yet been manifested what we shall be."

In this respect, as you know, " the Apostle and High Priest of *our* profession" stands alone. He is no lavish painter of His celestial treasures. As the blessed Archbishop of Cambray said,—this King is too *accustomed* to the splendours of his palace to dilate upon them. But how profound a character is this of truth! Of all artifices to secure success, the gratification of this curiosity about the unknown world, is (next to the gratification of present licentiousness,—if even second to *it*) the most obvious, and the most powerful. But the serene security of Omnipotence was above the employment of such seductions. He left it to the impostor of the East,—alas, that we should add, He left it to the lying legends of that superstition which corrupted His own blessed faith,— to devise those elaborate portraitures of the coming world in which heaven is formed on the model of earth, and glory is degraded to man, not man elevated to glory! With Him who came from thence to bring us thither, who even as He wandered upon earth was still " the Son of Man *who is in heaven*,"—it was no labyrinth of verdure and softness, of roseate bowers and unclouded skies; it was " the kingdom of the Father; " it was the vision of God through purity of heart; it was not " to marry or be given in marriage," but to possess " eternal life;" it was above all " to eat and drink at *His* table in *His* kingdom;" it was to receive the redeemed " unto *Himself*, that where *He* was, there they might be also." As He taught us, it seemed that the graces He preached were not merely the way to glory, but the very elements of it,—its primary notions were built upon spiritual not sensible experiences,—it presupposed such a change to be itself *intelligible*. As He seemed to state it, the life of God here was the antechamber to an eternity of God hereafter; here were to be learned the alphabet and rudiments of the language which was to be employed for everlasting. The *promised* world was but the full unveiling of that Sun by whose clouded light the Christian walks in *this*. . . Nor even in their boldest pictures, and in the use of *figures* that sensibly symbolize things invisible, did the Apostles once waver from the same high principle;—a beautiful (though less obvious) mark of the secret unity of inspiration. On the one hand, it was declared that "the working by which Christ was to subdue all things unto Himself" was to extend to the *body*, which was to be changed into the similitude of His pure and spiritual frame; while on the other,—if physical pain *was* said to be excluded, it was excluded (as you may observe in tracing the instances for yourselves) *implicitly*, and less in itself than as the dark shadow that waits on *sin*, to which it is bound by a terrible,—an irrevocable necessity. Nay, so complete is this superiority to merely physical gratifications, that our own St. John,—he who at one time symbolically speaks of the foundations of amethyst, the streets of gold, and the gates of pearl,—when he would indeed spring to the *full* height of the theme, discards all the glories of the material world, rejects as unworthy adornings the proudest group of Nature's daily and nightly magnificence, to bury himself in the depths of a purely spiritual illumination,—and tells us, that " the City had no need of the *sun, neither of the moon*, to shine in it, for the glory of God did lighten it, and the Lamb is the light thereof!"

Here, then, is in itself an answer to our question. " It is not yet fully manifested what we shall be," because that which we shall be is incapable of direct manifestation by sensible imagery:—or,—in another aspect of the same truth,—because " that which we shall be" is not to be expressed as severed from the whole course and current of Christian joy; it is not separately manifested because everywhere manifested; because every exhortation to humility, and joy, and love, is an exhortation to heaven itself,—and every congratulation upon the attainment of such blessed emotions, is a congratulation upon having already arrived within the verge of Paradise!

But I might say more. I might ask, if this minute and distinct anticipation of the world to come might not itself injure the completeness of a trusting faith? Am I too subtly refining upon the delicacy of Christian feeling, when I say that in the very obscurity,—the golden mist, that rests upon the features of the celestial landscape, there is in us now hovering on its borders, room for a more total and self-abandoning trust *in Him* who is to guide us for ever through it? The Father of the Faithful " went out," it is said, " not knowing whither he went!" And every true descendant in the lineage of faith will but rejoice in that ignorance which urges him to cling the closer to his Immortal Friend; which bids him gladly, for intimations which could but be obscure at best, substitute omniscience itself; and teaches him to cry,—" Lord, I know but faintly *what* it shall be, and I ask not to know! Only assure me that thou wilt be there; I have long been accustomed to gather my every conception of happiness around thy name; thou art to me the abstract and representative of it all; I will not insult the anticipation of thy presence with calculations of time and place. Be but thyself there; I know my only heaven in thee!"

Surely *this* would aid the discipline of the emotions into the obedience of a perfect faith! But suppose that faith realized in all its God-given strength and certainty; suppose that " walking by faith" had at length attained almost to " walking by sight;" that,—as the daily proverb proclaims that " seeing is believing," so the Christian could boldly reverse the thought, and almost dare to affirm, that " believing is seeing:"—Is *this* a state in which we could pronounce it well that it should be distinctly "*manifested what we shall be*"? I cannot think it. Man, though made for heaven, is made for earth also,—for earth, the trial-ground and seminary of heaven. Conceive him then, by the vision of a perfect faith applied to a perfect revelation, surrounded with, and lost in, the dazzling light of other worlds; the story of eternal life unfolded in all its minuteness; every separate source of felicity analysed and recorded; the melodies of heaven almost echoing in his earthly ears;—would such a man be fitted for the daily duties of life? Blinded by the lustre of the eternal noon, could he walk in safety, and with the gentle firmness of a Christian, through the paths of the spiritual life, strewn as they are with duties and demands? His eyes wildly and solely fixed upon the glory to come, would he not be apt to go astray upon the way that leads to it? . . . Yes, it *is* well that even to the perfect it should not be "manifested what we shall be;" that it should be a "glory that *shall be* revealed," a "glory ready to be revealed *in the last time!*"

But God is equally wonderful in His words as in His silence, in what He declares as in what He refuses to declare. And here He has told us not "what we shall be," and yet more than we could dare to dream! Heh as constituted *Himself* as the Image of our blessedness; and in so doing has confirmed the representations I have given, as well as secured the purposes of His revelation, with a depth of wisdom which I cannot but pause for a moment to contemplate. "We know not yet what we shall be, but we know that when He shall appear, *we shall be like Him.*"

What is God as apprehended by man? The aggregate of all conceivable human perfections carried to infinity. What is it to know this God? To believe that there is realized in existence a Being comprehending the full measure of these excellencies. What is it to love God? To adore with earnest and with grateful heart that impersonation of supreme perfection. It is of the very essence of such knowledge and such love, *to desire to resemble* its great object; and that desire will increase with every increase of that excellence in the worshipper's heart which it adores in God. Is it not then a glorious device of the Author of the Faith, to give us such a glimpse of the future world as must fall darkly and coldly on the eye of the unregenerate; but in the heart touched by a diviner glow must not only be at once intelligible, but must make a deep earnestness for possession,—nor that alone, but must actually increase that earnestness exactly in proportion as grace itself increases? So that as the heart rises in holiness, the reward rises in beauty; as the work of God in time becomes more consummate, the recompence of God in eternity becomes more attractive; and men can truly wish for heaven, only when they have its image already in their hearts! Can you not now perceive the force of the verse that immediately follows— " And every one that hath *this* hope in him, *purifieth himself even as He* is pure "?

I need not observe how this representation at once silences those who accuse the rewards of our religion as making it only a more prudent variety of *selfishness*. They know not of what they speak. Liberation from physical infirmities,— perhaps even a *moderate* participation in physical enjoyments, must indeed be elements of some value in every estimation of an ideally perfect state of happiness, to a being framed as man is framed; but if the essential blessedness of heaven be that which St. John proclaims,—the resemblance to its God,—it can only be a reward to those who covet to be like Him!

But is this sublime conception of the inspired penman a principle *exclusively* Christian? For all practical purposes it is; in idea and expression it is not wholly so. Bear with me for a moment longer, while from the very failures of human wisdom I would ask you to borrow a new leaf for the wreath that crowns your own adorable faith!

In that olden time when as yet " the Light" had not shone " to lighten the Gentiles," there were men who dared to conceive of human perfection as consisting in a *likeness to Deity.* The Christian pulpit acknowledges a sincere sympathy with every honest effort of man to rise above himself, and it need not be ashamed to repeat their reasoning. . . . They speculated somewhat in this manner. . . . Virtue itself,—what is it but the approach to some glorious ideal of perfection? God,—what can that mysterious Nature be but Itself the Cause and Fountain of all which we are accustomed to venerate as excellent or adore as lovely? These things then are not two, but *one;* and if man will raise himself to the highest point of his nature, he will make it the office of his life to *imitate God!* These were surely high and holy thoughts. Our nature may well be proud of them;—but, in sad truth, our nature was little the better for them. The reason was obvious. The object of Imitation was utterly disproportionate to man. When the first glow of enthusiasm had passed away, the proposal seemed extravagant, to copy the Infinite. The God who was only known as the mysterious Principle of the Universe, swelled into an immensity that defied all efforts at imitation.... But again,—every attempt to practically and permanently elevate, I will not say *the mass* of mankind (for that was never undertaken), but even a single individual, seems to be vain, in which *the affections* are not called into play. But where were the affections that could embrace immensity? Where was the love, or the hope, or the gratitude, that could fasten upon this dim and shadowy Abstraction? what emotions could the human heart own in presence of this mighty Principle of Power; except, perhaps, a vague and shivering terror, a blind dread, that froze and paralysed the soul, instead of animating it to the blessedness of adoration!

Brethren in the hope of Christ! *we* know how this problem has been solved. We know of a God, who, without parting with one ray of that transcendent essence by which He is alone in the Universe,—its Creator, its Sustainer, and its Governor;—who, without violating one jot of the truth of His own unfathomable nature, has yet so presented Himself to us, as to encourage even the faintest aspirations of the feeblest heart to repose in the bosom of a Brother. Consider this.

We can conceive since the fall, perhaps but two courses by which the God of mere abstraction could become the object of special and direct affection to an ordinary human heart. Let Him remain in His incomprehensible infinity, but mark a peculiarity in His favours, or let Him extend His favour to mankind, but descend from His infinity. He has done both. He has in *one* dispensation narrowed the field of His favour, He has in the *other* diminished the distance of His nature. Yes! we now know that there is a God whom it is no longer a hopeless enthusiasm to call on man to imitate;—one with whom, it would seem, a connexion so perfect may be established of heart and hope, that all the story of His earthly career is spiritually acted over in each of His earthly followers —who are declared to be "born with Christ," "suffering with Christ," "crucified with Christ," "buried with Christ," "risen with Christ," "exalted with Christ,"—until at length these analogies are lost in a deeper and more heavenly resemblance when, admitted into the sunlight of His glory, they catch the reflection of His eternal beams,—as they gaze approach, and as they approach become more and more completely invested with His radiance, are transfigured as they adore the God and Man, in the clear truth of His own unshadowed essence,— "are like Him, for they see Him as He is!"

That likeness, brethren, is even in this life begun, and begun from a similar process. We are "called the sons of God" even now; and no spiritual child of God is without the paternal image that authenticates and attests his descent. We are even already "predestined to be conformed to the similitude of his Son." The impulses and contemplations to which even faith attains, have in themselves a transforming energy. Clinging to Christ, we must in the very act of adherence to Him as our Redeemer, walk in His footsteps as our guide: and looking habitually upon His revealed excellencies, we cannot but love what we behold, and, in a measure, become what we love....Even in the ordinary course of human affections, do you not recognise this assimilating power of all genuine attachment? It is thus that two beings joined in mutual affection become each what neither was before; each catches from the other a tincture of that other's nature;—it is thus that through all the variety of the connexions and affinities of life, the changes of character reflect the changes of attachment. And to this, as to every other of the holier laws of the human heart, the religion of Christ presents its lovely counterpart. Christ has borrowed of us all that we ever had of innocence, our nature in its incorruption,—that He may bestow upon us in return, the likeness of His own perfections. And of this transcendent boon, I repeat, that even now, amid our trials and our tears, we possess the foretastes, the pledges, the opening dawn!

But why is not this transformation *yet more* complete? Precisely because the vision of this our Christ is not itself complete or accurate; because, conceiving our celestial King (as I before noted) by such elements of spiritual beauty as the grace of heaven enables us to find or to conceive in ourselves, rudiments of human imperfection inevitably adhere to all our portraits of these consummate glories. [And perhaps it was to something of this kind that the blessed Paul alluded, when, after speaking of having "known Christ after the flesh," he determined "to know Him so no longer."] But when the feeble conceptions of a too feeble faith shall have been exchanged for the full and accurate evidence of sight, no such weaknesses in the subject shall mar the beauty of the object; no distance shall diminish, no spot shall stain that everlasting Sun. It must therefore exercise a tenfold power of attracting, animating, illumining; all within its sphere must be robed in its beams, and present a copy of its light. Can you not then understand and acknowledge the force of our inspired Apostle's divine argument, when, building the resemblance upon the vision, he declared that "we shall be like Him, *for* we shall see Him *as he is*"? As Moses, returning from converse with his God, was obliged to veil a face shining with a light reflected from that living Light, so, and for the same reason surely, was it, that Jesus offered the memorable petition to His Father, "that they whom thou hast given me may be where I am, *that they may behold my glory*." (John xvii. 24.) Yes! blessed Lord! that we may behold thy glory, and be glorified with and by it; that after conceiving thee long and faithfully but dimly here, and to the last grieving over the dishonour our best conceptions do thee, we may at length "awake in thy likeness, *and be satisfied!*"

Ere that awful hour of manifestation, when Jesus shall be triumphant in His servants, and His servants triumphant in Him, a period must elapse to all; a period of whose length no man can dare to pronounce. We know that as He once appeared in humiliation, He shall assuredly appear in glory; we know that as the earth trembled at His resurrection, it shall yet tremble at His advent; that as the attesting sun was darkened at His death, so shall *He Himself* eclipse it by the splendours of His coming. "*When He shall appear*," we shall be like Him. Brethren beloved! as you would indeed prepare your hearts for that glowing image of God to be thus impressed for everlasting, cultivate the contemplation and the likeness of His nature now! If Christ is, indeed, "in you the hope of glory," oh! let Him be in you also the impulse and the example of a Christ-like life. The practical value of these views of the gradual transformation of our nature by the knowledge and the vision of God, lies mainly in this,—that they tend to give us some conception of the *inwardness and depth* of the spiritual change needed in man, and thus supply

motives to extraordinary measures of vigilance and purity.
"He that hath this hope in him, purifieth himself." He
knows that the resemblance to God is the great element of the
celestial state, and that the depths of the Spirit are the scene
and subject of that resemblance. He therefore labours that
God's image be so reproduced in his heart, that not merely
his outward actions, but his motives and principles of action,
may be such as harmonise with those of the august society he
anticipates. For the action abides only in its desert,—its
reward or its punishment; but motives and principles pass the
grave, they become part of our moral identity,—as they are
now, so will they endure for everlasting. We construct
ourselves for glory or for ruin; each day adds a new
element for good or evil to that nature which (as it were)
by its own elasticity will spring to heaven, or by its own
dead weight descend to kindred darkness. With this view,
learn to test all things by the standard of the sanctuary; of
each thought, and impulse, and purpose, and project, ask how
far it bears the impress of that likeness which is to be, in the
glorified nature, the ground and substance of eternal bliss?
How far is it recognised by angels; how far is it authenticated
by the example of that incarnate Son of God who came to be
to us the express image of His Father's glory? Thus living,
eternal life itself is begun in our hearts; thus, and thus only,
under the teaching and moulding of the divine Regenerator of
our nature, does the heavenly life in time, anticipate, and
herald, and prepare,—and blending with it at length is lost
in,—the life of heaven for eternity!

I have spoken to-day of the joys of eternity; I have now
to speak of the charities of time. As I before declared to
you, so do I now repeat,—he little knows the mystic bond
that unites the Christian motives and emotions, who can
conceive such a transition sudden or abrupt. I trust in God
your hearts will prove this day, that to lay the foundations in
the God of love, and in the world where His love is mani-

fested, is the surest art to build the fabric of charity. Yes, this union of joy and of tenderness *is* a wondrous paradox in the daily and hourly story of the Christian experience. Anticipations of unimaginable glory, themselves the very motives (and that from no sordid calculation, but from the native force of the feelings themselves,)—the very motives, I say, of humble, lowly devotedness! and those men who habitually live in a region of reposing expectation, compared to which the consciousness of royalty itself is a shadow,—the very men whose self-abasement is willing " to spend and be spent " in the cause, not merely of Christ, but of the meanest disciple that bears His name! It *is* a wondrous combination. Trembling hearts, that yet are bold to claim kindred with the Lord of a Universe! Resolute,—undaunted,—unconquerable believers,—men of panoply and prowess in the warfare with the powers of darkness, whose brows are bound with the wreaths of a thousand spiritual triumphs (" through Christ that strengtheneth them ")—who yet shall soften as children at the story of grief, shall gladly wear away strength, and health, and life itself at the bedsides of distress,—shall lavish all that is theirs to soothe a single pang, (these princely Pilgrims of Eternity!) and claim to themselves, as in the compass of an infinite benevolence, the whole sad inheritance of human woe! In hearts such as these (God grant they may be many here!) I still touch but one string when I " modulate " from the joys they anticipate to the sorrows they love to assuage; from the triumphant repose of immortality to the minute but all-important labours that in their own vicinity, as,—thank God!—in so many others, are educating souls by instruction, and precept, and example, to attain it!

Brethren in Christ! I have done. You now know the nature of our wants and our dependence. We have spoken largely this day of the image of God upon the soul of man;

and of its completion in the eternal world. Remember that when Christ would mark out His own from the mass of mankind, it was " by this sign," " that *they should love one another*." In this, then, above all things, save that love to God of which it is the product, rests the perfectness of the spiritual image in this world; in this, above *all* things, rests to ourselves the *practical test* and pledge that as we are " now the sons of God," so, " when He shall appear," and when we shall be admitted to contemplate and to study *Him*, the very essence of whose nature is love, we shall indeed " be like Him, for we shall see Him as He is."

SERMON IV.

THE HOLY TRINITY.

Revelation XXII. 1.

And he showed me a pure river of water of life, clear as crystal, proceeding out of the throne of God and of the Lamb.

This is a scene from heaven. It is a picture of the presiding Powers and Principles of heaven; a group of symbols expressing in the shadowy language of time and sense the ineffable realities of eternity. Eye hath not seen nor ear heard the true antitypes that answer to these images; thoroughly to know them is the experience of another form of existence, when new requirements shall bring new faculties; but it *is* given us to see, though as in a mirror darkly, yet as in a mirror truly; and from these representations, suited as they are to our present imperfect state, to collect the very substance and real being of things everlasting. These Personages that occupy the one undivided Throne of heaven, and before whom in equal adoration the heavenly worshippers fall prostrate; this bright effluence that proceeds from them both as from a fountain deep and central, and which, pervading the City of God, feeds and quickens the tree of life; —do these bring to you no thoughts that harmonise with that great Mystery in which the Church of the living God, the faithful conservator of the faith once delivered to the saints, calls upon her children "by the confession of a true faith to acknowledge the glory of the eternal Trinity, and in the power of the Divine Majesty to worship the Unity?" Surely it is no other than this Mystery of the threefold Deity that is shadowed to us in that Throne of the Father and the Incarnate Son, from whose depths is gushing the spiritual river of life,—that same river of living water, of which this evangelist has told us that Christ "spake it of *the Spirit* which they that believe on Him should receive." Surely it is nothing less than this, that the revealing Angel would exhibit to us as filling and glorifying the City of Peace, the new Jerusalem of God; even as the belief of it is now the glory and adorning of His Militant Church below. Long may that belief continue to animate and console us here; so shall we be meet partakers of those holy mysteries, when at length admitted to pass from faith to sight, and to study our celestial theology in the very presence of its divine object, whose " face " we shall then " see," and whose " name shall be in our foreheads!" Long may the Church, undismayed by the audacity of heresy, ... but I need not offer the prayer, for the Church's life is in Christ's promise immortal, and it lives but by this truth. It lives but by this truth; for its life is in the indwelling of Christ, and were Christ not God, His indwelling were a fable and a mockery, its life is in the abiding presence of the Spirit; and were the Spirit not a Person divine, how were He thus universally to abide and to intercede, without invading the deepest and holiest prerogatives of the eternal God? how shall not the Church adore these as God who do for her, and are to her, all that her highest conceptions can imagine her God to be and to do? or in what terms shall she define her God which shall exclude the characters and properties that Revelation ascribes to her Sanctifier and her Redeemer? Her life is blended with the life of Christ and of the Spirit; she breathes but by these divine Ministers of the divine Father; forsaking the blessed truth of their essential divinity, she abandons the very charter of her existence;—for she exists no longer, the spouse of Christ has no longer a being on earth, when surrendering the awful and glorious claims which St. Paul and St. Peter have not hesitated to vindicate to every faithful member of her body,—those of being "partakers of the divine nature," of being "filled unto all the fulness of God," she sinks into the cold creation of a human prophet, with no treasury of graces beyond the poor products of human faculties and human feelings!

Let us then return to our text; but return to it through an avenue that may open on either hand wider prospects of spiritual truth and beauty.

The Trinity in Unity, of Father, Son, and Holy Ghost, is presented to us in *two* aspects in the volume of revelation; antecedently to the incarnation of the Son, and subsequently to that event. Rightly to distinguish these, may clear our views, and by the simple force and symmetry of truth tend to obviate many objections. And first, of the first.

(1.) In the very first verses of the first Book of the Bible we discover plain manifestations of a threefold operation of Deity; the unapproachable Godhead creating by the instrumentality of the Word and through the life-giving efficacy of the Spirit;—and to this plurality (of which there is a faint image in our own nature) it is the all but universal attestation of the Church that the Deity refers when, as President of this mystic Council, he proclaims His will,—"Let *us* make man in *our* image, after *our* likeness!" The truest and safest comment upon the whole procedure, is the opening of St. John's Gospel, in which, with manifest reference to the parallel commencement of Genesis, and with the direct purpose of connecting it with the incarnation of Christ, and the new creation thereby wrought, he declares that "*in the beginning*" was the Word,—distinct from God, for He was "with God," yet one with God, for He "was God," the very Creator, for "all things were made by Him, and without Him was not anything made that was made." After the formation of man, thus framed to be an image of the Trinity, relations of course arise between him and his Framer; the drama (so to speak) of the moral history of the world is arranged, the

Personages are prepared, and the action of the eventful performance is to commence. And solemnly it does commence. In that mysterious Garden where the spotless infancy of our race was passed, *a Being* is alone with man, who wields the powers, bears the title, and publishes as His own the Law, of God. On the unveiled face of this Being Adam is permitted to gaze, the awful yet winning accents of this Being to hear and to understand; even as " the pure in heart" are promised once more to behold Him, and to grow brighter as they behold. But,—I catch a voice of many thousand years later which tells me, "*no man hath seen God at any time*, the only-begotten Son which is in the bosom of the Father, He hath declared Him;" and another which echoes and strengthens it, —that He is one "whom no man hath seen, nor can see." What! " no man *hath seen*" Him whom Adam saw alike in anger and in mercy, whom Abraham beheld and the Patriarchs, who proclaimed to Moses " *I* am the God of thy father,—I am that I am," whom the same Moses contemplated till his human countenance burned with the reflected glory of God, whom Isaiah beheld worshipped by all heaven? What! "no man *can see*" Him of whom it is distinctly promised that His servants shall " see His face," and " see Him as He is," insomuch that He shall be the very Light of the future world in the blaze of an omnipresent splendour? How shall we reconcile these things? Let Him declare who spake as never man spake! " Jesus saith unto him, Have I been so long time with you, and yet hast thou not known me, Philip? He that hath seen *me* hath seen the Father; and how sayest thou then, Shew us the Father?"—Let his Prophet declare, who names the Child of Bethlehem " the everlasting Father" as well as the Prince of Peace; let his Apostle declare, who tells us that " God was in Christ,"—that He is " the image of the invisible God," " the brightness of His glory, and the express image of His Person." *This* solves the difficulty which nothing else can ever solve. Every manifestation of God that has ever made our world a temple, was the manifestation of that eternal Word and Wisdom, who is "with God" and "is God;" the Father, or absolute Fountain of Deity, is Himself ineffable, inaccessible; no created thing hath ever beheld the Godhead of the Father save as it is one with the Godhead of the Son; or hath ever felt the quickening life of the Father save as it is one with the quickening life of God the Holy Ghost.

Thus, then, the Trinity glorifies the pages of the Law and the Prophets no less really than it glorifies the pages of the better Covenant. Thus, long before the divine Incarnation, the Word of God, not yet the Jesus, nor yet save in designation the Christ, was busy in mercy and in judgment among men,—visibly by Himself made manifest, invisibly through His Spirit. God was not pleased till the fulness of time to be "manifest in *the flesh*," nor "took He on Him," we are told, "the nature *of angels;*" in some mode distinct from these He contracted His infinitude to meet our limited faculties. The Prophets speak of this visible exhibition of the Son of God as outgrowing the powers of human or even of angelic endurance. Isaiah tells us that the seraphims veiled their faces with their wings at the insufferable glory of One whom St. John expressly declares to have been no other than Christ our Saviour; nor can we doubt when we compare a description of Christ almost verbally the same in the Book of Revelation (i. 13, 14), that the same eternal Word is shadowed to us in that "Ancient of Days" to whom Daniel saw the Son of Man approach, thereby foretokening that union of the human nature with the divine which was at length to found our redemption.

(2.) This brings us to the other aspect under which I have said the Trinity of Father, Son, and Holy Ghost is exhibited to us in the *New* Testament. It does not oppose the former, it is *founded* upon it; it only draws it nearer to our hearts in applying it to the immediate work of our salvation.

Christ then is the "Son of God," in another sense not eternal; God must consequently be his Father, in a corresponding sense not eternal; and the Holy Spirit is sent from both, in a sense not eternal but beginning and continued in time. In this way it is that these mysterious Agents operate directly in preparing us for glory, and it is in this secondary form that they are presented to us in the text. If this appear to you to require a little thought, you will, I am sure, acknowledge that the subject is one which deserves some reflection. The distinction I speak of, between the eternal Trinity and this subordinate manifestation of it in the work of our redemption, lies in fact at the root of the whole controversy between us and those impugners of the Christian verity, who are doubtless at this moment in more than one assembly of your city endeavouring to cloud and perplex the testimony of Scripture to the deity of Christ and of Christ's Spirit.

We observe, then, that at the incarnation of Christ, when God descended into Man, the whole Trinity, itself unchanged, assumed a new and peculiar position conformable to this wondrous revolution. The eternal Word, in being made flesh through the overshadowing of the Spirit, acquired a new title to being the Son of God; "*therefore*," declares the angel in St. Luke, "that holy thing which shall be born of thee shall be called the Son of God." In His *resurrection* again, as St. Paul more than once attests, His claim to this Sonship was confirmed and declared. The Son of God, then, and His eternal Father, have (so to speak) again met on the platform of this world, and there acquired new titles to Paternity and Filiation. While the Holy Spirit, coming among us as the Paraclete, proceeding from *this* Father and *this* Son, is no longer merely the Holy Spirit of the Old Testament, but a Spirit sent forth with powers before unknown, but derived from the incarnate Christ, of quickening, strengthening, and refreshing the children of the Father of Christ Jesus. Here, then, is the Trinity of the *new* creation, as the former was the Trinity of the old; it is the same in *substance*, but the colours are brighter, the attitude nearer and more endearing; the difference is only such as is between the God of the universe and the God that lives in the believer's heart. And this new, and to us even more interesting form of the Trinity, arising out of the incarnation of its second Person, is to last for ever; based upon the former, blended with it, and at last (though preserved) all but merged in it, at that wondrous period when, as St. Paul has told us, the Christ is to be subject to the Father, and "God all in all!"

With this distinction of the Trinity as viewed before and after the redemption, present to our minds, let us turn to the text,—let us turn to the Book from which the text is taken.

Whatever, in this wondrous Book of the Church, is obscure, *this*, at least, is clear enough; *this*, at least, humbly and patiently meditated, may win the blessing its last chapter promises to him "who keepeth the sayings of the prophecy of this Book." But I shall be brief and summary, as the time demands.

Suppose,—which I utterly deny,—that the reception of mysterious truths in religion could not be shown in any other way to affect the heart and life, is there not *one* way,—most important, most impressive,—in which they are calculated to exert a beneficial influence? If there be anything more than another in which the religious habits of our age are peculiarly defective, it is in the feeling of *awe*. We are not satisfied unless we have measured with the foot-rule of our understanding every side of every truth we profess; unless "our hands have handled of the Word of life." The finger must have been in the print of the nails and the hand in the side, or we will not believe. We have (I fear it) too much of the spirit of the heathen victor, who rushed into the Holy of Holies to discover *what was there;* too often (I fear yet more) like him we return from our scrutiny, contemptuously assuming that there *is* nothing where we have *seen* nothing. How in our times the rapid progress of natural knowledge may, and does, assist this spirit of proud discontent, it is unnecessary to insist. But, for the tendency in all its degrees, the revelation of mysterious truths is the trial, and, duly received, the remedy. In the old dispensation, religious awe was secured by means outward and occasional; the solemn Temple service, the frequency of miraculous interpositions, the prophetic teaching, the very obscurity of that shadowy region of types and forms in which their ceremonial religion lay;—in ours, where these things have been laid aside, the object is provided for by those fuller declarations which we possess of the properties of the Divine nature in itself and in its mystical communion with the spirit of man. And thus our God becomes more awfully unfathomable to the reason in proportion as He draws more nearly, more lovingly, more blessedly to the heart!

This statement applies more or less to *all* the mysterious disclosures of our system.

But this mystery of the Trinity forms the foundation, and the motive, and the strength of the practical life, in a manner so peculiar and eminent that it would be unpardonable to omit it; more especially as this very relation to practice is one of the most powerful scriptural proofs of the reality of the doctrine.

It is always somewhat presumptuous to affirm what are God's *final* objects in any dealing with man; Revelation, however, seems to encourage us in believing that the chief ultimate object of religion is to elevate man into affinity, and thence society, with his Creator. For *this* he was created in Paradise; *this* the new creation is to regain. This affinity can be founded only on resemblance or community of nature. Hence was he made at first in "the image" of God; hence are we perpetually reminded that the spiritual life on earth is conformity to the image of the Son; hence the glory of heaven is declared to consist in being "like Him," as "seeing Him as He is." And hence, as beings that *love* tend to likeness and imitation, so is the perfection of our religion *the love of God;* a love perpetuated into the next life, beyond the compass of faith and hope, *because* the likeness is meant to grow more and more perfect for eternity. To ensure this community of nature, we know that Christ came on earth in ours; in order that first occupying *our* nature, He might spread His own through us. So completely is this the great characteristic of our religion, so really does everything arise out of this and resolve into it, that the best index of its purpose, its surest expositors, its perpetual and living Scriptures,—its Sacraments,—are wholly meant to represent and to cement this very connexion. The idea of both,—not the only but the chief idea,—is the mystical incorporation of man with his redeeming God. Now mark,—through the entire compass of the New Testament, this mystical communion between man's soul and the Powers of eternity, is, without a shadow of distinction, referred to God,—to Christ,—and to the Holy Spirit as its objects. To unite with the one involves union with the other two:—as we have "the fellowship of the Father," so have we "the fellowship of the Son" and "the fellowship of the Holy Ghost;" as we are "baptized into the name of the Father," so are we "baptized into the name of the Son" and "the name of the Holy Ghost;" as God is our life, so is "Christ our life," and "the Spirit is life." That is to say,—the perfection of our nature, the final object of the whole work of God in redemption, is equally attained by blending that nature with God Himself, with God's Spirit, and with *whom?* A man, a brother man to Moses and Isaiah, to Paul and John! He that can believe this, may surely go a little farther and believe the Trinity!

If, then, the whole purpose of Scripture be, as they tell us, "*practical,*" I affirm that its practice is "rooted and grounded" in this our belief. I will not condescend to argue this great doctrine from debated text and isolated passage! I find it in every page of the New Testament; it is omnipresent in revelation, like the God it declares! Wherever it is not asserted it is assumed; it is not one thread in the web, but the ground of the whole texture. It is like the clouded sun at noonday; you cannot always see the very web, but you know it is *there* by the light it spreads! Everywhere,—we have seen it,—the Gospel points our aspirations to God; we rush forward,—and it is *Christ* that meets us! Everywhere it bids us pray to feel and know an inward God; we pray, we gain our prayer,—and " the Spirit " becomes ours! If these be but our fellows in creation, not one text,—nor two texts,—but the whole Bible is a mockery. What right have these inferior agents to interpose between us and our Father which is in heaven? What right have these subordinate officers of heaven to offer us God, and give us only themselves?

Dread not, then, brethren, in humble adoration to bend before the Son and Spirit of God, co-eternal emanations of the supreme Father, who are not the Father, yet without whom the Father hath never been. Fear not to worship where God Himself,—the "jealous God,"—has bid you kneel. This faith in the threefold Deity has been the one abiding glory of the Church in all its ages; it will be its glory for ever,—till the gates of hell shall have prevailed against " the great Prince that standeth for the children of the people." It has survived the shock of outward heresy, the peril of internal corruption. When every truth was more or less tampered with, this was respected; it was still the link that bound the Church's belief to heaven in even its saddest and darkest days; as long as it remained Christ was in the ship, and though " a great tempest" might " arise in the sea, insomuch that the ship was covered with the waves," and He, the Master, be " asleep on a pillow," not apparently interfering to rescue or to aid; yet though slumbering, He was *there*—there, to arise in His own time, and rebuke the winds, and say to the sea, "Peace, be still!" Brethren! once baptized into its name, hold fast to this belief; and amid desertion, and corruption, and calamity, God is with us still,—the Shechinah has not left the Temple! If the Trinity be in the creeds of all, we may hope that the Trinity shall be in the hearts of some. Children of the heavenly Father! believe it not only, but feel it too. If the apostles felt the Godship of Christ and of Christ's divine Spirit to be the ground of life spiritual and eternal, oh, shall not we endeavour to draw from the same fountains of unspeakable hope? Remember that every regenerate soul is itself the shrine of Father, Son, and Holy Ghost; that you are allied with the eternal God; and *that*, not through human or inferior means, but by the power of that Word that liveth and abideth within us. Heaven descended to earth, that earth might rise to heaven. It was not to tell us only of a world to come that Jesus came among us; it was to create in our hearts the heaven He preached; not to tell us of sanctity merely, but to sanctify; not to bring immortality to light only, but to immortalize. He came not to promise only, —the Baptist would have sufficed for that, but to *be* the thing He promised. This,—*this* is the difference between us who believe and them who cavil: *they* hold that the eternal God is beyond us, to judge merely and to reward; we believe that He is within us,—a Power, a Principle, and a Life! "In that day ye shall know that I am in you... because I live, ye shall live also." Therefore are we raised even now into a world infinite and eternal, whither no meaner belief can ever lift the soul of man; a world of thoughts, not wild and frenzied and enthusiastic, but calm and deep as the heaven they foreshadow. We are alone with God; the human nature is common to both, and He who is one with the Father, is one with us! Oh, blindness dark and fatal, which can see our wants, and cannot see that this union through the God incarnate is that alone which can ever meet them! Oh, hardness worse and more wicked than that blindness, which can see that this *is* very truth, and yet is not softened to perfect love by such a recital! When to lift us to a state like His own, God hath been thus among us; may His life and power quicken our dead and feelingless hearts, till the Trinity shall have become not the cold conclusion of the intellect, but the priceless treasure of the affections; the blessed foundation and the perpetual strength of the new and spiritual life! *What* was it that brought the eternal Trinity to glorify our earth, to tell us of themselves, and give themselves to us? *What*,—but love! love, — the one grace which is mutual between God and man; which made God human, and makes man divine! What was it that tore the celestial crown from the everlasting Son of God, to be replaced by the crown of thorns; that urged His weary steps through all that long labyrinth of pain, His earthly course,—and bowed His meek head, and yielded His agonized spirit,—what, but ineffable love,—the master grace of His own Gospel, the one pre-eminent virtue He came to exhibit and to diffuse:—that He might banish every narrow thought, and re-make the selfish world into one world of love!

SERMON V.

THE SORROW THAT EXALTS AND SANCTIFIES.

St. Matthew V. 4.

Blessed are they that mourn, for they shall be comforted.

THERE are many consolations in the Christian faith, my brethren; many sources of joyful hope derived from the eternal world of our expectation, much to animate the fainting spirit,—if genuine *belief* would but quicken the dull elements of our professed creed. Yet, after all, in some respects,—in its position in the world, in its tone of teaching, in *many* of its effects upon those who receive it,—the Religion of Christ *is* eminently the Religion of Sorrow! It presupposes a corrupt nature,—it purposes to subdue it: this in itself is a matter always of no slight difficulty, often of much anxiety and distress. It sets before us an ideal of perfection, which the feebleness of our natural constitution has, perhaps, never allowed any one disciple to reach, but which serves to keep alive a perpetual and melancholy sense of deficiency. It stands in the midst of a hostile world which it condemns, and which assails *it*. The very character of its Founder,—a "Man acquainted with grief,"—whose spirit pervades the whole, and who, Himself "separate from sinners," similarly separates His followers from the turbulent enjoyments of a world "that lieth in wickedness;" all these things—setting Christianity at variance with the scene in which it is for the present manifested—necessarily tinge it with a sombre colouring, give it that melancholy aspect which men so often observe and censure, and do, in truth, ally it, more or less, with sadness, perplexity, and pain. The ordinary representations of this, among men who know nothing of the practical operation of the religion, may indeed be exaggerated; but the fact itself, —that the spiritual life, based upon repentant sorrow, is (though brightened with heavenly consolations) accompanied with emotions of sadness arising from many sources, and constant obligations of self-denial often involving much distress, —no Christian, true and tried, can deny. As Christians we *are* self-crucified,—our faith is fixed to the cross. We must not shrink from an avowal which is our glory,—we confess ourselves the pilgrims of a land where little is to be found to content the wants or wishes of the heirs of eternity, and, looking to heaven as our only home, we acknowledge the loneliness of spirit which belongs to wanderers and exiles! "By the waters of Babylon" what *should* we do but "sit down and weep, when we remember thee, O Zion!"

On this day,* with which the Church opens a solemn season of sorrow and self-discipline, we may well pause to speak of sorrow,—its uses,—and its consolations. An immemorial custom has set apart this portion of our year as a consecrated time of subdued and serious thought, in which the children of heaven are specially called upon to humiliation and prayer. Let us, upon this its first day, join in meditating upon that mystery of sorrow out of which so much of Christian blessedness proceeds. Summoned to know and feel ourselves the dust we are, let us ask wherefore it is good for us to be abased,—good for us to chasten spiritual joy with spiritual sadness, and even in our happiest hours with God,—our high consciousness of adoption and sonship,—to own the lowliness of the creature, and still to sigh, "forgive us our trespasses!" We are invited to restraint,—mortification,—discipline,—to deepen the impression of the cross upon our hearts and lives. The precept is painful to flesh and blood, but it is wise;—let

* Ash-Wednesday.

us for a brief moment reflect upon its wisdom, that we may offer the obedience not of reluctant slaves, but of willing and reasoning men! We shall consider, then, the *uses* of affliction,—we shall speak of that mysterious *fellowship of Christ Himself* in this discipline of sorrow, which so gloriously exalts and sanctifies ours,—we shall endeavour to penetrate through these clouds, to the light of *consolation* beyond them.

The force and prominence which is given to the practice of self-denial in the New Testament is certainly, then, in its *degree*, peculiar to the Christian revelation. To die to the world in order to live to God, is nowhere else made the *fundamental* maxim of life. But we would err if we conceived that uninspired wisdom had not, in all ages, apprehended the necessity of restraint and the advantages of discipline. There is scarcely an attempt of thoughtful men antecedent to the publication of the Gospel upon the great question, "how man best may live," which is not built upon the recommendation of restrictions and denials; scarcely a project for public or private reformation which does not set out with the tacit or expressed acknowledgment, that to float with the current of common life is inevitably to surrender the proper dignity of man,—that peace of mind is not to be attained without severe and continued conflict,—that the high happinesses of wisdom are not the chance acquisition of lethargy and indolence, but the crowns and prizes of the triumphant champion. This tone of reasoning everywhere abounds among the uninspired teachers of the art of life. Mere caprice, or despair of high attainments, or the desire of originality, may now and then have varied it, and *did* sometimes disgracefully lower the standard of thought. But, on the whole, the testimony is plain and decisive. Conscience and reason gave no "uncertain sound;" and they whose practice fell below these lofty requirements were not (in their degree) without "the truth," but "held the *truth* in *unrighteousness*," as the inspired writer proclaims. How injudicious, indeed, is the attempt to disguise or deny a fact which is *itself* the highest testimony to the truth and importance of the revelation of the Gospel!

But while all these teachers speak of the duty of self-control,—praise, explain, describe it,—when we descend into their motives, we find a miserable poverty of inducements for a creature formed as man is. "Man should not refuse afflictions, difficulties, persecutions,—for it is a noble thing to be superior to that which enslaves the lower creation, a noble thing to be independent of all that fortune can do, a noble thing to rival the very inhabitants of the skies, and show them on earth souls as mighty as their own, a noble thing to strengthen the mind by occasional crosses when too much relaxed by ease and enjoyment." You see at once how little fitted was all this pompous array of motives to act upon the mass of mankind at all, to act upon *any* man with firm and constant practical effect. You see how directly it aimed at self-exaltation as its ultimate object and reward;—that is, how distinctly it perpetually said,—be humbled that you may be proud; be poor and persecuted, that you may despise your persecutors!... And thus the whole scheme eventuated in disappointment. It purposed to teach the art of happiness,—it taught the sure road to pride, isolation, and contemptuousness. And he knows little of human nature who does not know that, *wherever* happiness lie, *this* assuredly is not the path to it! No despiser of his fellows was ever other than despised of heaven, and an exile, not merely from spiritual happiness itself, but even from the temper most remotely connected with it!

"Blessed are the mourners," declares the Saviour. To this (as we have seen) even natural wisdom is not without bearing some attestation. "For they shall be comforted,"—*here* the illustrator of life and immortality stands alone,—alone in the clearness of the promise, alone in the authority of the Promiser!

Illumined by better light than earthly wisdom ever brought, let us once more, then, approach this holy theme of sorrow, and ask, in what spirit and for what uses a disciple of the Mourner of Gethsemane is to learn to grieve? And may the eternal Spirit urge these sad but healing truths upon every heart that beats before me! We are companions in a dark mysterious world; Christ spares not His people the trial and the tear; to *many*, life itself is one long "Lent" of spiritual tribulation, with glimpses of light faint and few; to *all*, suffering must more or less herald glory,—let us see if we cannot in some feeble degree penetrate the dark enigma of a Christian's grief.

If, then, the great condition of spiritual vitality be the union of the soul in time with the Lord of eternity,—if the nature of that union must mainly consist, on the part of the disciple, in humble and confiding trust,—is it not among the first requisites of the religious life that every obstacle should be cleared away which may prevent in the heart the full formation of that state of humble dependence in which the essence of its blessedness on earth is comprised? Now that the efficacy of *Sorrow* for this great work of self-abasement *is* mighty, scarcely requires a statement. Affliction is the very voice of God speaking to the heart of man its nothingness. Sermons may fail; but sorrow is more eloquent than sermons. It is not the Gospel, but it is the herald of the Gospel; it is the very "voice of him that crieth" in the vast "wilderness" of the desolated heart,—" Prepare ye the way of the Lord, make straight *in this desert* a highway for our God!" Surrounded by all earthly comforts, we may not comprehend the message, "comfort ye!" It may seem a superfluous consolation. We send it to the widow, the orphan, the captive. But when around us lie shattered the hopes and dreams of that fleeting prosperity, when we walk among ruins, ourselves a ruin,— *then* God's time is near, His hand is busy in that chaos, the "broken heart" is there which He has promised not to spurn, and His Spirit (which works by means and times and seasons) is even now about to weave of the dark substance of that grief the "garment of praise," of which His prophet has spoken,—the adorning meet for the everlasting kingdom! "Blessed," indeed, "are the mourners" to whom their mourning has brought humiliation; the raptures of eternity will declare whether that is "a repentance to be repented of!"

But, again, is there not *another* equally simple process discoverable in this mystery of the Christian's sorrow?—and shall we not *again* be grateful for the tears that teach the way to Paradise? You, of course, anticipate me when I speak of the power that lies in affliction not merely to humiliate man's *self*, but to avert him from the gloom of the world around him to the promised brightness of the world of hope. Surely I speak no novelty when I ask you, Have you not ever found that one stroke of sorrow carries with it, as it were, the condensed experience of years, and impresses with a truth, and depth, and reality never before known, the great fact that our pulpits are for ever publishing, and for ever publishing in vain, that the world is a traitor to our hopes, that its word is falsehood, its promise mockery; that however, in the calm of the summer day, we may float in lazy security upon its surface, it inevitably whelms us when the wind rises? But, oh, even sorrow itself is weak where God does not infuse His lessons in its sting. To no subordinate means will He depute His omnipotence! And oftentimes, just as the sinking seaman seizes in his agony the nearest support, so in our agony too *we* grasp at the hope next us,—some vain thought as idle as the one that wrecked us; some new dependence, that fails us as the old one did. And thus it is that we see so many wretched votaries of the world and of sorrow, who know happiness neither in enjoyment nor in promise, to whom earth is no heaven, and yet heaven no hope,—exiles of both worlds, and without claim in either! May God keep His Church from this last and worst perversion of His providential teaching!

Such,—not to pass into minuter discussions,—are some of the purposes and advantages of those chastening visitations to which the Church at this time more specially directs our thoughts. Such is the awakening, the purifying, power of sorrow,—in God's repository of providences, the great natural medicine for infirm and diseased spirits. ... It is remarkable, that in the work of *Christ Himself* upon earth, a certain power of necessary discipline is also attributed to His afflictions,—a mighty and mysterious subject which no man can approach without reverence and awe! But while fully to understand the nature of this qualifying process is perhaps beyond our capacity, the fact seems to admit of no doubt,— that it was, in the counsels of God, and the necessity of things, requisite, that the Leader of Salvation should be consecrated for His high office through a course of preliminary suffering. "Though he were a son, yet learned He *obedience* by the things which He suffered: and being made perfect, (that is, being thus duly consecrated for the dignity,) He became the Author of eternal salvation to all who *obey Him*." To reward obedience fitly, He Himself obeyed. To understand temptation, He Himself was tempted. To sympathise with man, He Himself became their Brother. Hence it is that He Himself connects the suffering and the reward in that question to the wondering disciples,—" ought not Christ to have suffered these things, *and* to enter into His glory?" and St. Peter, in like manner, combines the same double aspect of the office of the Redeemer,—" the sufferings of Christ *and* the glory that should follow," declaring them both equally the subject of ancient prophecy. Christ then is the bright and eternal model of suffering and its recompence; in His own divine Person He has immortalized their union! Is there not then a glory in rejection? may we not contemn content? Whatever be the intensity of sorrow that bows and presses the heart of man,—remember that for every grief you suffer, the meek and holy One suffered a thousand; that there is not in the spirit a dungeon or recess of anguish, however untrodden or lonely, in which the Lord of glory was not a mourning inhabitant before you! Does the victim know the loss of earthly comforts? Christ knew not where to lay His head. Does he regret the fall from wealth or power? Let him remember who it was that emptied Himself of the glory which He had before the world was, and left the throne of the universe for the agonies of Calvary! Does he deplore the *loss* of friends? Christ was friendless in His most trying hour! Does he bewail the *ingratitude* of friends? Christ was betrayed by His own familiar one! Finally, does he fear the coming of death, the torture of the separation? What death can he anticipate which shall approach the horror of the last days of his Redeemer? Thus, wherever we turn, whatever be our shade of grief,—we are but feeble *copyists* of the great Sufferer, who in His own person exhausted every variety of human sorrow!

But it may be asked,—in what sense not derogatory to the dignity of Christ can we conceive *Him* to have been additionally qualified for His office by a career of human suffering? Does *He* require purification, as we do? Could *His* knowledge be increased as ours is? Was *His* mind susceptible of gradual elevation, as *our* infirm and limited capacities are known to be? To what purpose discipline or preparation to a Being of infinite knowledge, power, and goodness?

To answer this *fully*, would lead me far from our immediate subject of contemplation. The solution is to be found in the distinction of the Divine and human natures, in the single personality of the Saviour. As God, the eternal Son was, doubtless, acquainted with all the varieties of human emotion; but the knowledge proper to Deity is not the knowledge proper to man, nor probably bearing any but a very remote analogy to it. As Man, the Lord Jesus was subject to all the sinless laws of humanity,—among others, to the gradual acquisition of knowledge, to the gradual heightening of character,—and to this peculiar law, that information acquired by experience is invariably more vivid and permanent than that obtained by any other channel. As still a Man, (though on the right hand of God,) our Lord does still, doubtless, preserve these principles of our common humanity inwoven in the texture of His nature;—does still know the more firmly, and feel the more intensely, and thence succour the more earnestly, because the knowledge and the feeling are no supernatural additions to His nature, but the knowledge and feeling gathered on earth, and now preserved for immortality, embalmed (as it were) in the divine essence that encompasses and eternalizes them!

To imitate this transcendent model the Church invites you;—by peculiar self-discipline *at this time* to essay the task. What is the object of self-discipline in all its varieties? What, but to bring the desires and habits wholly under control, so that they may learn to obey the slightest order of the spiritual reason and conscience? Every restraint,—every practice which tends to this end, is valuable in exact proportion as it attains it:—whether fasting or vigil, it is valueless in itself, valuable only in relation to this high and holy object. And, dearest brethren, when you remember to what a pitch of strength and health a human *body* may be brought by the steadfast maintenance of appointed rule,—does it not point to a mighty power of a similar nature capable of being exerted upon the spiritual part of man? Through dread of asceticism we are, I much fear, apt to pass into an opposite and more dangerous extreme of carelessness. Depending with an apparent faith, a real negligence, upon the agency of the Spirit of God,—we too much forget that the Spirit urges us *by* means, and to the *use of* means; that His object is not to supersede the prudence and the reason, but to disentangle it of encumbrance, and call it more forcibly, clearly, and constantly into action. Employ every means to rise from sense to faith;—if abstinence will help the work by conquering the opposition, abstain,—if watching, watch,—if any other of the varieties of mortification, boldly, honestly employ them. Consult with candour your own experience of your own temptations; and *then* the sincere prayer of faith will be heard, God will direct and overrule; and whether your spirits, qualifying under faith for the eternal inheritance, be led through the path of bodily mortification or not, a way shall surely be ministered for you into the kingdom of God and of His Christ.

Thither is *He* gone whom we, with our crosses, are to follow! "Blessed are they that mourn; for they *shall be comforted!*" consoled with that divine peace which He has won, and wearing those celestial diadems which He shall distribute! I speak on a day of solemn repentance; but through the saddest of Christian festivals joy *will* irresistibly force its way! The glorious object at the end of the vista flashes back its light upon the whole dim landscape of life behind it. No, —I will not again call it a religion of sorrow. In spite of all that life can bring to shake our calmness of enduring faith, we have something within us (if we be Christians indeed) which the world cannot reach. Joys,—secret but pervading joys,— are treasured in the believer's heart, though oftentimes he cannot himself measure the degree, or trace the source, of his own emotions! And in this gloomy night of life,—waiting for the everlasting day, we must have patience, even though we cannot yet catch the dawnings of the morn,—though we must live by sober faith, and be, for a while, the calm expectants of glory! . . . Think,—if we were Christians *indeed*, in what a spirit we would meet, this blessed hour! The Church bids us meet to grieve for sin,—the Church is right,—" If we say that we have no sin, we deceive ourselves." But in the blessed fellowship of the Father and the Son, the misery of our nature is irradiated and consumed in the light of heaven, sin cannot darken us with its shadow, and Lent itself becomes almost a season of rejoicing! We know not our own privileges! We are called into the family of God,—we are placed as guests at the banquet of heaven,—the treasure-cities of eternity are exhausted of their wealth to adorn and enrich us,—" He who spared not his own Son, how shall He not with Him also freely give us all things?"—But lonely, and languid, and loveless sit we! as if the poorest suppliant in this church who knows and loves his Saviour were not the hero of an eternal story,—were not a chosen brother to Him who is only " the firstborn among many *brethren!* " Come, then, we *will* grieve for sin! We *will* weep over that which made our Beloved weep! Morn and eve shall hear our sighs befitting the time of holy sorrow! We will mourn yet more as we approach nearer to that melancholy week when the " Man of sorrows " " having loved his own, loved them unto the end.". . . But, as " He was delivered for our offences," so was He " raised for our justification." Lent is brightened by its anticipated Easter! Amid all our griefs, a subdued and heavenly joy shall accompany us! Christ was crucified for us,—He is now rejoicing; we who have been crucified with Him, with Him will even now rejoice! And each day, as we read and hear of mournful things,—of the betrayal, and the garden, and the cross,—we will tell our friends that whether to grieve or joy we know not; for the gloom of the trial and the glory of the triumph are mingled in our thoughts. On the one hand, Christ is " set forth evidently *crucified* among us,"—on the other, we see " the heavens opened, and the Son of Man standing on the *right hand of God*." On the one hand, " Behold the Man!" and the crown of thorns,—on the other, " Behold the Man!" and the crown of glory, and the raptures of an assembled universe! . . . But, whether on the Cross or on the Throne, in Him alike and in Him alone will we glory;—He alone has " blessed " us as " mourners,"—and from Him alone (God grant to all His people the power to keep the resolve!)—from Him alone, in the midst of a flattering and seductive world, will we receive the promise as true, that such mourning shall yet be " comforted," —that they that mourn in Zion shall indeed receive " beauty for *ashes*, the oil of joy for mourning, the garment of praise for the spirit of heaviness,—that they may be called trees of righteousness, the planting of the Lord!"

SERMON VI.

THE PURIFYING POWER OF TRIBULATION.

Rev. VII. 13, 14.

What are these which are arrayed in white robes? and whence came they?... These are they which came out of great tribulation.

BRETHREN, how profound is the subtlety of the sinful heart; how perfect is that terrible science of self-deceit by which, from the dawn of reason to the hour of death, we learn to reconcile our worse and our better natures! Surely the "tree of the knowledge of good and evil" might well be to us a forbidden tree; for the knowledge of sin has only driven us upon the art of excusing it,—the wretched art of supplying apologies for predetermined crime,—the fatal power of preserving ourselves in an unbroken dream of imaginary safety from that wrath of God, which yet we cannot deny to be expressly "revealed against all ungodliness,"—of investing a perilous folly with the air of innocent playfulness,—of glossing over darker deeds with the poor pretences of passion and hastiness,—of, in one form or another, soothing a muttering conscience, and forcing reason, against its plainest evidences, to believe that an unimpressed, unspiritual nature can be *that nature* to which eternal Justice has affixed an eternity of rewarding happiness. Unable to question the solid reality of the glory revealed in Scripture, and equally unable to surrender our earthly shadows, we live in a miserable indecision between them. We would come to blessedness, but we cannot bear to walk the pathway that Christ has traced: we promise willing service to God in heaven, but we beg that the heart may have its own way on earth. And thus, day after day, instead of *being* the children of God, we waste our hours in persuading ourselves that we are so, or "special-pleading" with the Majesty of heaven to show cause why we are not!

Now, brethren, recur to the text, and see what encouragement it affords to these wretched infatuations. "What are these which are arrayed in white robes, and whence came they?... These are they which came out of great tribulation." A mighty scene is opened here. The scene which one day, when the curtain of eternity rises, will disclose itself to every one of you, is anticipated in this page. May we so gaze on the reflection as to fit us for the reality! Oh may we,—exiles as we are,—so feel and think of this celestial home, that our domestic affections may already cluster around our "Father who is in heaven," and our hearts and hopes be there, to "make ready the way before us!"

The Prophet of the New Testament tells you the things which he learned from the mouth of Christ and of angels, when he was (as may you be now, in a sense less miraculous perhaps, but not less important) "in the spirit on the Lord's day." He beheld hosts of the blessed (who can say—God grant it!—but that he beheld in that prophetic hour some of the very listeners who are now before me?)—"a multitude of all nations and kindreds," encompassing the visible throne of God and of the Lamb. How all that is loftiest in human conception—its learning, its philosophy, and its poetry—pale before one glance at such a scene! Sorrow had passed away, the unclouded dawn was begun. All that humanity groans for, all that man asks of nature and that nature cannot give, all that love (the essential Spirit of the universe) outpoured upon its chosen objects could bestow,—all was seen to be the bright lot of these blessed ones, and all was for eternity! The wandering soul had reached its centre, the ultimate perfection was attained, and human life ceased to be an enigma. The love of knowledge was satisfied in the perpetual contemplation of the substantial truth; the love of beauty in the unveiled source of all that is beautiful; the love of happiness in the enjoyment of secure and perpetual bliss; the love of the fellow-creatures in the society of holy and responding brother-spirits:—and this was to be for ever! ... John tells us little of his own feelings in his volume of prophecy; but we can learn from our own hearts what must have been the thoughts of the good disciple when he beheld this destined heritage of his regenerated human nature ... He referred humbly to his guide to learn the *history* of these happy spirits, and what was the reply? "Whence came they?" Was it from the haunts of idleness and folly,—was it from the tables where luxury robs the poor of their patrimony of charity,—was it from scenes of passionate excitement, the fever of partizanship, the struggles of rival ambition,—I am not speaking, you perceive, of open crime; I talk of ourselves, who say we "look for an heavenly country,"—was it from frigid and unthoughtful worship, from heartless prayer, and indolent duties,—that these sainted champions of the Cross ascended to their God? No, brethren, no,—" These are they which came out of great tribulation!" They walked a painful and laborious road on earth, before they reached the "City of Peace;" they ran counter to all the most cherished idolatries of their nature, before they were admitted to "see God;" they crucified every corrupted principle, before they obtained that better nature, which is at once the foretaste of eternal happiness, and its necessary qualification. If the portraiture of that undying felicity fires your hearts and imaginations, in the name of common prudence I call on you not to neglect the requisites. Peace is won through war; if you will have rest hereafter, you must not slumber now. The repose of mind which our faith bestows is no indolent lethargy; *this* is the "peace" of "the world," and it is "not as the world giveth peace" that Christ giveth it. The peace of a Christian spirit is not gained until after much contest, and where it exists it is eminently contradistinguished from all worldly principles of quiet,—first, in being not a passive principle, but a source of constant activity,—and secondly, in not resulting from the cessation of outward afflictions, but possessing a capacity of permanence, of triumphant vitality, in the very midst,—not seldom in virtue,—of those persecutions which destroy all worldly repose.

I repeat, brethren, that when I speak of the toils which must preface your everlasting happiness, or your Christian peace on earth, it is not to the open despisers of God that I am speaking,—to those whose whole life shows them beyond all the forces which we could *here* bring to assail them. No, brethren, it is to you who have learned the language of religion, and understand its feelings; to you who profess to fulfil in your life the pledges of your Baptism! It is to you who, living as others live, yet persuade yourselves that you " are not as others are;" and who, though on your deathbed you may not be able to summon from the recollections of a life, a single instance of an evil propensity conquered, a bright affection enkindled, a sacrifice endured,—yet have learned to repose serene in the confident conviction, that, beyond the chasm of the grave, you are to find the glorious form of the Redeemer waiting to conduct His tried and faithful servant into everlasting happiness. This is, indeed, the most irrational of all the delusions of the corrupted heart; and unhappily, in opposing it, we have to oppose an evil that in some manner is produced by the very spread of Christianity itself. It is not where the nominal profession of our faith is accompanied with *direct persecution*, that this monstrous expectation of securing heaven without a struggle against a nature radically corrupt, has place. It is where the religion is outwardly popular, where sincerity is untested and fortitude undemanded, —*there* it is that men dream that human nature can be subdued without a struggle, or that it requires not to be subdued at all,—*there* it is that we forget how those who are "clad in white robes" are "they that have *come out of tribulation.*"

Brethren, my object is to remind you that this self-deceiving forgetfulness is the deepest illusion of him who exists but to destroy you, of him whose principle of life is *hate*. My object is to rouse you to a conflict which you must rouse yourselves to encounter, or forego advantages which are bestowed only as the prizes of victory. And thence, —to suggest to you a careful retrospect in order to determine whether this contest has actually taken place, and to remind you, that, if it has not, if in some period of your life this internal struggle has not occurred, if you cannot remember a time at which you have earnestly prayed for strength, at which, becoming more and more aware of the difficulties and dangers of your state, you have cried aloud again for relief, at which receiving some consolation, you have risen,—and perhaps fallen, —and " being in an agony have prayed yet more earnestly," and have risen again,—at which, in short, you have gone through some, whether more or less, of the phases of this spiritual warfare ;—if, I say, you cannot recal (and recal with facility,— for to be genuine it must be of a felt importance which must make it for ever a prominent object in recollection) a series of changes like these, terminating in a better heart and higher affections,—then it is highly probable (not perhaps absolutely certain, but probable to an alarming degree) that your spiritual state is one of extreme and momentous peril, of peril great indeed at the present moment, but growing in intensity every hour you delay, from the operation of habit in strengthening the obstinate grasp of the world on your hearts. This is the inquisition I want you to make ; these are the signs of salvation which cannot deceive. These are " the marks of the Lord Jesus" which, as Paul bore them in the body, we should bear in the spirit. All the formalities of public, or even private, worship may deceive us as a token of the change,— scripture-reading may deceive,—religious society may deceive,

—habits of religious conversation may deceive,—even a considerable interest in the fortunes and progress of the Gospel around us may deceive,—but these things cannot deceive! To have struggled through our novitiate of religion,—to have sorely lamented and earnestly supplicated,—to have lingered on the borders of a worldly life, sorrowing — for that is human nature—to leave it, yet each hour feeling its ties relax,—to have, perhaps, been taught dependence by a lapse, and blotted out the record of it by a repentant appeal to the Saviour, and to have risen renewed from the failure, more strong because more cautious,—and fortified at length in determined holiness;—all these are experiences which he who has known has peace, which he who has never known may tremble for his final security. There may be immaculate exceptions from humanity who are independent of such a discipline, and who glide into Christianity as their native religion; assuredly few of us have ever seen even the image of such perfection in the natural man; and I suspect that if any such existed, they would be the last to perceive their own privileges, or to deny the necessity of that purifying "tribulation" of heart which seems the destined condition of spiritual perfection to every child of man.

[II.] For, brethren, upon what ground could you stand in resisting the necessity of this conclusion? that a work of *much and urgent toil*, wrought under the superintending grace of God, is requisite to secure your safety; and that, where you cannot cite such an experience, you are in deep danger of not having yet substantiated your claim to adoption in Christ as the sons of God.

Will you derive such a conviction from the nature and *condition of the human heart?* Oh, brethren, what hope can the indolent Christian discover here? Surely you cannot but perceive that if the religion of the Gospel be indeed *a restorative process*, which presupposes a fall from original righteousness;—if its purpose be to remove old objects of affection, and replace them by new ones; if, in doing so, it has manifestly to contend with the whole current of nature and habit; and if the customary life of an unconverted man possess scarcely an internal principle of action in common with that of a converted man, beyond a general sense of right and wrong; if the new heart is not merely a different heart, but a contrary heart,—if this be true (and few Christian men will deny it to be true, that this *is* the purpose of Christianity as an inward system), —can it be questioned that an operation, or series of operations, so fundamental, so extensive, so profound, are not to be achieved without difficulty, and perseverance, and prayer, and tears? It is surely nothing but the most melancholy forgetfulness of the real nature of the human heart, as contrasted with the objects of the religion brought to work upon it, that can leave us sunk (as thousands of us are) in the miserable illusion that we can be Christians by little more than naming ourselves such,—that we can reach our God without moving a step to meet Him!

But in answer to such statements as these, of the mutual relation of Christianity and the heart of man, it is said, "we have not to *destroy* affections, but *to change their objects* in this process; and this may be gradually effected without any very perceptible effort." Alas! this is the very reason why I insist upon the difficulty... Were the religious affections *essentially new*, we could assign no rules as to their entrance or their departure. They would be wholly out of the sphere of our calculation. It is in the alteration of their objects that we can understand the labour and trial of this great change. It is in *this* way that we can perceive that the education for the Christian profession is laborious, like that for every other "profession," which leaves the man and his faculties the same, and wholly alters their mode of operation. ... If our love of happiness—our desire, that is, of having the constant means of gratifying our various wishes—were to be changed into some feeling utterly unlike it, by the operation of religion, we could ill say whether a change thus inconceivable would prove a source of toil or of ease to ourselves. But if, our love of happiness remaining, its objects be made to suffer a total alteration;—if, loving happiness as before, we form to our minds a new species of happiness, a happiness whose Author and whose scene are beyond this world, a happiness which, as it can little turn upon our present experience, must (unlike our ordinary conceptions of the common objects of desire) be not known, but trusted for, that is, be the object not of sense, but of faith,—if this great revolution in the objects of our old faculties take place, then indeed we can perceive what a labour of mind is requisite to impel a new stream through these old channels, to fit the former machinery to higher purposes. And certain it is, brethren, that these higher purposes require a new "moving power,"—even the "Spirit of God.". . . But this point I waive; I only ask you, can it be doubted that a change of heart such as this supposes, is no alteration which leaves us *substantially* unchanged, but, on the contrary, a total transformation, and thence an epoch in every one's existence, —an era which, constituted as the world is in relation to the Christian disciple, can scarcely fail to be more or less prominent in the history of every human life? Have you, my brethren, yet passed this momentous crisis? If you have not, remember that, whatever be your fortunes in this world, it is but too probable that the only date that will ever be of importance in eternity is yet to come!

But, perhaps, this sort of argument in favour of the importance of this change, and the unremitting toil which is required of those who would realize it, may appear too abstruse and recondite; for, alas! how obscure appear all reasonings that we have no wish to follow! I refer you, then, *not* to the internal knowledge of the general heart of man, but to your own daily outward experience. You who think that the world can be deserted without a sigh, and heaven won without a struggle, I turn your contemplation to the world that surrounds you. If to secure mere physical comforts,—to gain a common livelihood (and remember one God is the God of all; His laws govern this world no less than the world to come),—such a weight of toil is required, such patience, such endurance, such incessant demands on the spirits and the intellect; shall we say that an eternity of happiness is to be won by no trouble at all? that for a good, uncertain in acquisition, and perishable if acquired, the providence of God has decreed the necessity of careful previous exertion; and that for a good, certain in acquisition and eternal in duration, He requires no cost or preparation of any kind, no discipline laborious or protracted, no sacrifice beyond what fashion or convenience may please to dictate?

But, brethren, this is a class of arguments that wears a more terrible aspect still! If it directs us to the conditions of our salvation, it also directs us to the terrible consequences of our sin. I have been asking you how it is that your eyes (ye who walk as Christians) can see the promises of Scripture, and yet be blind as to the conditions; and I have enforced the interrogatory by a reference to the conditional character of all the calculated happiness we can observe on earth. I now ask you, on the same grounds, how is it that no earthly power can secure your (let me not say "*your*," we are all one in this blindness!)—can secure our practical belief in the *terrors of its threats?* Does the course of *this* world justify the belief that its God holds the gates of the everlasting Eden open to His revilers or His neglectors on earth? What character do you discover in the God who governs you? We walk in this world through the midst of gloomy indications of vengeance. Take the palmary instance of the fact. *Death*, itself the wages of sin, is every hour reminding us of that cause which " brought death into the world and all our woe;" and yet, with death around us, we dream that God cannot punish! We who have been by that God permitted to read His word, cannot but know that we are mortal because we are sinners,—that the funeral processions which, as if by God's special appointment, in almost all countries are marked with a melancholy pomp, are but the solemnities of a legal execution, the grave fulfilment of the penalty that man incurred when first he separated from the Source of life! In misfortunes expected,—in sudden calamities,—in wars and pestilences,—in the very satiety and restlessness of prosperity itself,—we only read inscribed on the face of things the terrible justice of the God we have to do with! Nay, to such a degree is this character of condemnation graven on the earth, that there have been those who have declared they could recognise no trace at all of beneficence in the Creator, or at least but a slight and ambiguous one; that He has revealed Himself to His creatures as a Being of inexorable severity only; and that His very mercies were only apparent, and merely intended to deepen by momentary gleams of light the terrific darkness of His general dispensations. This is indeed a representation exaggerated, partial, and false; but who will say that such views are without *plausibility?* And this is all that the argument requires. If the evil of life, if its punitive character, be prominent enough to give currency to such a picture of the God who governs it; if, as we know, the gods of uninstructed nations (fair indications of natural convictions) are almost invariably personifications of the terrible; if in every cup bitterness enough is mingled to have the effect of thus poisoning the reason of men against their Maker;—I ask what ground is there for the hope that the justice of God is not answerable to His scriptural representations of it? What ground for the supposition that the mercy of God is boundless, in any sense which can set us at our ease in the ordinary negligent Christianity of daily life?

What then is the result of our argument, as far as it has yet proceeded? We are in the habit of denying,—that is, our conduct tacitly denies,—that we are bound in any sense to *labour* for eternal life, to "strive to enter at the narrow gate." We substitute the visions of indolence, an Epicurean Christianity, for the persevering activity of believing men. We reduce our Christianity to the miserable standard of custom, and we join with mankind to forget God in the easy decencies of religious observance...In opposition to this, I have urged that the very purpose of Christianity negatives such a mode of operation. If its purpose be to change the heart, the heart itself must be engaged in the work; and a long course of prayer and vigilance is needful to substitute heavenly for earthly motives and affections... Again, I have urged that the whole course of God's providence evinces that happiness is not to be attained by reasonable beings without the patient efforts of a faith reposing on the future; that, to put the thing in the most general way, pain, in some form or other, is the common condition of promised pleasure; and not only this, but that we are warranted by all around us, in denouncing the terrors of eternal ruin against wilful neglect. ...So far (and oh! how fatal is that familiarity with such truths which has rendered it almost impossible to impress them as they deserve!) I have but asked *your reason and experience* to accompany me in demonstrating, that those robes of unsullied purity of which the text speaks are worn only, or almost only, by those who have "come out of great tribulation," who have gained the rewards, because they have borne the toils of the conflict!

But here is an authority beyond reason and experience, and to that I would finally invite you! You who fancy that, under the ample canopy of the Christian name, you can dream your way to heaven, dare you appeal to the revealed purposes of Christ as He Himself has explained them? There is perhaps nothing which to a careful observer more eminently marks the divine presence of our Lord, than the constant union in His predictions, admonitions, and consolations, of great threatened affliction with great promised success. Two characteristics which *in a worldly* enterprise are almost irreconcileable, our Lord, from the commencement of His mission to its close, calmly predicts, and predicts without an effort to conciliate them. The religion is to be continually persecuted, and continually triumphant. And this declaration was derived from no previous experience: when the new faith had scarcely attracted the notice or jealousy of a single opponent, its Founder began to give it laws co-extensive with the world, to assign the mode of its future action, and to assign it on principles applicable to all the climates of the earth and all the ages of time. And still the two prominent characteristics were preserved,—the continued victory, and the continued persecution. And not only was this an external victory, an outward dissemination of the faith, but also an internal triumph, a spiritual happiness. " In the world ye *shall have persecution; but be of good cheer, I have overcome* the world." And I cannot but here remark that this difference is observable between the predictions of our Lord and of His apostles; that whereas they predict *mere facts*, as those who are instructed by another, He predicts the *whole operation of the Christian principles themselves*, as became the Author and Mechanist of the entire system; the apostles predict the persecutions as circumstances to occur, but Christ predicts the necessary operation of the principles that are to produce at once the persecutions and their consolation; the apostles declare facts, Christ declares laws and relations,—a difference so minute and refined, and corresponding so exactly to the different capacity and dignity of the persons, as I venture to say no possible supposition but that of strict truth can satisfy.

But what I am now insisting on is the inseparable scriptural connexion of the toil of attainment with the final happiness of the Christian. You remember how, in that succession of blessings with which so appropriately the teaching of Christ on earth is opened in the first of our Gospels, it is declared that they which mourn shall be comforted and that they which are persecuted for righteousness' sake possess the kingdom of heaven. And the same connexion thus introducing His mission, our Lord, as you know, unceasingly urges; consummating all instruction by His own example, in which affliction and holiness were so perpetually united,—affliction attesting holiness, and holiness sanctifying affliction. His apostles took up the same strain, and continually and earnestly declared that we "must through much tribulation enter into the kingdom of God." Nor is the succession of such doctrine lost through all the ages of the Church. How could it? for it is built upon the sameness of the corrupted human heart, and the sameness of the religion designed to restore it. And is it, brethren, in despite of such authorities as these, that we have constructed for ourselves a luxurious Christianity, in which the sacrifice of Christ is the *only* sacrifice we can understand, and His holiness the *only* holiness we deem required of God? Awake from this deadly lethargy, and in the midst of enormous privileges, cease to pervert your Christianity to an aggravation of your curse! Know that your self-deceit cannot deceive God; awake then, brethren, and know,—and that in whom God accepts He looks for the history of depravities painfully conquered, affections enkindled, patience exercised, and victory fairly won! If you cannot point to any such records; if, from birth to this day, you cannot name one hour of conflict with a world "that lieth in wickedness;" *can you* deem that you are qualified to be incorporated into that bright band which has come—and, while the world and the heart remain the same, must ever come—"out of great tribulation?" Can you arrive at that abode where "the Lord wipes the tears from all eyes," if you have never *shed* a tear? Can you, in one word, have fulfilled the terms of a profession which is, everywhere in Scripture, and on the most permanent grounds, designated as a warfare that tries every principle of the spiritual nature, without being once conscious of the presence of your adversary, or once engaged in anything like actual resistance? Is religion indeed a principle so *indefinite* that, if it come at all, it will pass like a summer-cloud, unheeded, over the surface of our hearts? Never imagine it! Be assured that the "white robes" of the blessed are not the robes of indolence, but the mantles and decorations of conquest! Be assured, also, that if (as the passage continues to say) these blessed spirits "serve God day and night in His temple," it is because their hearts have learned *here* the elements of that holy service, and their voices have been tuned on earth for the harmonies of heaven!

SERMON VII.

THE GROWTH OF THE DIVINE LIFE.

1 John II. 13.

I write unto you, little children, because ye have known the Father.

BRETHREN, the knowledge which St. John stated to be the basis of his exhortations, I am here this day to beseech you to provide and ensure. He wrote to "little children" because they had "known the Father,"—*I* speak to *you* that you may enable them to attain the same inestimable wisdom. He thought it not below the dignity of a pen which had transcribed the discourses of a God on earth, to condescend to encourage the progressive piety of children; Christians, think it not below yours to hear the story of their wants, and to meditate the means of their relief!

Yet how can I resume the topic which he left in this brief form upon his inspired page, without a moment's melancholy recurrence to the difference (too certain!) between the correspondents *he* addressed and the audience that I address? His letters, intended for the general Christian world, bore indeed no specific direction; they were the common property, as they are to this day the common heritage, of the Church. But we know what that Church was, when it received them fresh from the living Apostle. We know its enduring faith, its holy hope, its sufferings which were triumphs, its earthly defeats which were heavenly victories. They who are learned in the history of that wondrous time, have read of a love not only stronger than death, but stronger than the protracted death of a life of persecution. They know that peasants from the plough, and slaves from the market-place, achieved wonders of fortitude such as the proud philosophy of old time had scarcely dared to imagine in its brightest visions of human perfection;—that poor men—unconscious heroes who had never heard of heroism—not only sought the flames (*that* might be the weakness of enthusiasm), but—what no enthusiasm but that of God's eternal Spirit ever wrought—from the heart of the flames called for pardon upon the oppressors; so that the fires of persecution and the prayers of the persecuted rose, for vengeance and for mercy, to heaven together! Such was that early Eden of Christian history, before the enemy had darkened its glory with his shadow. We deny not—the Scriptures themselves deny not—that stains here and there might exist amid so vast and varied a body; weak brethren might fail, and false brethren might intrude; but altogether the effect was such as the world never witnessed before or since. In that new-born Church, human nature, as if recent from its contact with Deity in the person of the incarnate God, seemed once more to have issued in primitive beauty from the divine Hand, and again to have caught the original impression of the Maker. Eternal Purity had been on earth in the form of Jesus Christ, and, though He had passed away, the world where He walked was still fragrant with His presence! The Sun Himself had set, but the clouds yet burned with His glory, and twilight was still to defer the darkness to come!

Such was the Church that St. John addressed in the Epistle I have cited. I turn to *my hearers*, and I ask for that lovely image! Whither is departed this radiant glimpse of the heaven to come? Is it among you, brethren? or has it returned to the God who gave it?... Oh! if at this hour, in the throng that now listens to these words, I could feel myself addressing an assembly such as those holy conventions of old, that met—not in a temple like this—but in caves and sepulchres, to worship a God whom the world denied,—if, in surveying this fair array of stately and decorous Christianity, I could discover the hope that brightened the martyr's prison with visions of heaven,—if, in the crowd of pledged professors of the faith of the Cross set before me, I could behold the fitting successors of men who cast their whole earthly wealth into a common treasury of charity,—of females (the ladies of an age as rich, and, in many respects, as refined as the world ever saw) who cast their ornaments at the foot of the cross;— *if* I could believe this, or hope it, or imagine it, would I address you, as now I am doing, in the style that education and refinement demands of its orators? *or* would I not rather —trusting in tried hearts—spurn aside all the pomp of appeal and all the labour of argument,—and, speaking as my author spoke, and speaking no more, tell you that these " little children" whom I plead for to-day, endeared to you as they are by every local connexion,—if you will have them such as St. John would "write" to, or such as St. John's Master would adopt,—must by *you*, by you alone if at all,—by you, their natural protectors,—be taught to " know the Father!"

For them I have to speak, but not for them only. If you hear me on *their* behalf, you are also to hear me on your own. If I plead for children, I speak to *men!* Your hearts are indeed the tribunal before which I have to advocate the cause of this, your own parochial charity. But let me not forget that I have an office more momentous! They are also the tribunal before which, in common with your own accustomed minister,—with all other ministers on all other occasions,— I have to plead the cause of a charity more intimate to each of you,—that reflective charity, that holy compassion, by which the converted soul of a perishing sinner learns at last to take pity on *itself!*

For such an application I need not overpass the text—the pregnant text—before us. It presents two or three different aspects, and you will permit me to invite your attention very briefly to each. The "little children" whom St. John addressed, though here I have little doubt the term is to be understood literally, yet, you must remember, shared that title in the Apostle's vocabulary of love with all *humble* Christians of all ages of life. Nor was this phrase, in this extended sense, *peculiar* to St. John, though so often adopted by him, and so characteristic of his lovely nature. "Be ye therefore followers of God, as *dear children*," writes *St. Paul*. Again, "As my beloved *sons* I warn you,"—"I speak as unto *children*,"—and "my *little children* of whom I travail in birth." Christ Himself had authorized the beautiful metaphor, both by His express use, (John xxi. 5,) and still more, by the spirit of His teaching. Now, of *two* aspects under which the ascription of "childhood" to Christian discipleship might be viewed, it is observable how distinctly characteristic is the *separate* adoption by the two apostles,—how the tone of each character reveals itself in the employment of this simple term. The remark may seem somewhat refined,—perhaps overstrained,—yet surely it is in such minute and delicate shadowings that real genuineness best discovers itself. Observe, then, if St. Paul addresses his converts as "children," it is as *his own* children he chiefly regards them. The active, energetic minister of the Gentiles identifies his people and himself in the bonds of a familiar relation; and, justly proud of his fruitful labours in the Gospel, rejoices to think not only that the brethren of Ephesus or Corinth are the people of Christ, but that they are so through his instrumentality. But St. John,—gentle, contemplative St. John,—if *he* terms the members of the Church "little children," does so without any direct personal purpose. It is not as the children of his own apostleship, nor always as the children of even the heavenly Father, that he loves to regard them. The profound simplicity of his mind usually seeks nothing more by the term than to convey the general idea of innocence, dependence, humility, and love. How characteristic of two natures, which, both admirable, were yet admirable in ways so unlike!—two natures which, it is scarcely too much to say, are types to the Christian world in every age of two great classes of believers, that—each imperfect without the other—combine, when united in the fellowship of the Church, to exalt it to "the measure of the stature of the fulness of Christ." The one,—St. Paul,—ardent and impetuous, imprints his character upon every page, presents himself in presenting Christ, and throws into the cause of the Gospel the whole energies of a spirit, which in its highest exaltation is still St. Paul's. The other, in whom affection seems to have consumed in its heavenly flame, or assimilated to its own substance, every other power, loses himself in adopting Christ, and seems to speak to mankind from the mystical depths of another being, until it is no longer the man, John, we hear, but a half-beatified spirit, reiterating its lovely, simple lesson of love. The one, various, eloquent, "all things to all men," can never forget that his converts are the babes of his own spiritual fatherhood in this world, his special crown of rejoicing in a future;—the other, with but one idea, but that the highest of all, is himself so infantine in the character of his dove-like nature, as scarcely to wish to be aught but a child among these children of paradise!

Besides the *literal* use of this term, (to which I shall have again to return,—for I am to-day the advocate of no figurative or ideal childhood, but of real and immortal spirits schooling in this great academy of the world for heaven or for hell!) and the metaphorical uses—personal and general—which I have noticed, there is *yet another* figurative use of the term, which indeed many learned men have supposed to be intended in this very passage, but which at all events is frequent in the apostolic writings. It is that in which life—being no longer the growth, maturity, and waste of the body, but the "life of God in the soul of man"—is measured upon a higher scale than the course of fleeting years, even by the progressive strength of God's Spirit in the heart. In this sense the " children," " young men," and " fathers" of this passage, are regarded as symbolizing three great stages of spiritual advancement; and, whether St. John so intended it or not, such an interpretation of the passage contains a mighty truth. This brings us altogether out of the natural and visible world into that mysterious sphere of divine agency where God is alone with the human soul. It is not by the annual revolutions of a visible sun that the progress of *such* a life is noted, but by the advancing beams of the eternal Sun of the spiritual heaven. That " city"—and *the human soul* even in this world may in some respect be such—" hath no need of the sun, neither of the moon, to shine in it; for the glory of God doth lighten it, and the Lamb is the light thereof." (Rev. xxi. 23.) Now the passage, we see, attributes to this blessedness perpetual advancement,—advancement from holy to holier; and it is on this glorious prospect I would have you meditate, and perhaps assist you for a while to arrange your thoughts. For this internal life of God in the heart is subject, as everything perhaps but God Himself is, to the great law of progress. " Never man reached at once the lowest depravity," says an old author; Christianity shows us the fairer aspect of the thought in showing that man is not destined to be suddenly perfect. Everywhere it speaks of gradual development, of structures that are themselves the basis of new structures of holiness, of a journey prosecuted through many stages. The " truth" is *now* a life infused, *now* a seed planted and watered, *now* a light brightening more and more to the perfect day. It is the feebleness of childhood, the vigour of youth, the stability of manhood, the settled dignity and calm repose of age,—in all a continued identity of the principle of life, but a difference in its degrees of manifestation. " I speak unto you," says St. Paul, " as unto *babes* in Christ. I have fed you with milk, and not with meat; for hitherto ye were not able to bear it." (1 Cor. iii. 1, 2.) " As new-born babes," says

St. Peter, " desire the sincere milk of the word,"—evidently an early stage of the Christian life,—that for which the "milk" of the word is appropriated,—and that, too, not so much enjoyed as "desired." While, again, St. Paul looks forward to the glorious period when "we shall all come unto a *perfect man*, unto the measure of the stature of Christ's fulness." ... Reflect, then, a moment on this aspect of the passage, — on this progressive growth of the divine life; a point so bright with consolation to every traveller on the way to perfection,—to all who, "forgetting those things which are behind," would stretch forward, bating no jot of heart or hope, for the crown of promise. Surely, then, formed as man is, I cannot doubt that, in his present state, this principle of perpetual advancement, which supplies a constant motive for activity, and an object ever renewing in size and splendour as we approach it, is more suitable than even an inactive monotony of perfection,—if indeed, to a nature like ours, perfection were conceivable on such terms. When you remember how large a portion of our nature is made up of principles progressive in their very essence, you will be inclined to conclude, that if Christianity—that "truth" which is the supplement of our nature—be destined to feed the whole man, if this blood of life be meant to circulate through every vein and artery of the spiritual frame, then it is likely to be in its tendency an active, growing, or progressive system of inward holiness in order to suit a large portion of a system which, in this life at least, unquestionably *is* so. "Desires" exist, and they are in their nature active, energetic principles—seeking, coveting, aspiring. Now, if Christianity, which gives new objects and purposes to all our faculties, be formed to correspond to our "desires," it must not anticipate but excite them, —excite in order to gratify. This, then, supposes the divine objects of such holy desires to be constantly *increasing* in brilliancy and loveliness, in order that the desires of the purified heart may never expire in gratification, or fade into satiety. Now, what *is* holiness but this brightening presence of God worshipped by affections that thus grow as they gaze? Or view it in another way,—to love the perfection of the Gospel as personified in the Author of it, even the Father of heaven, is to see that perfection more thoroughly (for such is the very property of spiritual enlightenment, as well as, in a great degree, the property of even the natural mind, —to *see* excellence more vividly the more we *love* it). But must not the better sight of perfection quicken, in its turn, the very love that gave that better vision? And thus the object more prominent, and the love more animated, will perpetually call each other into new and brighter existence; every perception of God will set the heart on fire, and every burning emotion of holy love will in return bring God nearer to the soul; His presence will answer the demand of the adorer, and the adorer will rise, as his demand is granted, in prayers for a closer and yet closer presence; and where—where—shall this progress to infinite perfection *end?* Never in this world, —never, perhaps, in the next. *Our perfection* for eternity may be progress for eternity! Such at this hour may be the perfection of the angels. And the whole universe of pure born and regenerate beings may be conceived as scattered at different points along one vast highway leading to the light inaccessible where God dwells alone, in the secret sanctuary of His own infinite attributes; all travel incessantly towards the light which glows brighter and brighter on them as they advance, —for the progress is their happiness. *We,*—alas for fallen human nature!—are far back upon the course; but still it is a *common* course to all, and the good and great of every world are our fellow-travellers to God!

Am I intelligible to your hearts? Do you understand me when I speak thus of the Christian progress to God,—or rather perhaps I might say,—of that telescope of love by which he brings the light of God nearer and brighter to his soul? I do not ask you to agree with my *reasonings:*—God knows I state them with humility, and a deep sense how feeble is the grasp that the creature of an hour can lay upon the purposes or the processes of an infinite Providence. But I *do* ask you to understand the feelings and the experience to which I am appealing. Be with me in the *fact*, whatever becomes of the argument! Agree with me that to love God is to have Him present; that to have Him present is to love Him more and more; that to love Him more is to increase the glory and frequency of His blessed visitations;—allow this to be the record of your own experience, and I ask not what it proves,—whether religion be a progressive thing or a stationary thing; I only *know* it proves a point beyond all doctrines, or theories, or systems,—it proves that you are the children of God,—" *little children*" in the noblest and fairest sense of the phrase. But oh! if you cannot understand anything of all these details of the Christian's history, if they are colours to the blind and music to the deaf, then are you indeed " children" in the lowest sense,—children in the life of Christ,—babes who are still unweaned from the " milk" (as St. Paul calls it) of ceremonies, and observances, and worldly elements! Ah, brethren! if your closets have no account to give of rising contemplations, and quickening feelings, and those blessed visions which the " pure in heart" are promised, —if everything which tells of the neighbourhood of God is to your hearts, as perhaps at this moment when I speak of it, a strange, mystical, extravagant rhapsody,— *how* will you bear the blaze of His real and actual presence, that blaze which either glorifies the soul with its light, or scorches and withers it for all eternity!

Here, then, is the point. Is there one among you who has felt the first celestial breathings of the life of God, but felt no more,—an infant in the faith? Oh, my brother and friend! do you then feel no ambition to escape this poor and feeble childhood? to be no longer a minor in holiness? to " come of age," and assume the full rights and privileges of the heavenly citizen? Now that God's grace has made a rent in the barrier between you and Him, can you not catch a glimpse of the glorious scene beyond; or will you stand for ever at the *gates* of paradise? "For ever!" Alas, you cannot stand there for ever! Day treads on day, Sabbath on Sabbath, month on month, year on year; and if your deathbed finds you the same weakling "child" that this Sabbath morn sees you, can you expect to be the "perfect man" of eternal life? And is there a drop of more exquisite bitterness in the cup of everlasting perdition, than the knowledge how *near* you shall have been to the happiness you have lost? What spectres, in all its populace of devils, has hell itself more horrible, than the recollections of warnings given in vain, opportunities possessed in vain, exhortations heard to be talked of and forgotten? May God avert it! But we dare not disguise the truth,—is it too much to say that, at this very hour and in this very place, there may be those,—and they not the worst of my listeners,—who will one terrible day remember this morning's discourse? and weep bitter tears at the thought that, humble and feeble as was the minister, his words at least were true! But I pause. Perhaps I have too daringly raised the shroud that envelops terrors which it shocks to name. Pardon me, beloved brethren, pardon me, when you know that every word which I speak to you I feel to be still more awfully applicable to myself and my brother-ministers, who, offering ourselves as instructors, are guilty with a tenfold guilt if we forget our own lessons!

I have spoken to you of the "childhood" of the Gospel, in its various senses of approval and disapproval; and before I attempt once more to recal it to your hearts, I will ask you to consider for a moment the other phrase of the text,—which indeed can have only *one* sense, but that a sense of deep and glorious import. "Because ye have known the Father."

"To know God" or "Christ," in the dialect of heaven, is a term expressive of a peculiar operation directed towards the

Supreme Being, which in its entireness, as produced by the Spirit, I do not pretend to explain adequately, but on which, we may at least be certain, the understanding and the affections are both engaged,—the one informing, the others animating, much in the manner which I have already attempted to describe, when speaking of the progressive attainments of a Christian soul under the tutelage of divine grace. We find, or make, many divisions and subdivisions of our mind; we "know" with one part, we "feel" with another, and so forth; the Spirit of God regards these compartments very slightly, and with a single impulse converts the whole man to His purpose. Nor would I delay you among these minuter inquiries as to the import of a word, except for the purpose of drawing one important practical conclusion. It is that the use of the term, "*knowledge*" of God, to express the *entire* conversion of the *whole* nature to that Great Being, seems clearly enough to carry with it one important principle —namely, that the apostles considered that a right apprehension of God, if once obtained in all its perfection, drew with it by a sort of moral, or at least a *spiritual* necessity (a necessity according to the laws of divine grace), a real practical love of Him. "This is *life eternal* to *know* thee the only true God, and Jesus Christ whom thou hast sent." And a remarkable expression in Jeremiah makes it identical with the chief exercises of benevolence. "He (Josiah) judged the cause of the poor and needy; then it was well with him: was not this to *know* me? saith the Lord." (xxii. 16.)

But what is the extent or compass of this knowledge of God which is thus to purify the whole being? The text replies, when it declares "ye have known *the Father*." To know God as the Father,—of the world, of Christ Jesus, and, through Him, of the inner world and family of believers, —is to adore the source of so much that is wise, and powerful, and compassionate. To "know" here is to "love;" this light of knowledge cannot be without heat of affection. Remember, ye who read and dispute, and call your disputation "knowledge," that the knowledge of which inspiration speaks, is the knowledge not of a thing but of a person, not of a person merely but of a God, not of a God only but of a Father!

Yet, on the other hand, remember also,—that duly to know this God as a Father, you must know the facts by which His fatherhood has manifested itself upon earth; and that these facts are contained exclusively in one unerring depository. "Faith cometh by hearing, and hearing by the Word of God."

It is as the advocate of the diffusion of that Word of God in your own vicinity, among your own dependants, that I am here this day. God who has made faith depend upon the spread of His Word, has made the spread itself of His Word depend on causes even more human and secondary. I can seldom undertake a task like the present, even in the most restricted sphere of local charity, without astonishment at reflecting on the extent of this principle of mutual dependence of man on man in the universe of God!

Wondrous, complicated machinery of Providence! We know not what His real ultimate purpose may be with regard to these poor beings. We only know that, whatever it be, it will be wisest and best, since it will have been His. Nor does it militate against His wisdom thus to suspend man on man; nay, it redounds to His wisdom. A machine of infinite intricacy only proves an operator of infinite skill. Yet with all this, how awful it is to reflect, how astounding to capacities like ours, that the everlasting destinies of so many undying essences should in all human probability be suspended upon the apparently casual emotions of some hundreds of their fellow-creatures! that, under the high mysterious permission of Providence, a pang of wretched avarice in one person here may in the process of events condemn a soul to eternal ignorance of God; that another, to reserve the purchase of some paltry article of dress or ornament, may contribute to deprive one of her own sex of the instruction which one day would have saved her from degradation and ruin,—and thus may become in a manner an accomplice in the destruction of an unhappy sister; that another, because, as the phrase is, he would not be "talked out of his money"—ashamed of generosity, (for men *can* be ashamed of a good impulse) through some momentary caprice—should have it in his power quietly to sign the death-warrant of some miserable child, ill provided, ill instructed, abandoned to idleness, to profligacy, perhaps at last to public crime and public execution! Oh, may the God who has, for your own trial, left such powers in your hands,—may He, I pray, teach you on such occasions as these how to use them!

I have been discoursing of "little children" at great length to you, in all their figurative applications. When I thus come to the reality, I scarcely know how to proceed. But I must be their spokesman; they cannot speak for themselves; many of them know not the real value of the religious knowledge they are receiving, nor the terrible loss if they are to receive it no more. But oh! the world will soon teach these exiles from your charity that hell is open to receive those whom you have banished from the path to heaven! And in such an event, what shall we say of the *Judgment of God*, who has not given to any being in this church one farthing of wealth for which He is not exacting a rigorous account. Remember the parable of the talents; and remember that even the luckless wretch who "buried" his talent, may be outdone by him who squanders it in purposes of evil. The collection of this day is of vast importance to the success of the establishment; over and above your annual subscriptions, it is essential that you should be liberal now. Brethren! Christians! you must not shut your hearts upon these young creatures,—by every tie of neighbourhood the appropriate objects of your charity,— whose angels in heaven are watching this moment the changes of your minds? Shall Christ in vain cry aloud to suffer these children to approach Him, and will you forbid them?... I said, a while ago, that these purposes of generosity or avarice would be casual and accidental. But no,—they are not casual! It is no exaggeration to affirm, that, even in this matter, mighty agencies are at work at this moment in your hearts. The Spirit of love, and the hater of souls, who would rejoice to ruin you in ruining these little ones, are busy amongst you! The point to each may be a slight one, but it shows how the balance inclines as well as if thousands were at stake. Hesitate not, brethren. Follow the loving impulse where it leads you. And if I have told you aright this morning, of the progress of a Christian in the knowledge of God; and if, as I spoke, you aspired after such a progress; and if you believe with St. John that he who will love "God whom he has not seen," must be able to "love his brother whom he *has* seen"—then, in the name of the God of charity, look upon these objects of Christian affection, test the reality of your feelings by the reality of your works, and uniting as the redeemed of Christ in this holy tribute to the children of His love, teach, oh teach these young but immortal spirits to "know the Father!"

SERMON VIII.

LESSONS FROM A MONARCH'S DEATH.

(Preached on the Sunday after the death of William IV.)

EZEKIEL XXI. 26.

Thus saith the Lord God; Remove the diadem, and take off the crown!

THE religion which we profess, brethren, is at once the most peaceable, the most obedient, the most loyal, and the most levelling, equalizing, and humiliating religion in the world. While our whole faith breathes the spirit of submission to all constituted authority, and in confirmation of its requisitions declares that God Himself (doubtless to assist us in imagining to ourselves His supreme empire) has ordained the existence of governments and policies on earth, and while it thus continually adjures us by our loyalty to our God to be loyal to His officers and servants;—at the very same time it assimilates the prince and the peasant in *one lowly condition*, and its stated services witness, united in the community of their filial relation before the heavenly Father, the rich and the poor, the mighty and the mean. The Spirit of that faith, " whose service is perfect freedom," makes all its possessors obedient, just because it enfranchises them all; in liberating them from the dominion of Satan, it reconciles them to all legitimate earthly thrones. Christianity is indeed the religion of social order and genuine patriotism. The wisdom that descends from heaven is full of peace and promise for the kingdoms, as well as for the *individuals*, of our earth; it is the true bond and ligature of public subordination; it is full of loyalty and even devotedness to appointed authorities, at the very time that (in another sense and view) it rends the barriers that rank has established between men, and equalises all in the sight of a just and holy God. And not only do these apparent contrarieties coexist, but the one actually arises out of the other. The same unworldly humility which makes all Christians feel themselves on a common lowly level,—the same wisdom (holy and heaven-taught) which lets them see that all mankind are one in original corruption,—*these* qualities it is which, by natural consequence, inspire them with willing attachment to authorities appointed of their God. The spiritual Church of Christ is indeed the true republic political dreamers have only imagined; *there* alone the theories of universal equality are fully realized; but it is the very essence of this equality to produce submissiveness to all things but vice,—for it is the equality of hearts equally sinful, redeemed by a salvation equally gratuitous. The happy members of this great polity of believers acknowledge that they stand before God undistinguished save as His mercy may please to distinguish them; they exult in no privileges but the holiness which is the gift of His Spirit; and, even in their joy at the possession of that unspeakable blessing, they rejoice with unenvying humility, and ask not *which* is "to sit on the right or the left hand of Christ in His kingdom." In such a state of mind, (the true Eden of our souls, the true recovery of our perished paradise,) the differences that during this brief hour of existence are placed between man and man would become wholly indifferent, if these differences did not themselves imply *rights* which originate duties, that call for constant Christian obedience, and for the careful cultivation of the spirit of meekness, which alone can make that obedience to temporal superiors pleasing to the God who commands it, or a pleasure to man who renders it. Hence, the enthusiasm that supports with a rampart of hearts and arms the constitutions of free countries, is not merely justified, but *encouraged*, by our high and holy faith; and not only lives, but *lives best*, where Christian humility has made its home. Our faith is not formed solely for contemplative solitude, though it often loves and affects it; when once this vital principle has taken possession of the heart, it can animate and vivify *every* duty, no less public than private. It is as universal as the *light*, that so often is employed as its emblem. The Christian, brethren, is the true politician. No crisis or conjuncture can take *him* by surprise. His rules of action, in the storms of public commotion, are as simple and undeviating as in the privacy of his domestic life. In no case to prefer his personal interest to the public good; to hold the faith of his Lord and Saviour the main instrument of general happiness, and its diffusion the great object of social changes; and, as a part (and no unimportant part) of that faith, to stand by the forms of authority that time, law, and experience have consecrated, and regard disobedience to such a supremacy warrantable only when obedience to the higher authority of God (*plainly* revealed in His Scriptures) interferes to command it. Oh, brethren! if our hearts were but duly sanctified with the beautiful humility of Christ, how little would the busy casuistry of political reasoners disturb or perplex us! How little our fidelity to earthly dominations could be tampered or trifled with, if, abandoning the petty ambition that makes each of us strive to be his own king and governor, we could become informed by that Spirit of God, which, whether it move over a physical or moral chaos, is alike the Spirit of order, harmony, and peace!

I cannot believe, brethren, but that I have your sympathy in this line of observation. When the general mind is roused by recent changes, and the pulse of a nation beats quick with unwonted emotion, God forbid, if that emotion be a warrantable one, that the ministers of Christ should be dead to its impulses, that the pulpit alone should be *insulated* from the universal excitement. . . . Our religion teaches us no such maxim. In making us strive to be guides to our fellow-men, it does not make us cease to be *their* fellow-men. I say, God forbid that we should substitute for Christianity an unchristian stoicism! that when a nation is in tears, *our* eyes alone should be dry! that when it rejoices in the fervour of a renewed and augmented loyalty, *we alone* should affect a frigid indifference! Our Master did not feel so towards *His* country, nor do we towards ours. The Divine *Philanthropist*, who laid down His life *for the world*, was also the first of *patriots* when He wept over the *City of David*, as He was the first of *friends*, when, "having loved *His own* which were in the world, He loved them unto the end." No, the Christian philosopher knows too well the universality of his religion in its application to human hearts, to fear matching it with any conjuncture of human events; let me add, that the Christian minister knows too well his duty, not to feel that in all the changes of public affairs, in all the revolutions of public opinion, it is his calling not to disregard but to direct them;—that he is set as on a lighthouse in the midst of these waves, to hold out the light of eternal truth to the wanderers, and to hold it out only the more strenuously the more the waters rise and roar.

But, brethren, if on the one hand our faith thus strengthens the thrones of princes, and confirms peace upon the earth,—if it encourages generous devotedness to country and kindred by the example of Christ Himself, and sanctifies our chivalrous feelings of attachment to order and government by making them, as it were, *a part* of our chivalry to the Cross,—it also teaches another and a corresponding lesson. It is not less at home in the palace than in the cottage. It whispers in the ears of princes themselves the same doctrine of humble-hearted trust which it suggests to the poorest of their people; and to kings unceasingly urges, how awful is their duty to the King of kings! And in no position does the inherent supremacy of our religion appear more conspicuous than in its ministrations among the great ones of the earth. This is, indeed, the religion by which "every valley is exalted, every mountain and hill brought low." Where the just and becoming deference of worldly inferiority would scarcely venture to approach, the same inferiority, when ennobled by the high commission of the Gospel, fears not to come forward to threaten or console. It is the privilege of the appointed servant of God to be of no rank or of all ranks. He addresses not the outward and perishing man, but the inward man, the sinner, that in his community of sinfulness shares one nature with every child of Adam. Before his eye—if it be indeed single and purified—vanish all the painted pomps of earthly state,—these most useful, but *in themselves* unsubstantial accessories;—the real and permanent being (that is, the imperishable soul) only is seen; and in the conferences of the monarch with his spiritual counsellor, the hearts of two dying sinners alone converse with each other! The minister of Christ is the ambassador of a mightier Monarch. Is it for *him* to tremble while, bearing the credentials of the skies, and invested with the light of another world, he calmly unfolds the mystery of eternity to a brother spirit as eternal as his own? Is it for him to retrench the truth through fear or favour, when he knows that the anathema of Heaven is on him if he preach not the Gospel to every creature that is born of woman, and that is born to die? Is it for such an one to shrink from the blaze of human grandeur, whose eye has been familiar with "the likeness of the appearance of the glory of the Lord?".... And oh, brethren! with a more pathetic truth, I may ask,—if such an one know (as assuredly he *must* know) that the purple is no shield from *sorrow*,—that the bitter seeds of moral and physical pain grow with just as rank a luxuriance as elsewhere, in the courts of princes, and beneath the gorgeous canopy of regal bowers,—that higher power is *indeed* no more than "heavier toil, superior pain,"—under such a conviction, will the deputed messenger of Christ think his office to be less needful in the palace than the hovel? No, no! believe it (for all experience attests the truth), the poor countryman, who from hour to hour toils to procure a pittance that he cannot reckon on for the hour to come,—he, who in literal fact is "given day by day his daily bread," clinging to the outskirts of society, and (as it were) holding himself on to existence by hard, incessant muscular effort,—even he, in all his apparent wretchedness, does not more truly require the consolations of a world of future hopes, than the being who forms the glittering pinnacle of society itself. It is the same life carried on upon a higher level, the same heart beating under a different garment; nor does sorrow cease to be sorrow in its mask of pomp and equipage. The minister of God knows that while commanding obedience "for conscience' sake," the Bible recognises no human heart but one—a lost and ruined heart; and that, to regenerate and restore, it likewise presents but one universal and unqualified remedy.... And I cannot here but pause to remark, how happy in this particular is the constitution of Church establishments, in that they diffuse through *every* region of society the currents of truth; that they post their spiritual watchmen upon every ascending tier of the social edifice,—so that, if we have those whose duty it is to speak comfort in the villages of poor men, we have also those whose stately solemn rank qualifies and commands them to be the monitors of kings!...

Such then, my brethren, is the wide-spread authority of our religion over all ranks and callings of men. It addresses all,—it disturbs none. It does not alter the relative positions of men in time, but it purifies all alike for eternity. In commanding us to "render unto Cæsar the things that are Cæsar's, and unto *God* the things that are God's," it asserts the universality of its authority at the very time that it carefully distinguishes it from all earthly sovereignties. Our religion came not to disturb any empire but that of Satan; it dethrones no prince but the "prince of the power of the air." By the mouth of one of its greatest teachers, it exhorts "that supplications, prayers, intercessions, and giving of thanks be made for all men; *for kings, and for all that are in authority;*"

at the very same moment that it is busy in the palaces of those great potentates themselves,—reminding them through *whom* it is that they possess their power, that even absolute sovereignty is but a temporary viceroyalty for God, and addressing them perpetually in the words of one who was himself a king, —" Be wise, O ye kings! be instructed, ye judges of the earth! Serve the Lord with fear, and rejoice with trembling!"

I know, brethren, there exists in the mind of no rational man any calm collected persuasion that these suggestions of duty, and its eternal consequences, are less needful to the greatest than to the humblest of our earth. I know that no one past childhood will suffer himself to dream that princes are born to be immortal, or that the crown of earthly glory is " a crown of glory that fadeth not away." And yet,—it is vain to deny it,—the principle *is in our nature,* to be profoundly affected by the recurrence of instances of the perishable tenure of grandeur, far beyond any depth of emotion which death, in its mere abstract form, can command. We may know, with the most undoubting confidence, that no greater measure of life, no intenser vitality, is vouchsafed to royal veins, than increases—exults—glows—wastes—perishes—in those of the peasant on the hill-side; we may even conclude, with all the force of speculative conviction, that *happiness* is, after all, pretty equally diffused over all classes of men; and yet,—the event prostrates our philosophy! What! are not our daily obituaries crowded with names, every one of which may well be to our thoughts the index of hours of sickness and agony, every one of which the active imagination may multiply into hosts of weeping friends, orphaned children, and widowed hearths, and the lesser sorrows of a whole circle of intimates, until at last, at the extreme verge of acquaintanceship, the feeling fades off into indifference,—every one of which, I repeat, is the centre of a sphere of griefs; and are not our eyes each successive day saluted by these gloomy registries of mortality,—yet, where no personal interest is concerned, who reads them with even the shadow of an emotion? *But*,—when an exalted name has vanished from the earth, when that which once lived and breathed, the impersonation of power, has been borne away to be entombed in the stately sepulchre of history,—the general heart is arrested, the mission of Death seems to come direct from Heaven, and that decease, which is only the fulfilment of nature's universal law, startles us like a miracle, and seems to be an immediate interference of God.

It is not my purpose now to delay you with any protracted investigations as to the causes and reasons of this very interesting *difference* in the natural feelings, upon the occasion of misfortunes, the same in real experience, occurring to the great and to the lowly. Yet, perhaps, we ought not wholly to overlook the inquiry. It may sometimes be a mere form, or at least result, of the veneration with which we honour the authorities constituted in the land, which, if it be cultivated, may arise to a spirit of attachment that feels every grief of a virtuous public governor as its own. But the emotion is seldom thus unmixed. No doubt we cannot help, in spite of all our reasonings, constantly associating great happiness with great power; and the contrast of the supposed height of enjoyment with the depths of the feelingless grave, creates a mixture of pity and surprise which meaner instances cannot reach, because they cannot imply the contrast. And, even apart from any ascription of *happiness*, there is no doubt that the contrast between a power that subjected all, and a weakness that is itself subjected to the common lot, has a tendency to affect the soul with a great and unusual emotion. Again, loving power as we do ourselves, we cannot help in some measure sympathising with its possessors;—particular cases of envy, or jealousy, or such like, omitted, we naturally enter into their successes, exult in their exultation, weep with their sorrows, and are stricken with their fall. Instances of this are abundant. To such a degree of force may this sympathy arise, that in the days of the almost miraculous successes of the great tyrant of this century, there were men (and it is intelligible that there should be) who, in the fascination of his glory, and though included with their country as his enemies in war, almost forgot the ties of country and allegiance, and would in their delirium have given up all to one who seemed born the natural governor of the world. I need not refer to the striking instance of the same principle afforded in the arts of fictitious representation, where agonies that would lose their interest as the agonies of daily people, move us with the deepest pity as the agonies of kings. . . .

I will not detain you with any further examination of this point as a matter of theory; but I cannot forbear making one or two observations on it, as a matter of practice. In the first place, that where it exists merely as a consequence of the sympathy with power, it is often of the highest benefit to public stability; and that hence we may remark how admirable is the wisdom and goodness of Providence, who overrules a feeling in itself so questionable, to the best purposes of human peace and happiness. In the next place, that where our regret at the accidents of greatness arises from a veneration for legitimate authority, and for the great as bearing it, it is a feeling wholly to be encouraged and strengthened. And in the third place, that with all this natural devotion to power, it is truly melancholy to reflect how sadly the principle seems to expire just where it ought to act in its greatest vigour. Our Bible unfolds to us a King whom it styles "the blessed and only Potentate, the King of kings and Lord of lords; who only hath immortality, dwelling in the light which no man can approach unto;"—a Monarch whose power is infinite, and whose love is unbounded as His power; One whose holy sovereignty is formed to attach every better feeling of our hearts, and who sets us here with the sole view of disciplining and confirming those feelings:—subjects and soldiers, to vindicate His throne, and combat for His cause with "weapons not carnal." Yet the man whose heart beats for his country's cause, is dead to the patriotism of "a better country, that is an heavenly;" the man who boasts (and honourably boasts) that he loves and appreciates the free constitution of his birth, has no feeling or understanding for the magnificent polity of heaven; and he who would shed his blood to defend the kingdom of his earthly master, has no solicitude "to sit down in the kingdom of God." Alas! we worship the shadows of Power, and we have no adoration for the Substance! We pour out a world of feeling, treasures of rich and noble emotion, upon the instruments of authority, the mere subordinates of God,—and we have no loyalty for Him who moves the whole machinery, and from whom all force is derived, not more in the physical universe of matter and motion, than in the moral world of governments, powers, principalities, and laws!

You know, brethren, why it is that I address to you, this day, remarks and exhortations of this character. You know that since we last met in this place, a great event has agitated the public mind,—an event of the kind that makes epochs in the history of nations. At such a time the dullest awake to reflection; the reflective are quickened to keen and serious thought. Great events of all kinds are awful monitors; but, most of all, events that come about according to laws of regular succession;—*these* apprise us, with a power that cannot be evaded, of the unceasing flow of the time which we are all so deeply interested to employ to purpose. In being æras of *national* history, they also become to every individual æras in his own *personal* history. They force upon us the conviction that we are indeed in the midst of a system of universal change; that we ourselves are under this law of all created being; that every hour we too are changing for good or evil; until that last solemn hour when, in the Apostle's language, "we shall all be changed,"—to change no more! These are reflections which *every* great alteration in the story of nations must bring with it. We can arrive at *no* new landmark upon the long pathway of history, which will not summon such reflections as these.

But I would ill do justice to the subject of our meditations at this time, if I confined your thoughts to the general subject of earthly and successive change. This, brethren, is no common change. The inheritor of the throne of a thousand years has passed to his fathers. Death has been busy, reading once more his terrible lesson to living men; proving, in a new instance of power, that he is indeed "the last enemy that shall be destroyed;" and that no control (however widely recognised on earth) shall interfere with his supremacy, save *His*, who, "through death destroyed him that had the power of death." Alas! brethren, what availed it, that, placed at the summit of the first social system on earth, our departed monarch saw no recognised dignity intervene between himself and the beings of a higher world? What availed it that he stood (by the constitution of his country) *the source* of all the innumerable streams of honour and distinction that separate, and (like other streams) while they separate really unite, the divisions of society, in this vast and complicated empire? These things vanish as a morning dream, when from the secret throne where sits the Governor of all worlds, is heard the sentence of the text—" Remove the diadem, and take off the crown!" Of all the tributes that his subjects paid him, he takes with him from the world but one,—you pay it, brethren, in this temple! Yes! he for whom your prayers so often have risen to the throne of heaven, he for whose temporal and eternal welfare, each Sabbath-day, ten thousand ministers offered the incense of their supplication, —*he* is no more the subject of prayer: let us trust in God that he is gone to receive its fruits! Your labours here are true and permanent benefits; the loyalty of prayer is the support of monarchs when all other supports fail. "There is no king," says the Psalmist, " saved *by the multitude of an host*

... Behold, the eye of the Lord is upon them that fear Him, upon them that hope in His mercy." In the lovely relationship of prayer, the highest and the lowest may be invisibly united; those who could not aid their monarch in any other way, were rich in prayer; and often doubtless the devoted piety of some lowly subject, by its secret interest with Christ, has aided the ruler of millions in obtaining favour with the Ruler of the universe!

Sabbath after Sabbath, brethren, we preach to you of death and eternity. It is the great, the perpetual, burthen of our discourse. We cannot help its monotony. The sin that brought death into the world is in fault for that! When men are holy enough to hail the death that opens the pathway to eternity, we will cease the strain,—but not till then!... And with all our repetitions and variations of the one tremendous theme, how seldom we can enforce it upon men's hearts! how seldom we can fix a thought that will pass the doors of our churches! But *here*, brethren, you have circumstances themselves and history preaching to you! These terrible orators deal not in figures of rhetoric or artificial declamation. The stern reasoning of events is all they bring! Where we argue to the understanding, they address the eyes and the heart! And would to heaven that at this hour (how much better than a world of sermons!) it were given to us all to cast an eye upon the scene that now encompasses the perishing remnants of departed Royalty! The dignity of the sovereign still invests the lifeless form; it *is* fitting that the useful distinctions of time should follow to the tomb,—if they deepen the impressions of authority during life, they become still more touching instructors in death. Man, by a most just and noble instinct of respect, venerates the body for the soul; and honours the temple, though the God has fled. But *there* —night after night, and during days whose gloom is more melancholy than night—the stately vigils of a king are held! The magnificent chamber darkened to the likeness of a tomb, the long array of mourning watchers (mourning in truth as well as show,—for our monarch was loved by his people!) the sadness that hangs like a cloud over that majestic pile,—itself a monument of buried ages,—the dreary bustle of preparation for the final solemnities of a regal interment,—these are things that would move, if any thing could move. And if I dare unfold the page of a deeper sorrow, if I presume to point your eyes to the venerated form of that imperial widow, the woman of many virtues, whom her subjects knew but to love, —if I point to that form bent by a sorrow only the more affecting, because struggling to be repressed in the midst of that scene of crowded and stately woe,—it is not that I would idly intrude upon griefs too sacred for public utterance, but because I would beseech you in prayer to ask of the Comforter of mourners to be with her in her affliction. But, God be praised! we have reason to know that she is no stranger to that path of consolation.

Brethren, if it indeed be "good to go to the house of mourning," you have here ample means of familiarizing your hearts with plaintive and touching traits. Need I remind you that—as if to aggravate the contrast between the excitement and fulness of life on the one hand, and the perishable tenure of its glories on the other—our noble-souled monarch was sinking fastest upon the very day that his people were exulting in the anniversary of their country's greatest victory? that the pomp of mimic warfare in an hundred fields was animating the general heart with images and portraitures of lofty achievement, at the very hour when gloom was deepening over the couch of a king, and in those who hoped the longest, hope itself was wrestling with despair? Or shall I remind you,—for in such instances the minutest circumstances acquire a melancholy interest,—that almost his last beam of intellect was spent by our true-hearted monarch in a recollection of the glories of his country and of her chieftain;—his last bodily effort, in grasping the banner that symbolized her fame? But why do I introduce such topics? He is no wise man, brethren, who neglects the mention of such incidents as these, or disregards or repulses the emotions they tend to produce. They all—however slight in themselves, and often the more because they *are* so—aid in deepening the memorable contrast between all that this earth can afford,—its glories, its power, nay, its very virtues,—and the immutable attributes of the world to come. And even where they do not produce this determinate effect, they act to soften the heart with a gentle and benevolent sympathy,—the very soil that Christianity asks to be sown in!... And, therefore, I do not hesitate to remind you of the last and most touching of these contrasts, —that if *he* whom we lament had but lived a few days longer, had he but lived in health to see the setting of *to-morrow's* sun, the celebration of his commemorated accession,—his seventh anniversary,—was to have filled the nation with demonstrations of joy,—and, we may honestly say it, no feigned or unreal joy!... Let us hope that the joy which is silenced on earth is taken up in heaven! The temptations and difficulties of courtly life will not be forgotten in the estimate of a merciful judge; and if we trust the accounts of the calmness, serenity, and confidence of his latter days, we may hope that on that day, while we are walking in mourning garments and wearing the solemn hues of duteous regret, in the heavenly Zion there may be the "oil of joy" instead of our "mourning," the "garment of praise" instead of our "spirit of heaviness;" that the angels may there be celebrating a loftier "*accession*" to a *brighter crown*,—even the "crown of life, which the Lord hath promised to them that love Him."

Brethren, a *different* occasion now calls for the feelings of national joy which to-morrow's anniversary was to have brought. He is criminal, unworthy, unchristian, who refuses them. I have before told you that our faith not merely countenances but encourages those noble enthusiasms, which exalt the approbation of legitimate authority into an affection; and that it is in the best part of our nature to concentrate that affection for authority into a generous attachment to its bearer. But I am not here to call upon you to stand resolutely in defence of public order, whenever and however assailed. The weapons of this place are *prayers*... And he who, in the true Christian spirit, feels that all countries are great only in proportion as they make God their guide and governor,—thus perpetuating, as it were, a spiritual theocracy,—will surely not forget to make his morning and evening supplications to the Lord of all, that in His mercy He may direct the counsels of the young inheritrix of so glorious an ancestral possession; that He may inspire her with the practical conviction, that she is His deputy, entrusted with His authority, bearing His commission; that it is at once her duty and her privilege to support the public honour of His name, and the spread of His Gospel,—and the stability of His Church, as the means of both! May the God who has so long made Britain the modern Israel of His protection, still hold over it, and over her whose youthful arm now rules it, His helping and directing hand; that under the continuance of His special favour,—basking still in the brightness of His warming and enlightening beams,—our country may grow in the true prosperity of righteousness! And—for I would not that we should part without something of a character still immediate and personal—may we too be enabled to feel the importance, each of us, of his own position in such a country! to feel that the example of every man radiates farther than he can himself see or know,—and that it becomes him who professes a pure and holy faith, to evince by his conduct that purity and holiness which it prescribes, " that by well-doing he may put to silence the ignorance of foolish men;"—and thus to evince that, however malignity may misrepresent our divine faith, none is more unswervingly true to his earthly monarch than he who owns allegiance to " that *King* eternal, immortal, invisible, the only wise God,"—to whom " be honour and glory for ever and ever! Amen."

SERMON IX.

DYING TO SIN AND THE LAW.

Romans VII. 4.

Ye are become dead to the law by the body of Christ.

These words form part of a passage supposed to be among the most difficult in the writings of the Apostle Paul—one, it is thought, of those dark and involved argumentations to which the perplexed believer must apply St. Peter's designation of " hard to be understood," and on which the unbeliever is almost justified in sarcastically commenting that the Revelation requires a revealer, and that the mystery hidden from the foundation of the world is a mystery still. Though I cannot but think (as I will just now endeavour to show you) that the difficulty has here been most needlessly exaggerated, and that the perplexity in the scriptural student's mind is derived rather less from St. Paul than from St. Paul's expositors, whose conflict of illustrations produces obscurity (as opticians tell us that *interfering* waves of *light* produce darkness);—yet even *if* this passage, and many other passages that occur in the same profound page, were really as obscure as they are sometimes alleged to be, it might reasonably be questioned, how far the fact of such obscurity ought to occasion discouragement to the honest disciple, or can justify the negligent disparagement of the gainsayer. It is certain that, in the practical working of a revealed religion, if perspicuity have its general utility, occasional obscurity may be shown to serve most valuable purposes also;—that it manifestly (and to our daily experience) effects what no other obvious disposition of things could effect, by testing zeal for truth and sincerity of heart to a degree highly suitable to a state of trial; while it also provides for those gradations and diversities of spiritual knowledge so accordant with the character of variety observable in all the works and arrangements of God. It may also be easily evinced, that the objection would lie with nearly unabated force against every form of divine enlightenment short of that which would violently constrain belief; and it may then be candidly asked,—remembering our Lord's solemn declaration about the inability of even a visitant from the dead to overcome the infidelity of the heart,—whether we ought not gratefully to adore the mercy that saves from a measure of light which would leave us so utterly, so absolutely inexcusable? That men, under a demonstrative Christianity, would be better men, I think exceedingly doubtful; that, if unimproved, they would be far more guilty, no one surely can question.

Among the difficulties of Scripture study, there are some which plainly belong to the form and matter of the revelation itself; and these we are to receive, as we receive the earth itself, from the same bounteous hand for our *bodily* sustenance, —as the appointed material of necessary, honourable, and not unpleasing toil. "If thou searchest for wisdom *as for hid treasures*," says the great Master of Prudence, intimating at once the value and the difficulty, "then shalt thou understand the fear of the Lord, and find the knowledge of God." (Prov. ii. 4, 5.) But, as there are these inevitable trials in the pursuit of religious truth,—difficulties inherent in the nature and circumstances of the communication (difficulties, I may add, which no form or theory of Christianity, even Romanism quite as little as any other, has shown us how to obviate),—so there are difficulties extrinsic, superadded, and unnecessary, which we ourselves introduce, and for which our own prejudices, or vanity, or caprices, alone are answerable.

Among these sources of perplexity (as I am not now to think of *enumerating* and exposing them) there is one which is, perhaps, less observed than any other, and yet it would be hard to estimate adequately how far it has really operated to obscure and entangle the revealed record: I mean the effort to insulate the word in separate oracles, and then to make it say in each of them *more than it purposes*, perhaps, to say in all; to find (in something of the spirit of the old Hebrew critics) a separate mystery disconnected from all others, in every phrase and almost in every word. This— like so many of the most seductive extravagances in every department of action and of thought—is partly the exaggeration of an excellent principle, the principle of unbounded veneration for all, without qualification or exception, small as well as great, which the Spirit of God has given. But when to this is added the tendency of an impatient curiosity (another exaggeration of right principle) to pursue every glimpse of light which it fondly hopes will manifest in one flash the whole mystery of God; and when this appetite for a knowledge perfect and absolute has to work upon materials so *limited*, it is true, as are offered in the compass of the New Testament, but yet in which, at the same time, comprehensive comparison is so laborious, the result I speak of may surely be expected. We may expect that, on the one hand, the force of position will be lost; on the other, that phrases will often be overcharged with significances altogether transcending the simple purport of their inspired employers. You can conceive that, if a naturalist had but a single leaf or flower to study, or limited *himself* by some perversity to it alone, he would endeavour to discover *a world* in his specimen, and exhaust all the powers of the microscope to detect wonders within wonders without limit. How this tendency to find all things in all, is increased by the urgencies of controversy, it is needless to remark. If the botanist had to overthrow a rival theory of fructification, or to establish one of his own, you know how preternaturally augmented would become his powers of microscopic vision. Every visionary notion in religion boasts its text or two, and can boast no more; but its supporters hold the text or two so near their eyes that they hide the rest of the Bible.

Such remarks as these, bearing upon a very ordinary tendency in critics and interpreters, are, I believe, useful at all times. They are at present suggested by an instance of certainly very inferior *relative* importance, inasmuch as no special doctrine appears to have been based upon it; but which, nevertheless, as being part of a long and most momentous discussion which has formed the field of controversy from (as it would seem) the days of St. Paul himself, derives importance from its situation and connexions. The context that precedes the clause before us has been by many surrendered as hopelessly obscure; and yet I am inclined to think that the principal obscurity has been created by that closeness of inspection which lessens the field of sight, accompanied as it usually is by the compensating tendency to make *each* expression of the inspired record signify something above and beyond the simplicity of the sacred author's purport. I must now solicit your patient attention, and beg to refer you to your Bibles for the entire passage. I am mistaken, if a close examination of the whole do not evince at once the minute and perfect skill with which the reasonings of the inspired writers are constructed when they appear to cursory view least systematic; and the soundness of the great canon, that the first and best and most satisfactory of all investigations of Scripture is that which, not confining itself to isolated phrase, takes in the whole scope and connexion of the record as it lies. I must confess, however, that if a confirmation so honourable to the structure of our inspired volume, and if a simple elucidation of the word of life do not bring their own reward, I cannot promise you any in an inquiry that must necessarily engage the reason far more than it can excite the imagination.

St. Paul is engaged in the management of his great argument relative to the superiority of the Gospel dispensation above that of Moses, and the necessity inherent in the nature and connexion of the two, that the one should supersede the other. Now, there are two aspects in which the religion of Christ may be viewed, and we should never magnify the one at the expense of the other; as a principle of life and happiness, and as a principle of subjection and obedience,—life that quickens obedience, obedience that manifests life,—life that makes obedience delightful, obedience that makes life visible and practical. If you turn with me to the preceding, the sixth, chapter, you will find this representation a clue to the involutions of its rapid eloquence. That chapter is composed of the answers to two objections, and the objections and their respective answers (so often hastily confounded) are specially directed to special and distinct views of the Gospel. The former objection speaks of life, and it is answered out of the nature and characteristics of spiritual life and death; the latter objection speaks of subjection, and it is appropriately answered by citing the characters and contrast of the sinful and the righteous service. The one asks (ver. 1), shall we abide, or "live," (ver. 2,) in sin, that grace may abound? and the answer is that we are *dead* to sin, that the old nature is *crucified* (ver. 6), and that therefore it is unnatural, in the nature of things incompatible, that we should *live* to it. This death to sin is declared to be publicly solemnized in the expressive rite of baptism; and in it, as well as in the resurrection that follows it, we are declared to be copyists and partakers of Christ,—" baptized *into* Him," into His death, His resurrection, and His eternal life (ver. 3—11). The consequence drawn from this (ver. 12—14) is, that sin should not " *have dominion* over us," that it should not be suffered any longer to intrude its foreign tyranny upon the purchased possession of God; and this forms the transition to the topic of the second objection, which turns upon the cardinal idea of *subjection*, and asks—" Shall we sin because we are not *under* the law, but *under* grace?" The course of animated appeal that replies to this interrogatory (ver. 16—20) is fitted to it with exact and exclusive propriety. We are declared to be no longer " the servants of sin," but " the servants of righteousness;" that whereas, in the bitter bondage of nature and the law, men were " free from righteousness " (ver. 20), they are, under the dispensation of grace, " free " (or rather *freed*) —emancipated—(ἐλευθερωθέντες)—from sin, and formally articled to that holy servitude of godliness and love, whose " gift is eternal life through Jesus Christ our Lord " (ver. 23). ... Having thus concluded his double course of illustrative exposition, St. Paul now passes (ver. 21) to a further consideration, which results from both, and manifestly is framed to allude to both. He speaks of " the fruits," or consequences, of the ways of nature and grace : and to each he applies the notions, before so copiously treated, of *service* and of *life*. Now, the " fruit " of bondage is properly its " wages," the fruit of God's service is " a gift." And therefore it is, that, binding the whole argument and all its topics,—life and freedom, death and bondage, and the fruits of each,—into one summary, he declares, that " being *freed* from sin, and *servants* to God, ye have your *fruit* unto holiness, and the end everlasting life ; for the *wages* of sin is *death*, but *the gift* of God is eternal *life*."

We now arrive at the passage so much contested, the analogy of the deceased husband and surviving wife, in which so many have found an instance of what they are pleased to call St. Paul's " popular appeals," and " hasty comparisons," and " resemblances that must not be too closely pressed," but in which I trust to show you an apt and perfect sequel to the whole course of the preceding reasoning.

It appears, then, that the Apostle, having, as we have seen, in the close of the last chapter, united into one mass and interwoven in the texture of his language the two topics of that chapter,—the death to sin and the new obedience unto God,— opens this with a new and distinct illustration, in which he continues to represent this great revolution in colours yet more vivid, and with an outline yet more precise. The passage in which this is effected runs thus:—

(1) "Know ye not, brethren, (for I speak to them that know the law,) how that the law hath dominion over a man as long as he liveth? (2) For the woman which hath an husband is bound by the law to her husband so long as he liveth; but if the husband be dead, she is loosed from the law of her husband. (3) So then, if while her husband liveth, she be married to another man, she shall be called an adulteress: but if her husband be dead, she is free from that law; so that she is no adulteress, though she be married to another man. (4) Wherefore, my brethren, ye also are become dead to the law by the body of Christ; that ye should be married to another, even to Him who is raised from the dead, that we should bring forth fruit unto God."

The general purport of this illustration is, I suppose, manifest enough; it obviously describes a great change,—a dissolution of old connexions, and a formation of new ones; the government of the law and the espousal to Christ are manifestly contrasted; and the readers of the Epistle are pointedly warned of the duties that belong to that great and blessed engagement.... But when from this distant and rapid view we approach to a closer investigation, and (as is requisite in all comparisons) seek to appropriate to their due realities each person or object in the similitude, the case becomes more intricate, and this famous illustration, if we are to trust some of our expositors, is little better than those meteoric lights which, seen *afar*, are luminous, but under a closer gaze are found to be dark and rayless.

The Apostle, it is urged, would compare the union under the Law and the Gospel to the marriage-bond. The bond is severed by the death of one of the parties. The deceased husband is the Law now extinct, the second husband is Christ, the wife is the Church of God under the two dispensations,—that Church which, at the death of that Law (which was her former spouse), is released for a new and higher connexion. But to this is opposed the startling fact that in the application of the allegory by him who best understood his own meaning (in the 4th verse), it is the *Wife*—the Church—who is said to be dead,—" *Ye* are become dead to the law by the body of Christ;" and in the 1st verse,—the preamble and natural index to the purport of the whole,—it is said that "the law hath dominion over the person (for thus general is the word in the original, τοῦ ἀνθρώπου) as *long as that person liveth*," thus evidently resting the wife's right to liberation upon *her* death, upon her having ceased to live, and being thus emancipated from the power of the law. Innumerable have been the expedients adopted to escape this difficulty. Some have held that the words which we render " as long as he liveth," should be rendered " as long as it (the law) liveth, *i.e.* is in force,"—an opinion as old as the days of Origen, and advocated by Doddridge. Others have said,—to obviate the apparent inconsistency between the decease of the husband in the allegory and of the wife in the application,— that we are said to be dead to the law because the law is *dead to us*, and that St. Paul adopted this circuitous form of phrase to avoid offending the Jewish converts, who could not bear to hear it openly preached that the Law of Moses was itself no more. Such names as Grotius, Whitby, and Hammond have sanctioned this supposition. After what has been stated of the accuracy and precision of the reasoning of the last chapter, you will not readily believe that St. Paul is not the best guide to his own interpretation here; or that it is not our safest plan—without altering the natural force and signification of words, altering the venerable landmarks of inspiration—to try if we may not penetrate to an internal harmony more perfect, in the record as it lies before us.

For this purpose, I must recal to your remembrance the discussion that precedes the passage. St. Paul has established the two great characteristics of the new dispensation,—the *death* to sin which heralds the life to righteousness, and the *emancipation* from sin which gives the Christian freedman to the service of his God. With both these great ideas—prominent and governing ideas—in his view, he enters upon the passage under consideration. In reaching it, however, his mind passes through, and takes the tincture of, an important *connecting* notion,—the notion (as we have seen) of the "fruits,"—the results in hearts and habits,—of the dispensations of law and grace. When once his thoughts (guided by Heaven in their progressive changes) had come upon this great practical consideration, expressed in the metaphor I have cited, what was more natural or less abrupt than the transition into the peculiar form of allegory before us, in which these "fruits" are represented as the results of a mystical *marriage?* The mere suitability, then, of the ideas might lead you to conjecture that this passage is intimately connected with, and corroborative of, the discussion in the preceding chapter; but there is evidence more direct to establish it. In the fourth and fifth verses, you find the very term of which we speak (as a connective between the two trains of thought) employed in its new sense. It is there said that we are "to bring forth *fruit* unto God," instead of "bringing forth *fruit* unto death;" and this blessed result is declared to follow upon the espousal in the allegory,—upon our being "married to another, even to Him who is raised from the dead." This passage, then, confirms, repeats, all that has gone before; it does not alter its bearings or displace its relations. Like it, it speaks of a soul that once lived to sin and lived to bondage; like it, of a death which exalts the same soul to righteousness and to freedom. How, then, shall we dispose the personages of the allegory, to harmonize perfectly with itself, and with all that precedes and follows it? Shall we not say that *the wife*, indeed, the subject of the mighty change, represents the soul (whether individually of each Christian, or collectively of the general Church); that the *deceased husband*, whose claim and power expires, symbolizes, not the Law (as commonly held), but the principle of sin, to which the Law ministered, and to which so much of the preceding chapter describes the regenerate soul as "dead"—dead to sin, because sin is dead? And when St. Paul describes the woman as "loosed from the law of the husband," "free from that law," and "answerably *dead to the law*," shall we not plainly perceive that "the Law" in the parable is not represented by the dead husband, but by "the law of the husband," *the matrimonial obligation*, which kept the soul in bondage as long as sin was alive, but which ceases for ever when sin—the soul's gloomy consort and tyrant—has expired? Under this interpretation, all is complete and consistent. The Law—by the universal principle of law—has dominion over the woman as it has over all, as long as life lasts. But with death the obligation terminates; over her that is mystically dead the condemning Law loses its stern control. How then is this death produced? The second and third verses purposely tell us; with a view to preparing the way for the new connexion that is to follow that mysterious death. It is itself a result or necessary accompaniment of the death of the husband; here is the momentous peculiarity of this case; the husband is the principle of sin, and the death of sin in the soul is the death of the soul unto sin. In this way, conformably to the Apostle's assumption in the first verse, the power of the Law—that is, in the allegory, the old matrimonial bond—expires, in point of fact, by the simultaneous death of both the parties, but mainly (for this is the chief scope of the whole) by the death of the wife, as he had said above (so exquisitely harmonious is the management of the figure all through)—"the one that is *dead* is freed from sin." Thus is she freed from the obligation of her miserable bondage; she is enfranchised by Him who has slain her accursed companion through His victorious sacrifice; she is "dead to the law by the body of Christ." The death of sin and unto sin liberates from the law, and opens the way for the new and celestial union. The law bound the wretched soul in servitude to sin, for "the strength of sin is the law" —it gave sin its sinfulness, and gave no power to escape it; nor could this terrible espousal to evil be broken, in the nature of things and God's providential dispensation, except by that decease of sin, which left the soul correspondingly "dead to sin," "dead, then, to the law" (which can only govern the living), and free to form the new and sacred union. The main subject of the allegory, then, is not the death of the law, but the death of the soul to sin and the law: it is this which assimilates it to the reasoning it follows, and incorporates it in the mass and current of the Apostle's discourse. How strongly the interpretation which considers the deceased husband to be the conquered principle of sin, is confirmed by the form of expression in the fifth verse, I need not now remark. But it is worth while to call your attention to the sixth verse, as a proof that the two great subjects of which I spoke at first were never out of the Apostle's calculation, through all this comparison, and hence as a proof how closely it is connected with the entire. Summing up the past discussion before he proceeds to a new one, he recals again the two main characteristics of the gift of God which he had bound together in the illustration,—the death to sin, and the new service to Christ. "We are delivered from the law"—that, namely, sin, being *dead* (or, "we being dead to that")—"wherein we were held; that we should *serve* in newness of spirit, and not in the oldness of the letter." Surely this, a professed *inference* from the passage we have discussed, evidences that that passage itself must contain these elements,—must embody in one forcible example the fundamental doctrines of the spiritual death to sin as the great initial step in the Christian course, and the fruits of *obedience* to God as the manifestation of the spiritual resurrection.

But after all, it may be asked, whether it must not be admitted that St. Paul's illustration would have been clearer and simpler, if he had symbolized the expired law by the expired husband, and regarded the soul not as itself dead, but as living and liberated by the death of its party in the nuptial contract? It is at all times exceedingly dangerous to imagine improvements upon the Spirit of God; but in this case I have no hesitation in replying that such an alteration would dilute and enfeeble the strength of the whole parallel. St. Paul—(it is one of the loftiest characters of genuine inspiration)—abounds in expressions and arguments that seem forced and overwrought, until inward experience has raised us to the level of his language. And as I do believe that the great power of this remarkable passage eminently consists in its representing the soul of man as resigning the very principle of the earthly life and its condemning law before it can combine with Christ, in its thus bringing up a dead bride to this solemn spousal to receive from her beloved a new life of grace as her nuptial dower, therefore do I feel—and I know that I do but too feebly feel—that to lower this relation of the parties would be to weaken the true and thrilling purport of the original. In the sixth chapter he had spoken of *death to sin;* he now presupposes that death realized, and he shows that death *to the law* is its necessary accompaniment,—for that the law hath no control over the dead, that they are beyond its powers of cold command and inflexible vengeance. And if you would trace the force of this connexion or (in a manner) this practical identification of sin and the law so conspicuous in all the theology of St. Paul; if you would see how he clears the law of sinfulness, yet shows that to us it must be "the law of sin and death,"—you will find it exactly where it is demanded by the symmetry of the whole discussion, in the reasoning that follows the passage before us to the end of the chapter.

Into this I cannot now undertake to conduct you; indeed, I fear you will think that I have too long detained you among these more minute and elaborate inquiries, which are seldom popular, because they demand something from the listeners as well as the preacher. Let us then, before we part, rise for a while from discussing meanings to feeling them!

"Ye are dead to the law" and "by the body of Christ,"—a phrase which imports Christ's incarnate nature in general, but more eminently that nature as *sacrificed*,—as in that of Col. i. 22, "He hath reconciled you in *the body of His flesh through death*,"—or in the very perfect parallel of St. Peter (ii. 24), "He bare our sins *in His own body*,—that we being dead to sins should live unto righteousness," which gives us the same ideas in the same connexion. "You are dead unto the law"—unto the law considered apart and unaccompanied, as the organ of command and punishment—that ordered and avenged. "You are dead" to that which exhibited your God as a God only of terror and retribution, who gave you "statutes that were not good, and judgments whereby you should not live." (Ezek. xx. 25.) You are dead to the law as a sole covenant of life, for it is "the ministration of death;" you are dead to it as a *principle* of life, for "the letter killeth" and "the flesh profiteth nothing." To this law you are "dead" in being dead to sin, you stand in the same relationship to it as those whom men call dead, but who indeed are "alive unto God,"—who, "through the grave, and gate of death," have passed into another world and a higher form of existence. The law—solitary and terrible—was, as such, an element in the old world of sin and weakness; it was the curse suspended over the head that could not stir to escape it. All perfect indeed, for it was a copy of the mind of God; but dreadful to behold, for it was above the strength of man. It was the presence of Jehovah in a world unworthy of Him; and it consumed where it shone. To this frowning and fearful avenger you are dead,—"the body of Christ" has wrought this glorious decease, the lightnings of heaven have fallen on Calvary and expired there, and you can now triumph by *death* as He has done!

"Ye are dead." This spiritual death must surely be in some profound sense—so often and so earnestly is the phrase reiterated—the mystical image of that death from which it derives its name. Whither does death conduct us? "To-day thou shalt be with me in paradise," said the Lord of life to the dying penitent. He Himself "preached to spirits in confinement,"—preserved in the secret citadel of God,—a world where, as He declared, "all live unto Him," and whose happier region perhaps is typified in that "bosom of Abraham," which the Jews employed to express it, and which our Lord has consecrated by His adoption. His servant, "absent from the body," expected to be "present with the Lord," desired "to depart and be with Christ, which was far better,"—to "die unto the Lord," and "whether he waked or slept, to live together with Him." The triumphant fulness of heavenly glory seems to demand the body no less than the spirit; and may we not fairly deem, with many of our sagest and holiest divines, that there is beyond this scene, in some lone region of the illimitable universe, a home for the spirit unbodied, or clad, it may be, with some finer and invisible materialism, where in the calm expectation of consummate bliss it learns the art of higher happiness, and trains its faculties for coming glory? Is there not a world of spirits—the antechamber of heaven—where the eye, long accustomed to the gross darkness of the flesh, is gradually couched for the luminous presence of the ineffable One, a gentle twilight between the night of this life and the morning of immortality? Thither, doubtless, often descends from the throne of His glory,—there, perhaps, more constantly dwells by some unimaginable Shechinah,—the Man Christ Jesus with whom "our life is hid," and who, by promise and earnest of the fulness to come, teaches His expectant people that they have indeed "a building of God eternal in the heavens." And as in all our physical changes, spiritual changes more intimate and essential seemed pictured, I cannot but think that as our death represents the spiritual death that opens the Christian's course, so this intervening state of holy anticipation seems eminently to represent the peculiar blessedness that follows that "death to sin" and "to the law." Few are our intimations of the condition of the saints departed, but these few breathe of profound repose, tranquillity whose stillness nothing further can disturb. They are "asleep in Jesus." The bodies that arose at the crucifixion were "the bodies of the sleeping saints." They are blessed, "for they rest from their labours." "We now groan, waiting for the adoption, to wit, the redemption of the body;" but when the first great step towards it shall have assured all the rest, we can afford in joyful peace to "wait." And if such a state be real (and some such state can scarcely be denied), peaceful, though till the final resurrection incomplete, full of quiet hope and calm confidence that blessings possessed are the heralds of blessings far greater to come,—if death does release the children of God into this, or some such, happy territory,—how, think you, do its tranquil people look back upon the life of this world—that restless and unhappy tumult in which they once were struggling? They may remember it, —faintly recal it as some confused and painful dream; but the motives, and principles, and practices of that shadowy state can have no further relation to them, and their thoughts wander no longer among its sorrows and its guilt. They are "dead" to that world, "dead" to its sin, "dead" to its avenging law. It cannot cast its shadow across the grave; it cannot prolong one pang of bitterness, one touch of temptation. Its waves are broken beneath the walls of that sheltered paradise. These are the franchised of Christ and of death; dust has returned to dust, that the spirit might return unto God: they have died into His eternal life! Brethren, such is the story of the dying saint, such his oblivion of the past,

—his glory ever growing and gathering for the future! Such is his entrance into a new world,—serene and lofty as the heavens spread above the storms, changeless and eternal as the heart of God. This is the story of the dying saint; such dying saints must you even now be, if you would live even now with Jesus. Such a death to a world of embodied wickedness,—its principles, its habits, and its hopes; such death to a law of terrors, that you may rise to a law of love; such dissolution of the old tie,—accursed not in itself, but its object,—that it may be renewed in a tie of everlasting sanctity; such an end,—final and irrevocable,—to that deadly wedlock with the principle of evil, that the marriage-feast may be held which all heaven shall sanction, and the "King's Son" receive his bride! Widowed she comes, but not joyless; for she remembers that her widowhood is her glory! Some faint remembrances of that dark espousal may linger; she may still hesitate to exchange the weeds of her mourning for her bridal robes; we will not speak harshly of the weakness, for we know it must pass away. Are these phrases strange? Why should they not be, when they speak of changes vast, and startling, and momentous? what ordinary language shall fitly characterise these hidden miracles of the soul? They are the phrases of God's Spirit, and not mine; "take heed how ye hear" them! But *you* know they are not strange, who have ever beheld the glory of God in the face of Jesus Christ, that "glory" which is mercy, forgiveness, and immeasurable love; and who, dying—yea, long since dead—to the law of fear, and coldness, and distance, and repulsiveness, have, even in the midst of this daily world of aim without object and labour without profit, found within you a loving power to live in his spiritual, and prepare for his immediate, presence. To you may the sternness of command be more and more lost in the suggestions of grace; and the law, substantially unchanged, brighten into the spontaneous dictates of gratitude and love! Dead to the law as the gloomy legislation of death, may you live to it as the "law of the Spirit of life," knowing it in that nobler shape in which it is but the type and form by which love joyfully moulds itself, the standard to which the spiritual affections delight to conform, whose only compulsion is "the love of Christ *constraining*" them! May you be enabled to make the law your model, not as the servile task of your bondage, but as the will and very image of Him whom you adore, and in adoring *imitate* (for imitation is the perfection of worship), being "as obedient *children*,"—they are His own words, or who would dare to utter them?—" holy *as He* is holy," "perfect *as He* is perfect," "pure *as He* is pure," "doing righteousness *as He* is righteous," "walking in the light *as He* is in the light,"—inasmuch (to blend all in one word,—our hopes, our happiness, our life) "as He is, *so are we in the world!*"

SERMON X.

THE RESTORER OF MANKIND.

JEREMIAH XXX. 17.

I will restore health unto thee, and I will heal thee of thy wounds, saith the Lord.

THE words that were spoken by Jeremiah to console the hearts of *Israel*, had a deeper significancy for the Israel of all ages. The ministers of *Christ* stand forth with a heaven-sent commission to restore; it is the leading character of all their teaching. It is even felt to be so by those who *reject it*. And I know no more melancholy contemplation than is afforded by the sight of the numbers who, feeling the necessity, and even believing the reality, of this restoring efficacy, support with all their hearts and souls the existence of the Christian churches that are formed to minister to its operations; acknowledge in all their words, and in many of their actions, the beauty and perfectness of our doctrine, as distinguished from all other kinds of moral instruction; contend for it earnestly in conversation, public and private; declare unreservedly for Church-teaching, in preference to all other teaching; and yet—as if no churches existed, as if no real change had come upon the spirit of things by the preaching of Olivet and the death of Calvary—live and move, devoted Christians, without Christianity!

Now, brethren, what I would propose, on this occasion, to your consideration, is *this*. How deep are *the wants* which our faith supplies, and how wide is *the feeling of the beauty and power of the remedy!*—both (in combination) supporting the permanence and (so to speak) the *popularity* of that faith; both, without spiritual assistances and deep earnestness of effort, incapable of advancing us one step in realizing its blessings. What the *lessons* from such a consideration of this world's outward sensibility and inward deadness to Christianity *ought* to be, it would be unnecessary to declare. You can surely deduce them for yourselves. May God enable you to do so, and you will have little cause to regret the time I may have to detain you here. You have doubtless then, brethren, often meditated, *what* is the definite business of a Christian teacher. You have reflected in what especial regard it is, that he is expected to differ from every other real or pretended instructor. Reflections of this kind have been forced upon you by the most obvious outward appearances of the world we live in. As the citizens of a *Christian country*, it is impossible but you must have often defined to yourselves *what* that peculiarity is—what its nature, and what its value—which justifies the establishment of a legalised ministry, and thus constitutes a distinct class in society, that in its most important and constant character—that of preaching and teaching —was utterly unknown to ancient times; which constantly calls for new churches and new officiators; which more or less tinges the conversation of almost every circle of friends; which more or less mingles itself with political calculations of every description; which occupies half the learning and research of half the countries of the world; which, in short, by all kinds of publicity and prominence, challenges universal attention. You conclude that it must be something of corresponding, that is, of enormous, importance, that explains the existence or necessity of institutions so deeply rooted in society, and branching so widely through and over every portion of it. You feel that it can be no trifling distinction that has created clergies and churches; that has asserted to itself an exclusive right to one order of men, and a pervading influence over every other order; that demands in its outward observances a seventh part (at least) of your lives,—in its inward influence does not hesitate to demand *the whole!*

Nor does it satisfy such reflections to dismiss the entire matter with the negligent conclusion, that all this machinery, and all its past and present operations, form but one among the many follies of mankind; that the public and national ordinances of *one remarkable religion* which (circumstantially different it may be, but, in the source they claim and refer to, substantially the same) now exist all over the civilized earth, —are but fragments of unenlightened antiquity, clouds of the night that still are suffered to hang upon the morning, harmless customs that will arise in countries, one knows not why or wherefore. On the contrary, you cannot be ignorant that no such dormant or lethargic existence is permitted to this marvellous visitor; you cannot but know that it is the perpetual object of jealousy and conflict, and *that* directly in proportion as it asserts its distinctive character; that the nations are continually invited, by men not at all deficient in eloquence, ability, sagacity, or influence, to expel its very name from their social system; that its genuine professors are seldom safe from a persecution more or less virulent; that (whatever may be said of the slumber of the middle centuries) *these*, at least, are times in which the antiquity of a custom is not likely to fully satisfy men for its continuance; and that in despite of all this (surely the very opposite of an inactive or permissive condition) it still, by some inexplicable vitality, lives undestroyed in the midst of destruction,—it recommends itself by some internal necessity to the hearts of nations,—*people will not do without it*,—and though in the drunkenness of a national frenzy they may insult, and revile, and trample it, they are soon found to return cowering beneath its feet, and offering it up an adoration not always the purest, indeed, but still an adoration, and still sincere! We must look *further*, then, if we would find the charm that attaches even the worldly to some form of our faith.

Nor, again, will it solve the problem to reply (in a more reverent, but still a mistaken spirit) that a corps of moral instructors is felt by statesmen to be expedient, and by good men to be obligatory. There is some truth in this, but it is far indeed from the whole truth. The pertinacious vitality of Christianity (I speak, you will understand, only of its secondary and earthly causes) depends neither on statesmen nor on good men. The statesman is too careless and too interested to labour continuously to preserve it; the good men are too weak and too few. No; Christian establishments, the general organization of Christian services in countries, are built upon a broader basis than occasional policy or even occasional virtue; Christianity can only be universally recognised, because it speaks to universal humanity. We may curse it in our wickedness, and flout it in our folly; but we cannot wholly tear it from our hearts. It is based on too firm a foundation of knowledge of man's wants and weakness; the chord it touches is too genuine; the aspect it displays is too exquisitely adapted to console our miseries; it speaks too direct a language to our common unhappiness, to be ever wholly and irretrievably rejected by the general people. All history confirms the fact. Nations have run through the whole cycle of caprices. They have chased and abandoned a thousand cherished pursuits. But I know not of one that ever *permanently* rejected, after enjoying it, the blessing of Christian worship. Ambition may forget heavenly in the pursuit of earthly greatness, rank may feel too fortified in position, and wealth too strong in gold, to feel the constant necessity of the great Physician; but, as of old, " the common people " will still " hear Him gladly." And then,—as to *moral education*,—" if that were indeed *all* that was required, have we not our men of fancy, and our men of thought? If a corps of ordained philosophers would suit the wants of an unhappy world, the numbers ambitious of distinction in the pursuits of mind would always be sufficient to supply the demand. But the world, in all its corruption, nevertheless feels and knows that such guides would leave its wants ungratified. They may expound the malady, but they can poorly tell the cure. They can ally themselves with every folly as well as with every virtue; and whatever influence they may have over our hours of calm, they are lost in the tempest of the passions, unheard or despised when " deep is calling to deep," when the flood-gates are burst, and the winds are up.

What, then, is that which these teachers cannot bring, and which that higher and more hallowed order of instructors professes to bring? What is that which, in spite of corruption and frailty, in spite of evil speakers that aggravate the corruption, and evil-doers that exemplify and disseminate it; what is that which, even in its very perversions, has a power not wholly perished, and in its severest censures a secret and impressive commendation to the very hearts that practically reject it; what is that which has revolutionized the domination of selfishness in the world, till in times of trouble and change we hear the people cry aloud that they will stand by their teachers as long as *they* stand by their teaching, and that they will never consent to exchange them for the frigid apostles of a pretended rationalism? Brethren, the answer to the question is supplied in the assertion of the doctrine taught. Christ has the power, because, even in its lowest form, it preaches hope and restoration to man; because even the most negligent feel that it speaks the words of the text— " I will restore health unto thee, and I will heal thee of thy wounds."

But if this great peculiarity of our teaching, which thus separates the ministry of the Church from all other incorporations of instructors, *do possess* this power over even unconverted souls,—if Christianity *has* this hold over the affections, even when they are in neglect and uncultivation,—is it not pitiable that it should have *no further* influence over the hearts of men? is it not deplorable that they who so warmly and earnestly assert the claims of a national Christianity, should live without its internal spirit? Is it not to be lamented that the Christ who, by universal consent—nay, *at the universal demand*—is preached in our pulpits, should be so little the Christ that is prayed to from our hearts? Is it not melancholy that where all nature and all experience thus testifies in favour of our doctrine, and of the great subject of our doctrine, *the crucified Redeemer*, we should not carry out our honest prepossessions, and learn more closely to reflect that those very tendencies only prove how many are the principles of our nature to which it is formed profoundly to appeal? Assuredly the masterpiece of the wisdom of that God who constructed the human heart, will not be found wanting in perfect and beautiful applicability to its weaknesses and failings. He who formed the heart capable of temptation, has provided the remedy for its foreseen fall; and we may be confident that the structure of the mind itself will not be more wondrously wise than that of the remedy for its lapse . . . *If*, on the sixth day of creation, God solemnly called upon the Persons of the Trinity to unite in the formation of man,—saying, " Let us make man in our image,"—in due time also He called upon the same Trinity to unite in the work of his restoration,—the Father accepting the sacrifice, the Son achieving it, and the Spirit for ever sanctifying the redeemed. Nor was the former work more glorious than the latter; indeed, if we did not know that in the Eternal Mind those things which we call *means* are themselves ends, and that our subordinations and dependences can seldom be relied on as those of an infinite God, we might almost conclude that the very *creation* of man was in the Divine purposes only a work preparatory and subservient to the mightier work of his *restoration*. However we may stimulate our fancies with the glories of God's outer world, if we would indeed enjoy " the light of the knowledge of the glory of God," we must seek it where the Apostle found it, " in the *face of Jesus Christ*."

What then, brethren, is it to preach restoration to man by " Christ crucified?" Consider, first, what it *is* to preach Christ crucified? and you will perceive. It is to preach Him in His sacrifice as the sole atonement of sinners, and in His obedience as their great example. It is to write His name upon the front of all teaching, to found all exhortation upon the principles of His truth. It is to instruct the world to look upon Him whom their sins have pierced, and by habituating the eye to seeing Him upon Calvary, to prepare its weakness for seeing Him in glory! It is, in short, to faithfully deliver the message of God; for the whole scheme of religious truth, all that we are and hope to be, our beliefs, our confidences, and our love,—all spring from, and return to, that momentous hour in which Christ became " Christ crucified," that hour in which, exalted between heaven and earth, as it became the Mediator of two worlds, He intervened alike on the part of God and of man, and *first* looking up to his Father with a prayer of pardon, and *then* " bowing his head" to the sin-laden earth, reconciled *both* for ever!

Let us, then, see *what* it is which fortifies Christianity among a people's hearts, and yet leaves it so sadly uninfluential upon their lives; what it is which approves, and yet *rejects*, this doctrine of Christ crucified; what that strange character may be which assails the affections without binding the practice, which makes mankind unable to live wholly without Christ or wholly with Him, and renders (under Providence) the external Church imperishable, even while the internal and spiritual Church is in trouble and adversity,—even when the mystical Woman of the Apocalypse has to fly " into the wilderness, where she hath" (glory to divine mercy!) " a place prepared of God, that they should feed her there." (Rev. xii. 6.) Brethren, the reason is, that the doctrine of the Redeemer appeals to the universal *wants and anxieties of man* with a supernatural wisdom and power of application; and that hence, even while Christ is rejected, He is recognised,—even when the express prayers and regular offices of a believer are forgotten or unknown, yet the want, the craving desire, for truth is felt, and, as the Psalmist phrases it, "*the heart and flesh cry out* for the living God."

Look, then, to the doctrine of a crucified Redeemer (the seminal doctrine of Christianity) in its remedial character; and may God teach you, as you feel the want, to apply the remedy! I here appeal to your own experience, and to it alone. I am not to tell you now for the first time, what are the lessons directly derivable from this central tenet of the Gospel. I am not (after eighteen hundred years of its preaching) to undertake to invest them with novelty. I cannot say, with the prophet, " New things do I declare;" but they, brethren, who have obtained the "new Spirit," are able to feel that these things are never old. They can say, with Jeremiah, " The Lord's mercies are new every morning;" and, in a subject of inexhaustible extent, can for ever find freshness in the offices of praise and worship.

If, then, there be any character more especially marked in the Scripture accounts of Christ's advent among men, it is the character of a *Restorer*. " He healeth the broken in heart, and bindeth up their wounds" (Ps. cxlvii. 3). He is the " Sun of righteousness, with healing in His wings" (Mal. iv. 2). He applies to Himself the prophetic account, and declares that "the Spirit of the Lord hath sent Him to heal the broken-hearted, to preach deliverance to the captives." And you know how, on one occasion, He attributes to Himself the character of one commissioned specially to recover the lost or languishing victims of this world : " They that be whole need not *a physician*, but they that be sick " (Matt. ix. 12). All these expressions show clearly that He comes to purify some presupposed corruption, to repair some antecedent ruin, to satisfy some preexisting wants. "What, indeed, were the mass of His miracles but types and images of those moral and inward restorations, by which He makes the blind indeed to see, and the deaf indeed to hear?" And, as is easily shown, it is the feeling of these wants which in the minds of men perpetuates the corresponding feeling of the necessity of the remedy; and it is *this felt necessity of remedy* which supports the character and claims of Christianity in the world; while, at the same time, it is the *slowness* of men to embrace with sincerity and practical earnestness the proffered remedy, thus felt to be required and felt to be real, which renders the faith in the crucified Saviour inoperative and unfruitful.

For, 1st, the faith in the Christian sacrifice and its attendant revelation of the Divine character, alone answer the demands of the heart and reason of man for a higher state of moral perfection. I am well aware how feebly this voice is heard in the ordinary course of the world. Man could scarcely be deemed a fallen creature, if the consciousness of his fall were so universal as to prompt the continual demand for his restoration. But it would also be an over-statement to say that we have not a desire for something *better*, as well as for something *happier*, than this earthly state admits. Men do weary of the wickedness of the world as really, though not indeed so frequently, as of its disappointments. This is not the place for laboured discussions; and I will simply refer you to one powerful instance of this anxiety for a better and holier condition. I allude to cases of *private and personal injury*. Reflect upon your emotions in such instances. There is surely something more than mere resentment; there is a strong sense of injustice, and, naturally connected with it, (as the mind calms and diffuses its feelings,) a melancholy impression of the lost moral balance of the whole world, and a correspondent yearning for abodes where righteousness shall be a principle of universal action. I specify these cases, **not** because the feeling is there more *real*, but because **it is more** *intense and defined.* But, brethren, all these aspirations are in our faith met and satisfied. Is it not its preeminent character to unveil before our eyes a kingdom where immortally dwelleth righteousness? Is not its great Sacrifice the corner-stone of the *equity* of the whole moral universe,—the Sacrifice that enables God to be at once "just, and the justifier of him that believeth in Jesus?" Here, then, is the preaching of Christ crucified, recommended to the reason and to the heart. Here, in the beauty of its holiness, is a cause of its lingering power over the better affections even of those who have no strength to realize its commands. It establishes a righteous Governor upon the throne of heaven; it develops the symmetry of all His judgments; it answers the inward appeal of the frail and wretched beings, who can "know the better," even while they "the worse prefer."

2. But again, Christianity offers to maintain *a communication* between this world and that eternal world of holiness and truth. Here is another want satisfied; the aspiration of weakness made not merely a privilege but a duty. It would be easy to show how this elevation has been the crying demand of human nature in all ages, how it has produced and supported even false religions, and how (in its proper character) it is only satisfied in the true one. For the "*prayer*" to which I allude, as making Christianity attractive even to the frailest,—in adapting it to our better affections,—is obviously not a prayer for enjoyments similar to those of daily vice. Yet such was and is the prayer of the Heathen. The prayer of a Heathen is the miserable deprecation of a cowardly piety; for as is the Deity, so will be the prayer. And thus, too, the purer knowledge of God which Christianity unfolds, creates a parallel purity in its prayer. It is no longer to avoid momentary misfortunes, or to call down ruin upon transient enemies; but to be preserved unspotted for a future world of glory, and to be assisted in vanquishing the one sole enemy

that a Christian recognises as such. And thus (as before) it attracts even the most negligent by the beauty of its provision for our real exaltation. And who can doubt that it *is* the exaltation to which reason really (though feebly, perhaps) points? We for ever seek a happiness beyond the reach of chance,—Christian prayer beseeches it; we seek repose from incessant troubles,—Christian prayer is the stillest exercise of soul; we ask, even by blind impulses of nature, for pardon in the wretched consciousness of depravity,—Christian prayer encourages our timidity into confidence. Here, then, is a provision which (rightly considered) is really peculiar to our faith; and which so truly utters the wants of our condition, that it is, as it were, but the direction of nature in the channels and currents of grace.

3. Another particular in which this blessed faith commends itself to our wants, is in its confirmation and direction of that principle of *hope* which, even in our daily and worldly life, we are perpetually forced to substitute for happiness. It leaves the tendency, but it alters the object. How prominent this principle is in our Christian life, I need not remind you. "We are saved by hope." That is, we are saved by the exercise of a principle which we are in some measure instinctively inclined to make the source of our earthly happiness, but which, as yet, we have known as little more than the harbinger of disappointment. That our hope in Christ is no such delusion, I am not now about to argue. I am only inviting your attention to its admirable aptitude to our condition, as employing that machinery of hope and trust, which nature before possessed, for higher objects than nature ever contemplated. The author of the Epistle to the Hebrews describes Christians as those "who have fled for refuge to lay hold upon *the hope set before them;* which hope they have as an anchor to the soul, both sure and steadfast." The hope

which deserves such characters is in its nature, as a feeling of the soul, the same as that which we waste upon the emptiest dreams of time; but it was He "who is our Hope" that first taught the feeling to be sure and steadfast, that first made it indeed "the anchor of the soul," *because* He first made it (as the passage goes on to say) a hope "which entereth into that within the vail."

4. But above all its recommendations to the wants and solicitudes of man, the Gospel commends itself by the adorable *object which it presents to our affections.* The pining attachments which find no earthly being commensurate to the magnitude of their own nature, cannot wholly resist the attraction of the Being whom the Gospel reveals. The God who in His character of a Providential Governor is inaccessible to our conceptions, and coldly present to our reason, is in Christ a Friend who is more than a Brother. The language which inspiration gives our lips upon this subject transcends the natural understanding, and yet even the natural heart can find some dim echoes to the celestial call. The devotion with which we are encouraged to regard this great God and Saviour of the New Testament,—the affection with which He has contemplated us (for "we love Him *because* He first loved us"),—create a new and holy and eternal bond of love, such as in its fulness, indeed, our fallen humanity could never have anticipated, yet such as becomes an answer to many of the profoundest wants of the soul. And the worldly themselves (so great is the influence of such a system of belief among us) may be struck by reflecting, how enormous would be the desolation of the universe to even their minds, if the God of the Gospel were suddenly to disappear from their habitual convictions, and the Gospel itself to be detected as a dream! A sceptic could allow the horror of "a fatherless world;" but those who (even practically feeble and remiss) have ever contemplated the purity and beauty of the Divine lineaments visible in the Christ of the Gospel, can conceive a something

not less terrible in the dismal vacancy of a "redeemerless world!"

Thus, brethren, we see that, even in its most superficial view, the faith that we preach has its attractions. Thus we see that even to the godless wanderer, its restoring promises, its soothing and sympathising aspect, make it a something from which he would not willingly be divorced. There are those, indeed, to whom it is seen only in its terrors, and to whom it brings but a heart of desperation and a tongue of curses. But I speak now of the general complexion of our ordinary society. And I call upon you to press upon your hearts the lesson, that all this promptitude to admire and to support the faith of Christ in the world, is but an aggravation of guilt, if your inward hearts nevertheless prefer the world to the faith of Christ.

And now, brethren, I beseech you not to misunderstand me, as if, when I thus speak of the manner in which the faith commends itself to the wants of man, even in his natural condition, I could mean to imply that it can make any due or deep impression without *higher aids than nature ever gave*. This is *not* my reasoning,—most emphatically it is not. No; but from the felt beauty and perfection of our Christian scheme of teaching, I take occasion to press you to make the great restorative truly your own *by the appointed means of spiritual enlightenment*. I beseech *you* to beseech God your Father, that He would, of His own transcendent grace, quicken into earnestness that passive reception and merely verbal approbation of its claims, which I have been all along describing. All these excellences are formed, indeed, as the text has it, to "restore health unto you, and to heal you of your wounds;" but to *heal*, they must be received by *faith*. And faith is—*the gift of God*. Is it then a vain or daring course of the Christian minister, to attempt to analyse the medicine in order to show its suitableness, as long as he teaches that it can successfully operate only through a God-given acceptance of it? To *deny* that we may reverently look into these things,—on the ground that God alone can apply them,—would, by a false humility, be to enthrone the sovereignty of grace upon the ruins of reason. No; examine all, learn all, search all,—as long as you remember that, whatever be your admiration of the plan of the Gospel, "no man cometh to Christ, except the Father draw him."

Finally, my brethren, and before we part, reflect how the religion of Christ (considered as we have considered it) regards the world into which it enters? As a vast *hospital*, crowded with every wretched variety of sickness. From the burning fever of violent passion, to the cold palsy of heartless neglect, it contemplates all, and understands all, and is adapted for all. The sovereign restorer is busy among the throng; the diversities of misery are familiar to its diversity of powers. It interprets their griefs for those whose miserable restlessness betrays the disorder they cannot themselves comprehend; and it interprets, only to *restore*. And, brethren, what the world at large is, *this assembly* is also. Is not this very room,—and every other crowded temple of our city this morning,—an hospital of the heart? Every Christian congregation is but a miniature of the Christian world. Am I mistaken (would to God I were!) when I say that here, too, there sit at this hour more than one sufferer by the maladies of our miserable nature, aggravated by the pestilential atmosphere of the world we have to live in? Am I deceived (would to God I were! but the pulpit is not the place for flattery) when I say that even here, there are at this moment more than one who come to ask for a remedy they will not accept, and to worship a God whom they will not *serve?* Oh, brethren, if any of you there be who feel the feebleness, and require the cure, beware of saying to the ministers of Christ, as Job did to his friends, "Ye are forgers of lies, and physicians of no value!" When you come to the church of

God, you come to the great dispensaries of heavenly health. Pass not from ours this day without profit. Our Master, brethren, was assailed because He healed on the Sabbath-day; but to us (as to Him) it is not only "lawful to heal on the Sabbath," but the Sabbath is peculiarly *appropriated* for the blessed work. May the serious thoughts and holy aspirations of this day, register ours in heaven, as one distinguished in the history of souls restored and regenerated for eternal glory!

SERMON XI.

THE TRUE FAST.

(Preached for the Mendicity Institution, at St. Stephen's Chapel, Dublin.
Sunday Morning, July 23, 1837.)

ISAIAH LVIII. 6, 7.

Is not this the fast that I have chosen? .... Is it not to deal thy bread to the hungry, and that thou bring the poor that are cast out to thy house? when thou seest the naked, that thou cover him; and that thou hide not thyself from thine own flesh?

BRETHREN, the passage which I have just read to you, and which, I trust, you will feel to be practically appropriate to the occasion on which I have to address you to-day, is one of those in which the purity and holiness peculiar to the Gospel seems to be foretokened in the morality of the prophetic canon. Isaiah has been termed the Evangelical Prophet; and he is so, not more in the transcendent clearness of his predictions of evangelic facts, than in the corresponding brightness of his anticipations of evangelic holiness. As the inspired writers approached the great centre of purity, they became more and more deeply tinged with the glory they were approaching. The twilight clouds were red with the coming Sun. The odour of celestial sanctity which filled and encompassed that Divine Person who was essentially and inherently holy, diffused itself (as in those eastern islands of which we read) far along the wide extent of the Old Testament records; and might have given to the Jewish reader who travelled among them constant and beautiful notices of the fragrant scenery—the balm of still more ethereal doctrine —he was approaching, and of Him, its presiding Spirit,—

Him who (as the sacred song mystically has it) is, above all, "*perfumed with* myrrh and frankincense."

I do not, indeed, mean to assert that the moral illumination of the prophets always increased in direct proportion to their proximity to the age of the Lord whom they predicted. Such an assertion would be hasty and ungrounded. No such law is discernible in the distribution of prophetical inspiration. When Moses predicted the Prophet that was to succeed him at the distance of centuries, he was, perhaps, vouchsafed a vision of the glory to come more perfect than Isaiah ever possessed, and an apprehension of eternal goodness more unclouded; when the father of the faithful "saw the day" of Christ "and was glad," the feeling of joy which our Lord represents him as experiencing, in the perception of the blessed vision, seems to point to a degree of spiritual exaltation beyond, perhaps, that of the most favoured of his followers in the lineage of faith. Isaiah himself surpasses those who succeeded him. And, therefore, when I speak of moral illumination growing with the nearness of the prophets to their Lord, it is a different sort of proximity or distance to which I allude. It is no measure of time or space that can mark the position of a prophet's spirit in relation to the God who illumines it. It is on the scale of a more mysterious spiritual measurement, that we are to compute the comparative distances at which it pleases the Source of all excellence to hold the minds whose ecstasies contemplate, and whose words reveal, the dispositions of His future government. He to whom "a thousand years are as one day," can extend the arm of His power and the breath of His Spirit as well across the chasm of a thousand years as across the narrow interval of a single day; just as He to whom "one day is as a thousand years" can, in the unexpected turns of His providence, cover the events that a single day is to bring forth, with the mystery that shadows those of a thousand years to come!

When, therefore, I say that *the affections* of the prophetic messengers were inflamed by the same glorious Source that enlightened their *understandings*; when I profess to trace in their writings a parallel growth of *knowledge* and of *holiness*, and to see, in the hearts of those who were admitted into the more secret sanctuaries of the Divine counsels, all that deep veneration and all that practical piety which befitted such a privilege; it will be obvious to you, my brethren, that I refer to no nearness in place or time to the God who inspired them and whom they adored. It is the deep intimacy of the Spirit that I allude to; the internal contact of God with man. I call them *nearer* to God, when their vision of His glory was more perfect; even as we count ourselves nearer to some earthly object of admiration, when our dim and shadowy vision gives place gradually to distinct and definite perception. But these are idle comparisons! What earthly object, however magnificent, can suggest the feeblest conception of what *they* beheld? Supposing the mind to be previously unaffected, what earthly object would, by the mere perception of it, produce such terrors as those which Daniel describes in narrating that awful vision by the river Hiddekel; when, as he tells us, "I was left alone" (for his companions, though they saw nothing, had fled with an inward and mysterious terror), "and I saw this great vision, and there remained no strength in me; for my comeliness was turned in me into corruption, and I retained no strength: yet heard I the voice of his words"? or that of St. John the divine, when seeing the Lord Jesus in His glory, he "fell at His feet as dead;" until the same Christ who had made him His chosen friend on earth, became his Friend also in this awful crisis; and, in the same tone with which He addresses the timidity of every trusting believer, said—"Fear not! I am the first and the last"?

I am not now, brethren, about to carry this profound and mysterious subject to any farther detail. I am not about to argue (as I might, perhaps, do) that these prophetic visions—these wondrous intercourses between the uncreated God and

His creatures—are a mighty testimony to the high capacities of our mental nature. I am not about to insist that they form a positive, direct, and palpable evidence that our souls are made capable of the presence of the eternal Spirit; and that, though compassed by the evils of mortality, and frail through their dependence on a frail body, these souls are formed to repose in the courts of heaven, and fitted for the audience-chamber of the eternal God! Yes,—I might argue that if to us the influences of the heavenly Spirit are inconceivable, yet Moses spake to his Maker—substantially *the same Spirit*—" face to face;" that if the agency of the celestial upon the earthly be ever a temptation to the agonies of incredulity, yet " of old time ... holy men of God spake *as they were moved by the Holy Spirit*," and that their inspirations are an instance and a proof *to us*, of what it is within the laws of the spiritual world to effect! Oh, Christians, " who sorrow as those without hope!" ye whose temporal unhappiness have so clouded your religious horizon, that in your earthly troubles you lose the guiding star to heavenly peace,—becoming infidels in misfortune, and misdoubting the Spirit of consolation when most you need Him to console,—turn, I pray you, to the prophetic records, and learn, and be wiser as you learn, how the captivity of the prophets of abandoned Judah was illumed by the glorious presence of the Spirit of God; how those very " rivers of Babylon " by which the people " sat down and wept "—the " river of Chebar " and the " river of Ulai "—were made the especial theatre of some of the most magnificent manifestations of the Lord Jehovah's helping and consoling presence, that are contained in the whole series of the prophetic visitations! ... But (as I said) it is not to these subjects, profoundly interesting though they be, and though the text before us might naturally invite such considerations, that I would now conduct you.

I return to the point. I recal to your contemplation how closely allied—the text is an instance—are the supernatural illumination and the moral elevation of the prophets of God. The more their souls were opened to the future, the more they imbibed its holy influences. Christ Jesus—the Messiah who was to bring in an everlasting righteousness—was present not more to the vision of such men, than to their affections. Living in the august presence of God, their practical life took its complexion from their habitual society.... True it is that, now and then, the Lord of holiness, for His own mysterious purposes, suffered the accents of genuine prophecy to pass from profane lips; but He gave to such no continuous commission to instruct His people. They predicted not by rule, but by exception. If all prophecy be miracle in relation to the common laws of knowledge, theirs was a miracle even in relation to the scheme and world of miracles.... In every age of His dispensations, it has been the undeviating law of God to combine together the real knowledge of real truth with the habits and feelings of real goodness. He has made the pathway to His truth to lie through *the heart;* He has made, in all ages, the practical devotedness of a good life to be at once the preparative of belief and the consequence of it. How it springs (in all its rich varieties of charity) *from* a knowledge of the truth, I need not now detail; how it leads *to* such a knowledge, I leave Him to convince you who has declared, " If any man *will do His will,* he *shall know* of the doctrine whether it be of God!"

Here then, brethren, is the reason why I have insisted on the moral elevation and personal holiness that characterised the prophetic calling. *Here* is the reason why, in selecting a passage of deep practical import for our consideration on this festival of charity, I have thought it right not only to declare to you, as a mere revelation of truth, what the Spirit of God spoke through the lips of Isaiah, but also to remind you *at what time* the Isaiah lived who delivered it, and *in what manner* he and his prophetic brethren were wont to live and act in virtue of their high privileges I have told you that in the exact proportion in which they obtained glimpses of the truth of God, they manifestly increased in love to Him and to man for His sake. I have told you that the nearer they stood in their hours of vision to the unveiled glory of the coming Messiah, the more ardently burned their hearts, and the more fervently were fixed their resolutions of unwearied practical charity. I have reminded you that the blessed truth of the text was spoken by one whose soul was familiar with the laws and designs of Providence, and, as it would appear, in the very spirit of that prophetical familiarity; and I have selected this very passage out of a host of similar passages (for, blessed be God! the whole Bible is but one long revelation of the essential beneficence of our Maker), in order to impress upon you the glorious identity of the eternal principles of Scripture morality in every age—before Christ, and under Christ, and after Christ. Christians, need I make the application? Are your hearts able to receive it? If those who lived in the shadowy realms of type and vision could feel the force of maxims so pure and benevolent,—if a promissory Christ could create so fervent a flame of charitable zeal in the breasts of the prophets,—what becomes *you* who have (as the Apostle applies it) "the word *nigh you, even in your mouth and in your heart; that is, the word of faith* which we preach?" Had those men visions of God? What then? do not we, if we possess faith, "*endure as seeing Him who is invisible?*" Had these men spiritual gifts? What then? have we no Spirit to enlighten us—no privilege of prayer that secures His presence? Brethren, "there are diversities of gifts, but the *same Spirit*." The prophetic messengers—these "holy men of old"—had no monopoly of the infinite Spirit of holiness; their gifts are recorded not to dishearten, but to encourage us. If such blessings were bestowed in the old time, what will be done—what *is* done—in that which is preeminently the dispensation of the Spirit; that in which, in literal truth, (how we *can* slumber in the midst of such truths—"dark with" our very "excess of light!") the Spirit of God forms a ready and perpetual channel of communication between our hearts and the Source of all holiness,—a ladder, like that of the patriarch's vision, from earth to heaven! If formerly that Spirit bestowed isolated gifts of practical holiness on isolated individuals, is He not now, as it were, the Sensorium of the entire Christian system, the ineffable medium through which it receives the impressions and impulses of that divine Essence which is evermore around it, in which "it lives, and moves, and has its being!" Brethren, with such *an aid as this*, are *we* unable, with our distinct apprehensions of divine truths, with *our* unclouded knowledge of the essential goodness of the Divine character as revealed in His incarnate Son—are *we*, I say, who possess the harvest that ages were spent in maturing (for it was decreed "that they without us should not be made perfect"), are *we* unable to realize the unworldliness, the benevolence, the charity that the prophets of the elder time, seeing their God through a cloud (of *radiance* indeed, but still *a cloud*), could preach, and practise, and perish as martyrs to support in the world?

You see now, brethren, why I brought Isaiah before you, and his brother prophets,—these men who were holier, and heavenlier, and richer in the works of love, upon an anticipated Christ, than we are in a Christ already our crucified example. These men of God knew no divorce between belief and love; between living perpetually in the presence of a benevolent Lord, and imitating His benevolence to their fellow-creatures! As it is the Spirit of truth that has solemnised the union of the principle of faith with the works of charity, so it is, and in all ages has been, the master-policy of the spirit of evil to effect their separation. But what "God hath joined together let no man put asunder!" This same purpose of separation, which in darker ages (as we call them) the enemy of man sought to accomplish by making faith stand for a catalogue of superstitious observances,—similar to the *fasts* of which the

Prophet speaks in the text,—he now attempts to accomplish by exaggerating and perverting its more legitimate signification. The former cheat became impossible when the Scriptures began to be *read;* the latter, I trust, will become equally rare, as the Scriptures begin to be *felt* ... So subtle is the dexterity of the human heart in evil, that even from the most salutary truth it can extort a poison ... The principle of religious dependence which in the Scriptures is called "*faith*,"—that principle which begins in a making to feel and know a Redeemer (that is, a pardoning and restoring God) to be needed and to be provided, which continues in habitually depending on Him, and making a communion with Him the business and happiness of life, and which naturally *acts itself out* in works of love to men,—that principle which, restoring the communication between fallen man and his Maker (a communication for which his unfallen nature was originally made), must obviously be the highest and purest state of minds on this side of the grave,—that principle which is nothing more or less than the general religious principle as exerted by a frail towards a perfect nature, turned into the channel of Christ's redeeming work and regenerating promises, and matured to a simpler purity by His gracious Spirit,—that principle which is thus in its inmost essence a principle of unworldly and absorbing devotion, in its very nature a *liberalizing* principle; for what will liberalize our hearts as to worldly possessions, if continued converse with a higher sphere of being does not, and what will make us actively loving and merciful and charitable towards every breathing thing, if habitual confiding access to a God whose essence is love, and who charges us on our loyalty and gratitude that we make ourselves the ministers of His mercies, do not?—This principle, I say, thus in its essential quality formed to be obviously the master-spring of the whole system of life's duties,—this principle, by which the Spirit of God, who bestows it, may in a manner be said at the same moment to justify and sanctify us,—this principle which, in a word, puts our human souls in the full sunlight at once of divine favour, and divine holiness,—a principle which is in itself so noble, and in its necessary results so pregnant and productive, —this (by the miserable ingenuity of the depraved heart of man) has been perverted into a barren act of speculative conviction, an audacious assumption of divine favour, and a secret internal justification of indolence, covetousness, and unspirituality. This subject (*practically* simple enough—else how was "the Gospel" ever "preached to the poor?") has been so beset by the thorns of controversy, (another device of Satan,) that I suppose it may be necessary to say that in making these melancholy assertions, I allude to no professed sect, party, or denomination whatever. No, Christians and brethren; the only sect I allude to, is that terrible and widespread sect which began at the Fall, and will, I fear, continue to the Judgment,—that sect whose birth is in the unchanged evil of the human heart, of which the devil is arch-heretic and founder,—that sect without a name, which in one form or another has in every age compromised between heaven and hell, by giving its beliefs to the *one*, and its conduct and heart to the spirit who governs the *other!* Oh, brethren, whatever outward modification of Protestantism you embrace, avoid this master delusion! Let no man lull your constant "diligence to make your calling sure," on pretence of selling you a cheaper talisman for heaven! Let no man persuade you that heaven is to be won by anything which does not necessarily bring with it the "purity of heart without which" no soul "shall see God!" Let no metaphysical subtleties (the misfortune of our age) about the cause, or the essence, or the period of justification, cheat you into dreaming that anything can be a principle of justification before the tribunal of God, which is not also, in its necessary results upon your hearts and life, a principle of sanctification fitting you for His divine approval! Be content to "hunger and thirst after righteousness," to live habitually in the presence of Christ, to verify constant faith by constant love,—and you can afford to resign to the God of the universe the mysteries of *His providence* in the work of salvation.

Brethren, our work of love this day has warranted my enlarging on this everlasting connexion between your faith as believers, and your development of that faith in universal charity. I will go yet further, and suggest, that your habits of benevolence in this life,—those habits which this day we are calling upon you to exercise,—are intended as a training for a *love more perfect* which is to the glory of a future state, a love concentrated upon a diviner object! Bear with me a moment while timidly, indeed, as becomes a feeble fellow-sinner, I would dare to speculate on that world which you are now educating your hearts to enjoy! Yes, the tenderness of soul which strengthens in this morning's act of charity, may be disciplining itself for a higher sphere; this day may bear a fruit to eternity!

The whole religious providence of God towards man in every age has been a system operating by the combined influences of faith and love,—both directed towards His own perfect essence. In the Old Testament dispensation (as you read in the noble summary in the Epistle to the Hebrews) faith was the leading principle,—faith dependent on a God who appeared as a rewarding and avenging Power. In our dispensation, where God has allayed the terrors of His power in the mercies of Jesus Christ, love mingles largely with our devotional states; and, as I believe, in the dispensation to come, faith will fade before the absorbing lustre of her sister grace, and LOVE, consuming and transforming all to its own substance, rule for ever the glorified spirit of man! In our existing condition, what is faith but love relying on support? What is love but faith forgetting the support in the supporter? Now, in a higher state of consummate perfection, a higher motive will be ours than the *consciousness of a feebleness that requires constant support*... Admitted to the presence of the eternal Source of all good, the answering affections of the purified heart will secure allegiance by their own independent exercise. " Underneath will be the everlasting arms," as before; but we shall be *too* much engaged in looking on the glorious countenance of the Supporter, to be much engaged in relying on the support! If even in this world we can, as St. Peter tells us, " become partakers of the divine nature," can we doubt that such a participation is meant to form the main glory of the next? and if this be so, is it not remarkable that this celestial principle of love (which seems to be the final perfection of man and the central principle of the Gospel dispensation) is really the only one in which we can perceive the possibility of a reciprocation between our God and ourselves? If *we* rest upon God by *faith*, yet He cannot rest upon us; if we pour ourselves upon Him in *gratitude*, yet He cannot return gratitude to us; if we approach Him in *fear*, yet He cannot fear His creatures;—but in love alone our God and we are fitted to combine! there alone the human and the divine nature are one! " We love *Him*, because He first loved *us*." In His other affections, as pictured in the Gospels, we talk of the " *human* " and the " *divine* " nature of Christ coming prominently forward; in the daily manifestations of *His love* alone, we know not which nature it is that speaks, for that lovely principle belongs to both alike!

So far, my brethren, for the love of man to his Creator. I hope sincerely that such views will not appear to you a cloudy mysticism. The truth is, that in our happier moments, these things strike us with all the force of absolute demonstration; but in the busy turmoil of the world the transparent waters are shaken, and the reflection of heaven is lost. The delusions of daily life act as the ministry of Satan to hide these glimpses of a higher life from our hearts!

Still, it may be said, this love of God is the contemplation of supreme excellence; how can the love of the creatures—

the practice of benevolence towards frail and faulty mortals—form a training for so holy and so lofty an emotion?

I cannot now pause to discuss this at any length. I can only afford time to observe,—if you remember that God *is* love, and if you combine with this great revelation the fact that in proportion as we attain a quality of goodness, we learn to estimate and love those who possess it, you will soon see that every progressive step in attaining habits of compassion and kindness upon earth, must necessarily be a step towards estimating and loving Him who is the essential Spirit of benevolence.... And besides this, doubtless, the earthly affection resembles in some mysterious way the heavenly, else the same title could scarcely be chosen for both. Yes, the love of man is the type and shadow of the love of God,—the first step upon a pathway that conducts to paradise. The people of God are here engaged with the rudiments and images of those affections which are to be the duty and the happiness of their eternity!

And therefore it is, brethren, and with a view to this final glorification, that we are placed in this world in the midst of scenes formed to elicit and consolidate the habits of mercy and compassion. Among the many reasons for the existence of moral and physical evil, is not this a reason of force, that the miseries of mankind form a school for the education of the people of God? Our heavenly Master has not chosen to spare Christian climes the curse of poverty; but the genuine Christian can convert the curse into a blessing. To His own disciples He declared, "The poor *ye have always* with you." He came not to turn the world into a heaven, but to make it the path to heaven! Wherefore do we move in the midst of destitution, but because we move in the midst of trial and discipline? Wherefore are you, all who hear me, made the stewards of God and ministers of His wealth,—the mediators between God and His poor,—but because in His mercy He would give you opportunities of " laying up treasures in heaven, where neither moth nor rust doth corrupt?" Oh, brethren, turn not your riches into curses! You who possess the means of diffusing earthly blessings,—woe unto you if you forget the responsibility that attaches to the possession! Woe unto you if, concentrating them all upon your own persons, you shut your ears to the cries of the myriads that starve at your gates, and, labouring to make the earth a heaven for yourselves, leave it (as far as *you* can do) to be a hell for the wretches who surround you! Such warnings are addressed to all. There is *none* who cannot spare his proportion; there is none who is not a creditor to God for every particle of wealth he possesses; there is none who, in denying aid to the destitute, is not presuming to cheat his heavenly Master out of His own entrusted property!

You are aware, brethren, on what account it is that I speak to you in this tone to-day. The melancholy notices that cover the walls of your city have already apprised you that the strength of your Christian principles is to be tried in the preservation, from imminent peril, of an Institution whose object is to secure your destitute fellow-creatures from starvation. It is no slight toil for Christian ministers to be called on continually to perform such duties as this; and yet I feel that we ought to forget the toil in the unequivocal honour it does to the Christianity we preach. It shows, however our faith may be undervalued, the world cannot easily do without it. If man was born into a paradise prepared for his reception,—if he was to pass his hours in perpetual festivity,—he could afford to forget, and he would soon forget, the very existence of the religion of the Gospel; but where there is sorrow to be relieved, where the exhausted treasures of charity are to be replenished, where helplessness solicits support, the Church is the ready resource, and Christian feeling the only security. Misery is the remembrance of our faith; while there is beggary and wretchedness on earth, the religion of love will never be forgotten!

Of the state of the Institution which I call on you this day to support, it will be sufficient to say that, by a statement laid before a meeting of its committee, on the 27th of last month, it appears that (as compared with this time last year) its inmates have increased by 830,—its applicants for admission during six months by 1,537; that the prices of provisions consumed in the Institution have risen to an alarming height; and that the subscriptions received, to meet these accumulated difficulties, have been constantly decreasing in a ratio even greater than the increase of expense. It would be needless to go farther into calculations which you can all easily obtain and verify for yourselves. This is the miserable summary of the case that appeals to your feelings this day; this is the case which, if you are backward in your duty as Christians—nay, as human beings—this morning, will force the managers of the Institution to cast loose upon society the army of paupers —not far from 3,000—that its invaluable care now secures from offending your eyes and persecuting your feelings! I appeal to your *personal interests*,—will you not save your city from this inundation of misery, and of its consequent vice? I appeal to your *hearts*,—will you suffer your ill-fated fellow-creatures—morally your equals—to starve upon the steps of your mansions? I appeal to your *justice*,—will you permit the whole expense of an Institution that forms a public blessing, to fall upon a few whose Christian benevolence makes them your victims? I enter into no laboured defence of the principle of the Institution: suffice it to say, *it exists;* and whatever was its original policy, its failure *now* would be a public calamity, a pestilence of poverty! ... A day or two since, I visited this receptacle of outcasts, while its officers were in painful uncertainty as to the possibility of maintaining its existence; and as I contemplated the disemboguing of the mass of mendicancy I have witnessed, in one flood of misery upon the town, I thought of that terrific passage in which the prophet declares the fate of the abandoned city of God,—

"The people shall be cast out into the streets because of the famine... and they shall have none to bury them.... If I go forth into the field, then behold the slain... and if I enter into the city, then behold them that are sick with famine." Brethren, this must not be. Talk not of coming *poor laws!* The God of Israel has already settled that plea, when He bade the Israelites not refuse the poor man, because the seventh year (the Jewish poor-law) was approaching. (Deut. xv.) Suspend not a claim of life and death on the chances of prospective legislation! The contribution of a single individual this morning may be the saving of a life from the agonizing death of hunger! Where is the Christian that on such terms will close his heart and his purse? Oh, brethren, in such a case, I would invoke you by *Him*, who for ever consecrated poverty by living as a poor man upon earth, to honour by your tributes the state which He honoured by His life! May He who gave Himself a willing sacrifice for you, incline your hearts to imitate in some poor degree His beneficence, by making *some* return from your earthly abundance for the ineffable blessings He bestowed!

SERMON XII.

THE WAY TO DIVINE KNOWLEDGE.

(Preached for Peter's Schools, Peter's Church, Jan. 28, 1838.)

JOHN VII. 17.

If any man will do his will, he shall know of the doctrine, whether it be of God.

THE version which in our public translation is given of this passage, appears—at least in the *present* use of language—to be faulty from ambiguity. The auxiliary word, "will," which is *sometimes* (as when we say, a man "*will take* a journey," or "*will purchase* a possession") employed as a sign of a *real action* to be performed from the voluntary effort of an agent, and *sometimes* for the *voluntary purpose* or desire only, is here, as well as in some other kindred passages, used in a manner which leaves the English reader in some doubt as to *which* of the senses was intended, a doubt which may very materially obscure the real import of this momentous declaration. You are to observe, then, that an appeal to the original language of this Gospel at once determines that the declaration is, *not* that if any man *will actually perform*, or continue to perform, the will of God, he shall "know the doctrine," *but* that if any man *sincerely wish* to perform that will, he shall discover the divine original and descent of the doctrine. The knowledge in question is not, in the first instance, suspended upon the cordial voluntary performance of God's will, but purely upon the purpose to perform it when once discovered; a qualifying condition for this great gift of knowledge, much more merciful, because much more limited.

Our blessed Instructor, then, has here taught us that a sincere desire, intent, and purpose to execute the commandments of a pure and holy God, from whatever source they be made known, will in hearers of the Gospel be inevitably attended with a knowledge of the true source,—that is, with a recognition of the real character of His own teaching as an authentic message from heaven. "If any man wills to do His will, he shall *know the doctrine*" (for thus it is better, because more literally translated), "whether it be of God."

It would not be easy to imagine a declaration of more moment to man in every age, but above all to man in an age of high and cultivated civilization. While in its direct form, as I have read it to you, it exhibits to the humble spirit a promise of surpassing mercy, and altogether worthy of our God; on the champions of an arrogant enlightenment, its *converse* flashes a terrific denunciation of guilt and dismay. For if it be certain that the unfeigned desire to serve God is necessarily attended by a knowledge of His truth in Christ, it must be equally certain, by strict and inevitable consequence, that a *rejection* of the faith—or, by similar reasoning, a disparagement of the faith, or a neglect of the faith, or a carelessness about its influences, its advancement, its perpetuation—must arise from an absence of solicitude to please God in His chosen form, or any God in any form,—that is, from a radical atheism of the heart. Such is the unalterable connexion that this great proposition establishes between purity of will and the knowledge of truth—between ignorance, or contempt of a preached Gospel, and real inward obstinacy. Casting upon unbelief all the criminality of wilful disobedience, dethroning it from its airy supremacy in the intellectual part of man,—where it sits sometimes in the form of a gift of keener *acuteness*, sometimes in that of a superiority to vulgar prejudices,—to a low and vile position among the worst corruptions of the heart, it destroys at a blow all the most cherished flatteries of humanity,—it crushes on their very shrine the idol that, when all others are broken, man would last resign—the idol of his intellectual ambition.

I invite you, then, in a cautious, humble, but earnest spirit, to consider the real scope and foundation of this statement. The discussion of this great law of Christian knowledge will form a fitting preparative for that work of large but pressing liberality,—liberality directly devoted to sustaining and diffusing the means of this same religious enlightenment,—of which I am set here to be this day the organ and the advocate.

In order to clear our course of superfluous obstructions, and to narrow its limits, let us define the legitimate *compass* of the doctrine. You will observe, then, that the declaration of our Lord applies only to those who, by whatever means, have been brought within the circle of Christian admonition. This I conceive to be implied in the words of the text. It is true that it states, in a form of the widest generality, " if *any man* wish to do His will," but then it also states that " he shall know of *the doctrine*." Now, " doctrine," or teaching, supposes a teacher; that is, supposes this prompt servant of God to have come under the ordinary influences of religious instruction. You may, perhaps, perceive that I make this remark in order to obviate the extravagant conclusion which a well-known modern enthusiasm is constantly deriving from such promises. If—in order to establish from this declaration the tenet that a distinct revelation of unknown truths is made to every worthy heart—it be answered that *the Spirit* may be the supernatural Instructor here intended, I need only reply, in addition to the obvious argument from the context, that such an interpretation would militate against the fundamental principles of those who propose it. The very nature of the immediate revelation for which they contend is to be self-witnessing, and, as to its claims of divine origin, irresistible. Now, to suppose *such* a revelation of unknown truths *here* intended, would certainly be to suppose the possibility of their being unrecognised by the recipient; inasmuch as, whatever be the "teaching" contemplated, our Saviour most manifestly suspends the apprehension of its divine origin upon the previous state of the receiver's heart; that is, He would, upon this hypothesis, state that perception to be a *contingency* which it is the very essence of their theology to represent as an irresistible conviction, as a light which publishes itself, and which it would be contradictory to conceive as requiring the assistance of an illumination no brighter than its own. . . . It is, then, to no such mystic manifestations of undiscovered doctrines that the present statement refers: its subjects are that vast mass of mankind whom God's providence has placed under instruction in Christian elements; and the office of the Spirit of God on such is, not to enrich them with new revelations, but to impress and vitalize the old.

Having thus ascertained the *range* of the doctrine, let us next examine the *character* it supposes. "If any man *will to perform the will of God.*" The obvious—and I suppose the usual—interpretation of this passage, states it as intimating that the true source of unbelief is to be found in a carnal disinclination to make the sacrifices that the Gospel peremptorily requires in every real believer. And truly this is a most valuable lesson, and, as I have already hinted, unquestionably implied by strict consequence in the declaration of our Lord. Yet it seems to me even more profoundly instructive to look at this assertion in its positive than its negative form; to follow it word for word, just as it fell from the lips of Jesus; and to consider rather the glorious consequence of belief that is *directly* stated to result from the existence of the condition, than the terrible conclusion we must draw where that belief is rejected, as to the absence of the condition that would have brought it. . . . . "If any man will do the will of God, he shall apprehend the doctrine, whether it be of God."

There is in the expression (both original and translated) a *repetition* of the same word "will," which (except for purposes of mere explanation) cannot be omitted without, as I think, a great injury to the perfection of the sense. " If any man *will* to do *His will*,"—that is, if there be a constant breathing after a union of the human will with the divine, a zealous resolution of the one into the other, an anxious absorption of the desires of the man into the purposes of the God,—then let that soul, thus disciplined for truth, but catch one glimpse of Christian teaching, the glimpse will gather to a blaze, spread and swell into noonday, and the divine credentials of the Gospel reveal themselves in characters of ineffable lustre. In the words of St. Paul, (Rom. xii. 2,) by being " not conformed to this world" (which, as the " friendship of this world is enmity with God," nearly coincides with the resignation contemplated in the present text) such a spirit will " *prove* what is that good, and acceptable, and perfect *will of God*."

But, it will be objected, how can such a state of mind be conceived as *altogether prior* to Christian instruction? It might be sufficient to answer, that to us the question is really of no practical moment,—to all, certainly to most of us, there was *no period* altogether prior to Christian instruction. And therefore, even though the objection were founded upon truth, it could still afford no excuse to us to whom it cannot possibly apply. With you and me the dawn of reason and of religion was the same; among the earliest forms of sound to which our infant breath was moulded, " Our Father, which art in heaven" had a place. Your objection—were it founded—might perhaps tend to acquit the unevangelized Indian of the guilt of his unsubdued and rebellious heart; it cannot, by any ingenuity of delusion, be applied to acquit *you*.

But, in truth, the objection has little foundation in any point of view, if the distinction with which I commenced be remembered,—that it is not obedience, but the wish to obey, that is stated in the text as the condition of illumination. A man who once believes that a God exists, (and this, you know, is presumed in the expression, "if he will to execute the will of *God*,") unquestionably may—under the guidance of the Spirit of truth—imbibe habits of practical resignation from his studies in the volume of the world, no less *truly* than from his studies in the volume of the word,—though not indeed with anything like the same reasonableness, devotedness, entireness, purity, and fervour. Affliction (for instance), the great medicine of Mercy, may compel him to his knees; on his heart, thus softened, the Spirit of grace may take its opportunity of impressing a deeper subjection; and thus, this holy preparation of a will prostrate before the Will that rules the universe, will be found (in consonance with our Lord's assertion) to make ready the heart for the perfect teaching of the Gospel. But, to consider this great subject to any profit, it will be necessary to consider the entire matter a little more comprehensively than in the form of an answer to an accidental objection.

The great characteristic of Christian illumination,—that in which it is essentially distinguished from every other scheme of instruction,—is in the force with which it insists upon the great—and, as a fundamental point, the novel—principle, that the path to all *knowledge* of righteousness lies through the heart. I have expressed the *peculiar claims* of the Gospel— including, of course, its prophetic precursors—to the publication of this principle, with cautions and limitations; because I am well aware that in all the writings of the thoughtful, in all ages, occasional apprehensions of such a truth are discoverable. Founded, as it is, deep in human nature, it was impossible but that it should sometimes reveal itself to those who spent their lives in *analysing human nature*. But it is often (and above all, in such subjects as these) a much greater positive discovery to perceive the relative importance of truths, than to perceive the truths themselves; and it is in *this* view that Christianity asserts its claim to an important innovation upon the errors of mankind, when, instead of suffering this great fundamental principle to lie immersed among a heap of other relics of human thought, false at least in its position, though so momentously true in itself,—it declared from the very outset, and declared as the master-law of its teaching, that the knowledge of spiritual truth was only receivable by the preparation of the Spirit; that the vision of divine things required undiseased eyes; that it was only " the pure *in heart* " who were qualified to " *see God*."

Conformable to this representation is the employment of the term " *knowledge* " in the various writings of the Christian revelation. It is used in two senses,—one of which is almost invariably either accompanied with actual disparagement, or referred to a very subordinate rank in the education of a disciple; and the other of which, exalted among the glorious attributes of his highest earthly possessions, very manifestly includes, in its very essence, an ardent purity of the *affections*. To the former—the exclusively intellectual sense—may be referred, for actual *disparagement*, such declarations as that in 1 Cor. viii. 1, that " knowledge *puffeth up;* " and for a statement of *inferiority* in the gifts of grace, the affirmation of St. Paul, in the 13th chapter of the same Epistle, that a man may have " all knowledge " and yet " be nothing," and that " knowledge " of this kind " shall vanish away." In the 15th of Romans he acknowledges that they are " filled with all knowledge," yet declares that nevertheless he must write to them to counsel and to warn; and prays *not only* that they may believe, but that they may be " filled *with joy and peace* in believing." In the same manner, in 2 Cor. vi., out of eight or nine successive gifts that the ministers of God are besought to manifest, their " knowledge " is but one; the purified affections absorb the rest. And, as if to show *on what basis* this knowledge (to be of any profit) must be raised, in the most animated and fervid of all his writings (Eph. i.), he prays that his converts may receive " the spirit of wisdom and of revelation,"—but it is " *after* he heard of their faith in the Lord

Jesus, and their love unto all the saints." Such, then, is the position in which inspiration has placed our intellectual (even a *miraculous* intellectual) knowledge of religious truth, when considered in itself as an isolated gift of providence or grace.

But the studious and purposed employment of the same (or much the same) term in, as will be evident from the contexts, another and loftier sense, throws *additional* light upon the argument; because it not only confirms the former reasoning, but it establishes a further principle of the deepest importance. It not only proves that knowledge *by itself* is *nothing*, and that, *joined* with the glorious graces of the heart, it is *inferior;* but it also proves that, nevertheless, even while we admit it inferior, we must also remember that to call out and support the others it is *necessary*. And it thus raises a barrier against intellectual pride, on the one hand, and against that enthusiasm, almost as dangerous, on the other; that "zeal not according to knowledge," which, not comprehending how harmoniously adapted is the Gospel to the entire man, and in an affected anxiety for the religion of the *feelings*, would banish the intellect from all participation in the business of the Christian life, and thus act as wisely as those who should remove *the fuel from a fire*, under the pretext that it is an insult to the dignity of that noble element to suppose it to require such support.

I say, then, that the real value of "knowledge," when reduced to its due place among the Christian acquirements, is easily collected from that selection of the term which I now proceed to exemplify, to express some of the very loftiest attainments which humanity can conceive, or can expect to reach, under the choicest influences of the Holy Spirit. Whatever be the nature of these attainments, and whatever other and higher elements they may include, it seems most undeniable that they presuppose an element of *knowledge*, as otherwise it is inconceivable why the term should be selected to express them. It is not more certain that the term contains much more than the ordinary sense of knowledge, than it is certain that it contains *it* also.

When St. Paul declares, in 1 Cor. xiii., that he shall in the future world "know as he is known," and that such knowledge shall be to the present as the knowledge of a man to that of a child, who can deny that in the difference of these degrees of knowledge there is yet a similarity; that between the partial knowledge that "shall vanish away" and the perfect knowledge that shall abide for ever, there is at least so much of sameness, that any faculty that is busy in the former may be expected not to be laid aside in the latter, which is not the opposite of it but the completion? . . . But again, on the other hand, when he declares that there are men ever "learning, and never able to come *to the knowledge of the truth*" (2 Tim. iii. 7), it is evident he must mean something much more than a knowledge of *understanding*, against which (in a case so simple as the Christian creed) no such hopeless barrier can be conceived. When St. Peter exhorts the Christian converts to "*grow* in grace and in the knowledge of our Lord Jesus," he speaks of a *progressive, a growing* clearness in this spiritual perception of Christ, wholly inapplicable to any ordinary knowledge of a body of truths relative to any ordinary person or thing; a remark which may also, perhaps, be justly applied to the prayer of St. Paul for his Philippian correspondents, "that their love may abound *yet more and more in knowledge* and sensibility" (i. 9). Now, you know, without any great expense of reflection, that there is this capital difference between that which concerns the understanding and that which concerns the affections; that the former is incapable of any increase as long as its object, truth, remains strictly the same; while of the latter, the object may continue unaltered, and yet the degree of fervency indefinitely advance. The conclusion is inevitable, that the knowledge here contemplated is a combination of intellect and *affection ;* in short, that it is *that* of which St. Paul elsewhere declares, that " God hath shined *in our hearts* to give *the light of the knowledge* of the glory of God" (2 Cor. iv. 6). The famous expression in Eph. iii. 19, " *to know the* love of Christ *which passeth knowledge*," has often been cited as an instance of singular obscurity; but this view of the double significance of "*knowledge*" easily resolves the difficulty. It thus appears, that St. Paul prays that his beloved at Ephesus may be taught " to know" (in the high and peculiar sense of the term) " the love of Christ which passeth knowledge," (in the *common* sense of a mere intellectual perception,—the arrogant knowledge, γνῶσις, of the early " Gnostics.") That " love" is indeed connected with this spiritual apprehension of divine things, you may collect from St. John, who teaches us that " he that loveth is born of God, *and knoweth God*" (1 John iv. 7). And, to pass from the pupils to the Master, with what an energy of affection, far surpassing the perception of any person or thing, does our Lord declare that He " knows His sheep, and is known of His!" and with what melancholy denunciation of moral guilt does He attest that " the world has not *known*" His " righteous Father," but that " *He* hath known Him!" Yes, blessed Lord! Thou hast indeed " known Him!" In the mystic Sonship of a past eternity, Thou hast studied and loved that volume of all perfections! Thy shrine was the bosom of the Everlasting; and there Thou hast read, inscribed upon the very heart of God, the secrets of that righteous administration which is without beginning and without end. Nay, —what, after all, was this vision but *reflection?* Was not this union to the celestial Parent such, that to contemplate *Him* thou hadst but to gaze,—oh, mystery transcendent!—to gaze in conscious glory upon *thine own* all-holy Essence?

Brought to this point, we can perhaps attempt to trace to its foundations, in the constitution of nature, the great law of Christian " knowledge," in that highest sense of the term which makes it a loving, adoring, and ever-growing recognition of the inexhaustible perfections of God ... God is the centre and substance of moral perfection,—of goodness, of wisdom, of justice. He is "love," says St. John; He is "only wise," says St. Paul; " Justice is the habitation of thy throne," says the Psalmist. Now, every man knows in proportion to his experience, and adores in proportion to his knowledge. The more, therefore, the soul of man rises in the experience of conscious purity, the more will his adoring knowledge increase of Him who is the perfection of purity; the more he resembles God, the more he will contemplate Him; while again, in proportion to the contemplation, the resemblance itself will increase, according to that of St. Paul, that they who " with unveiled face behold the glory of the Lord, are changed into the same image, from glory to glory." . . . That the reverse is similarly true, that without inward holiness a man is without the very *idea* of our God, it is, I hope, now superfluous to insist on. A man cannot *compose* a conception of which he never had the very elements! As he who has no idea of power cannot conceive omnipotence; so he who has never realized holiness can have no conception of that God who is " of purer eyes than to behold iniquity." He talks of "God," but he worships an idol.

So far, then, you perceive how it is that the " knowledge of God" must ever be a property rather of the heart than of the understanding, and also that it is a grace susceptible of indefinite, indeed of infinite, increase. The application of this principle to the declaration in the text requires a more minute, but still a very simple, train of reflection. Let us devote one moment more to pursue the process by which the bright conclusion is wrought out.

The declaration amounts to this,—that if any man make the will of God his will, *he* shall recognise the divine origin of the Gospel. Now, I assume that the man in question was supposed by the divine speaker to have already attained a general notion of God as a Being of supreme excellence; *otherwise* it is most certain, in the first place, that our Lord could never have supposed him to attribute the Gospel to God as its Author, the moment he came to hear it; and, in the second place, that the rewarding illumination to which Christ referred could never have been destined for one who entertained low conceptions of the Deity,—who conceived of Him, perhaps, as a merciless and unholy tyrant of the universe. Resignation is a virtue only when its object is noble. Resignation to the spirit of evil is the last stage of sin; and resignation to God, under the impression of His being the patron of unholiness, is no better.

The subject of the present declaration, then, already conceiving God to be (according to his best notions of perfection) pure and holy, is next represented as resigning his whole will to the will of that Supreme Governor. Is it not evident that such a man, the humble worshipper of his own best idea of perfection personified, has already attained a high state of moral sensibility? On that "honest and good heart" (to use our Lord's own words in the parable of the sower) the seed is now cast. The GOSPEL, "the doctrine," is now exhibited to him. He sees, and he adores! It is the very completion of all he had but faintly and imperfectly drawn in his own heart. But being, from his state of humble resignation to God (a state built upon the belief of God's entire supremacy in the sphere of goodness), already habituated to refer to Him everything morally excellent as to its primal source, he naturally, inevitably, connects this new and glorious apparition of truth with *Him;* and when it is proposed as indeed the genuine offspring of the Divine Mind, joyfully accedes to the claim, recognises the credentials, and embraces the messenger! His moral honesty assents to Christianity; his humble resignation attributes it to Heaven. And THUS IT IS that "if any man will to do the will of God, he shall know the doctrine, whether it be of God."

But more than this—if it be not too daring to conjecture: as such a man "grows in grace," his growing "knowledge" (making Christianity yet more worthy of God) and his growing resignation (ascribing it yet more completely to God in proportion to its proximate excellence) draw closer still the link that unites Christianity with Heaven,—the Lawgiver on earth with the Lawgiver above; until, at length, they approach, they merge, they are lost in each other; and recognising in Christ Himself nothing less than the whole circle of perfections he had been wont to adore on the throne of the universe, he sees in the Messenger, THE VERY GOD He proclaimed!

Farther than this I will not ask you to follow. The angels who veil their faces before the throne, may take up the history! It is for them to say, whether there be stages of knowledge that rise above this adoring perception of Christ as the true image of divine holiness in the temple of the heart. It is for them to tell whether their hearts, animated by a yet more ardent flame of love, have lighted their apprehensions to a yet more perfect intelligence of God; whether, as they have knelt before the throne in ecstasy of adoration, a ray hath ever broken forth from the mystic cloud that encompasses the Godhead, revealing secrets of the Divine Nature beyond the apprehension of *man*, and inflaming all heaven with a glow of wonder and delight too powerful for *human* frames to bear. . . . But no,—we will not disturb their repose of joy with our questionings! We can afford to tarry, —can we not? The time shall come when WE too shall " sit at the feet" of God, pupils in this heavenly school of happiness! Yes, the time *shall* come when He who willed to be glorified in the human nature will set us on a level with the angelic. " Father," said the Divine Sufferer, as He closed that dying prayer of His last evening, " I will that they also, whom Thou hast given me, be with me where I am; that they may behold my glory which Thou hast given me!" (John xvii. 24.) Oh, brethren, spirits for whom He died, it is by gazing on that glory here ("as through a glass"), you will be fitted on that day to behold it in the reality! Study His perfection; gaze on it till it fascinates you into its likeness. Yea, "be perfect *as* your Father who is in heaven is perfect." Feel and know that the only way to feel and know Christ is, to be Christ-like! Be assured that every step you rise in inward holiness, you are obtaining a nearer vision of that God who is holiness itself; and that no other organ than purity of heart can ever behold Him. Burst, therefore, the shackles of a mere dogmatical religion, a theology of phrases and periods. Can you be saved by a proposition in Euclid? Believe me, you can just as well be saved by a proposition in theology. Creeds are valuable only when our hearts say them. Love God, and love each other as the children of God; and the God of love will teach you divinity.

What are the simple conclusions from the whole? To those whose *hearts*, rich in Christian experience, and whose *understandings*, patient to examine the doctrines of eternal life, have endured to follow me thus far,—*two* conclusions will, I trust, manifest themselves, both equally and forcibly applicable to our immediate business of this day. THE ONE,—that the great prize of Christian enlightenment is to be sought by a humble subjection of the powers of the soul to the master-hand of God,—that by a profound submission to His service to the extent of your light, that light will be enlarged; and, surely, among the *earliest* duties of that subject will,—those which peculiarly designate a heart fitted to recognise the lineaments of God in Christ,—is found that lovely obligation of *benevolence* to which I now invite you.... THE OTHER,—that with all these preparations of the heart, it is nevertheless certain that the "knowledge" of God—the holy intimacy with Divine perfection, which I have shown you the Scriptures understand by that term—doth necessarily suppose some previous acquaintance (in the ordinary way of the faculties) with the great truths of the Gospel system: that is, that it requires, in more or less proportions, the very teaching, the very vigilance, the very training, the same humble ministry of the Bible-class and the school-room, for which I have this day to implore your aid. The *one* shows you what your FEELINGS ought to be, *benevolent*,—for *you* at least well know, that " to will performing the things that God wills" is to be so; the *other*, with as powerful an appeal, displays the proper OBJECTS of your benevolence,—those who, in training for the great science, " to know Him, and the power of His resurrection," are even now learning the necessary conditions of that knowledge, the alphabet of the Gospel, in the crowded schools of your parish. . . If you have indeed inhaled the spirit of these holy hopes and expectations of which we have been discoursing, let not, I beseech you, that spirit in a moment evaporate, and once more uncover as it passes away, the narrow niggard avarice of this world's daily prudence. Think you, that in these deeper discussions of the knowledge that is born out of humility, and fed by hourly holiness, I was for a moment forgetting the cause of these children of poverty and of the Gospel? No; but I was also remembering *you!* I would not *betray* you into benevolence, or deceive you into a spurious and momentary charity. I would treat you as rational, immortal, thinking beings: I would appeal to your reason in its calmness, and I trust in God you will show, this day, that you are not unworthy of being so appealed to.

SERMON XIII.

THE ASCENSION.

(The Ascension Day.)

Acts I. 9.

While they beheld, He was taken up; and a cloud received Him out of their sight.

In Christ Jesus all possible states and conditions of sinless being are hallowed. Poverty and contempt are sanctified, for Christ preferred them. Torture and uttermost agony are sacred, for Christ endured them. The grave is a holy thing, for He rested there. Glory and supreme triumph are resplendent with a light such as earth never gave them, for He has assumed them as His own. He has travelled through all varieties of being, and has left in them all the impress of Himself. So that, whereas the whole life of man was a thing defiled and unholy, it is now and for ever consecrated as a shrine or temple of the God who hath dwelt there. "He took not on Him the nature of angels, but the seed of Abraham." The angels have the holiness of creation; redeemed humanity has the holiness of occupancy and indwelling. *Those* have come from the hand of God, and are as they came, blessed; *these* have carried God within them in the Divine Representative of the race. The Manhood has borne the weight of Deity undestroyed,—it has held within it the lightnings of heaven, and not perished. As it is the mightiest boast of our race that we have thus been inhabited by a Divine presence; so it is our loftiest office to sympathise with all the high destinies of that Person who thus incorporated us with Infinity, who introduced us into the very sphere of supreme Deity, and who carries our fortunes with Him when He traverses the adoring heavens, and, while millions of worshipping seraphs are prostrate as He passes, teaches even them to adore in Him a *Man* no less truly than a God.

Those, then, are not to be heard who would suggest to us that man was higher and happier in his unfallen state than he can ever hope to be, and who perpetually lament as an incurable woe the ancient exile from Eden. It is true that the day when "the man was driven out," was the birth-day of affliction to the resolute enemies of God; to such it was the beginning of sorrows, the twilight of that darkness whose midnight is not even yet come. But to man, as a race,—to the regenerate, as individuals,—that love of gloom was pregnant with glory. Had there been no fate, there had been no redemption; had there been no redemption, humanity were the *creature* of God, but it could not have been the *contained* of God. Never could it have filled so wondrous a page in the story of the universe; never could it have thrilled the angels with " desire to look into" the marvels of the people of dust. We might have been the children of a divine Father, (are the saints less so *now?*) but we never could have pointed to a *Brother* on the throne of heaven! We never could have known a deeper interest in all the doings of the empire of God, than a general approbation of the workings of holiness might bring. We could scarcely have ventured to assume an anxiety about the decrees of Heaven, confident, and calmly confident, in their wisdom,—and, perhaps, judging it a presumptuous intrusion to attempt farther inquiry; we could not have felt, as we do now, that we are inseparably linked with all that is loftiest in the economy of the universe,—that there can be nothing effected or undertaken in which *we* are not personally interested, as effected or undertaken by Him, who, in one divine manifestation of His nature, has been pleased to bind us for ever to Himself.

It is true that, in answer to all these cheering and elevating convictions, there are those who would insinuate that *we* are too diminutive a speck in the array of worlds thus to claim, in the ascension of God into the highest heavens, the union of *our* interests with the counsels of Deity; that it is an unwarrantable arrogance to claim an exclusive right to the special favour of this universal God: but that which we assert—the glorification of our nature in the glorification of Christ—rests upon no such principle; it would not be diminished though shared with millions! The very immensity of divine power, providence, and love, which alone forms a ground for the objection, suggests at once its solution.

How far the Redeemer has multiplied Himself in the work of redemption, I know not; through how many desolate worlds He has sent a message of life, I know not. Whether the restored sinners of other orbs may also claim their own in that infinite essence, and talk of their Bethlehems and their Calvaries, their Nativities and their Ascensions, it would be vain to conjecture; and it cannot in one jot alter the reality of *our* eternal union with Him. For myself, I own no jealousies in the common happiness of races and of worlds. I believe the heart that beat at Gethsemane large enough to hold a universe in its love; and I should no more envy the redeemed of a distant planet than the redeemed of a distant continent. It is the prerogative of a divine affection that it can multiply through new thousands without abating to each; like the light of the sun which diminishes not to surrounding objects because you open to it the windows of a dark chamber till then unvisited by its radiance. I should rejoice to see that brow which bled beneath the thorns crowned with the victories of ten thousand worlds! I should feel that it was with higher exultation, and more assumed confidence, I could answer to the cold question of the doubter, "What is thy beloved more than another beloved?" that He was, indeed, "the chiefest among ten thousand" (Song v. 9, 10). Nor should I approach Him with a more total and unmingled affection, with a more thorough devotedness, or a more exclusive confidence that I, the meanest of His creatures, enjoyed the fulness of His love, in the midst of this host of His adorers; or with less tenderness utter the exquisite expostulation of the repentant Apostle, " Lord, thou knowest all things!" and, even in the midst of these innumerable worshippers from every region of creation, " thou knowest that *I* love thee!"

These speculations, as to the relation of an incarnate God to the other innumerable regions of the universe, need, therefore, give us no real alarm. In the present state of our knowledge of the immensity of creation, it is almost impossible but they must arise; and more especially in reflecting on the great mystery we celebrate to-day,—a mystery which obliges us to contemplate Christ as at once the enthroned Monarch of the whole infinity of being,—of suns and systems that are scattered in millions along the paths of space " as the sand which is by the sea-shore, innumerable,"—and at the same time a Man, and bound by ties intimate and everlasting to one little corner of the universe, one little island in the ocean of immensity, one little speck, small in its own system, and invisible beyond it. We can well afford to admit Him not only by right of creation the natural, but even by right of redemption the *spiritual*, King of this multitude of peopled worlds. Our property in the affections of this infinite heart is in no respect limited by any supposition of this kind.

Whatever be the boundlessness of the restorative energies of Christ, whatever the extent of that agency which the Second Person of the Trinity is qualified and commissioned to exert, with equal earnestness will the man of spiritualized reason and affections dwell upon every element of His story. Enough it is that the infinite and eternal God is on the stage of this earth manifested as *our* Redeemer; that, in the consummation of that redemption, He has assumed *our* nature into His own, and thus identified *us* with all His acts,—enough is this to fix us with anxiety upon all He has done, and still does. I believe it to be the characteristic of *divine* love that it is unaccompanied with that jealousy which is consequent on exclusiveness, and which assuredly works its temporary purpose upon earth, but has no place, because no utility, in the higher system. Even in the *Christian love* of *this* world I see the principle manifested, in the absence of narrow-minded and partial views, just in proportion as *it* is realized in each believing soul. And hence I think it of the very essence of the divine affection that it should rejoice, not in separation and individuality, not in proportion as the worshipper is a "first object" with the worshipped, but in proportion as happiness is multiplied, as the adorer sees his own feelings reflected in the mirrors of surrounding hearts. *Thus* it is that Christ, while to us He is eminently *our* Christ, may receive the adoration of innumerable tribes of sentient beings, and be *our* beloved, in proportion as He is the beloved of all the redeemed of all spheres. Thus it is that *we* can rejoice, as He bore our nature into heaven, not the less, yea, much more and more intensely, because He may have diffused an equal felicity over the immensity of the rational universe. Thus it is that we may admit that the Son of God,—the Eternal Offspring of an Eternal,—has not limited His quickening agency to our world; and yet, knowing that *we* for ever are His, that He bears *our* nature, will judge *us*, feels with us and for us, is Son of *Man* no less than Son of God; thus it is that we can sympathise with every event of His history,—with His birth as *we* are born, His growth as *we* grow in mind and body, His trials as *we* are tried, His death as *we* die, His resurrection as *we* are to rise, His ASCENSION as *we* also are to be "caught up to meet the Lord in the air." It is said that the Apostles "*looked steadfastly* towards heaven as He went up,"—methinks it is so that we also, as we read or hear this wondrous event, should fix eye and heart upon that heaven which He, the First-born, has pre-occupied, that we should feel that in Him a portion of *ourselves* has departed thither, a sinless type of humanity which keeps its place for the rest; and that our heart, in Christ, being already there, all else should struggle, with holy impatience, to follow.

The Son of God ascended into heaven invested with a human body. This is the great fact of the day and of the text; this is the first heavenly stage of Christ's redeeming work. That "plant of renown" which (if the thought be not too fanciful for the theme) had first to fade and wither on the day of suffering, which was sown in the grave, which rose above earth in the resurrection, is glorious in "bright consummate flower" in the ascension, as it is in *fruit* in the day of gifts and blessings, "fruits of the Spirit"—the day of Pentecost. But while you maintain the truth of the Manhood, remember that His Divinity is boundless as ever; beyond all restriction as beyond all conception. They are much mistaken who imagine that we would confine that being beyond all beings, when we pronounce that it assumed, and still preserves, attached to its divine Substance, a human frame. There is no incompatibility between the two; no inconsistence between an essence of infinite power and a material structure; no contradiction between a Being who, as God, is everywhere, and, as Man, is subject to the usual restrictions of humanity. . . . The body with which Christ ascended possessed unquestionably peculiar privileges; such as the spiritual body of man is hereafter to possess. But that it was the same body as had walked on earth in sorrow and toil, Christ Himself had earnestly impressed on His witnesses. Whether subsequent changes may not have still further altered His frame, to suit its new abode, we have no certain means of determining. But while yet among us, He had evinced, by the most "infallible proofs," that the glorified body was identical with the suffering body, that the signs of suffering were immortally impressed upon the impassible frame, and consequently that He carried with Him into heaven our nature, the pledge of our futurity; and not merely our nature, but our nature crucified: such a nature as, bearing with it the ineffaceable impress of His own divine sufferings, might at once introduce us into heaven by mercy, and secure us there by justice. . . . Of all, then, which I have endeavoured to impress, this is the sum: that this ascension of Christ is the great pledge and proof of our eternal state; that our nature is for ever identified with His, so that as long as He is *Man* we must be happy, as one *with Him;* that the great value of this transcendent fact is, not merely that it is an *example* of our future ascension, but that it is our ascension *begun*—we in Him having risen to heaven, we in Him being at this time present before God, we in Him being united with the eternal plans and procedures of Heaven, so that we are for ever blended with Christ, His property, His purchased possession, the very members of His body; insomuch that they who succour His suffering disciples in this world shall be pronounced to succour Himself: and that Paul, who persecuted the Church, was said, by the Church's Head, to have persecuted "Christ." And further, that whatever similar benefits the same Divine Person may, in the depths of past eternity, have wrought for others, *our* claim is in no degree diminished: infinite power and love may have extended itself in innumerable manifestations; but we only know it redeemed *us*, and we are content to know *this!*

That there might be no shadow of doubt as to the permanence of Christ's manhood after the ascension—the manhood in which, "because He is the Son of *Man*," He shall come in judgment — He purposely gave His followers mysterious glimpses of His own state as it subsists in the eternal world.

We know that — subsequent to His disappearance from Olivet—in the same nature (so as to be at once recognised) *Stephen* beheld Him " standing (in readiness to assist) at the right hand of God." We know that *Paul* declares that he " saw the Lord," and places his dignity of apostleship upon this very basis. We know that *John* beheld " a Lamb *as it*

had been slain," before whom that new song was sung,—
" Thou hast redeemed us to God by thy blood, out of every
kindred, and tongue, and people, and nation ;" and, " Worthy
is the *Lamb that was slain*, to receive power, and riches, and
wisdom, and strength, and honour, and glory, and blessing."
So completely did Christ bear into heaven the badges of His
sacrificial work on earth. As His last step on earth was upon
that mount which had witnessed His agonies in the garden, so
even beyond the clouds did He bear us, and our sorrows, and
their remedy. The very imprint of suffering upon hand and
side is still visible to all heaven, and bids many an astonished
angel cry aloud (as the Jews of old), " Behold, how He
loved them !"

And if this be so,—if Christ Jesus has thus borne with Him
our nature into the inmost sanctuary of heaven; if He has not
hesitated to wear the form that Adam wore, in that Holy
of Holies where angels tremble as they gaze,—what ought to
be our feelings as we reflect upon this astonishing transit?
How ought we to be animated as we remember that a body,
spiritual indeed, but yet tangible and visible, a nature immaculate indeed, but yet human and *ours*, has been uplifted by
the energy of indwelling Godhead, and set in the centre of the
Paradise of God? If this fact be believed, it is impossible it
can leave us as it found us. It is a thing so surpassing in its
importance, that no human spirit can receive it and be unmoved. To hear this story of a common acquaintance, and to
hear it on grounds that left its truth unquestionable, would
occupy our every thought for hours, for days, with minds more
reflective for a far longer period. But to know that it has
happened mainly with a view to *our own* future exaltation;
that it is but the prologue of a drama which is to take in the
whole blessed company of the redeemed; that it is a preparatory measure which is to introduce an endless procession of
future entrances like itself,—saint after saint rising into the
glory thus secured by this Captain of salvation, and each met

at the threshold by Him who thus has scaled the skies that He might be there before us!—to know this, and to believe it, is to awake to emotions that annihilate earth, and open heaven *already* to the exulting soul! Think, then, for a moment, what *are* the feelings that the follower of the Lamb should own, when he ponders this passage of his Leader into the highest heavens,—turn to your own hearts and ask,—are such feelings there?

If Christ ascended to obtain "gifts"—spiritual blessings—for His people, (a purpose everywhere expressed both by Himself and His prophetic heralds,) who cannot see that at least one attitude of the believing soul is to be found in earnest supplication for their bestowal, or grateful welcome of their presence in the heart? If, when He sprinkled the mercy-seat of the eternal Sanctuary with His own blood, when the "It is finished" of Calvary was once more uttered in presence of the accepting Father, and all the preliminaries of the ministration of the Spirit were thus completed; if then He was entitled to take, and took, from the treasury of heaven its choicest graces, and held them liberally forth for all who sought them; is it not incredible that, with the knowledge of such things, a cold inactive heart should still insult God by indifference to His proffered blessings? Christ has risen bodily into heaven, that He may be spiritually present in the earthly heaven of the Church; the bodily ascension and the spiritual indwelling are two aspects of the same act.

There is among us, ever since that wondrous day, a power beyond all powers,—a strength to nerve the feeble heart, an unction to anoint the sightless eye, an energy to revivify the spiritual dead. It is around us as "the wind that bloweth where it listeth," but not capriciously dealt; for prayer can charm that invisible essence into every soul that believeth. There is a secret, subtle, unseen Power, mightier than all that fabling romance ever dreamed of *its* magic; it is near us if we will but know it, within us if we will but call it: *this* is the heritage of the believing world ever since that day of Olivet. But oh, Father of mercy! how despised is Thy celestial gift! Oh, Son of glory! how neglected is the prize of Thy conquest! There is no dream too unsubstantial to be preferred to this reality; no lie too glaring to be preferred to this everlasting truth. It is written of David (2 Sam. vi.) that when he had brought the ark of the covenant to its home, that ark which was in all its particulars a manifest type of the Messiah; and when he had sung that Psalm which St. Paul has applied to the ascension of Christ into heaven, he bestowed his gifts " to the whole multitude," says the sacred writer; " to every one a cake of bread, and a piece of flesh, and a flagon of wine." Gifts such as these were received with joy; but their divine antitypes are spurned as worthless. The mystical David from His own high home dispenses His own flesh for the life of the world, and that spiritual bread which he that hungers after righteousness shall eat of and be satisfied, and that " fruit of the vine" which is even now to be drunk in the earthly " kingdom of the Father." But few are they that hear His invitation; and the promise of joy and peace is as carelessly spurned as if the world were not groaning under sorrow and disquiet. A message of happiness such as meets every want, such as supplies every yearning of the heart of man, such as moves all his natural affections by natural motives, and strengthens, and enlightens, and directs the whole by supernatural assistance,—*this* is received with a coldness which would be unjustifiable were we in Paradise itself, and already encompassed with all, and more than, such a message could promise!

I know how all these representations are ordinarily met; and in what tone the men of this world are wont to receive this doctrine of the spiritual blessings won for the souls of believing men by the sacrifice of Christ, and dispensed in consequence of His ascension to glory, — let me rather say, manifesting themselves in the Church of Christ as the natural and necessary result of that spiritual presence which is one with the ascension. Some, indeed, evade our pressing instances, by the convenient theology which would confine this whole wondrous benefit to the apostles themselves and their immediate followers; and which pronounces, that, beyond the special purposes of that age, such assistances were neither promised nor required,—an assertion so directly contrary to the whole tenor of the New Testament, to the positive declarations and the implied assumptions of all its writers, that no charity can designate *that* as less than wilful infidelity which professes to uphold it. Whether viewed upon grounds of natural propriety or of inspired promise, the same conclusion forces itself forward, that " the manifestation of the Spirit " was not more for that age than for every age. The *whole bright circle of the Christian graces* are ascribed to the gift of the Spirit sent from the right hand of God by Christ, who evermore dwells there;—and are *they* less required now than they ever were? The " fruit of the Spirit " may indeed once have been the recal of the dying from the gates of death, of the lame from his motionless misery, of the blind from darkness. We know that the apostles " spake with other tongues, as the Spirit gave them utterance:" that " God bare them witness both with signs and wonders, and with divers miracles and gifts of the Holy Ghost according to His own will." But we know also, that " the fruit of the Spirit is in all goodness, righteousness, and truth " (Eph. v. 9). We know that it is " love, joy, peace, longsuffering, gentleness, faith, meekness, temperance." We know that " the love of God is shed abroad in our hearts by the Holy Ghost;" that men are " justified by the Spirit of their God," and by Him " sealed to the day of redemption;" that men are " saved by the washing of regeneration and renewing of the Holy Ghost;" that the entrance into the divine kingdom is suspended upon a birth " of water and *the Spirit;*" yea, that the pervading influence of the same awful power so extends from the beginning to the end of the story of God in the soul of man, that "no man can" even "say *that Jesus is the Lord* but by the Holy Ghost." Things take their titles from their essential characters, and the religion of Christ is declared to be "the ministration of the Spirit." If holiness be the garb of a believing soul, if the lapse of centuries leave, on the one hand, this requisite unaltered, on the other, the power and mercy of God undiminished,—so that the want remains and the supply remains,—then was the coronation largess of the Son of God, enthroned in heaven, no temporary gift meant to astonish a single generation, or two or three generations, and then leave the world in darkness the deeper for that momentary light. "He gave gifts to men" worthy of Himself, and as Himself omnipotent and eternal! He sent forth a Spirit, which should be His Vicegerent in the Church; and as long as the Sovereign reigns in heaven, His spiritual Viceroy reigns in human souls. They are correspondent and correlative one to the other. If I *go not away,* said the Saviour before He ascended, the Spirit cannot come; if He *be* away, then the Spirit is in the Church; the absence of the one is the presence of the other: let me rather say that there is *no* absence, no distance, no departure, no separation! Christ *Himself* is one with His own Spirit, and with Him templed in the heart of His mystic body. As Paul declared of himself, we "know Him no longer after the flesh,"—we know Him not by sensible perception or miraculous vision, but by a deeper, a better, an inward and abiding sense. We are habituated, from the natural influences of the body, to think that the knowledge of sight or hearing is the knowledge of all others surest, distinctest, and best: but an object to *be* seen and heard must be at a *distance* from eye and ear. Better far is that inward apprehension in which knowledge and possession are one, which makes us know Christ in giving us Christ, and allows us to speak of Him not as an object of distant perception but of internal consciousness. "*Touch* me not," said Jesus after His resurrection, to weeping and astonished Mary;

"*for* I am not yet ascended to my Father;" and, among all the conjectures which have been expended upon the significance of that singular prohibition, is it impossible that He might have alluded to *this spiritual* contact which was to be the consequence of His ascension, to this inward grasp which the abiding of His Spirit was to allow,—so that those who of old had seen and heard the Lord, were thenceforth to know Him as it were by touch and feeling, by direct and palpable apprehension. Nor this alone. There is a sense even more inward than touch itself, though accompanied by it,—the sense of *taste*. I surely need not remind you, that in the most determinate of all Christ's expositions of the mode by which He was to perpetuate His presence in the Church, entering secretly into each believing heart and there abiding, the perceptions of *this* very sense are eminently employed. We are to "eat of His flesh and drink of His blood:" our whole spiritual life is to be preserved only by doing so. Here then is the last perfection of the inward presence, and thence the inward knowledge of Christ. Himself incorporated with us as our spiritual nutriment, He is present to us as our spiritual object. Though on the right hand of God, He is not the less with us, for God Himself is with us. "Ye are the temple of God." He has ascended " above the highest heavens," but He has bowed the highest heavens to us. "If any man hear my voice, and open the door, I will come in to him, and will sup with him, and he with me." And, indeed, it is remarkable how by every form of phrase, the sacred writers labour to express the total identification of the interests of the Church and its Founder, and the perpetuated indwelling of Christ through the Spirit, subsequently to His local ascension to the immediate presence of the Father. They seem to represent a sort of *reciprocal* action between the heart and its Lord. Sometimes *we* ascend into the abode of Christ, and our life is said to be "hid with Christ in God:" sometimes *He* descends to us, and "we live, yet not we, but Christ liveth in us." Sometimes *we* are "raised up together, and made to sit together in heavenly places in Christ Jesus:" sometimes He is *in us*, "if we be not reprobates." What other than this mysterious communion was it which the old patriarch saw at Bethel, when "he dreamed, and behold a ladder set up on the earth, and the top of it reached to heaven; and behold, the angels of God ascending and descending on it,"—and when he rightly deemed that the place indeed was "dreadful," but yet that it was "none other than the house of God, and *the gate of heaven?*"

That gate is open now and for ever! It is open ever since the day when the choir of angels sung, as the Victor rose to receive his crown,—"Lift up your heads, O ye gates; and be ye lift up, ye everlasting doors; and the King of glory shall come in!" He—ascending "into the hill of the Lord"—"shall receive the blessing from the Lord, and righteousness from the God of his salvation." That gate is open now, and all the powers of hell and darkness cannot close it upon those who close it not on themselves! The Forerunner is gone on "to prepare the place," for which nothing can unprepare us but our own resolute wilfulness. . . . Remember the awful words of the "men in white apparel" that stood upon the mount, as the Apostles gazed after the disappearing form of their Lord,—"This same Jesus, which is taken up from you into heaven, *shall so come in like manner* as ye have seen Him go into heaven." We stand midway between the two awful manifestations,—the ascent to glory and the descent to judgment. Between the two epochs lies the history of the world. There are those,—and they are men of deep thought in many instances,—who believe that the second of these great events is not so far distant as the unbelieving world would gladly deem,—who think that "the thief in the night" is already on his way, that "the good man of the house" had better set his watch and bar his doors. I enter not now into such calculations. Such expectations have often been held, and often deceived; but it is a miserable folly which would thence conclude that they can never be realized; and which, from the poor experience of a few hundred years undisturbed by miracle, would take occasion to ask,—" Where is the promise of His coming? for since the fathers fell asleep all things continue as they were." It does, indeed, seem to be a providential arrangement of God that at almost *all* periods the expectation of the coming should be preserved in the Church. Ages have, it is true, proved the fallacy of these immediate hopes; yet the hope itself " springs immortal;" and still, with unrelenting earnestness, the brotherhood of Christ strain eye and ear to catch the distant gleaming of the advent light and the sound of the chariot-wheels. From their very *failures* they gain (and not unjustly) a ground of hope; for that which must at a definite (though unknown) period be accomplished, and has not yet been, must, in virtue of those very disappointments and in proportion to their number, be judged the nearer. And were we to judge by the analogy of the first advent of the same mighty Personage, we would expect an undefined *anticipation*, mingled with much disbelief, to herald His approach; as if the human heart felt itself beat quicker, it knew not why, at the approach of so tremendous an event; or as if all nature (like the pulseless calm that precedes an earthquake) silently owned a secret terror, as the Creator again descended into His work! However the dispensations of God be arranged,—and of that which the very angels of heaven know not, nor even the Son in His human and prophetic capacity, I dare not to pronounce,—our path of practice is equally sure. If it is given you to believe that " to be absent from the body " is " to be present with the Lord," you will rejoice as sincerely to seek Him there, as to *await* Him here. The grave may receive every frame that now breathes before me; darkness and the worm may be the destined lot of all that now glows with life; but you know the Apostle's inspired promise to such. He taught those tremblers of old, that they who remained alive to the coming of the Lord were to have no privilege before the dead that slept in Jesus; that the grave could make no divorce between the Saviour and the saved; yea, that a *precedence* was even to be given in the work of the heavenly introduction to those whose Christian deathbeds had in all ages preached immortality to the survivors,—for that " the *dead* in Christ were to rise *first.*" Oh, beloved, as you feel and know the importance of these things, let your life of holiness be " meet for this inheritance of light!" *Then,* when the mighty hour of final triumph shall indeed come; when *the second* ascension shall take place,—no longer the solitary Christ vanishing in the cloud from His lingering followers, but the royal Judge encompassed by millions of His saints,—then, indeed, shall you be able (oh, may this assembly furnish a goodly contingent to that glorious army of the just!) to cry again, with the Psalmist, " God is gone up with a shout, Jehovah with the sound of a trumpet. Sing praises unto our King, sing praises!" . . . Now, indeed, and of very truth, " the Lord reigneth, let the earth rejoice; let the multitude of the isles be glad! . . . The Lord is great in Zion; He is high above all people!"

SERMON XIV.

THE FOLLY OF MORAL COWARDICE.

2 Timothy I. 8.

Be not thou, therefore, ashamed of the testimony of our Lord.

This present world, my dearest friends, is to be considered as a grand field of battle between the powers of good and evil. In this world the forces on both sides are arranged in perpetual encounter; and that contest, the fame of which occupies the universe, is perhaps on this narrow globe to be finally decided. That the conflict of sin and holiness has ever extended beyond our earth; that through the immensity of worlds like our own, which throng the infinite space around us, there has ever been anything at all similar to our fall and our redemption, we have at least no direct grounds to suppose. For all *we* can tell, this world alone is the field of contest and the prize of victory; and bears much the same relation to the grand dispute between good and evil, which in our earthly politics any small district, made the temporary scene and occasion of war, bears to the rival interests of vast and powerful monarchs. The district itself may be limited, but it is the theatre of a mighty contest; it may be the same speck in the map of the world which our world is in the map of the universe; but yet a tremendous question is brought to issue on it, and the importance of the question communicates itself to the scene where that question is at stake. If among ourselves men will make a pilgrimage of curiosity and admiration to any scene where nations have met in the terrible embrace of battle,—a Leipsic or a Waterloo,—with what a depth of interest may we conceive that this world of ours shall hereafter be regarded by the hosts of heaven,—this world where the last great conflict was fought between the armaments of heaven and of hell, and the crown of undisputed glory for ever secured to the Messiah of God!

But the most wondrous thing about this great conflict is its deep silence! The battle of God and of Satan is raging around us every hour,—we are in the thick of the encounter; and yet we scarcely hear it. There is no " noise of the captains" nor " shouting." " Every battle of the warrior," says the great Prophet, " is with confused noise, and garments rolled in blood," but *here* there is a silence as profound as slumber! It is not that the *name* of religion and of the heavenly warfare is altogether unheard. Of names and watchwords we have indeed abundance, of busy controversy no lack, of bitter ill-will in the name of Christ, an overflowing measure. But the matter of which we speak, the real warfare of good and evil, has no connexion with these formal follies and miserable delusions. The true contest, that which includes the winning or losing of *hearts* to God, the inward securing of blessedness or condemnation,—*that* contest is lost and stifled amid the busy bustle of man's interests and passions. It goes on, but it goes on unnoticed. Yes; the disputes of a neighbourhood, the momentary encounter of rival interests, are loud enough to occupy every ear and every mind: the conflict of heaven and hell, the strife that fills the whole length and breadth of eternity, is around us, nay, within us, and not one in one hundred has even really known of its existence.

But what infinitely heightens this wonder is, that in this very contest we are ourselves the combatants. Were we mere spectators, we might slumber in the contemplation; but we are ourselves the soldiers in the fray. The leaders indeed are not of us,—the Captain of salvation and the spirit of evil. But under the rival standards we are, every one of us, arrayed; each busy in manifesting allegiance to his master, and earnest in spreading his empire. There is not one being present here —those, perhaps, excepted who are upon the turning point of change—who is not silently registering himself as the resolute warrior of Christ or of Satan; and who is not at this moment acknowledged in the rolls of heaven or of hell as such. You are all fighting for your chosen cause, whether you know it or know it not. This is a truth you cannot evade: may the Spirit of God teach you not to *try* to evade it! ... And the warfare *never ceases!* Return to privacy; *there*, in your conversation, your conduct, your expressed opinions, you are earnestly labouring for Christ or for His enemy. Go forth to public life; *there*, amid the tumult of the throng, remember that you, in common with every member of that throng, are personally contending for the extension of the empire of God or the empire of evil. Reject domestic life and public life, and mingle among your friends and acquaintance; *there* the tremendous responsibility still follows:—by your words, by your deeds, by the mere influence of example, you are combating as zealously for Christ in person or for the devil in person, as if with your bodily eyes you could behold the Redeemer and the destroyer, and all the army of angels and fiends that accompany them; and with your bodily ears catch the words of encouragement they issue, the notes of joy that from heaven hail the repentant, and the horrid mirth with which the tempter rejoices over a ruined soul! ... Oh! does not this matter concern us? If such be the condition of man, that, by the mere fact of being a gospel-hearer, he enters his name and takes his side in this awful contest; if there is, and can be no neutrality, with what eagerness ought we indeed to inquire,—What party have *we* espoused? where is our place in the campaign? If the veil were suddenly raised which hides from the bodily eye the good and evil spirits that are around us, in *which* array would we be found?—among the friends of God, or among those who, for a while, have gathered their forces against the monarchy of Christ, but are destined to be consumed by the brightness of His appearing?

The scene of this conflict, then, is the world; and of the world, specially, the human heart. The instruments, therefore, by which the warfare must be conducted can only be the *motives* that influence the human heart. This is only to say that the means of attack and resistance must be suitable to the nature of the country. "The weapons of our warfare," as St. Paul expresses it, "are not carnal;" they are of a spiritual nature, because they are to be applied to a spiritual substance. The sword of steel pierces the body,—" the sword of the Spirit is the Word of God." The shield may protect the outward frame; but that to which the Apostle invites our attention, and our prayers, is "the shield of faith, wherewith ye shall be able to quench all the fiery darts of the wicked."

Can we, then, do better than call over a few of the weapons in the armoury of *Satan*, by which *he* is enabled to conduct his attack with a success so appalling? Can we do better, when about to appeal to Christian charity for the means of resisting the ministry of darkness by the message of light and life, for the means of making "the poor of this world rich in faith," of spreading and strengthening the kingdom of Christ among you,—can we do better, on such an occasion, than revert to the powers that resist the work in our own hearts, and in the hearts of those on whom we press the Gospel? Let us make our enterprise of Christian love the occasion of earnest self-inquiry and self-humiliation, and God will accept and bless it. One of the most powerful of these adversaries of God, in the heart of man, is (as we shall see) alluded to in the text; but it will reward our pains to introduce it by a very short notice of some of its sister delusions.

The *first* place in the melancholy catalogue belongs to disbelief. In other words,—a vast proportion are in the bondage of irreligion because they have never *believed* the Gospel. To believe the Gospel is to believe a great deal. It is to be firmly persuaded (whether by argument or any other means) that there was a period of our world at which a series of events occurred wholly unlike everything that engages our attention in the daily course of experience: to be persuaded that there was a time when, to remedy human sin, the Creator of the world descended into His own creation in order to become its Saviour; that, for this purpose, assuming all the weaknesses incident to our flesh, sin alone excepted, He was familiar as a daily friend with the creatures He had made, and died at length by their hands; that, rising again, He demonstrated the fulness of His triumph over the powers of darkness, and, sending the gift of His illumining Spirit, founded upon earth a society whose office it is to look unto " the Author and Finisher of their faith," and live as those who expect the return of their absent Lord to establish a kingdom of everlasting righteousness. *This* is to believe the Gospel. You see that it brings you wholly beyond the limits of common experience; it calls you into a new and spiritual world, governed by laws unlike any to which you are here habituated. Brethren, I am forced to ask,—How many of us can sincerely say we are "*believers*" of these facts? How many of us have any but a faint and transitory notion that all this ever happened? How many of us can honestly say that we have as clear a conviction of the life and resurrection of the Lord Jesus as we have of any the most distant incident of our own past lives? Is it conceivable that truths so tremendous could really be believed,—truths in which we are all so profoundly concerned,—and yet produce not the slightest result upon conduct and feeling? No, the unchristian in practice is an infidel in theory; he feels not because he believes not; he believes not because he attends not; he attends not because the spirit of darkness is ever busy blocking up every access to his mind with the shadowy fears, and hopes yet more shadowy, of a ruined and perishable world. But the spirit of darkness has other engines as destructive as unbelief itself:—

For instance, there is the agency of *indolence*. Belief is here arrived at, perhaps; a speculative conviction of the truths of the Gospel: and there are, accordingly, some symptoms of life, admissions of the enormous importance of religion, abstinence from ordinary vices, efforts towards a more diffusive charity. A suspicion is also entertained that a mightier change is required; and that all this, though it be among the fruits of the regenerate nature, is yet not the regenerate nature itself. Occasional prayers are now offered to God for His assistance in this greater work; purposes of commencing it are made, and repeated, and made again; yet how is it? years follow years,—the soul is hastening to judgment,—and the change never comes! It is prayed for now and then; it is asked with very tears, now and then; under the urgencies of a powerful preacher, or of a faithful friend, it is acknowledged to be the one eternal truth of God;—and yet the change is not come, the step itself which brings the spirit of a believer into the circle of the people of the Lord is not effected! There are times—and at some period or other they come (awful to think!) in, as I believe, the lives of nearly all hearers of the Gospel—when the light of divine truth seems to shine with unspeakable glory upon the soul,—it may be in affliction, in prayer, in contemplation, or when listening to the preaching of the word, for the outward occasions are many; there are times, in the life of almost every man, when earth half disappears, and heaven is nearer to the mind, and at which a sanguine or susceptible temper is apt to believe that it could for ever resign heart and life to the dominion of God; and, nevertheless, let the occasion pass away, and the emotion passes with it,—the tide ebbs, and leaves the heart dry as ever,—and the momentary Christian goes forth into the world, through sheer indolence, once more a worldling, gaining nothing by the temporary piety but a confirmed distrust in every return of better feeling! ... Dear brethren, if this case apply to any of you, in the name of Christ and of your own salvation, I call upon you to receive such visitations of the Spirit of God as pledges of His abiding presence, and encouragements to *progress*. If any of you have known such hours of blessedness, oh, relinquish not by indolent neglect these bright promises of the heaven that awaits you! They are the twilight of the celestial dawn, the foretaste of Paradise. If God has thus drawn near to you, will you not indeed cultivate His glorious acquaintance? By being visited with such feelings you have been specially marked out, as having in you a something not wholly unfitted for the kingdom and presence of God. The eye of that God is lovingly upon you. The hosts of the blessed are anticipating your companionship in their own holy regions. Will you by indolent neglect, and that wretched indecision which hovers between sin and holiness till death cuts short the question, forfeit the inheritance of glory which was more than ever your inheritance from the time that the Spirit of God called at your heart and made you feel the value of your inestimable privileges? Called, as all are, to be the children of God, you are called in a special sense to whom God has even for the briefest period made Himself known, in feelings of piety sent by Him, in tenderness of spirit sent by Him, in holy hopes sent by Him, in deadness to the world sent by Him, in humble happy dependence, His, and only His, invaluable gift!

We have spoken of the terrible power of indolent indecision as an instrument of Satan for preserving the spirits of men in captivity to his will. The text intimates another yet,—shame, or the fear of man's opinion. And truly I believe that no snare ever invented by the adversary of man has secured a larger array than this of recruits to the army of evil. Disbelief is blind to the Gospel; indolence evades it; but shame alone deserts and degrades it. "Be not thou," says the Apostle to his convert,—" be not thou, therefore, *ashamed* of the testimony of the Lord." Feel no shame in executing the honourable office of witness to His truth. Chosen as a minister of the Gospel, exult in your high commission, and let the world perceive that you value the reproach of Christ above all *that* world can offer! For my own part, I, Paul, "am not ashamed, for I know in whom I have believed;" or, as he expresses it elsewhere (Rom. i. 16), "I am not *ashamed of the Gospel* of Christ; for it is the power of God unto salvation to every one that believeth."

That there *is*, then, such a feeling—monstrous though it be—as this, of being ashamed of goodness in every form, but more especially of being ashamed of professing discipleship to Christ, it is, I suppose, unnecessary to remind you. (All of us may see it in the world; not a few of us, I fear, may detect it in ourselves.) We all know that there are those who, incapable of shame in the commission and the avowal of the grossest profligacy, will yet blush to be convicted of having yielded for a moment to a transient impulse of religious emotion. The fact being certain, I ask you to contemplate the utter extravagance of this perversion of feelings. And if there be here any who recognise, in any of its degrees, this weakness among their own, I beseech them to reflect how utterly irreconcileable it is to any principle even of that common reason which we all acknowledge as the guide of life. . . . And, perhaps, the simplest mode of effecting this—for I would address you with studious simplicity—is by comparing our views of worldly and of heavenly things, and showing how strangely the wisdom which governs us in the things of earth, deserts us when once we pass to the higher platform of the eternal world.

To any listener, then, who would be a Christian, but dares not,—to any whom a miserable dread of his fellow-sinners prevents from avowing his terrors or his hopes in Christ,—to any who would tremble before God only that he trembles before a brother worm,—to any who, in whatever degree, (for this folly is of many degrees, and few wholly escape it,) is " ashamed of the testimony of the Lord," I put it simply, but earnestly,—How is such a feeling justifiable upon any grounds of *reason?* I do not now oppose it as opposed to the express commands of Scripture, though these, indeed, are reiterated and impressive; I oppose it merely upon the ground of its utter inconsistency with the principles which you yourselves recognise as the governing principles of this our daily life and experience.

For, in the first place, you who are ashamed of your fellow-men to avow the profession of Christ, is it that you are ashamed *of believing certain established truths,* such as the Gospel comprises? Are you ashamed of confessing that, however the half-learning and entire corruption of a few wretched objectors have laboured to sap the mighty basis of the Gospel revelation, you still can perceive, in that wondrous story, the lineaments of truth,—a power and an evidence such as falsehood never possessed? Is it of this *conviction* you are ashamed? I will not tell you that such shame is a foul desertion of a cause you cannot disbelieve; but I *will* ask,—Is this to be *the only* conviction, the possession of which brings shame and timidity? Does shame attend the deep convictions that regulate daily conduct? Has any man, upon any other subject, ever been ashamed of avowing a belief founded upon adequate testimony? ashamed of employing his intellect in the discovery of truth, and arriving at a satisfactory conclusion? I will state an instance. Has any man ever,—fallen as humanity is,—has any man ever (supposing him of common honesty) learned, upon unquestionable proofs, the certainty of a deed of friendship done him by a disinterested benefactor—a deed noble in all its circumstances, important in all its results—and blushed to avow his *belief* that the deed was truly done? Conceive him snatched from awful danger at the peril of a life; conceive enormous debts freely discharged; conceive him rescued from the horrors of a prison; and can you imagine the rescued man *ashamed* to avow his *knowledge* that he owed it all to the free, unconstrained compassion of a friend? Who here would not shrink from the *meanness* of such falsehood of heart? Yet, behold, in this Gospel story we have all these very circumstances acted upon the great theatre of eternity; we have a rescue from peril by the very death of the Rescuer, and a security offered of everlasting life; we have the free cancel of debts never capable of discharge by us; we have the precious purchase-money of redemption paid, even the blood of the Lamb without spot; and yet, in the company of our brothers and sisters of the dust, we have the inconceivable meanness to evade admitting our *belief* in the reality of these inestimable blessings! We cannot shake off the conviction, but we would hide it! We cannot burst the bonds of our belief, but we are heartily ashamed of the disgrace of being convinced by the Gospel!

But, again, you who blush to be thought a Christian,— Is it of the *prudence* of your course you are ashamed? of the fact that, while others are dissipating the short allowance of life to no purpose, you are laying up treasure where the moth does not corrupt nor the thief plunder? I ask not what the Word of God declares of your cowardice, but I ask what judgment *your own daily practice* passes upon it. Is, then, a prudential regard to a man's own welfare so universally discredited upon earth that you should tremble to be detected in evincing it? Are you ashamed that men should know that from morn till night your thoughts are busy in securing the wealth of this world for yourself or your possible descendants; that at every hour there burns in the temple of your heart the fires of that idolatry whose god is "the god of this world;" that every second thought is devoted to the great purpose of augmenting possessions, extending connexions, advancing your personal importance? Or, on the contrary, is it not certain that no character possesses more of general esteem than he who, from the cradle to the grave, has lived exclusively for such purposes as these, if he have but pursued them without any striking violation of the common rules of honesty? Such is worldly prudence and its estimation. Now, change the scene, expand the prudence until it takes in the concerns of an eternity, and is the estimate to be altered? Alas! you value yourself upon the long-sighted prudence whose calculations are bounded by the grave; you are ashamed of that which comprehends the happiness of immortality; you glory in pursuing a wealth that withers in your hand; you blush to be known as a speculator in the treasures of heaven; you exult in doubling that income which, after all, no accountant would assure to some of us for five years, or four years, or a single year: but when the calculation swells till it embraces the territories of God's coming kingdom, an inheritance that cannot fade, a crown of glory, immortal in the heavens; when the " bidding" is for the fee of a celestial estate, it is no longer " prudence" to pursue the speculation, it is " enthusiasm," and " fanaticism," and " hypocrisy," and the rest,—and you are ashamed to avow it!

Again; if indeed it be not of the *prudence* of your religious calling you are ashamed, is it of *your superiority to common temptations*, of hopes that place you above the pleasures of this world, and a serenity unaffected by its troubles? There *are* those who have even attained to this pitch of habitual piety, and yet, melancholy to say, have still the weakness to dread the scoff of fools, and who would willingly evade the topics they love in solitude, when engaged among the societies of unbelieving men. You are ashamed, then, to publish your very superiority, to let men see and know the purifying power of the principles you profess! But was ever man, on any *other* subject, similarly ashamed? It is a total mistake to suppose that Christianity is the *only* profession that requires a superiority to temptation. The truth is (and it is an awful truth, as it tells upon our state before God) that men *do* commonly, for the purpose of securing earthly distinction, endure a series of preparatory trials, and difficulties, and self-denials, at the very least equal to what would have vanquished a corrupt nature, and secured, under the blessing of Christ, a high place in the everlasting world. There is probably not an individual here who cannot remember that, within the past week or month, he has, through respect for man or for his own future advancement, laid himself under restraints precisely the same in severity as religion is perpetually asking, and perpetually asking in vain! So much for the common excuse derived from the power of temptation and the corresponding mercy of God; so much for the expectation that God will pardon us in consideration of the force of a temptation which the presence of a single bystander would have ensured our triumphantly conquering!

If, then, it be certain that every worldly pursuit requires for success a superiority to temptations of some kind, is it not most inconsistent to see no glory in the *Christian* conquest of difficulties, and all that is splendid and attractive in the conquest of them for the poor purposes *of earthly advancement?* When we see the young labourer among yourselves who, for years, toils through the dull difficulties of his preparatory study on the faint, uncertain hope of reaping future fame, we sympathise with his hopes, we wish good speed to his courageous perseverance; it is so in every profession and pursuit of mankind, but one! Extend the hope to the skies, exchange an earthly for an immortal scene, let the crown which hangs in view be not this world's,—an apparent crown of glory to the eye, a real crown of thorns to the brow,—but such as Christ wore,—thorns for a while in this world, glory in the next; let *this* be the prize for which the ambition is aroused and the struggle made, and all the admiration vanishes; and the combatants themselves, in this heavenly conflict, become half ashamed of exhibiting their own victories, or being known in the grace and power of God to have achieved them!

Once more I ask of you who tremble at the sarcasms of man, are you indeed ashamed of *communion with God;* of that high and holy privilege which enables you, even in this life, to traverse unchallenged the courts of heaven? Do you dread that man should know that the Holy One who inhabiteth eternity has deigned ere now to sanctify your heart with His presence? Do you fear it should be whispered among men, that to you hath been fulfilled that bright promise of the Saviour to His people,—"If a man love me, he will keep my words; and my Father will love him, and we will come unto him, and make our abode with him." (John xiv. 23.) Alas! in *this* instance, *too*, how strange is that perversity which alters every principle of ordinary life on the field of *religion!* Men are respected in the dignity of their acquaintance; to be familiar with the great is, in a manner, to share their greatness; and even beyond wealth itself is the peculiar power of rank, and of association with rank. But shift the scene, as before; instead of the transitory splendours of earthly greatness, let the curtain rise upon the unclouded Majesty of heaven; let the Monarch of the universe (of whom all earthly authority is but the image) be the acquaintance sought, or the guest received, and—oh, incredible impiety, lost in still more incredible folly!—men regard with contempt or neglect the being thus favoured (and every genuine follower of Christ *is* thus favoured); dignities like these have no attraction; the God of all glory wanders through His own world almost unacknowledged, or is abandoned to the hospitality of the poorest and most destitute hearts; and it is well if even these are not driven by the contempt of their fellows to secrete, in very shame, the Divine Inmate who honours them!

Such, then, is the "scandal of the Gospel,"—such the being "ashamed of the testimony of the Lord." The Apostles, who were placed among *professed unbelievers*, had many *additional* causes; to which, of course, in addressing a Christian congregation, it is needless to allude. The marvellous humiliation of the life of Christ, and the ignominy of His death, were common subjects of heathen, as they are to this day of infidel, sarcasm. I need not tell you (I trust) that these are the very circumstances which raise to its highest sublimity "the mystery of godliness,—God manifest in the flesh.".... I have preferred to consider this cowardice in our Gospel profession as it exists among ourselves,—among us who boast to be Christians, but so seldom boast to be Christ-like!

I know that this dread of man's opinion is not without its causes. I know that the world loves to be undisturbed in its indulgencies; that the surest way of being so is to set the tone of public fashion against that public disturber, the Gospel of Christ; and that everything thus unfashionable is, to feeble and unsteady minds, the subject of shame. I know that unbelief represents the aims of religion as shadowy visions, without base or substance; that for such purposes constraint seems preposterous; that the Gospel, which calls for such restraint, is therefore despised as a delusion, or repelled as a nuisance; and that, even for the humble believers who look for the coming of Christ, and who know that this world is but the antechamber of another, it is hard to war—short and preparatory though life be—against the absence of sympathy and the presence of contempt. All this I know; but I know, also, that it is all destined to form a portion of that necessary trial which alone can confirm in habits and principles meet for heaven. I know that "whom He loveth He chasteneth;" that not one affliction is visited unnecessarily upon the children of the heavenly Parent; that, hard as this trial may be, yet we are called upon "to endure hardness as soldiers of Christ." If there be any among you who feel the severity of this ordeal,—who, consecrating the earliest energies of life to the cause of Christ, yet dread the scoffs of the unhappy rebels against that cause, that surround you; still more, if there be any who, with a lingering disposition for religion, are yet deterred from being all that the Spirit of God could make them, by the fear of some wretched bystander, who selfishly spreads his own sin for fear of being himself discountenanced and deserted in his vices; if any such cases be now before me, I point then to *the future* as the glorious compensation for all! *Such* are on the borders of the kingdom of God: may no power of Satan, may no influence of example, no indolence of delay, no return of unbelief, no advice of evil counsellors, no *scorn of fools*, prevent them from achieving the passage! They may be scorned,—what matter? they will be saved! To each and all let them answer with the Apostle, who endured worse than they can ever be called to endure,—" God forbid that I *should glory save in the* cross of our Lord Jesus Christ, by whom the world is crucified unto me, and I unto the world!" Ashamed of Christ!—of Him who has redeemed man's nature from wretchedness, and first given to the race a security of immortality, an interest in an eternal world! Ashamed of Him who is the "express image" of God; "in whom dwelleth all the fulness of the Godhead bodily;" "by whom the worlds were created," and who still sustains the worlds from annihilation by the power of His might! Ashamed of Christ!—of Him who was *not* ashamed to endure all the bitterest mockeries of sinners for my sake; for my sake to exile Himself for long years from the immediate glories of heaven; for my sake to wander among the lost and ruined of the earth; and still for my sake to close a life of sorrows by a death of bodily and mental torture! Ashamed of Christ!— of Him who rose triumphant from the grave; and though no fleshly eye can behold Him, even now sitteth at the right hand of God, "in the glory of the Father;" yet, amid all His glories, pleads for my sake the obedience of Gethsemane and the Sacrifice of Calvary!.... Oh, may many here be enabled to return such an answer as this to the calumnies and reviling of the world! Happy are they, and yet more happy in all that outward unhappiness which fortifies them more and more for everlasting bliss! Happy, indeed, are they who thus live, confiding that, however it may be delayed, a time *shall* come when the truth of that Scripture shall be proved,—" Behold, I lay in Sion a stumblingstone and rock of offence; and whosoever believeth on Him *shall not be ashamed!*" (Isa. viii. 14; Rom. ix. 33.)

SERMON XV.

THE WILL OF GOD TOWARDS HIS CHILDREN.

Matt. XVIII. 14.

It is not the will of your Father which is in heaven, that one of these little ones should perish.

It is in behalf of those "little ones" of whom the Redeemer spoke that his minister has this day to address you,—the "little ones" whom the Father wills not to perish. God knows I can say, with the deepest sincerity, I heartily wish they possessed an advocate better qualified in strength of mind and of body to plead their cause; with yet deeper feeling I will say, would to God the audience who hear me were all sufficiently exalted in the simplicity of Christian affection to be independent of the outward and accidental qualities of the advocate; sufficiently partakers of "the mind which was in Christ Jesus," to feel that, in the simple words which I have just read to you from one of His heavenly discourses, there lies a power of appeal which as no art should be permitted to lessen, so no art ought to be capable of heightening. Oh, beloved brethren, rejoicing as I do to see, in defiance of some difficulties, so many of you assembled to-day upon this holy work, I cannot, nevertheless, forbear to put it to you,—How shall we answer it to ourselves, how answer it to God, that, on any occasion like this, motives of various shades and kinds— for I will not take upon me to analyse them—should draw us together to prayer and to the word, and yet that the same facilities of prayer, the same eternal Gospel, fresh from the lips of Jesus, should be before us every successive day of our lives, yet that the prayer should so often be cold or neglected, the Gospel so often unread; because the one must be offered up in that solitude of the heart where God alone is present, and the other, the Gospel, is presented, not in the artificial form of a preacher's discourse, but in the naked simplicity of Christ's own divine eloquence? But, dearest friends, whatever be the spirit which has prompted us to assemble here this day, there *is* a Spirit which can convert all our motives into impulses of blessedness: may He, at this hour, enlighten our souls to a full intelligence of that word of truth which is no subject of momentary display or of momentary excitement, but the very law of life, whereby you, and I, and all of us, shall in a few more years be tried, and on the love, or the neglect, of which are poised the destinies of an eternity! I have this day to implore you to a work of charity; but my duty extends farther. In remembering these children of the Gospel I am not to forget *you*. I am not to forget that, in beseeching you to provide for the souls of your fellow-men, I am also to call upon you to provide for your own. I am not to forget that, in asking you to contribute to this small work of occasional charity, I am also pleading to immortal souls for their own salvation; entreating spirits born for eternity not to forget their own high heritage; beseeching my fellow-sinners (so many of whom I have known in all the intimacies of private acquaintanceship) to forget the advocate in the cause he pleads, and (even under a ministration so feeble) to "awake,"—if not before, yet *now*,—" to awake, and arise from the dead, and Christ shall give them light.". . . For such a purpose I need not go beyond the beautiful passage which I have selected for our thoughts upon this day. I chose it because it bears an obvious and simple reference to our immediate business of educational charity; but, in truth, it bore with our Lord, and should bear with us, a far deeper and more comprehensive meaning.

When our Divine Instructor declared that "it is not the

will" of the Father "that one of these little ones should perish," He understood by that tender title something far more than the infancy of nature; He meant to typify the lonely childhood of a Christian soul. The "little ones" of this heavenly Parent are they who, with the gentle dependence of children, cling to Him as their sole support, and, with the pure-minded innocence of children, "keep themselves unspotted from the world.". . . In this view, then, let us (invoking the directive grace of God upon our thoughts) dwell for a while upon the power and importance of the revelation made to us, in this passage, of the words of Him "in whom were hid all the treasures of wisdom and of knowledge." (Col. ii. 3.) Remember from what lips these momentous words fell; remember that they are, indeed, the words of Him who "knew the Father," for He was one with the Father; and whose sole object in uttering them was that He might sanctify you, in common with thousands of the blessed, to a meetness for the inheritance of His own everlasting kingdom.

The text, then, answers the two questions that most concern mankind; it declares the character of *God*, and it declares the character and qualifications which He considers necessary in *those* whom He wills to be eternally happy.

I. To any human being capable of reflection, and believing in his own immortality, there can be no subject of so vast an importance as *the real nature of the divine character*. Were life to terminate in *this* world, could we indeed be certain (and you know that the infidel himself cannot be *certain*) that the dust, which is all that remains to the eye, of departed man comprised all his immortality—could this be proved, which never can be proved—there *might then* be some poor ground for carelessness as to the disposition of the God who rules so pitiable and momentary a scene. We might say (as millions *do* say—the practical infidels of Christian countries) that we are content to live as our fathers have lived, trusting to experience and to our own natural sagacity to guide us through the circumstances in which nature or chance has placed us: much, in short, as the illiterate classes in a nation trouble themselves little about the details, or the machinery, or the character, of the government that controls them.... *But* if it be certain, or probable, or possible, that, after the brief and disturbed dream of this life, we are, every one of us, destined to pass into a scene of which, apart from Revelation, we can only form faint and shadowy conjectures; if it be certain that the character of this scene must depend directly upon the character of the Being who has created and ever governs it; if, to resume the comparison I just employed, the poor man were made certain, that, whatever be the tone of the government under which he *now* lives, he must shortly pass into a country where his whole prospects of advancement depend upon his suiting himself to that character, whatever it may be—*what* would be his, *what* ought to be our, intense curiosity to catch even a glimpse of the real nature of the administration on which we are all thus awfully suspended! how earnestly ought we to inquire, with how passionate an interest ought we to ask of any who profess to know, *what is the real disposition of this mighty Governor?* if we are in His favour, how shall we preserve it? if so miserable as to have lost His countenance, how, oh, how shall we appease Him?... I pause, and ask,—How many in this assembly have ever *seriously* put that question? how many have ever, have *once*, in their whole existence, distinctly asked of themselves, their Bibles, or their Minister, what is the temper of the God upon whom they are to rest their whole prospects of eternal happiness? Oh, brethren! how zealous is the curiosity with which you study the minutest details of ordinary political intelligence: with how earnest a countenance, and how animated a spirit, do you ask and discuss each day's report of the progress of earthly policies! nay, there are *names*, mere names, connected with such subjects, which, were I now to pronounce them, would at once divide this assembly into hosts of eager and resolute partisans; yet *here* you have before you the politics of a universe, a government that stretches from eternity to eternity, an administration upon which every soul is dependent for an everlasting issue: we go among you, we tell you "the news" of this great kingdom; we tell you of the stability of its laws, the wisdom of its management, the riches of its resources; we tell you of that *revolution* in its affairs at which angels themselves shrink in astonishment, that revolution which sent the monarch of a boundless empire beyond the stars, to die by the hands of his own rebellious subjects, that no soul here should perish; we tell you all this,—we repeat it,—we reiterate it,—you know that it is all true, that prophecies and miracles, and the tortures of martyred thousands, are pledges of its truth,—what then? you listen in silence, or impatience, or listen not at all, and turn to devote the faculties that God meant to contemplate the mysteries of the policy of a universe to the politics of nations contending for a few fields a thousand miles away from you, or to the politics, almost as exalted, of the village and the neighbourhood at your feet!

Let me suppose you, however,—may God's inworking Spirit verify the supposition!—let me suppose you alive to the tremendous importance of discovering God's real character and purposes about you, thrown as you are on His mercy for eternity. Now—not to be minute—there are two obvious sources from which you may have a chance of deriving such intelligence,—*the world* around you (as far as your experience of it extends), and the express *revelation* of God Himself, if such a revelation exist. Regard, then, the former of these sources. Alas! its answer is not only precarious from our very limited knowledge; but even, as far as it goes, clouded and comfortless. In a world lost and ruined as ours is,—a world which, perhaps, among the infinity of worlds that occupy the depths of space, is the only one into which the pestilence of sin has entered; in such a world there is much to darken our apprehensions of the essential goodness of God. The terrible prominence of evil around us, the afflictions that encompass and harass even the best, the facility of ruin, the difficulty of recovery, the uncertainty of all, these are the signs and tokens of (as it would appear) a government of terror and of vengeance,—a government in which severity is the rule, and mercy the exception. To those who patiently regard the scene around them it must always, indeed, be evident that the Ruler of the world *might* have made all mankind far more unhappy than He *has* made any of them; but yet it must also be quite as evident that it was in His power—as mere power—to have made them far *more happy* likewise. And, unfortunately, it is just in proportion as sorrow presses heavily upon the heart,—that is, just in proportion as consolation is needed,—that, to the uninstructed mind, the darkness of God's dispensations appears terrific, for we all have experienced how the mind reduces everything to its own colour: that as the Spirit of God has said, that "to the pure all things are pure," so to the sorrowful all things are sad; until to the weary and despairing mourner—do I speak to none who can sympathise in this?—the world blackens into one tremendous midnight, and God Himself seems but to assume the features and attitude of an Almighty Avenger.

If such be "the faint and uncertain sound" with which the world answers to our demand upon it to reveal the character of its Maker, we must then turn for instruction to a less distorting medium for the light of Divine truth—to the express declaration of that God Himself in His Word. I suppose you, of course, to be, at least speculatively, believers in the Divine authority of that Word. I address professing Christians. I suppose you to have learned the few and simple proofs by which for eighteen hundred years it has silenced infidelity; and established itself to be the very image and portraiture of the mind of God. Let us, then, examine the original by the image.

I take my stand upon the text which the business of this day has put before us. Hundreds crowd upon my mind, but to see clearly we must contract our circle of vision; and *this* holds the essence of the gospel character of God. Yes, the world may robe our God in the terrors of an avenger, and Revelation itself may confirm but too certainly the truth that He will avenge; misfortune may darken the spirit and dim its prospects of heaven; the traces of ruin (moral and physical) that everywhere encompass us may affright: but as long as faith enables the trusting Christian to hold in bright remembrance *this* publication of the will of the God of all this apparent evil, that Christian cares not. "It is not the will of your Father which is in heaven, that one of these little ones should perish." Here, then,—casting aside all the dark and troubled speculations which partial views of this world may create,—*here* is the character of the God with whom you have to deal! The whole mystery of Providence is not, indeed, solved; trials, uncertainties, evils apparent or real, are left as they were; but through them all the eye of faith (seeing all by the light of promise) penetrates, and still beholds, presiding over the disorders of the world, a law of love, even the power of that God, who, armed with terrors for those who wilfully despise Him, yet wills not that one trusting believer, one of the "little ones" of His own family of faith, should ever perish from the way of life. And THUS it is that our text answers the first question—the tremendous question as to the character of God. There is such a doom as "perishing," it is mentioned in the text; there is such a law as God's decreeing that the guilty should perish, it is intimated in the text: *but* there is of the same God a determination and a purpose, that those who love Him should be His, and His for ever—for that is the direct object of the whole to declare.

II. With *such* a God as this, who would not rather be in alliance than in warfare? Here, then, is a *second* point of vast moment.

I told you that the text declared *more* than the character of God. It declares *the character and qualifications of those whom* He selects as His chosen people. Would you belong to that bright and holy band? Have you, indeed, no ambition to secure a place among the redeemed people of God—among those who from age to age have passed from the grave to glory, and who *now*, witnesses of that truth in heaven for which they toiled and suffered on earth, are perhaps contemplating your career, and sympathising in your trials? What avails it that God should publish Himself as a God who wills the happiness of every creature, if the obstinate perversity of our own hearts render us deaf to all His overtures of mercy, and generate a character to which it is absolutely inconsistent with the majestic harmony of all His own high attributes that He should be *able* to extend favour or protection!

What, then, *is* the character which the text supposes? The Father wills not that "THE LITTLE ONES" should perish, —the confiding and childlike dependents on His mercy. The humble in heart, then, are they on whom the special power of the promise rests... Here is the marvel and the mystery of this Gospel which we preach. Here is that tremendous pass at which it breaks company with the whole throng of this world's daily maxims. Here is the point where you are to examine to *which* train and procession do you belong,—the procession which is gorgeous with all this world's glories and animated by its pride, or that lowly company of the saints whose glory is to carry the standard of the cross, and whose pride is to be ever nearer and nearer to the humility of Him who died upon it! Self-exaltation is the master-principle of the world; self-annihilation must be yours, or you can never hope to see the rewarding smile of Him who has declared that "he that humbleth himself shall be exalted;" that "the poor in spirit are blessed, for theirs is the kingdom of heaven;" that though He be "the high and lofty One that inhabiteth eternity, whose name is Holy," yet He "dwells with him that is of a contrite and humble spirit, to revive the spirit of the humble, and to revive the heart of the contrite ones."

This awful truth, that between the world's glory and God's glory there is a variance which no art of self-delusion can reconcile; that no human heart can idolize the one and truly adore the other; that if you will, indeed, struggle for the eternal prize, you must silence every pulse of worldly ambition, tear from the soul every longing desire for the miserable excitements that consume away your years; and, receiving a new nature, cast yourselves, in trembling hope and all the lowliness of infancy, as "little ones" at the feet of God; this seems to many "a hard doctrine,"—"Who can bear it?" To some it is "enthusiasm" (the world never wants a name to stigmatize a truth with); to some it is "fanaticism;" to some again it is "hypocrisy." Brethren, we cannot pare, and shape, and fashion Christianity to suit any man or body of men. It is the unalterable decree of God, as promulgated in His Word, that the sinful nature can never behold the sinless glories of His kingdom; that it is only as justified by the humble faith which is the characteristic of these "little ones" of the divine family, of whom we are speaking, that man can enter into life; that this humble faith works a change in the whole tenour of the life and habits; so that the believer is one who walks in a new world, encompassed by new objects, and seeing by new and gifted organs; that to the contemplation of such a one, all the boasted glories of this world of a few seasons are a withered and melancholy pomp; for to his vision—whether in prosperity or affliction, in business or retirement, in crowds or in solitude—there is ever present a glory before which the loftiest mockery of greatness the earth ever offered is pale and colourless, even that glory which the dying martyr saw when he exclaimed, "Behold, I see the heavens opened, and the Son of Man standing on the right hand of God!" (Acts vii. 56.)

I cannot now pause to *reason* the matter more minutely. Do

you believe, in spite of all the sneers of a Satan-prompted world, that this is indeed the better course, to join yourselves in humility of faith to the little family of the children of God? Why delay, then, *an hour* to resolve upon the change which is to change an eternity? Have you so little experience of the seductions of the world, that you think their weakness admits of delay? Or rather, do you not know, from old experience, that the terrible probabilities are, that many here, now moved, it may be, by the terrors of the warning, will not have passed from this church, and entered once more upon the world, for one hour, when old habits will resume their course, old companions their power, this admonition vanish as a dream; or rather, let me say, the severed dream of life will reunite again, the slumber recommence, and sink as deep as if it had never been broken? And must it indeed be so? Must eternal spirits be lost in the midst of all the richest graces of God— His word, His sacraments, His services, the prayers of His faithful people? No; I will dare to hope for better results. I have told you of the character of the God who is to judge you and me,—how that He is revealed in the Gospel as one who waits for you, who beseeches you, who wills not that the "little ones should perish;" I have told you of the humble holiness which must form the character of a child of His family; I have implored of you to remember the awful necessity of this mighty change, and the still greater awfulness of the short uncertain period allowed to effect it: and I *will* hope that all this is *not* in vain. It may be that another time may come when we shall rejoice over even this morning's humble labour. Yes, it may be; and such hopes are among the few earthly consolations of the Christian minister's course; that, in that holier world where the redeemed of Christ are hereafter to meet, where friendships more durable than this world's are united, and "the communion of saints" is complete, some one of those that are now before me may recur to this very occasion as one upon which for the first time the heart was, under the Spirit of the living God, touched for higher things, and from which it retained the impression, until, after prayer and anxiety, faith had at length effectively laid hold upon the incarnate God of Calvary, heaven became a known and felt reality, and the Christian's triumph was secured for eternity. Would to God it might be so; deeply should I rejoice at the message which brought me here this morning to invite my fellow-sinners to that God who will not have one trusting believer disappointed of his hope of immortal blessedness!

But I must pass from these exhortations to the more immediate business of this morning. I must leave them to the Holy Spirit of God to preach to your hearts. Remember, it is not that I would waive them, now, or ever. I had rather (and I take upon me to say that, with all their ardour for its welfare, the managers of this charity had rather) that one soul purchased by the blood of Christ were really aroused to its high calling by these words, weak as they are, than that uncounted thousands were cast into its treasury. But the more direct purpose of our meeting calls me to provide for *it;* the young disciples of Christ, who rest upon your liberality, require me not to forget *them*,—the cause of pure and scriptural education bids me remember its demands.

I am here this day to ask of you to support the claims of one hundred and fifty pupils receiving in this place, under careful guardianship, the means of an independent livelihood in this world, the means of securing an everlasting inheritance in the next. I am here to ask of you, rich, and prosperous, and enlightened, to step between these poor children and the chances of temporal and eternal ruin. I am here to beseech you, whatever be your denomination of Christianity, to respect and support establishments where those Scriptures which we *all* in common acknowledge to be the direct effusion of God's Holy Spirit, and the unerring test of religious truth,—for to the Scriptures all alike appeal,—are made the great basis of instruction in the law of eternal life. . . . Those who have had but the poor lessons of *worldly* experience, know how dependent are the fortunes of life upon its commencement: they know that those lives of crime, and those deaths by legal punishment, which pollute the records of our unhappy country, and which curse its beauty as with a pestilence, that these are directly traceable to the wasted summers of boyhood, to our peasant youth without education, and to their education (when it comes) without religion. These are the maxims of the commonest *worldly* prudence. A statesman who was an atheist would prefer that the people he had to control were believers in God and His futurity; a landlord who was himself the slave of profligacy and of folly would yet prefer that his tenantry were a moral race, and would gladly give to the people the virtue he himself rejects. Such is the everlasting word, the eternal bridal, which God Himself sanctified of old, between holiness and happiness, that even in this world the way of its peace is often the way of God; and "righteousness," still, as ever, "*exalteth* a nation." And thus taking the matter upon the lowest grounds,—looking upon you, not as the elect of Christ, but as men concerned, for your own sakes, in the welfare of the thousands who every year swarm into life around you; not as Christians, but as Irishmen and Irishwomen, to redeem your country from the pollution of blood, from being the anathema of the civilized universe,—I call upon you this morning, largely and liberally, to support an institution that would educate its starving and shivering poor. . . . Do I desire to address you upon narrow or exclusive principles? God knows I do not. Shall they be Romanists, or shall they be Protestants? I say, make them *Christians*. Call them by what *name* you please; but teach them, oh, teach them, from the full measure of God's own pure and holy volume, unclouded, undiminished, unmutilated, that man's life is precious in the sight of God; that souls are indeed immortal and destined for immortal recompenses; that the blood of the murdered calls to heaven for vengeance: teach them that the God who sent His own and only one to die for mankind, is no God of a party or a faction, but a God of love, and who would have all mankind brothers in love. Teach them this; show them how all the law of Christ, and the story of Christ, declares such lessons and exemplifies them: be sure that in heart and soul they understand it, and I care not what you term them, in what division of the catalogue of party you class them; I only *know* that so trained they are trained to be "the children of God, and heirs of the kingdom of heaven."

Here, then, is the simple story with which I am this day attempting to interest you. It needs no artificial colourings. A hundred and fifty eternal souls dependant for their guidance to immortality upon your wish to secure it to them. Oh, surely, of all branches of charity that which most truly approaches the celestial charity of Christ Himself, is charity to the *souls* of mankind—charity of education! Were the bodies of the starving poor to perish in heaps at your doors while you were revelling within, you would, indeed, be criminals before God; yet even this criminality is not equal to that of the professing Christian, who, with the sacred words of Divine love ever upon his lips, can see around him the *undying souls* of his fellow-men in training for ruin, and yet not cast one coin (beyond what *shame* extorts) into the purse that Christian charity is collecting to guide those souls to salvation. Can you, indeed, believe that to the never-fading glories of God's right-hand there is but one way, that that "way" is Christ Jesus (as He has declared); that that way cannot be known unless it be exhibited; that it cannot be exhibited unless you yourselves step forward to invite? I will add no more. May the Spirit of God take up the cause of these children in the hearts of each of you! May He enlarge your feelings, strengthen your liberality, and, in His own glorious hour, reward you in the everlasting kingdom of the just in glory!

SERMON XVI.

STRENGTH AND MISSION OF THE CHURCH.

(Preached at Leeds Parish Church, Nov. 21, 1841.)

ISAIAH XIV. 32.

The Lord hath founded Zion, and the poor of His people shall trust in it.

SUCH, brethren, are the encouragements that consoled the ancient city of God in the day of her trouble. Harassed by her rude neighbours of Philistia, her garrisons already stormed, her armies scattered before the idol-worshippers, her own very sanctuary threatened with violation, she was bade remember her Eternal King, and take comfort in the thought of that watchful Guardian who sooner or later would assuredly avenge her wrongs. Often was she taught the same lesson; and often, in despite of her own froward and unbelieving heart, was the prediction realized. The Lord still " loved the gates of Zion;" the streams of His holy " river still made glad the city of God;" and He was " known in her palaces for a refuge." But a gloomier hour at length arrived. Even Divine patience has its limits; and the last dread crime of Zion could only be expiated in her ruin. Blood had flowed beneath her hands, every drop of which was worth a universe; and she had invoked its curse upon her own head and the head of her children. And now, behold, in the fearful words of her own prophets, "the lion is come up from his thicket, and the destroyer of the Gentiles is on his way;"—" Jerusalem is ruined and Judah is fallen; because their tongue and their doings are against the Lord, to provoke the eyes of His glory."

But what? is this the city of which such glorious things are spoken—that "the Highest Himself should establish her, that she should not be moved?" Where are His mighty promises of perpetuity? Where is that foundation which no power should ever shake—that Zion, in whom "the poor of His people were to *trust!*"

Brethren, look around you, and you behold the evidences of its existence, and of the eternal faithfulness of Him who is pledged to its immortality. A greater than Zion inherits her name; a greater than Zion bore it in the far-reaching scope of the prophetic vision. That "city of the great King" was but the perishable emblem of a "city whose builder and maker is God." It is true, she was honoured by His symbolic Presence, and sanctified by His sacred worship; it is true, that for ages she alone, in a world of darkness, held the precious lamp of His truth: but what are these characters of honour to hers whose every living stone is quickened with His indwelling energy; whose worship is no more in type and shadow, but in spirit and substance; whose preaching and teaching, no longer shrouded in obscurity, and limited to a corner of the earth, spreads over all lands, embraces the whole family of mankind, and makes even the course of that sun whose "going forth is from the end of the heaven, and his circuit unto the ends of it, and from whose heat there is nothing hid," a faint image of the power with which she diffuses, through all nations, "the light of the knowledge of the glory of God in the face of Jesus Christ?"

What destiny God may yet have in store for His ancient people it is not for us to fix with precision; but this of unbroken perpetuity, as His earthly dwelling-place, is plainly not theirs. Few candid students of prophecy can indeed doubt that a great destiny is yet reserved for the earthly Israel; that if the fall of Israel brought the beginning of blessings to the human race, the restoration of Israel is to be the means of their consummation; that God will yet bind together the two severed dispensations, making them give and receive mutual lustre; will vindicate "the law" and yet more "the prophets," but most of all, that Christ to whose final triumph they and their nation shall again minister, not in rejection, but acceptance; not in guilt, but glory. Still, in even this high destiny all the fulness of prophetic announcement is scarcely realized. The unbroken continuance of presence and blessing, so often predicted, has in their instance been fearfully interrupted. Israel after the flesh is referred to the distant future for her glories; we must then sometimes seek a Zion for David and Isaiah, whose glories are present, abiding, perpetual. In that element of His inheritance the spiritual Israel takes the place of the natural; the new Jerusalem of the old; the mount Zion, which includes "the general assembly and church of the first-born," of that which bore but the children of unhappy Judah. And thus, "even that which was made glorious had no glory in this respect, by reason of the glory which excelleth. For if that which was done away was glorious, much more that which remaineth is glorious." (2 Cor. iii. 10, 11.)

Why do I impress these things upon you, brethren? Because I would gladly lead you to feel the importance of your position as the members of this divine society—the Holy Catholic Church of Christ—in order that you may feel the community of interest which unites each such member with all, and may recognise the claim that every province of the great empire of Christ possesses upon the affectionate consideration of the rest. I am here to speak of the great necessities of a sister Church; of her labours in the cause which you love; of her difficulties with which, I can scarcely doubt, you will be prepared to sympathise. Something of such matters I must say; but though charged with her interests, I can scarcely in this place think of entering into *minute* details of her position. Another opportunity will, with the divine permission, offer for that. This is the place for the broad princip'es of the truth; and I know well that, if you but feel them as they deserve to be felt, the rest will follow of itself. Once learn to love Christ in His Church, and the Church as in Christ, and every source and channel of charity to His destitute members will spontaneously open.

Mark, then, what the text affirms. "The Lord hath founded Zion;" this is the guarantee of His love and her stability;— "the poor of His people shall trust in it," or, as the margin has it, "shall betake themselves unto it;" this is one purpose of her divine mission upon earth,—the care, the teaching, the education, the guidance of the poor.

I. The strongest, most fundamental title of protection is creation. Even among ourselves no one frames an object in order to destroy it; he who makes, makes that he may preserve. A man has mixed up his own labour with his own manufacture; it becomes a portion, as it were, of his being; and to destroy the immediate creature of his own hands becomes a sort of indirect suicide. It is thus that men justly delight in achieving those lasting performances which perpetuate themselves after death; it is thus, (and standing in this noble structure I can urge the conception with all the vividness of reality,)—it is thus that good men rejoice in the opportunity of accomplishing works that shall endure when their own course is over, and multiply the blessedness which they are no longer at hand to diffuse. These permanent monuments of usefulness are, as it were, the heirs of their purposes, the executors of their benevolence; and silently represent for them their plans, their hopes, their desires, to posterity. And if this be so in human nature, shall there be nothing to compare with it in the Divine? God, indeed, who is eternal, can require no successor to whom to devise His purposes of love; but all the claims that "the thing framed" can have on "him that framed it," hold with tenfold force when the object is not, as in our humbler works, the mere apposition of pre-existing materials, in which nothing is ours except the order of arrangement, but is itself, alike in matter and in form, the

direct offspring of His own inexhaustible power and goodness.
It is hence that the creation—wherever the creation is incorrupt
—looks with trust and confidence to the Parent of all; knows,
by instinctive conviction, that what He called into being He
is resolved to preserve in being; boldly denies the natural possibility
of absolute annihilation in any region of His universal
empire; and though it admit that when evil—the only thing
that God has not made—intrudes, weakness accompanies it,
and that rebellion dissolves the implicit compact between the
Father of holiness and His offspring, yet, even here, sees in
all the partial changes of sin and death only the working out
of some more extensive and immutable plan, in which evil
itself shall yet be shown to have performed some merely subordinate
part, and, as an unconscious or reluctant slave, to
have contributed, on the grand balance of the whole, to the
ultimate glory of the One Supreme unchangeable God.

Thus is the Maker bound to the made; thus is creation in
itself a presumptive title to protection. And it is abundantly
plain that the strength of such a bond will ever increase with
the toil expended on the object produced. Your own manufacturer
will tell you that the result becomes more precious
with the capital invested; that the hopes and interests of the
artist are more and more interwoven with the work in proportion
to the time, and the thought, and the labour, and the
expense its construction has involved. As he gazes on the
consummate result, it represents to his mind the whole mass
of these the whole elements of its formation; he feels that
more of himself is contained in it, and he identifies its success
and its reputation with his own. Shall we venture to apply
this also to the Supreme Architect of the world? We can
scarcely do so. The Scripture, in condescension to our capacities,
has represented the Omnipotent as resting from His six
days' labour; but the same Scripture has taught us that such
a phrase is but a figurative one as applied to the sublime
repose of a Creator who " worketh hitherto," and merely

expresses the cessation of a particular form of His ever active energies, when it speaks of Him as "the Creator of the ends of the earth," who "fainteth not, neither is weary." Are we, then, to admit that here *no* claim remains; that this most touching ground of protective mercy is inapplicable to the God of the Bible? Not so. He has so provided that this too should be an argument of our undoubting dependence; unable to know pain and weariness as God, He has become Man that He might do so; and He who without the lifting of an arm called a universe into being, has shed His own life in agony to create a Church.

Behold, then, how, as His own, "God loved *the world;*" how, as not only His own, but His own in pain and anguish, and endeared to His inmost heart for ever as such, God hath loved His Church. He spoke to bid the one, He died to make the other, exist. The Lord hath founded Zion; so too hath He the world: but this (as Jericho of old) was "founded in the death of *a first-born;*" the streams that make glad this city of God are the water and the blood that flowed from the pierced side of the Founder. When He beholds His Church He sees in it the monument of His own inexpressible sorrows; as mothers are said to love with special tenderness the child whose birth was one of peculiar anguish and peril, surely so does He feel this offspring of His divine agonies drawn closer to His eternal heart by the thought of all it cost to give her being.

Then, again, in this Church of His is His own *honour* pledged. He hath not covenanted with the world that now is to immortalize it; but He has passed His own Word for the perpetuity of His Church. Nothing so framed was ever framed to perish; He has infused into it His own Spirit, and His Spirit is life. Even this were security enough; but His *oath* is securer still. That the Church of Christ should fade away from the earth, would fill even heaven with dismay; for it would perplex the very angels as to the changeless truth of

Him who has promised it immortality; yea, heaven's own foundations should totter if that Church, which is the antechamber of the kingdom of glory, which is, saith St. Ambrose, "the image of the celestial," were to wane and disappear. It may be corrupted, it may be enfeebled, it may be persecuted, or worse—it may persecute; it may be ignorantly enslaved in one division, or insolently turbulent in another; it may, in short, be all that the subtlety of the tempter, during his permitted hour, can make it: but it cannot perish. Its day of purification must come at last. The Church may forget Christ,—it is nowhere promised that she shall not; but Christ cannot forget her! "Thy sun shall no more go down; neither shall thy moon withdraw itself: for the Lord is thine everlasting light, and the days of thy mourning shall be ended. *Thy people also shall be all righteous;* they shall inherit the land for ever, the branch of my planting, the work of my hand, that I may be glorified." [Isa. lx. 20, 21.]

But even more, is not this Church, in its ultimate perfection, set forth as the very *reward* of all the sorrows of its Lord? and shall He be defrauded of His recompense? To "see of the travail of His soul and be satisfied" is His destined crown; this "joy set before Him" was that which enabled Him to "endure the cross, despising the shame." Every one of you, then, that lives in faith and purity within this holy society, becomes an element in the happiness of Christ; and, glorious thought! can make heaven itself to Him more blissful. Every one of you that resigns a world of corruption for the holy simplicity of the Christian life, adds a new joy to the joys of even an enthroned God. And if this be so now, what shall it be in the day of the regeneration? The Church that shall end, as it began, with none but saints its members; the Church that shall be by Christ presented to Himself "a glorious Church, without spot, or wrinkle, or any such thing;" how shall its solemn entry into the prepared kingdom fill the heart of its almighty Guardian with an ecstasy which, even amid all His accumulated glories, it is yet reserved for Him to experience!

Yet, why insist upon these things? All these relationships are below the truth. There is more than creation to bind the Church to Christ, more than promise, more than reward; there is communion, oneness, identification. A man may desert his child; he cannot desert himself. Even though the Redeemer could forget His espoused Bride; even though He could deny His plighted promise; yea, though He could abandon His own reward; He cannot abandon His own body. The people of Christ, once received into His covenant, and there abiding, are interwoven into His very nature; "we are members," declares the Apostle, "of His body, of His flesh, and of His bones." With such a union there can be no separation; if Christ be immortal the Church is so; when He dies she shall perish, but not till then.

Such is the Holy Church of God, her dignity, her promises, her privilege. Let not such expressions as these be weakened in your estimation by any distinctions of visible and invisible Churches. For my own part,—I would not dictate to others upon a point on which many of our holiest and most gifted divines have been divided; but, as far as my own researches have extended,—I know of but one Church in the New Testament; that which was visibly founded on visible Apostles, Jesus Christ Himself being its visible chief cornerstone; and I confess I cannot but regard it as eminently unfortunate that any other conception of the Church of Christ should ever have gained currency within her borders. It is true that Christ's promises are conditional on repentance and faith, to all who are capable of exercising those graces; it is also perfectly true, that those alone who fulfil the conditions really, and in spirit, adhere to the Head; but this, surely, no more constitutes these happy and holy believers a "Church," in the scriptural sense of that term, than the loyalty of a few members in a disaffected corporation constitutes them the corporation, or the fidelity of a few soldiers in a mutinous army constitutes them the army itself. That the Church should be corrupt does not annihilate its existence, or destroy its essential being as a society. That the body should be all more or less infirm with the exception of a single arm, does not make it necessary to call that arm the body; still less, to rob the sickly frame of its appointed rights—its sustenance for the present, its hopes for the future. I should not have mentioned this point at all (because I have no time to do it any justice) were it not that it bears directly on my business here this day. For one of the evils of this refinement of the Church into the ideal company of the Elect is, that it cuts all the tenderest nerves of sympathy between godly men and the visible Church of Christ around them. It is impossible for them to sympathise, on purely scriptural grounds, with a society which they have been taught to imagine is nowhere — or scarcely—recognised in Scripture. It may be a valuable community, but it is not *theirs*. They admit it to be a useful machinery, perhaps,—a tolerable instrument, as times go, for spiritual benefit; but they do not see in it a direct appointment of Heaven, an immediate object of divine superintendence, a society intended to engage and to foster their affections, dear for its own sake, and for Christ's. And these being the considerations that impress godly men most deeply, the Church thus loses her highest, holiest, and most engaging claims. Calculation takes the place of a bright and happy enthusiasm; the Spouse is regarded as a useful servant, not as, amid all her misfortunes, the still cherished Bride of Christ. And thus, instead of the topics that Paul has given us, and Isaiah, and the Lord Himself, we have to descend to low calculations of economic utility. Not that we dread such inquiries as to the social value of the Church; but certainly we would rather not be always obliged to stoop to them.

But I must proceed; for I am aware I cannot venture to detain your attention at present beyond a limited period. I turn, then, for a moment, to the other branch of the text;—to that which predicts that this Zion of God shall be the resort of His poor, and the object of their trust.

II. How does the Church of Christ fulfil this promise? In what capacity does she present herself as the appointed guide and friend of the poor? This is of moment to my case; for it is to enable her to be such that I desire to engage your exertions.

Brethren, the Church of Christ is one vast institute for the benefit of the poor. He who loved all, eminently loved them; professed Himself eminently *their* gospel preacher; declared that the heaven He preached, though open to all, was still peculiarly a heaven for them. And His Church has ever, even in her darkest days, retained much of the character He thus impressed. There were times when, in her overweening secularity, she taxed the rich to supply her undue ambition; yet, even then, to do but justice to those ages of arrogance, she had still an open hand for the poor. But it is not of her temporal charities I speak now. It is in the doctrine she preaches, and the way she preaches it, that the Church is indeed the poor man's consoler. It is in meeting his sorrows with tidings of glory to come, in brightening the gloom of his humble home with the hallowed light of eternity, in soothing his days of hard and heavy toil with her peaceful sabbaths, in watching over his bed of sickness with a patience as unwearied as if his poor chamber were gorgeous with gilded ceilings and silken tapestry; it is in these things that the Church carries on that loveliest attribute of her Lord,—" Thou hast been a strength to the poor, a strength to the needy in his distress!"

And then the truths she teaches him,—how elevating, how enlarging, how fortifying, how exalting! I thank that God of grace that there are within her precincts hundreds upon hundreds of pastors who have no other feeling; men as sincerely devoted to the work of Christ as any Church in the world can produce. Brethren, you must not desert this Church of Ireland; you must learn to love this poorer sister. A common interest ought to endear us to each other; for what are we but the outpost in a contest which you will yourselves have to endure? But why do I speak merely of the Church of my country? I tell you my country herself asks for scriptural education; the poor Irishman loves it, when he dares. That noble country, that land of generous hearts, what does she want to make her worthy to accompany you in history but the uncorrupted truth of Christ that you possess? Will you not unite in the blessed office of diffusing it? Will you not awake among yourselves and your friends a holy enthusiasm for this high enterprise, now that it is undertaken with auspices that authenticate it to your understandings no less than to your hearts? You may allege, that you are too often appealed to on these Irish charities; that you cannot distinguish between their rival claims. Brethren, it is not for me to criticise the principles or the operations of bodies, which, no doubt, all mean well; but I must be permitted to say, that the authority by which this Society is presented to England sets it far above every other, however ardent or devoted. Its connexion with the legitimate governors of the Irish Church affords a security to which no other can pretend. The Educational Society of the Irish Church, the Society of her Bishops and her Clergy, is this day recommended to your affections; I trust in God, recommended not in vain.

SERMON XVII.

THE INGRATITUDE OF THE JEWS.

(Preached at St. Stephen's Church, June 4, 1837.)

MATTHEW VIII. 34.

And, behold, the whole city came out to meet Jesus: and when they saw Him, they besought Him that He would depart out of their coasts.

THIS verse, my brethren, is part of a passage which connects together two very remarkable scenes in the life of Christ. Short as it is, and perhaps of no great apparent importance, it is nevertheless not to be lost and consumed in the wonderful tales of miracle and mercy which precede and follow it. The story of the Gospels, rich in abounding usefulness, is scarcely more instructive when it describes the conduct of God, than when it recounts the corresponding conduct of *man;* and to enter fully into the spirit of the whole, both must be taken in, as correlative parts of one all-important narrative. The Gospel has a double nature, like its Author. And not when the omnipotence of the Son of God flashes out in the miracles of the Son of Man; not when His prodigies of healing and sustaining are heaped before us in all the bright profusion of a benevolence almighty as it is benevolent; not when (raising others from the dead as a foretaste of that last grand "declaration according to the Spirit of holiness," when He rose Himself triumphant over the tomb), He cried, "Lazarus, come forth!" or to the corse of the ruler's daughter, "I say unto thee, Arise!" —not even in such wonders as these lies a deeper spring of thoughts than in the parallel narratives of the emotions and feelings of the frail and mingled crowd that heard Him. If the one class of memorials seem now and then (in happier moments) to exalt us almost beyond what we *are*, the others too truly *inform or remind us* what we are; if the consciousness of participating in spiritual unity with such a Being as our Prince of Peace sometimes lifts us beyond the lowly level of humanity, the consciousness, confirmed by the same faithful pages, of sharing in the corrupted nature of those who neglected, or despised, or persecuted, or *murdered* Him, may well restore us to the grave sadness of a Christian humility. Thus is Scripture perfect in its combination of records and its balance of motives; thus is it profitable not more for "doctrine" than for "reproof and correction." In truth, the richest harvest of godly knowledge lies not among those demonstrations of divine *power* which were presented by our blessed Lord; the heights of those omnipotent examples (though far indeed from *barren*) are perhaps too lofty to admit of general or easy cultivation; and though I firmly believe not a wonder that is recorded of Him is without a deeper significance than we commonly imagine, yet the readiest, and most abounding fruit of instruction, is to be gathered in the lower territory of the Gospel, in that region where the divinity seems to lose itself in the manhood,—in the discourses of the divine Preacher Himself, and in the doings of His majestic lowliness. And (as I have said) not least of all is instruction to be gained from the recorded conduct of the mixed multitudes who came within the sphere of this Light of the world; and by some of whom the rays of His celestial influence were happily absorbed into their very being; by some, flung back ungraciously to the source itself of the illumination; by some received, indeed, but received only to be distorted in passing through a thousand fallacious and perverting mediums of passion, and prejudice, and precipitation.

The results of the preaching of our Lord were, indeed, individually various. His own heavenly teaching was not without its fruits; although the task and the glory of immediate conversions were principally permitted to His ministers. There were those who besought Him to remain, as well as those who " besought Him to depart." In one place we read that " the people sought Him, and came unto Him, and stayed Him, that He should not depart from them," (Luke iv. 42,) and just after that, they " pressed upon Him to hear the word of God." (Luke v. 1.) The honest-hearted officers pleaded to the Pharisees that " never man spake like this man," (John vii. 46;) and " many of the people said," on the same occasion, " of a truth this is the Prophet." But the general complexion of the case is sadly different. The occasional virtues of individuals are lost in the criminality of the nation. The impulses in His favour were few and incidental; the current against Him strong and steady. And the request in the text, that the Lord of life should depart from their too-honoured coasts, was only one of the earlier incidents of that drama, terrible in its consistency of crime, which ended with the suicidal imprecation, " His blood be upon us and upon our children!"

My present object (in accordance with the remark which I have already made relative to the importance of considering the human and corrupt examples, no less than the divine and holy Example, of the Gospel narrative) is to lead you to reflect how complete and how melancholy is the portraiture presented to all following ages in the histories of Christ's rejection: an example which is so perfect in its development of the profound depravity of our nature as to induce me to think that the season, the place, and the other circumstances of the Great Sacrifice, were selected out of the mass of historical situations and possibilities which lay before the divine Disposer, with an express view to the formation of so tremendous and unparalleled a warning of the heart's deceitfulness and desperate wickedness, to all who were to follow the age of Christ's appearing.

For, brethren, (to illustrate the nature of such reasonings more fully,) we are not to imagine that, among the unnumbered and careful preordinations of God in relation to the *personal* office and achievements of *Christ* in the great event of human history, the precise time, place, and other similar circumstances, even to the minutest particular of time, and place, and circumstance, were not every one of them matters of divine forethought and prescription. When we find not only the *country* of His birth foretokened, but the very *city* of it; when we find not only His descent from *Abraham* proclaimed, but His descent from a special *tribe* of Abraham's family—and not only from this special tribe, but from *a particular royal line;* when we find the *state of the general world* at His coming not obscurely shadowed forth, and, still more, the *very year* of His great sacrifice predicted, and the accompanying *condition of the former but forsaken nation of God* declared; can we doubt (seeing thus the particularity of the prophetical annunciations) that there were reasons in the divine counsels for every *further* specialty of His history, though not prefigured in the prophetic canon,—that the world was duly prepared for Him no less than He for the world,—that the precise condition of the people among whom He came, and no other *condition* of that people, and no other people of *any* condition, suited the exact designs of Heaven? And if we suffer the impulses of such reflections to extend, they will surely end in an assured conviction, that there is not a detail (of whatever apparent irrelevancy) in the histories of Christ which may not have had its *definite reason* in relation to the entire plan of redemption, as it assuredly had its general fore-ordination, or foreknowledge, in the eternal purposes of an all-purposing God.

There is one class of purposes, then, which is of all others the most easily comprehensible; the purpose of *example and admonition*. If you remember that the high providence of God has seen fit to leave His Church no infallible external guidance peculiar to them beyond the writings of the New Testament, it will tend to impress upon you the exceeding importance of every line in such a volume so circumstanced. Such a volume is not likely to contain much that is irrelevant. And it is in this way that I believe that the Scriptures of the New Testament were in the deep purpose of God so arranged, in their historical part, as to fitly become to us very much what the typical details of the Old Testament ought to have been to the Jews; an outward and palpable representation of deep and eternal moral truths, a visible external detail, confined to a special race of mankind, of that which is invisible, internal, and universal as the human heart. So that the realities of the ancient types become themselves instructive types to all future times. The story of Christ incarnate in Judea is the story of the Christ that spiritually visits every natural heart of man.

I say, then, that the age of the world, and the peculiar position of the chosen people at the time when our blessed Lord came down to tabernacle in human flesh, were of all ages and national positions the most admirably formed to call out the excellencies of the superhuman Sufferer and the corresponding character of the unregenerate soul; that thence (through that divine and adorable mercy which works good from evil) the history of *such a being so placed* becomes an example surpassing all other supposable examples, for the everlasting instruction of posterity.

I must content myself, this evening, with offering only one or two very simple illustrations of a proposition which your own research will easily extend, or which some future opportunity may enable me to accompany you in extending.

In the first place, then, (to commence this melancholy exposition of criminality,) regard the political condition of the people among whom the Lord of glory was manifested in the flesh. The royal philosopher has said that "it is better to go to the house of mourning than to the house of feasting," and that "sorrow is better than laughter; for by the sadness of the countenance the heart is made better," (Eccles. vii. 2, 3;)

and these sayings, no less true than beautiful, are confirmed by general experience. But there are exceptions to the rule; and the fallen condition of the kingdom of the Preacher himself was destined to form a prominent one. It may, perhaps, be said with truth, that the state of mind in which—all requisite previous instruction being supposed — sorrow is found to indurate rather than to soften, in which the most powerful of all moral medicines becomes a poison, and in which the spirit, instead of being broken and contrite by affliction, becomes habitually impenitent, and desperate with its woes, is that condition of human nature which (if we were to select among the varieties of depravity) is actually the farthest from God. Now and then this frightful condition is on a large scale developed upon earth in famine, and plagues, and other such visitations; and those who have witnessed it want no explanation of what the misery of *hell* consists in. In cases of extreme and urgent misery, however, when life itself is to be struggled for, it would be vain to offer instruction or consolation; and where the contrast is to be exhibited, and the corruption that refuses the consolation to be displayed, an instance must be sought of less immediate and crushing anguish. That instance was furnished in the Jews. When the Messiah appeared, they were an oppressed and unhappy race. Possessing little national consequence, and only a shadow of independence, they were continually forced to see their ancient religion reviled, (and we know the miserable heroism of their attachment to it!) their hallowed services mocked by the brutality of a ferocious heathen soldiery, their rights of property violated by the officers of a foreign oppression, their very lives endangered; for did not Pilate "mingle their blood with their sacrifices?" Their own rulers only aggravated the general misery. Contentious, arrogant men filled the chairs of the prophets; and the venerable high priesthood had become the reward of successful bribery, or more sanguinary audacity. Such an instance of national depression, in contrast with former grandeur, was at that period—at any period—not to be parallelled on earth. In the midst of such a scene appeared the promised Restorer. The Spirit of God moved over the chaos of their fortunes, and would have harmonized the whole for ever. But the Messiah invoked His countrymen in vain. They had no heart for the happiness He could offer them. Like many in every age since theirs, they could sigh for national regeneration, but they could not begin with individual reform. Here, then, was consummated the depravity. The sorrow that should have prepared their hearts for the good seed of the word left them harder, more obdurately vicious, than ever. They could follow their Theudas and their Barcochebas, but they could not accept the lofty and beautiful emancipation which Christ proclaimed. They could worship the false lights of false Messiahs,—they went astray while the Light of the world was among them. They " turned from all He brought to all He would not bring;" and refused allegiance because the Lord of Eternity would not condescend to accept the paltry honours of an earthly throne.

Here, then, is the point. That the condition of the Jewish people—reduced to the lowest ebb by afflictions, and, nevertheless, only more abandoned in iniquity as individuals as they sunk deeper in calamity as a nation; covered with sores and weakness, yet unable to recognise and adopt the Physician—presents a specimen of the hopeless ruin of the human heart, such as no other nation or age could (in this definite and tangible form) have presented; and that (as I conceive) such a condition of things was chosen by the supreme Disposer with a view to impress the terrible example upon our hearts. These things were " written for our learning, that we, through patience, and comfort of the Scriptures, might have"—shall I say—" *hope?*" Yes, truly, for those who have already learned the discipline of that "*fear*" which is " the beginning of wisdom;" for those who already know how to walk in the " fear of the Lord" as well as in the " comfort of the Holy Spirit."

(Acts ix. 31.) Hope? Yes, but hope only for those who realize the beloved Apostle's indications of a genuine hope, when he tells us that "every man that hath this hope in him purifieth himself, even as *He* (Christ) is pure." (1 John iii. 3.)

The Jews, then, were an example, or type, of slavery that would not accept real freedom. I said that they were an example of this unfruitful affliction *in a definite historical form*: and I said so because I would not have you to dream that they stand alone in their folly. The Christianity of our time has little cause to exult over the legal righteousness of the synagogue; as little, to reproach the Jews of that day with sorrows that brought no profit, and opportunities neglected. Did they alone groan under intestine dissensions? did they alone groan under a foreign tyranny? Alas! is not every unconverted heart an abandoned Israel, perplexed with the conflicts of internal passions, and ground down by the incessant tyranny of a despot more merciless than any earthly governor? Wretched disguise of hollow happiness! Those who have watched the manners of the slaves whose necks are cursed with the tyranny of American freedom often tell us that there is a remarkable, and, at first glance, a very surprising peculiarity in their habits. The stranger does not discover, as he expects, the gloom and reserve of sullen despondency, but rather an excessive levity, a reckless gaiety of spirits, that seems to contrast most inexplicably with their miserable situation. But the wonder soon disappears. The gaiety is quickly detected to be an irrational mirth, the most horrible result of despair and degradation. Hopeless, thoughtless, feelingless, they snatch the momentary respite from the whip, and endeavour to make up by an overstrained effort of compulsory joy, for the shortness and uncertainty of their unhappy festivity. Their miseries breed their vices; and profligacy is but the refuge from despair. I have never read such descriptions as these without thinking how truly they picture the general aspect of the world. The same unmitigated slavery, the same transitory reprieve, the same feverish excitement, the same profligate abasement, the same dark and dreaded punishment, overhanging the whole!

Such is one admonitory aspect of the Jewish example. The subject is fruitful of *many* warnings; but we must pass rapidly on.

If time permitted, I would more particularly wish to enlarge upon the peculiar opportunities which the state of the Jewish RELIGIOUS system afforded for calling out the various perversions of truth,—hypocritical, free-thinking, and mystical,—under the notice, censure, and correction of our blessed Lord. It would not be difficult to show that, in our own day, perversions exist almost literally parallel; so perfect is the Gospel type for the Church's instruction. But the subject is too extensive for any incidental treatment. I hasten to a point more simple and quite as instructive.

I affirm, then, in the third place, that the history of the mission of Christ, as connected with the Jewish people, presented an instance—a "prerogative instance"—of the mass of INGRATITUDE which mingles in the corruption of the human heart, such as no other connexion could have furnished in any age or country of the world. Whatever doubts may have attended the former reasoning, here we argue with absolute certainty. The elder revelation, which we receive as the only revelation of its date, stands alone, because the people it concerns stand alone; and if the people were not a *solitary* instance of ingratitude, that revelation (which assumes the peculiarity of their position, which again is the point on which we found the ingratitude) *could not be true*. On this point, then, (as to facts and circumstances,) we are left in no perplexity of hypothesis or conjecture.

It is true that all living beings are indebted to the Creator for the original and basis of all blessings, the gift of existence. It is true that, *so far*, all human beings are bound to gratitude. But though existence may be a necessary groundwork upon which alone blessings can be wrought, and in this relation may be itself regarded as a blessing in being preparatory to possible blessings, yet it is very certain that it may likewise be the ground of misery, and thus prove, in this relation, eventually a curse. Our Lord bears out this language, in speaking of one to whom " it would have been good if he had never been born." And in such cases a feeling of gratitude is plainly incompatible with common consciousness; that is to say, gratitude except for *possible* advantages, a feeling too indistinct for notice, not to say too rational and collected for a state of the turbulent and agonized depravity I am adverting to. But suppose the existence adorned with the usual mercies of Providence: even then general obligations, which are participated with the universal world, at best produce but little impression. The beneficence which is divided among so many seems proportionably lessened to each; a supposition, indeed, wholly inapplicable to an *infinite* Benefactor, but not the less common on that account. Besides, they are felt as *laws of nature* rather than as acts of nature's Lawgiver; and we are as little affected by them as by the physical ordinances that the earth should revolve, or that the sun should give its light. The chief reason is, however, that, applying to God the littleness of man, we cannot conceive the immensity of a love that can extend to all the earth, and yet be a personal friendship to every individual. But the belief of *special* favours, the knowledge that God has done for us what He has not done for any but us, the conviction that He who governs others by general rules of providence has chosen us out as the peculiar theatre for the display of distinguishing graces, this individualizing of divine favours is that which powerfully moves to gratitude, and, in the natural course of things, demands a rich return from the heart. And so it ought to be. For though others who have received *much* ought *not to relax* in gratitude at the sight of greater favours denied, yet, assuredly, those who have received *more* ought to *increase* in gratitude at the enjoyment of greater favours received. All nations were reasonably—and are at this day in reason and conscience (the reason of the heart)—bound to worship the unseen Cause of benefits which, however ignorant in particulars, they at least felt, and feel, to be *provided* for their use, not produced by their *power;* nor should the invisibility of the Giver diminish the gratitude for the gift, any more than it would diminish it in any parallel instance of *daily life.* He who receives an *anonymous* charity is not the less deeply affected with gratitude because the donor is unknown; the gratitude is generated in the heart irrespective of the object; the winged feeling lives and breathes, though it knows not where definitely to rest and settle. And thus it was that the unknown God of the Athenians claimed by a perfect right the acknowledgment of the natural heart, even before Paul had declared Him whom they "ignorantly worshipped."

But all these vague uncertainties of feeling centre upon a *revealed* God. The Jews had lived upon a far higher level than I have described, both of heavenly knowledge and of heavenly favour. They *knew* the Benefactor, and they knew Him *their own peculiar* Benefactor. In the beautiful language of their legislator,—" The Lord's portion is His people, Jacob is the lot of His inheritance," (comparing Him to some great king—as in the preceding verse—who, after dividing his realms among his chieftains, selects some one lovely and favoured spot as his own special domain and royal residence.) " He found him in a desert land, and in the waste howling wilderness; He led him about, He instructed him, He kept him as the apple of His eye. As an eagle stirreth up her nest, fluttereth over her young," (you remember the resumption of the metaphor by our Saviour in a still gentler form,) " spreadeth abroad her wings, taketh them, beareth them on her wings; so the Lord alone did lead him." (Deut. xxxii. 9—12.) Truly might the Psalmist say, " He hath not dealt so with any nation.'

(Ps. cxlvii. 20.) Their whole history had been one tissue of divine interpositions, their blessings were rewards, their misfortunes punishments; and that temporal scheme of providential justice, which is vainly sought on this side of the grave in all other histories, was almost realized in the Jewish. As the fulness of time advanced, the prophetic messengers foreshadowed the breadth and freeness of the evangelical spirituality; and this left the people without excuse in retaining the narrowness of national prejudices. No *honest* reader of Isaiah could escape feeling that a time was to come when the Spirit of God would demand the *world* for its inheritance, and the slender stem of Judah's mercies swell into a cedar whose branches should cover the earth. Yet Jesus, the substance of all the ceremonies of the law, and the fulfiller of all the morality of the prophets,—Jesus, " to whom give all the prophets witness," not more in precise predictions than in the whole cast of their thinking, (as some reflectors give back an *accurate image* of the sun, while others give *a general diffusion* of his light,)—Jesus was (as those prophets had foretokened) "despised and rejected of men!" But had He been rejected of others—had Athens rejected the great Teacher for her philosophers, or Rome despised the Captain of Salvation for her warriors—we had lost a mighty document of human depravity. No; "He came unto *His own*, and His own received Him not!" They who, through a long course of centuries, had been educated into expectation of the ever-blessed Visitant perverted the expectation, reading it by the corrupted glare of their own ambition; and though miracles more wondrous than those of their greatest leaders were performed before their eyes,—miracles that identified the Saviour with the Angel and Guide of their whole past history,—yet the infidelity of the heart prevailed to poison the reason, and they rejected Him!

Nor is it to be said, to countervail the accusation of *ingratitude*, that they preserved their allegiance to God while they refused Christ, whom they did not recognise as His Messenger

The circumstance thus pleaded is the very one which constitutes or heightens the special charge of ingratitude. For the Messiah's ministry was so arranged as to form a perfect trial of the heart; and it was the blindness of heart alone which was unable to perceive the Godhead under the veil. There was no possible proof refused, whether internal or external, in demonstration of the truth of the Mission, except *one* which the corrupted heart demanded, and which, *because* the Mission was to be a trial of heart, God on that very account denied; I mean the direct and continued display of earthly majesty and dominion. This was refused, because he who could not recognise and adore a Saviour without the accessories of worldly distinction was not deemed worthy to receive Him at all. In external condition humble as the humblest, the Divinity broke out in flashes of exceeding splendour to those whose passions would allow them to interpret it; and Christ walked the earth an enigma, whose solution lay in every honest heart. The " mystery of godliness" was addressed to the godly. What evidence, consistent with the general plan of redemption, could be offered of the true Messiahship of our Lord which was not liberally given? and shall we excuse His persecutors of ingratitude, because that tumult of passion, which was the very source and fountain of the ingratitude, continually interposed to cloud the conclusions of their reason? The reason was proclaiming Him the Deliverer, while the passions were refusing allegiance; and to say that the enemies of Christ were not *ungrateful* in assailing Him, because they persisted in not perceiving Him to be the Messiah, would be to say that ingratitude to Christ only then becomes possible when circumstances have rendered it *impossible*. For my own part, I believe that Jesus *was largely felt* to be the true Prophet, both before and after His death; but that the hostility of vice was so unconquerable, as that the belief was overwhelmed and buried in the abyss of passion. The men that saw Him scatter miracles around Him, and radiate mercies as the sun does light, assuredly *knew* Him to be the Messiah, though they could not bring their hearts to confess it. Holding, then, that the reason and conscience of Israel knew their Lord, while its passions and depravity refused Him,—holding that every opportunity of identifying the Lord Jesus with the promised Deliverer was bestowed, short of a direct concession to vice, I proceed to build, upon the *very circumstances* of His manifestation, that testimony to the extent of human ingratitude which I conceive to have been designed by the divine counsel as a tremendous lesson to every future age.

The main force of the ingratitude, then, lay in the very *humility* of the Redeemer's condition. He came among His countrymen as a poor and humble dweller in their native Galilee,—the fires of His omnipotence suppressed, the "glory which He had before the world was" left behind Him in the eternal bosom of His Father. Here, then, was a trial of the heart,—the evident God of their fathers (at the lowest, His evident Messenger and Friend) asking the hospitality of His ancient people. Here was the *one only instance*, the solitary opportunity, that has ever occurred, or can ever occur, from the creation of the world to its conflagration, for man to return a personal acknowledgment of benefit to his God. The God who had filled their sacred records with glory was among them, and "had not where to lay His head." I repeat that unbelief must not protect them, when the unbelief was itself a crime of the heart. Had he come as He once appeared to their lawgiver on the Arabian mount,—the mount "that burned with fire," in "blackness, and darkness, and tempest;" had He come as His Angel descended on the host of Sennacherib; had His advent been with all the insignia of worldly dominion,—a rival Cæsar,—who *would or could* have refused Him? and where would have been the ingratitude of rejection? But no; He came to try whether His own would receive One in whom the rest of the world could take no pleasure; He was received with the crown of thorns and the cross!

If such a point as this singular example of ingratitude can receive any further illustration, we might easily suppose a fitting parallel. Imagine that our own native land had been placed by divine Providence under a similar course of protection; conceive that in its battles the powers of heaven were seen manifestly interfering; suppose that its rulers were guided by an undeniable divine impulse, and its moral education conducted by commissioned messengers of Heaven encouraging or reproving the general mind, and all referring their authority (fortified by miracles and prodigies) to one celestial source of power and knowledge. But misfortune reaches our land,— the fatal recompense of carelessness and crime. After many days a wondrous, but not unpredicted, event takes place. In our streets and fields appears a Being not of this world, a meek Omnipotent, spreading blessings by no tardy mechanism of nature, but with the direct and rapid strokes of almighty power. His own declarations, joined to all around Him, proclaim to those good hearts who can read the language of His actions, and to the reason of all men, that He is, indeed, the Being from whose inexhaustible beneficence the past recorded glories of our people had sprung, whom some mysterious ordination had sent to take refuge among us. Yet we have no mercy upon the merciful; we seize the advantage of His human form, and through His assumed mortality afflict Him with the death of robbers and murderers. Can you bear the thought of such atrocious ingratitude? Is it in your nature to conceive the actual commission of it by your own hands? To be unmoved by a friendship that passes all examples of devotion; to be hardened to reasonings of exquisite applicability and truth; to deny the day when the light is shining into your eyes,—is this conceivable? Christian brethren, remember Nathan's reply to David. As near as it is possible for any living being to approach the sin of Israel, so near do those approach who, in our time, desert the banner of the Redeemer. You cannot directly insult His form on earth; you cannot weave the bloody coronet for the brows of the King of kings; you cannot, with your own hands, nail Him to the accursed tree: but you can (an Apostle declares it) " crucify to yourselves the Son of God afresh, and put Him to an open shame." Do you take advantage of the terrible privilege? Do you exult in this figurative crucifixion of your Lord, and thus identify yourselves with His murderers? Oh, fellow Christians, before every one of you this night hath " Jesus Christ been evidently set forth," as before the Galatians, " crucified among you." Will you learn the awful history only to copy it? Opportunities abound for the crime. He who persecutes the least of the disciples of Christ persecutes Christ Himself. He who reviles the Gospel, reviles Him who sent it; and cries, " Crucify Him! crucify Him!" evermore from the depths of his heart. If the wretched Jew had the visible Christ to assail, have not we the Christ that is accurately reflected in the Gospel? if he had a Christ to *behold*, have not we a Christ to *contemplate*? But no; you will, with God's blessing, cherish better thoughts. You will not begin by bidding " Christ depart from your coasts," and end by crucifying Him. Nay, rather let me trust that you will learn more and more to be " crucified *with* Christ," as the Apostle says he continually was; that, like him, you will learn to " crucify the flesh with the affections and lusts," until at length you reach that sublimest point of all with which he closes his Epistle, when he declares that, by the Lord Jesus Christ, " the world is crucified unto him, and he unto the world!" Such a state of heart and soul *prayer* alone can bring; and to prayer, and the God of prayer, I leave you.

SERMON XVIII.

THE ADVENT EXALTS HUMAN RELATIONS.

(Preached for the Western Lying-In Hospital, Dublin, December 2, 1838. Advent Sunday.)

LUKE II. 7.

And she brought forth her firstborn son, and wrapped Him in swaddling clothes, and laid Him in a manger; because there was no room for them in the inn.

WHEN you remember, my dear brethren, the peculiar and very touching occasion on which I have been requested this day to address you, as well as the solemn introductory festival which the Church celebrates on this day, you will have no difficulty in conceiving the association by which the passage I have just read is connected with my present labours. Blessed Christianity! Few, indeed, are the occasions of benevolence to which it does not furnish motives, or impulses, or examples, or suggestions. Few are the forms of human sorrow, demanding human relief, which will not be found represented, in a shape more affecting and more exalted, in those pages of which the divine Hero was "a man of sorrows and acquainted with grief." And common as, in one form or other, is that work of charity which I am now called on to perform among you, let us not forget, let us rejoice to remember, how exclusively it is a *Christian* work, this business of public appeal for public benevolence upon religious grounds and motives. Antiquity knew nothing of it; we ourselves know nothing of it until every lower motive either fails in strength or is misplaced in application. As long as the ordinary business of the world is in progress, worldly motives are sufficient to keep the wheels of the vast machinery in ceaseless activity; now and then they may have energy for even a better sphere of operation; men, from a sense of interest, will be just, from a natural affection will be sometimes sincerely kind. The enthusiasm of *party* will often incidentally urge to vast and real sacrifices; and men will do good to some of their fellow-creatures, to vex and exasperate others! But these are low motives, degrading motives, at best weak because occasional and limited, motives; and when *more* than this poor and perverted benevolence is wanting, when deeper springs of mercy must be sought, and demands more pressing urged upon the heart, the lever that is to stir the mass must be fixed upon the *Gospel* as its fulcrum. A new body of motives must be summoned into action. "The powers of the world to come" must be brought to vivify the cold and deadly feebleness of the world that is now. If earth is to be regenerated, heaven must be opened; and the form of immortal love that is there enthroned must be disenshrouded of its veil of clouds, to transform, by the penetrating power of its glories seen and known, the adoring heart into His own image and likeness.

And I have to speak to you this day of claims thus elevated by every heavenly consecration, as well as endeared by every human tie. We approach in time, let us also approach in thought, the sacred season of Bethlehem, the announcing angels, and the worshipping sages. Let us upon this advent festival feel ourselves where we are—in the early twilight of the Christian dawn; the clouds faintly tinged with the promise of the yet unrisen Sun. Such a time, and all its crowd of recollections, will plead for those for whom I can but feebly plead. And having to speak for woman in her most touching character, her most fearful earthly trial, I thought it well to remind you of *Him* who was pleased to enter upon humanity as you have done, to connect Himself in the relationship of childhood with an earthly mother, and in the voluntary humiliation of His birth to sanctify that destitution, (that poverty embittering the natural agony of the hour,) which you are this morning called upon to respect and to relieve.

Let us, then, pause for awhile upon this great model thus beautifying every natural relationship, and entering into the world He created in order to re-create it after a diviner fashion. Let us regard Him as He came among us, a Man among His brethren; so mysterious, yet so simple, yea, the more mysterious in His very simplicity.

Why, then, was it that the eternal Son, when He abandoned that "glory which He had with the Father before the world was," and determined to be " the Man Christ Jesus,"—why was it that, instead of wonders in the heavens and the earth attending His coming, the convulsion and terror of a universe attesting the descent of the Godhead into His creation, He was pleased to make His apparition on the scene of the world even as others do; to be the infant and the child before He was the man; to be subject to the filial obligation in the fulness of its legitimate extent; and to be all this in a situation in which such ties were stripped of all that could recommend them, apart from their own intrinsic value,—a situation in which wealth could not adorn, nor authority dignify them?

Not to delay upon other explanations of this fact, and to dwell more forcibly upon that which more directly concerns our present purpose, assuredly one prominent reason was that, separating, by means so much more intelligible than argumentative statements, what was essentially excellent in human nature from its depravations and corruptions, He might bestow a special dignity upon those primary connexions of human life upon which the rest so mainly depend, and in which the tenderer and better affections of the heart find, and were meant by our Creator to find, their peculiar sphere of exercise. Nothing can more truly show that nature and revelation came from the same hand, than the assumption into revelation of all that is innocent in nature. When God, as Creator of the world, bound together all the variety of human connexions by all the variety of corresponding affections, He wrought a work destined for everlasting; dispensations may change, but these things are not meant to change: the second and higher revelation did not purpose to obliterate them,—it presupposed them, it encouraged them, it consecrated them with the blessing of the skies. And thus it is that, when from the perusal of the New Testament a man descends into the charities of social life, things do not seem changed in their position, but wonderfully beautified in their complexion; a diviner glow rests upon them and a holier sanctity. There is a change, but it is a change that adorns without disturbing. It is as if a man who had lived in a twilight world, where all was dimly revealed and coldly coloured, were suddenly to be surprised with the splendours of a summer noon. Objects would still remain, and relations be still unbroken; but new and lovely lights and shadowings would cover them: they would move in the same directions as before; but under an atmosphere impregnated with brighter hues, and rich with a light that streamed direct from heaven.

Now, as I have intimated, by what means could this high result have been attained with such force, directness, and certainty, as has been effected in the adoption by our God Himself of those very connexions? "By their fruits ye shall know them," was His own maxim, and He was willing to be its perfect illustration. How feeble was the commandment of the elder law, " Honour thy father and thy mother," compared with the tacit command and overwhelming inducement which the believing Christian recognises in the fact that God Incarnate Himself was obedient to His earthly mother, and voluntarily subject to even a reputed father! How stern the aspect of that precept which, under implied conditions of punishment, declares the inviolability of the marriage connexion, compared with the softening grace with which the presence of the Lord hallowed a poor man's marriage at Cana, and the consecration which, in adopting it as the emblem of His own immortal bridal with the Church of the redeemed,

He has for ever cast around the ceremonial of a Christian union!.. Yes, it has been said that the burial of Christ has sanctified the grave; it may as truly be said that the life of Christ has sanctified all the relations of human existence. If in passing through the grave, on His return to the throne of heaven, He left there the odour of His transitory presence, as truly has He, in passing, whether literally or spiritually, through all the holiest connexions of the human heart, left in them an ineffable sanctity, recast them under holier auspices, baptized them with (as it were) the very "waters of life," and regenerated them into the types and symbols of immortality!... If *we* were to conceive a God upon earth, we would surround Him with that which seemed to *us* the most to befit His presence, as the most to declare His attributes. *We* would enshroud Him in the lightnings of the skies, and make Him speak in its thunders: if He descended at all to the level of humanity, it should be in the state and equipage of a monarch; He should move encompassed by an imperial retinue,—the angel-warriors of heaven; and His very favours should be distributed with that sovereign goodness in which the *sovereignty* is at least as clearly manifested as the goodness, and he who receives is made to feel that he is indeed a receiver. But when God would indeed be man,—when, having of old "seen that all was good," He now saw that *almost* all was evil, and would once more behold it as He made it, when this high resolve of Heaven was indeed to be realized,—He looked abroad to see what in humanity was worthiest His assumption. The splendours of an earthly, a *provincial* monarchy could not attract Him who was familiar with the dignities of an adoring universe. But there *was* that which even He could regard with approbation. From *that* store He selected His human attributes; in *that* dress He invested His earthly nature: *that* was the true mantle of His royalty. The love of the son to the parent which He exemplified; the love of the brother to his brethren which He felt;

the love of the husband to the wife which He approved and typified: these were the elements of humanity which their Creator did not think unworthy of acceptance; and to display which, in the long course of daily life, He selected a position among the varieties of human existence in which, apart from every shade or colouring of interest or ambition, they alone, in truth, purity, and fervour, might be simply and unaffectedly exhibited. And to those who can read His divine story as it ought to be read, not even when He shall come hereafter in the "glory yet to be revealed," surrounded by all those beings of light whose very light shall be but the reflection of *His* radiance,—not when the whole elemental system shall, as we are led to believe, by some unimagined process, "dissolve with fervent heat" before the terrors of His presence,—not even *then* shall a more celestial glory rest upon His form, than when, "a first-born infant" in the arms of His spotless mother, He was laid, amid her tears, in that wretched hovel, assumed the feebleness of infancy, and the tender subjection of childhood; and in showing us, by His own inestimable example, what sinless man should be, left us every pure affection unbroken, and only fastened their ties more permanently by linking them all in one blessed bond to the love of God made visible in Him!

So far, then, you can perceive a strong reason for the manner of Christ's incarnation,—for His advent among us in the simplicity of our ordinary manhood. You can perceive that it conferred an inexpressible dignity upon the relation, above all others, of the mother and the child: and I would add that of His design to exalt this as well as the other natural relations, to make them high and sacred elements in the religion He was about to establish, a most lovely proof is insinuated in the constant employment of all these connexions and feelings to symbolize the eternal realities of the spiritual world. We may easily believe that, for such a purpose, only those elements of earth would be adopted which possessed a kind of natural holiness, preparing them to be the types of these celestial connexions. *Love* itself, in all its forms, would seem to be the type or image of some still diviner affection of which man is susceptible towards God; so that the earthly exercise of this (and similar) virtuous emotions, might be a kind of preparatory discipline for, (at least a shadowing forth of,) that future exhaustion of the whole soul upon the supreme excellence of God manifest in Christ, in which it is, over and over again, intimated that the perfection of celestial blessedness consists. To some such training of the heart St. John would appear to refer in those well-known words, " He that loveth not *his brother* whom he hath seen, *how can he love God* whom he hath not seen?" ... And, in intimating the nature of these eternal relationships, I have sometimes thought it observable, that the very connexions peculiarly insisted on by Christ, were those in which He Himself was *not* pleased temporally to manifest Himself upon earth. The relation of *fatherly affection*, in which (as displayed to man) His divinity unites Him with His own divine Parent, is one of these. "The sons and daughters of the Lord Almighty" is (as you know) a peculiar title of the faithful of Christ. But a still more constant and emphatic instance of the principle is the relationship of husband and wife as applied to the everlasting union of Christ and His Church; on which I need scarcely dwell, as you must be aware that through every part of the prophecies, through remarkable parables, detached expressions, and even miracles of Christ Himself, and through the apostolic Epistles, this remarkable figure is employed. Does not this lavish use, as applied to the redeemed, of the very titles which, in any literal sense, He rejected, seem as if the Blessed One, while here on earth, had purposely withdrawn Himself from these peculiar connexions, in order the more completely to concentrate the undivided affections of His human nature upon His redeemed followers for all eternity? And it is remarkable that while *He* rejected this literal union upon earth, His followers, to whom it is permitted upon earth in His absence, are to be without it in heaven, where it is expressly affirmed that "there is neither marrying nor giving in marriage," but where it is also declared that " the marriage supper of *the Lamb* is prepared, and His wife hath made herself ready!" ... There *is*, then, there is in the world to come a state of being which shall display to man the realities among whose shadows he is here and now a wanderer; there *is* something which shall not deceive, which shall not disappoint, which shall not disappear; something which shall meet the full impulses of the human affections, shall raise them, by raising their objects, shall give them a sacredness such as even in their present beauty (and it is great) they cannot dare to claim: there *is* an object for whom we are made, and out of whom we cannot rest; who is the secret want of our hearts even when we go astray from Him; and whom we desire when we know it not!

If Christ, then, sanctified some of our affections in this world by assuming them, He still more gloriously exalted others by making them the representations of the attachments of mortality. On *this* occasion you are addressed in reference to that peculiar condition of human nature which forms the common basis of all the subsequent relations of life; and surely I do not err in believing that the Christian, thus appealed to, will feel a new claim upon him, in considering that *he* manifests respect for what Christ respected, that *he* assists those to whose peculiar circumstances God Himself, when He adopted our nature, was pleased to add inconceivable dignity, in allowing that nature, though miraculously formed, to be nevertheless not formed as Adam was formed, but, in the language of the Sacred Record, " made of a woman."

Yes; the passage before us speaks of *her:* it speaks not merely of the " first-born," but of her who bore Him, and whose mysterious agonies were unsupported by the aids of wealth and the appliances of luxury; who was rejected when she would have given to the immortal Infant the common comforts of that trying hour; and who had to place among the beasts of the field, less insensate than man, the "life of the world" thus cast forth to die!

But what was this but the echo of a distant prophecy heard across four thousand years? As in Adam all died, so in Christ were all to be made alive; and as in Eve was the occasion of the fall, so in a daughter of Eve was the occasion of the salvation. The "seed of the woman," destined to "bruise the head" of the mystical serpent, promised so long, was at length upon the earth; the powers of hell trembled at that little sufferer ill-protected from the inclement winds by one poor Jewish maid; and the angels of heaven pealed forth songs of rapturous exultation over Him who was rejected at His birth, as He was rejected in His life, rejected in His death,—as He is at this hour rejected by those who call upon His name but have never imbibed His love, by them (beloved!) who with a Bethlehemite spirit, and with hearts closed to the distresses of sisters, in that fearful trial, cannot pity the sorrows of those who are weeping as His mother wept.

But we will not dread from a gospel pulpit to speak of *her* as she deserves. The melancholy perversion of the faith, which has since so largely afflicted the Church of Christ, has ascribed to that "blessed among women" distinctions scarcely less than divine. But let not this re-act to tempt us to refuse the promised tribute of honour to her whom "all generations" were "to call blessed." Identified, as we are, with our divine Master, it is impossible not to receive into peculiar and holy intimacy that honoured being to whom the Son of God was so long subject, and whose will (within due limitations) He was so long pleased to make His own. The adoring disciple of Christ, whose imagination finds its happiest exercise among the sacred abodes of Nazareth, learns to love almost as a parent her whom Jesus loved as such; and joins in spirit that sainted disciple whom Christ made, as it were, His inheritor in filial affection (" Woman, behold *thy son!*") and who, commissioned by the dying Redeemer, bore the maiden-mother to his own home.... How wondrous, how unfelt before or since, the communion of that mother and that Son! With the full remembrance of His supernatural descent, to sit at the same daily table for all those long and untold years that preceded the public ministry of the Great Prophet; to tender all those thousand gentle offices of life, which a mother alone can know, to a divine Child; to recognise in Him at once the babe of her bosom and the God of her immortality; to catch, ever and anon, those mystic echoes of eternity which the deeper tones of His converse would reveal, and to behold, plainer and plainer as He grew, the lineaments of the God impressed upon the wondrous inmate of her humble home,—glimpses of the heaven that was within, traces of the language of the skies, (she still, with that serene observance which seems to have been her special character, " keeping all these sayings and pondering them in her heart;") surely, *these* were experiences to dignify that mother in our thoughts; yea, to give a glory and a hallowing to maternity itself for ever.

One point, above all others, added a peculiar interest to that wondrous connexion. The Virgin and her Son stood *alone* in the world! alone, in the long line of the human race! He with whom she was so awfully, yet endearingly connected, could acknowledge no earthly father, no author of His humanity, but that overshadowing Spirit by whose mysterious operation He had been invested with our nature. " She brought forth her first-born Son," and, as though she were a widowed mother, none stood by who could soothe her sorrows and share her love for the new-born infant with the anxious sympathies of a father.... I know with what virulence this divine mystery has been of late assailed. I am aware of the unceasing efforts of what is ostentatiously called Unitarian Christianity to undermine the scriptural proofs of a fact to which (as you all are aware) the Record bears such evidence that it can only be questioned by questioning the genuineness of the Record itself; and which is, in point of reason and the nature of the case, manifestly required in consistency with the whole purpose of the advent and the atonement of Christ. To enter into such discussions is not my object now. Though, it is true, the great fact in the text, and the natural connexions of the object on which I have been commissioned to address you, might warrant them, I would be unwilling to trespass on what is, after all, the more special theme of another and greater festival; even if my time permitted these minuter inquiries. It may suffice to say that, on an occasion like this, I cannot venture to detain you beyond a very limited time; and yet, *shall* I pass the subject without a word? To oppose the uniform belief of the Church, (which, indeed, has rather inclined to exaggerate than to depreciate the dignity of the virgin-mother,) to oppose the unequivocal testimony of Scripture, there seems to be (except the utterly unsuccessful attempt to discredit the genuineness of the narration) but one universal objection,—the same to this as to all other doctrines that transcend ordinary experience,—that the thing is an incomprehensible "mystery." The Church is in this holy season peculiarly busied with her mysteries; I cannot, then, but pause, while speaking of the great mystery declared in the text, to ask, are we, indeed, the fools these men would paint us to believe such? *They* would have a Christianity purged of mysteries, or none; a Christianity without trinity of persons, or duality of natures, or miraculous conception, or atoning redemption, or sanctifying Spirit; and all these exclusions equally, because they are mysteries. They are told that the object of this religion is to bring together earth and heaven,—a world which we know little with a world of which we know nothing; and they expect to have the details of such a conjunction level to their capacities. They are told that God has interfered with the fortunes of man; and they expect the mighty transaction to proceed as simply as an ordinary treaty of peace. They admit that God has condescended to enlighten His creatures; yet they are obstinate in refusing to take anything from Him on trust. They concede that the preliminaries of ages were not considered too much to herald the advent of this great epoch; that that "day," seen through the vista of two thousand years, was enough to make glad the heart of one patriarch,—nay, that the patriarch of the human race himself was permitted to see in it the source of all his consolation; that a polity, singular in the history of the world, was for centuries maintained for the sole purpose of evidencing, and illustrating, and preparing it; that miracles and prodigies, each enough to make the foundation of a separate system, were, aggregated together, only worthy to be the faint precursors of this Master Wonder; that figures, each worthy alone to occupy the full breadth and height of an ordinary painting, were only the accessories of the mighty and prominent form of that mystic Being who fills the foreground of the Christian picture: and yet, admitting all, or nearly all, this; obliged to confess that, explain it as we may, the whole subject comes to us from on high and clothed in the light of other worlds, these objectors,—though drenched in mysteries, when they come to the scriptural testimonies to the miraculous conception, and personal dignity, and mystical offices, of Christ, —suddenly assume the utmost minuteness of sceptical caution; set to work every refinement of criticism to extort inanity out of expressions the most positive and unequivocal; stamp folly on the Old Testament in order to rationalize the New; contend implicitly (in this endeavour to *unmiracle* the advent and the person of Christ) that the vast organization of Judaism was, after all, a preparation in which nothing was prepared, a porch without an edifice, a cypher without a solution: in short, after groping through a labyrinth of preliminary mystery, refuse to acknowledge *that* mystery which alone can make all the rest cease to be such.

But you, my friends, I trust, have not " so learned Christ"

or Christ's Gospel. You are willing to concede to your adorable Master that dignity which really exalts our nature by exalting His: you are willing to admit that He, and she who bore the hallowed title of His earthly mother, were connected in ties such as they alone have ever held : you are willing to acknowledge that in that awful hour of Bethlehem there must have mingled with the sorrows of the outcast virgin the trembling joys of one who knew herself the supernatural channel of the Hope of the human race ; and that, though she might own to the feebleness of the woman in that hour of trial, and deplore amid the unworthy accompaniments of such a scene that " low estate " of " the handmaid of the Lord" which had reduced her to them, yet that, as she gazed upon that eternal Child in whom was bound the regeneration of Israel, of the world, " her soul *could* magnify the Lord," " and her spirit rejoice in *God her Saviour!*"

If you can indeed reflect those feelings, and sympathise with that blessed mother in her fears, her hopes, her joys, your hearts are attuned as I would have them: and your thoughts from her sorrows will descend without difficulty to those sorrows, which are like hers in their agony, but not like hers in their consolations. The terrible decree, " In sorrow shalt thou bring forth," might be considered in some degree alleviated or counterbalanced in her case, by the high consciousness of a supernatural destiny and the confidence of divine protection it naturally included. But there are those around you, and among you, who have no such internal restoratives. There are those who, with all the physical terrors that in all ranks belong to such a period, labour under the additional horrors of a poverty far deeper than that which afflicted the mother of the Lord of life ; those to whom the shed at Bethlehem,—miserable as it was,—would at least afford an undisturbed retreat, would offer shelter from the wind and rain. But God alone, and those whom, as missionaries of charity, the benevolent purposes of this or similar institutions conduct into the darker retreats of destitution in this city, know what is the real extent of human wretchedness around us,—to what unutterable depths human life may sink, and yet exist! Crowds immured in a single house, separated, —and scarcely separated,—by crumbling walls and floors; not one of whom can perhaps count with certainty upon the food of a single day; creatures whom misery has almost deprived of the feelings of that common nature which seems to have deserted them as outcasts. To this condition the perpetual fluctuations of trade will often in a week reduce men, who still are prevented from common mendicancy, by lingering feelings of independence; who, though they cannot "dig," are still "to beg ashamed." But, in such a crisis, a *man* can still make head against utter despair; though the cheek be wan with hunger, and the limbs feeble, and the heart sick with that sickness which no medicine can heal, and the demon be at hand to whisper crime, yet the energies of a man are not to be crushed by a blow, there is a faint vitality in the darkest misery, that, till nature fails, preserves a spark of hope. But when, to that sex whose delicate organization is always more susceptible of impressions, the terrors accede of an hour which even the best aids of prosperity are weak to lighten; when in the midst of cold and starvation, and the multiplied forms of misery, the heart-broken mother knows that the time is come when she is to add a new victim to the mass of wretchedness around her; and when amidst the distraction of the scene, the noise, the discomfort, those "pangs of a woman in travail" become hers which have been employed by blessed lips to express the extremity of human anguish, —what a situation is hers! how she learns that there *can* be a misery more deplorable than poverty, more acute than hunger!.. When the blessed Virgin brought forth in poverty, "she brought forth her *first-born* Son;" but, oh! with the majority of these whom you are called upon to aid, how different is the case! Surrounded by the previous heirs of poverty, the miserable mother, in these gloomy abodes of destitution, has the embittering feeling that, to a family already outgrowing the means of subsistence, she is adding a new, unwelcome claimant; and in the dark, perverted, feelings of want (which so disnatures man!) who can doubt that, to her anguish, is often added the bitter sarcasm of the wretched husband, or the still more wretched children, who murmur that the fraction of food should be still diminished to provide for the wants of a stranger! . . . Brethren, how *can* I think of such scenes as these, and not recal the difference of position in which the same trial finds those whom Providence, of its free mercy, has placed in your *rank* of society, and gifted with your command of resources? It is true, *no* earthly power can rob that agony of its sting; the primal curse made no distinction of classes; and God fixed that terrible transmission of punishment on grounds too radical and permanent to admit of evasion by human skill. But to the lady of affluence, who reclines in the midst of a silence which even the stealthy tread of the attendant fears to break; whose slumbers are encouraged by all the soothing appliances of medicine, and before whose muffled doors the very streets are carpeted lest they should ruffle her repose; to her, above all, whose languid eyes, when they do unclose, rest upon those who, undisturbed by the contracting calculations of poverty, are ready to make every conceivable sacrifice to buy her a single hour of peace, and whose affection, always earnest, is quickened in intensity, and attempered to a more refined delicacy of attention, by the circumstances in which she is placed,—to *her* the terrible trial, when it does come, at least comes lightened of all its external terrors, and alleviated by the very consciousness of the love it calls into action. I would not claim,—it is not the will of the great Author of rank and subordination,—that comforts so high and peculiar as these should be the comforts of all; but I *would* claim, that the common necessaries of life's most trying hour,—the few days of undisturbed repose, and the ordinary aids of medical science,—should be unprovided to none. I *would* claim, that the offices of this most benevolent charity,—whose sphere is a population of 70,000 human beings (for *all* are equally interested in a mother's health), occupying nine entire parishes, the poorest in your city,— should be aided in their work of mercy; that, after alleviating the sufferings of 1,570 of our poor sisters during the five years of its existence, it should not now be enfeebled in its resources. Notwithstanding every effort of economy, the poverty of the district so often demanded its aids, that, although sacrifices most creditable were made by the medical officers, the debt of the institution is now considerable. This *might* have been evaded by the cold severity of determined rejection; it might have been evaded by turning away the eyes from the misery that surrounded them; by hearing without pity the shrieks of the destitute, and resolutely suppressing the compassion which even the practised experience of the physician cannot help feeling, at some of the forms of human woe; had *this* been done, you might have been spared this appeal, but would you have it so? Conceive, then, that you are each of you tendering your relief to that individual case whose expenses your contribution will enable the institution to defray. Imagine that you *see* the misery, which, whether you see it or not, is truly around you. Mothers! remember your own hour of peril, and sympathise with your sisters in sorrow! Fathers! remember *your* anxieties, your fears, your hopes! and think of those who can rival you in anxiety and fear; but who have no "*hopes*" but those which this day is to bring them. But why do I delay upon these lesser claims? *Christians*, of whatever sex, or class, or calling, remember *her* who was agonized as these wretched mothers were and are agonized; her who bore her "First-born" as the poor bear theirs, and thus for ever dignified maternal destitution: remember Him, who even in infancy " had not where to lay His head," and to whom no retreat like *this* was open; but who, assuredly, when that great day comes, at which we shall all meet again, and when the love to the disciple is accepted (He has promised it!) as love to *Himself*, will not forget that *peculiar* form of charity, which, along with all its other claims, may recal to His divine remembrance, the weeping mother of Bethlehem, and that Infant who was "laid in the manger, because there was no room for them at the inn!"

SERMON XIX.

DANGER OF BACKSLIDING.

(Preached at St. Anne's Church, Dawson Street, July 2, 1837.)

REVELATION II. 4.

Nevertheless I have somewhat against thee, because thou hast left thy first love.

WHETHER the exhortations contained in the second and third chapters of the Apocalypse were primarily directed to the *Churches themselves* which are there specified, or to the *presiding bishops exclusively*, who are in each case entitled the "angels" of the respective communities, is a point which has occasioned much discussion. Perhaps the truth may lie in a medium between both. On the one hand, there can be no doubt that the title "angels" *is* intended for the superintending ministers of these Churches; the metaphor (from the heavenly to the earthly ministers of God) is itself natural; and the application is confirmed in this instance by the general consent of the ancient Church. On the other hand, there are expressions in the exhortations themselves which seem to overpass an individual application; and the Spirit seems to make constant transitions from the condition of the minister to the condition of the flock, or rather (perhaps I might say) to identify the fortunes of both, and interweave together the contemplation of their destinies.

In the sentence I have read, this doubleness of application is certainly both possible and instructive. Every one knows —too many by melancholy experience—what it is to abandon the "first love" of the adoring Spirit; what it is to have known the bliss of entire communion with a heavenly Parent, awful as God, but tender, too, as man; to have withdrawn the heart from everything transient and perishable to fix it in undoubting faith upon the Immutable and Eternal; to have felt in the very novelty and wonder of the emotion a proud confidence that it could never pass away; and yet to have known it pass away gradually but utterly, the world again insensibly returning, the poisonous waters again filling every one of their old channels, the chain again tightening round the heart, and the emancipated freedman of God once more lying down in contented slavery. There are those, the great Teacher has declared, who "hear the word, and anon *with joy* receive it; yet have no root in themselves, but endure only for a while." With such cases we are all familiar; they are the standard subjects of the unhappy mockeries of infidelity; as if our divine Master had not with a pencil of light drawn the portrait of such, and forewarned us that these things were to be.

Now, as the application to the individual is but too clear and justifiable, so is the application to the general body of the Church, or of Churches, fraught with terrors scarcely less impressive. And it is in this point of view that I mean this day to consider the case. I do so, brethren, in direct reference to the peculiar occasion on which I have been requested to address you. The work which I am to ask you to promote, is a work which eminently recals us to the principles and the obligations of our Church Union; which sinks the individual in the community; and which I will not stoop to asking you to further on any grounds but those of that sacred tie that binds you in the unity of the Body of Christ with any the humblest baptized believer. I ask you to support and shelter these fatherless little ones, *not* merely because you are individual believers in Christ, and thence bound to works of mercy, but because of a relation above and beyond this,— because no believer (if I might so speak) *is* individual; his individuality is merged in his membership; he is one of many, of many who are one. I would recal to you those enormous obligations, so often disguised or forgotten, which in God's sight you owe to that holy Catholic Church, in the most favoured division of which you are born, to its laws, to its ministers, to its members,—yea, to the humblest and weakest infant that has ever been borne to its font, and baptized, as you were, into the Father, the Son, and the Holy Ghost.

The passage before us supplies a ready, God grant it may be a profitable, opportunity for the application I propose.

What an example of the melancholy frailty of human nature is presented in the fortunes of these famous Churches of the Apocalypse! Planted by apostles, nurtured with the blood of martyrs, animated by the effusion of the Spirit in miracle and prophecy, ministered to by the most conspicuous saints of the first age of Christianity as their bishops and pastors, constantly visited by the inspired messengers of God, and (as here) admonished in express terms of the consequences of a lapse, and stimulated to persevere, they, nevertheless, yielded to the seductions of the enemy of their peace, gradually lost every remnant of primitive purity, and, deserving the threatened vengeance of God, were left to so utter a desolation, that for many an age not one hymn of praise has been heard within those walls which St. John and St. Paul hallowed by their presence and their prayers. A few poor relics of ancient sanctity still lie scattered among some of them, but relics that only the more sadly attest desolation. Remembrances of former glory have excited the piety of some of the modern residents to attempt to erect churches and gather congregations; to renew in the seats of these ancient communities of holiness a faint image of that fervent and willing activity which in elder times distinguished them; but such efforts, few and desultory, have not gone near to remove the heavy cloud which divine justice has cast upon these once favoured localities.

"Their glory has passed away." The services of an antichristian imposture—of Mohammedanism—have invaded the very soil upon which the sacred buildings rose; and the ground where Christ was once so ardently worshipped, the very materials of which His temples were formed, are now desecrated to the gross superstitions of a lying and sensual creed.

Among all these Churches thus living in the light of God's peculiar mercies, perhaps none was so eminently favoured as the Church to which the reproof of the text was addressed. *Ephesus* is a distinguished name in apostolic history. In St. Paul's second missionary voyage we find him engaged there, strenuously "reasoning with the Jews," upon whom the efficacy of his labours appears to have been attested by their earnest requests that he should "tarry with them." Some time after (at an early period in his third voyage) he arrives again at this great metropolis, and the whole of the 19th chapter of the Acts is taken up with the history of this visit. You remember that it was on this occasion that the great Apostle baptized in the name of the Lord Jesus, and gifted with the Holy Ghost those disciples of John, who till then "had not so much as heard whether there be any Holy Ghost;" that it was on this occasion that for three months he spake boldly in the synagogue, and afterwards, when assailed by enemies to the doctrine of the Cross, disputed daily in the house of a private disciple,—continuing for two whole years to preach, so as that all Asia "heard the word of the Lord Jesus." You remember that this Ephesian visit was accompanied by "special miracles" of the most striking kind; that it was here and now that the evil spirit was permitted to overcome the presumptuous sons of Sceva; and that it was here that God also manifested the mercies of His good Spirit in converting to the way of truth numbers, who (among other depravities) devoted to the miserable impostures of divination, at length "burning their books before all men," learned to seek for truth in the holier divining books of those prophets who had foretokened the coming of the Redeemer. Finally, you remember that it was here that avarice befriended idolatry; and that, in vindicating the honour of Diana of the Ephesians, the "craft in danger of being set at nought" was (as often since) made the adversary of Christian truth. A great Church had, however, by this time been erected, and in the following chapter, Ephesus is again strikingly introduced to our notice. I need not remind you of that pathetic charge which Paul at Miletus addressed to the elders of this Ephesian Church; how he tells them to "take heed to themselves and to all the flock over the which the Holy Ghost hath made them overseers, to feed the Church of God which He hath purchased with His blood;" or how, with melancholy prophecy, he warned them that "after his departing grievous wolves would enter in among them, not sparing the flock." Too truly has the terrible prediction been realized. But a more glorious page belongs still to Ephesus. To *this* Church, yet in its primitive bloom, was addressed that Epistle which of all the writings of its author contains the fullest and deepest revelation of the Christian mysteries, an Epistle in which the writer seems animated by a peculiar and unwonted energy of inspiration, and which, it is obvious to any reader of its congratulations and encouragements, could scarcely have been addressed but to those who had already enjoyed the richest treasures of grace. The Apostle does not command them, but confers with them; he places them on his own level in Christian attainments, and rejoices with them in a common salvation. He does not so much speak *to* them, as speak *on behalf of himself and them*. If he declares "*we* have obtained an inheritance," and "*we* should be to the praise of His glory who first trusted,"—he adds, "in whom *ye* also trusted;" if, reversing the order, he reminds them "*ye* walked according to the course of this world," he takes care with deep humility to add "among whom *also we all* had our conversation." I need not enlarge upon this characteristic of the Epistle to the Ephesians; which you can easily establish for yourselves, and which cannot be easily established by anything but personal investigation. You will find that, all through this noble display of gospel truth, the writer addresses his correspondents as those who had been elevated into a participation of the mysteries he described; as those to whom specific moral commands were less necessary than exhortations to the continued and increased cultivation of the Spirit that animates and vivifies them; in short, as those who might expect, by perseverance in prayer, that "being rooted and grounded in love," they "might be able to comprehend with all saints what is the breadth, and length, and depth, and height; and to know the love of Christ which passeth knowledge!" These were attainments too high for *novices!* No beginner in the school of the Spirit could dare to hope for a learning in the things of God so vast, so comprehensive, and so profound, as this.

Such, brethren, was the Church of Ephesus in its primitive years. No cloud rests upon the mirror which these earliest records present of its primal purity. Our Christian contemplations may dwell upon it as a holy association of ardent yet patient children of God; a paradise in which Satan might indeed lurk, (for he lurks wherever there are human hearts,) but in which, as yet, he could not dare to ravage or destroy. Though alone and discountenanced in the midst of a profligate and idolatrous metropolis, doubtless they were deeply and truly happy! At peace with themselves, and loving, with the unmeasured affection of Christians, all around them, the terrors of the stake and the lions could not ruffle the bright tranquillity of that peace and love. The glory of the inward light spread on all that circled them, and as it fell upon their afflictions, turned them to a joy better than this world's most seductive pleasures can bring. Despised, stricken, oppressed, calumniated, they smiled upon the tormentors, and praised God in the midst of the torment: for the holy ardours of the "first love" could to the triumphant spirit overbear the flames of martyrdom. And surely it was a singular testimony to the omnipotence of the Spirit of grace, that in the very capital of Eastern idolatry—in the place where Satan had set up the most superb of his idol-temples, in order to blind men to the truth that God "dwelleth not in temples made with hands;" even *here* arose, perhaps, the noblest and purest of all the early Churches, flourishing uncontaminated, in the midst of corruption and vice. Alas! Churches, like individuals, may mourn over the lovely recollections of childhood. The freshness of early spring belongs to the history of both alike. Each has its period of unforgotten innocence. The fervency that glories in opposition, the kindling enthusiasm that consumes before it every paltry and unworthy feeling— these are the characteristics of the youth of Churches, no less than of their individual members.... And even as a man overworn by the cares and perplexities of busy age, often gladly reverts to the uncorrupted hours of his dawning life, to their happy confidence, their guiltless desires, their boundless hope, so may the advanced age of Churches; so may *we*, brethren, who in our day forget our God and neglect His word, turn back an eye of sorrowful remembrance to those times yet glowing on the page of history, when *our* Church, though cradled in the furnace of persecution, seemed, as it were, to borrow from the furnace its fire, and like that flame, rising as it kindled, to struggle still upwards to heaven.

The *first* scene in the history of the Church of Ephesus is closed. It leaves a solemn and deep impression of unmingled happiness. Christianity is seen in action; faith in the Lord Jesus, *working by love*. No rude dissensions disturb the beautiful calm of hope and peace; heaven is reflected upon earth; and the angels of God, as they pass and repass on their missions of mercy, acknowledge that their own holy societies can scarcely surpass the blessed communion of regenerated human hearts.

The *next* scene opens in the passage from which the words of the text are derived. That passage is the last notice of happy and favoured Ephesus, contained in the Scriptures of the New Testament. A mighty censor had been among its congregations. John, who had resided for years as superintendent of the Asiatic Churches, and whose affectionate heart had been deeply interested in their welfare,—now an exile in a lonely Grecian island, banished, as he expresses it, " for the word of God and for the testimony of Jesus Christ," transmits to the growing Church at Ephesus the admonitions of the Spirit of Truth. Yes; the man to whose unsealed eyes the Lord Jesus Himself was revealed in His glory as He had formerly been in His humiliation, the man who became the organ of prescience to the whole Church of Christ, till time shall be no more, he, thus honoured and exalted of Heaven, was at this hour a banished exile under the proscription of all earthly authority. Who can but pause upon such a contrast? The mighty of this world laid their interdict upon the humble Christian teacher, they cast him out of their coasts, and refused him all but the existence which they did not leave his brethren long; but they could not debar him the society of God Himself! Truly, the inspired exile *could* endure their frown, when the Lord of the whole universe *smiled* upon him; truly, he *could* bear the absence or the discountenance of the haughty nobles of Asia or of Rome, when the hierarchy of heaven were with him in his wilderness!

Such an inspector as this was not likely to overlook the traces of corruption or decay in the congregations of Ephesus. He had been too familiar with infinite Purity to lightly brook even the earliest rudiments of evil. But a mightier voice than *his* spoke in the message to the Church of Ephesus. " He that holdeth the seven stars in His right hand" addresses it in this solemn exhortation. In its tenor we can but too plainly perceive, that a declension *had been* detected in the community once so humbly resolute in its holiness. The

Ephesian converts were still, indeed, a noble body. Would that our existing Churches reached the height of even *their failure!* But the seeds of ruin were sown for a future development. These Christians could still withstand the terrors of persecution by the might of prayer; but the prayers were less frequent and less ardent, and the world had stolen in between them and their God. Hear, then, what the Spirit saith unto the ruler of this Church, and in him, doubtless, to this Church itself,— " I know thy works, and thy labour, and thy patience, and how thou canst not bear them which are evil: ... and hast borne, and hast patience, and for my name's sake hast laboured, and hast not fainted. Nevertheless I have somewhat against thee, *because thou hast left thy first love.* Remember, therefore, from whence thou art fallen, and repent, and do the first works; or else I will come unto thee quickly, and will remove thy candlestick out of his place."

The remaining history of the Church of Ephesus is not written in the Scriptures of God; it is to be collected from the uninspired records of the time. From these we learn that St. John himself resided there till the close of his long life; and taught his lessons of love to the last. For many succeeding years it existed in the mixed condition of good and evil which our modern Churches exemplify. The great martyr Ignatius, on his road to martyrdom, addressed it with affectionate zeal; and bore testimony to its (as yet) continued holiness. At the close of the second century it was still the head of Asiatic Christianity, and, under its venerable bishop, feared not to question even the growing sovereignty of the Church of Rome. But it is needless to extend the inquiry. I must not pause to analyse its ruin. A darker season came on the Church of Ephesus. It decayed with the general decay of vital godliness; and it at length attracted the threatened vengeance of its neglected Master. What then?—does history bear out the fulfilment of the divine menace? I will not tell you to ask the question *now* among the ruins of Ephesus

Many ages since you might have asked, whether the lightnings of divine wrath had stricken that ill-fated city and its Church; with the Book of the Revelation in your right hand, you might have entered the site of its streets and interrogated the city which was the light and glory of Asia, whether the vengeance of God is indeed inevitable in its visitation of sinners; and the melancholy echoes from fragments of the desecrated sanctuaries and fallen temples of a lost Christianity alone would have answered your question with a terrible affirmative!

Now, brethren, with such an example as this before you,—with such an example written in the Scriptures of God and in those pages of authentic history which are, as it were, the Scriptures of His general Providence, I ask you, is it not wise to pause upon the awful tale, and question ourselves, how far it is applicable to our own condition, and what lessons as to the dispensations of Providence it presses upon our thoughts? I am not about to attempt extracting remote and novel conclusions from the facts of this striking case; let me but assist your minds to travel in the natural course of simple and unlaboured meditation.

In the first place, then, does it not forcibly remind you, that the Providence of God oversees with special care the fortunes of *Churches* no less than those of individuals; that Christians are regarded by their Master in their collective capacity; that He delights not more in the growth of the separate plant than in the growth of the *garden and the grove?* Brethren, I cannot impress this point too forcibly upon your recollections. Churches, visible and regulated Churches, even more than scattered instances of individual piety, are the great objects of divine favour, if we may trust the records of the New Testament. The spirit so prevalent in our day, of regarding individuals wholly apart from their place in *a Church or communion of Christians*, really finds no support whatever from the documents of our faith. I need not tell you in how many cases the Apostles address themselves to the communities, and

not to the single members; and how by every variety of
argument and illustration they impress the necessity of those
subordinations and dependencies which constitute the distinctive features of Churches. Nowhere are individuals addressed
in a way that would separate them from some organized
association of believers. None of that abstracted and independent piety which connects itself with no visible system of
ecclesiastical governance, none of that unregulated religionism
which holds itself at liberty to join with any party of worshippers just as caprice or convenience may dictate, is recognised in the ordinances either of Christ Himself or of His
commissioners, the Apostles. In the passage before us and its
context, we have the Churches brought under view wholly
irrespective of particular individuals, they are themselves individualised as the direct objects of divine superintendence;
and all the attributes of distinct personal existence are conferred upon these aggregates of Christian men. So certain is
the fact, that, as from the beginning Christ knew *who* were to
be "His own" in a special sense, whom "the Father had
given to Him;" so, from the beginning He also purposed and
ordained the existence of a visible republic of His professing
people. The eternal God consecrates the principle of order in
making His own earthly kingdom a system of order. There is,
as I believe, no more doubt that Christ meant that a temple
should rise on earth, external in its construction and visible to
all mankind, and enlarging perpetually with new fronts and
new chambers, than that He also, from the first, fixed the omniscient eye of His love and approval upon those special portions
of the structure which were durable enough to last for all
eternity, those separate pillars which were afterwards to be
made "pillars in the temple of his God." The visible Church
of Christ, the Church Catholic,—including all who in united
worship call upon the name of the Lord, and even in frailty
attempt to follow His laws, is the framework and mould for
that perfect Church of the latter day, which is to be formed

of devoted hearts alone. In the days of primitive purity and persecution, the visible Church and the " invisible Church " coincided in extent, they were pressed into one by the weight of persecution; we know too well that they have since occupied a widely different compass; but assuredly we are not therefore justified in casting away the exterior frame of the visible kingdom of Christ. Brethren, it exists with a view *to the future!*—to that time when every outward believer shall be a believer in heart, and when once more, as at first, (and perhaps through the same instrumentality of persecution,) the visible Church and the body of real believers shall coincide, to separate no more. But even then, that Church of perfect holiness shall be not the supplantation of the present, but its continuance. It will be that same body, in perfect health and with every particle renewed to a firmer substance, which is now existing in weakness and difficulty; but the body will, though changed in every particle, still preserve its organic identity. There will be the same form and structure of the temple, but its pillars will then be based upon every continent of the earth, and its dome will reach to heaven! I cannot, before leaving this part of the subject, avoid remarking how complete a contradiction this whole context presents to the mistaken enthusiasm of some of the honest but most deceived advocates of what is called " close communion in the Church" in our own day. Those who would eject from their meetings every one of whose personal character they were not previously satisfied, and who refuse to meet at the table of the Lord such communicants as our Church gladly welcomes there, seem most strangely to forget the spirit of our Lord's injunctions through St. John. The whole tenor of these messages is to preach not expulsion but repentance. If Ephesus have failed, it is told—not *to cast out the feeble*, but universally, the evildoers and all—*to "repent."* If Thyatira have been guilty of the grossest crime, it is said to the criminals, not at all that they should abandon their place in the worship and offices of the Church, but that they should "repent of their deeds." Sardis, again, is almost wholly lost; it is said to be "*dead;*" righteous only in "a few names:" yet are these few commanded to congregate in solitude and exclude the rest? No such thing. The Church at Sardis is still considered as composed of the entire mass of good and evil, and warned to "remember," to "hold fast," to "repent." It is obvious in this case that if Christ considered all the Church annihilated except the "few names that had not defiled their garments," there could be no room for telling the Church to repent lest eventually ruin should fall upon it. And so of all the rest. They are all evidently considered as mingled masses, as not the less real Churches on that account; but, on the contrary, as passing through a course of discipline which supposes a variety of stages of good and evil, without once losing during the whole trial either the character of a Church or the right to each of the members of membership and communion.

On the whole, I would recal to you, my brethren, that the portion of Scripture before us, implies and enforces the great principle of *Church unity* in evincing that God directly oversees the destinies of Churches, that He addresses them as individual beings, and that while (as in the case of *Sardis* just quoted) He *selects* from among them to "walk with Him in white" the "names that have not defiled their garments," He yet regards them also in *the mass*, and as a mass or aggregate, exhorts, or threatens, or punishes, or rewards them.

But, dear brethren, this passage of the Word of Truth suggests reflections still more touching than any general exhibition of the divine will as to the formation or government of Churches. It reminds us that these Churches, however beautified by early piety, may by degrees sink from the glories of their first estate, and deserve and experience the vengeance of God. Brethren, I cannot address you as a Church, but I can address you as the *members* of a Church. Would to heaven that I could adequately press upon you the duty that in such a position devolves upon every one of you! Will you suffer that Church into which you have been baptized, to come under these terrible condemnations of the Invisible Ruler of *all* Churches? Inasmuch as each of you neglects the worship, or despises the ordinances, of God, so far does he aid the fall of the Christian communion to which he belongs, and add to his own loss the crime of injuring the holy influences of the entire Church of Christ. We cannot stand alone in irreligion. Man extends the image of his vice far beyond the sphere of his personal presence. The example of crime multiplies itself; and the folly of a careless hour may produce in endless succession (and, if you weigh the point, *does produce*) a perpetual generation of increasing sin, that gathers on from age to age, till a single being becomes literally the ancestor of the guilt and punishment of an infinite multitude and an eternal duration. Oh, brethren, do I overcharge the matter when I press upon you the enormous extent of your responsibility towards the Christians who join with you in worship and praise? Remember that if example be powerful for evil, it is also powerful for good; and that the same principle which may make each of you the parent of an infinite succession of guilt, may also make you the source of never-ending blessings. I know not a consideration which ought more deeply to stir the heart of every Christian brother than this extension of his capacities of beneficence to people and ages that he has never beheld or even imagined in the warmest dreams of hope, and the glorious reflection that all this long posterity of virtues, whose existence was primarily traceable to his example, will one day, doubtless, be set before him, as the crown and reward of his labours! It is most true and consoling, to remember that great examples of our faith are *sown* in the various ages of earthly time, to germinate from century to century unto a thousandfold produce, and extend branches into eternity itself. Every action that we perform in presence of others, every word that we speak, is in some measure creating our own likeness around us. Shall it be for good or evil? The happiness or sorrow of an undying soul will one day answer the question to every one of us.

Surely, brethren, you can plainly see why it is that in the present case I feel it so pre-eminently necessary to remind you of your *personal influences*. You are members of a Church rich in great examples, and you are called upon in your turn to requite it the service it has done you in affording them. In being members of the Church of England, you are introduced to the noblest association that man, under God's guidance, ever constructed. If you deem that at this age the warmth of *its* " first love," like that of Ephesus, is indeed abated,—what is *your* duty? To rekindle the flame in your own hearts, and by the fervour of your example and your teaching to spread and support it. Believe the experience of all ages, that the truest way to aid the cause of religion is *to be religious!*

Brethren, were I to ask you to point out the probable causes of the declension of the Church whose history has engaged us this day, what could you name but the very characteristics which are prevalent among *ourselves?* Putting aside all merely external influences, what trait of guilt could be cited which our own sad experience cannot parallel? Alas! if the mercy of the Most High had not been eminently exerted to preserve among us the light of early truth, would not our negligence have ere now merited its extinction? If wandering and unfrequent prayers, if frigid and heartless services, if a surrender to casual conveniences of man's loyalty to God, if *these* were the ruin of Ephesus, its ruin may *yet* not be alone in the world! Our reformed Church's "*first love*" carried it unscathed through the fires of an almost unexampled persecution, (for Christians have improved in the science of persecution upon their heathen masters!)—could *we now* endure the terrors of another such trial? " Another *such* trial," did I say? Can we endure for the sake of Him who bled for our salvation, to surrender even the least of the superfluities of life? Can we sacrifice even trifles for Him who sacrificed *Himself* for us?... Brethren, I say, beware lest the Church whose cause you desert, be left to perish in the desertion. In the admonitory instance before us this day, you saw how God avenges His justice upon Churches. If ours—in its forms the purest existing depository of scriptural truth—be still to flourish, still destined to accompany and illumine the future history of our country, secure to yourselves the glory of being among those for whose sake the Lord Jesus loves to strengthen and support it; if (which Heaven avert!) it be doomed to fall, (in dread requital for the sins of the people it vainly strives to govern,) *be your hands guiltless of its ruin!*

SERMON XX.

THE WORD OF GOD.

(Preached at St. Stephen's, Mount Street, June 18, 1837.)

Luke V. 1.

The people pressed upon Him to hear the Word of God.

I suppose, my brethren, there are few present who cannot even, as I have read them, make the personal and practical application of these words. When the members of the clause are separately regarded, that is, when it is considered, that the "*people*" in question were a portion of that ancient people of God, which had been so often illustrated by His favours, but which, at the period here noted, had, by a miserable progress in degeneracy, become even a more hard and heartless generation than ever their fathers had been; that this people, thus mighty in recollections, thus debased in actual habits, are said to have "*pressed*" on the great Teacher, to hear His exhortation,—the Author of the scriptural promises thus becoming their Interpreter; and that that which they heard was the "*Word of God;*" it requires but little exercise in the reflective reading of revealed truth, to call to mind the corresponding circumstances of OUR PRESENT STATE. The self-love which makes us continually apply to ourselves what we read of the advantages or the misfortunes of others, should not be permitted to slumber where it is most required. And it is no unwarrantable demand on your powers of meditation, to ask you to remember, what is the character (or the diversities of character) of the "*people*" who are listeners of *our* day; with what degree of energy they "*press*" to listen; and what, or how great, ought to be the practical effect upon our minds of that most providential preservation of the Sacred Records, which allows us at this hour, after the changes and chances of so many centuries, to read and hear in substance the same "*Word of God*," which these men of Galilee pressed to hear.

Such inquiries as these, brethren, are pre-eminently important in the days upon which we are cast; days in which, by an overweening and injudicious zeal for the authority of the visible Church of Christ, attempts so formidable and so seductive have been made to depreciate the supremacy of the Word of God as the sole external organ of certainty in divine knowledge: I say that it is necessary that it should be fully perceived, that (whatever may be our visionary speculations as to what God *ought* to have done) He *has not* seen fit to present to man any assured guidance beyond the recorded inspirations of His evangelists and apostles; and that we should be evermore reminded that the presumptuous body which undertook to assume the place of that supreme authority, proved by its wretched self-contradictions and its still more wretched moral failures (springing directly from its position), that it had assumed a height never meant for man, that humanity is not formed to breathe in such an atmosphere of exalted power, and that confusion and perplexity are the vengeance of God upon those who dare to challenge His attribute of omniscience. *Such* are the fundamental convictions with regard to the great theoretical question of the "Word of God." And whatever may be the progress of opposing views, we are not without some striking practical developments of our convictions. Wherever we would spread our faith, we come armed with the sole authority it recognises. And surely this *is* an æra diffusive of Christianity. The missionary societies of Britain have reached its antipodes. Every month ships, freighted with the materials of illumination and happiness, leave our ports. The sun, which never sets upon the territories of Britain, is but a type of that sun of brighter beam, which she seems determined shall be as extended in its radiancy. And what is the watchword of all these legions of Gospel colonizers? The Bible, and it alone! "We ask no more," they cry, "than the records of John, and Paul, and the rest of their band, to follow up their work, and plant Churches, as they did, through every part of the unbaptized world." . . . And yet, brethren, with all this brilliant activity, with all this confident assertion of our sole dependence on the Bible, are we quite sure of our own condition with regard to the use of this revelation? While we preach to others, are we quite safe from being ourselves castaways? Are our sole energies to be emissive and external; and are we, after all, destined to be like that sun of which I just spoke, which is the source of light and heat to the whole world around, but is said to be itself internally a dark, and dull, and frigid mass? What matters it that the Word of God should be elucidated with comments, and flattered with praises, and multiplied among the heathen, if it be not laid to heart by those who explain, and praise, and disseminate it? what matters it (except to *increase* his condemnation) if he who (in the Apostle's metaphor) beholds his "natural face" in this perfect mirror of the human heart, " beholdeth himself, and goeth his way, and straightway forgetteth what manner of man he was?"

We are not, then, brethren, shrouding ourselves in convictions of personal or national excellency, (for a man's national pride is often only his diffused selfishness,) to blame the preacher who, going back to the very elements of duty, would enforce on you the need of individually applying to the study of the truth. Alas! it is the melancholy identity of human nature in every age, that has made the business of your preachers, from whatever quarter this comes, still unchangeable. Would to God that the time were come, when our sermons of appeal, and censure, and exhortation, shall be all but unintelligible! when the path of perfection shall be so universally trodden, that men will not be able even to *understand* the perversity that could seek any other! In this *present* mingled state, however, when our forgetfulness makes a constant appeal to first principles needful, we have but to adore the merciful providence of God which has made the most necessary truths always the simplest to learn.

Regard, then, as the text naturally directs you, the "*Word of God*," that is now preached,—the existing *urgency* to hear it,—and the "*people*" who are its favoured (and too often its forgetful) hearers. . . . Consider the Word of God, its origin, progress, and arrival among us.

By the wisdom of a God who works the interests of the universe on a scale of policy proportionately vast, we are placed here, brethren, in a position which it would be madness to deny, *is* a very dark and mysterious one. He can have, indeed, very little knowledge of himself who can regard himself without wonder and curiosity. Around us is mystery, and within us is mystery; and there really is not a single branch of knowledge of which the most accomplished thinker may not say, as Paul said of the subject of his teaching, that it is the "wisdom of God in a mystery." So limited are our faculties, that we cannot conclude the ultimate reason of any one thing we see; and our highest exercise of philosophy goes not beyond superficial analogies, and resemblances, and consequences; but, *to the full reason of nothing*. The unbeliever may chafe at the mysteries of faith; I beseech him but to remember the mysteries of *reason*. . . . In the midst of all this uncertainty and limitation, and while man, who could be content to be ignorant of all things else, is miserable not to know himself, his nature, or his destinies, a slender thread of light pierces our obscurity. At various periods, at one period especially, of the history of our world, that which reason might have conjectured, but could never confidently calculate, took place, and a communication, amazing in all its particulars, *was* effected between us and the world above or beyond us. By what causes these communications were regulated, why till then delayed, or why then given, no human mind is competent to determine: suffice it to say,—we are made to believe testimony, and we know by unanswerable testimony, that the communications took place,—that the shroud was for a moment withdrawn, that the cloud was rent, and the secrets of eternity lightened upon our eyes. When the great Consummator of these communications, the One to whom it appears they had all been subservient, passed away, the cloud again closed, and since that day we have been left without further guidance at once immediate and visible. But though this be so,—though our immediate guidance is not a visible one, and our visible guide is not an immediate one, —yet the promise then given has not been broken; and the God of miracle fulfils His engagement as the God of providence. Means were employed, — means both natural and supernatural,—to cherish and preserve upon earth, in the chosen vessels of grace, the blessed light thus mysteriously bestowed. The history of these means is the history of the Church of Christ.

Among these means, if not the most important and remarkable (for to *the teaching of the Spirit* of God must ever belong the highest title), at least the most easily traceable in its history and fortunes, is that which, in obedience to its own authority, we term the " Word of God,"—that revelation of the divine will preached by our Lord to the Jews, and to us, through the exceeding riches of divine mercy, ever since preserved. In preserving this, however, there have been no miraculous interpositions, no "wonders in heaven above, and signs in the earth beneath," little which we cannot trace to the ordinary laws of nature and of human motives. But the object (even *we* can see) was too mighty a one, not to make it a prominent consideration in the divine counsels. Providence has been invisibly regulating all, with a governing power, only the more wondrous in its perfect secrecy. The machine of the universe is so known to its Creator, that He does not require to interfere with the mechanism for His own purposes; He only interferes when interference is requisite in order to summon our attention. Through the divine control, which, inscrutably operative, supports the Church as it supports all things; nay, supports all things in subserviency to the Church; (for as the dead unorganized world is maintained with a view to the vegetable world, and the vegetable with a view to the animal world, and the animal with a view to the intellectual world, and the intellectual with a view to the moral, so the moral world itself exists with a view to that spiritual state, between which and the Spirit that gives it, even angels are not worthy to be the interval!) I say, then, *through this divine control*, that book which is the book of our hope, and faith, and consolation, has been preserved to our age and country. How strange, how providential has been its history! and how deep ought to be our attachment to a book so mercifully made our inheritance! From the Churches of the primitive times it passed (as ecclesiastical tyranny grew strong and would not brook a collateral authority) to the seclusion of monasteries, for many a long and barren century; but God was with it through the darkness, and He brought it forth in His own good time; it was like those seeds of which naturalists tell us, that lie for ages dormant and unfruitful in cells beneath the earth, but whose *vitality has never been lost*, and which, when brought upon the surface, shoot up with vigour into all the beauty of luxuriant vegetation. Such has been the story of the written Word of God; and if we would but remember what that volume contains,—if we would but lay it to our inmost meditation, that that book holds within its leaves the only authentic record that, from one end of the earth to the other, exists, of the will and purpose of the Being with whose will and purpose we are to be concerned for all eternity; I do not say that we would adore or consecrate the volume, but I *do* say, that not a sabbath, not *a day*, would pass from us without bearing its burthen of prayer and thanksgiving to that God, who, while myriads sit in the shadow of death, has, in His special favour, given to us that commandment which is " pure, enlightening the eyes." " The entrance of Thy words," cries David in a holy ecstasy, " giveth light; it giveth understanding to the simple. I opened my mouth and panted: for I longed for Thy commandments." (Psalm cxix. 130, 131.) Oh, Christians, shall we who live after the Advent of the Redeemer, and beneath the full effluence of the Spirit, the Comforter, be outdone in fervent desires by him, who, however blest, could only in prophecy look for the future and distant appearing of his Saviour?

But men have said—you are fortunate if you have not in this day, and among professing Protestants, heard men say,— nay, brethren, we are fortunate if the infidelity of *our own* hearts have not often prompted to us to urge some objection of the kind—that it is scarcely conceivable that in *this way*, through the medium of a volume formed like every other volume, through written characters and ordinary study, we should have to learn the eternal truth of heaven: that it is hard to believe, that matters which concern the interests of an eternal existence should be acquired in the same way, and suspended upon the same outward chances, as any common detail of temporary knowledge. These things are wonderful to those who forget that all things are wonderful:—above all, who forget that the matter of their objection is the greatest glory of the wisdom of God, inasmuch as His highest providence is evinced not in the sudden emergencies of miracle, but in governing the whole tendency of human affairs so as by means of every one of them (and, as it were, in spite of every one of them) to bring about His sovereign intent. How do we answer these objections? We answer them by appealing to *facts*. If the fact be, that the truth has actually been preserved in all its integrity in this way, and been made beneficial to thousands, who will be extravagant enough to impugn the mode of communication because it is not a visibly miraculous one? . . . But it will be urged, as I have more than once heard it urged, If the truths of our salvation were taught us, not thus through a book and through its human preachers, but through some direct interposition of Heaven, man would be roused to exertion, God would be honoured, and His standard would be followed by many more than these thousands. Perhaps so! but who taught the objector that it was God's secret purpose that there *should* be more? The same line of argument would go to object to the course of Providence because *all* are not believers, it would object to everything which could endanger the chances of happiness to every man; that is, it would end in objecting to a system of probation of any kind, on which all religion proceeds, and thus would modestly terminate in objecting to religion its *very existence!* Is it necessary to answer such wild and guilty extravagance? Far better and more profitable is it, to observe by what external machinery our heavenly Ruler preserved His truth in preserving the "volume of the Book," through all ages of its history; so that amid all the tempests of a thousand revolutions this ark of our salvation rode ever on the surface of the waters. The diffusion of His own truth was not forgotten by the great Dispenser of all, when He taught their beautiful art to the first inventors of printing. For what is every branch of discovery but *the teaching of God?* Is it not *He* who instructs the astronomer to develop His disposing wisdom in tracing the courses of the stars? Is it not *He* who sits by the chymist when he detects the exquisite organization of the smallest masses? Is it not the same God who guides the intellect of the physiologist to find in his own frame those traces of wonderful design which prove the Deity that formed it? Every mind that discovers is but a pupil of the Infinite Mind! And that views of the future spread of His kingdom were before the Deity when He permitted us to possess that invaluable art which multiplies our thoughts, and His thoughts, through every clime, it is surely no presumption to infer. ... But, brethren, a weightier personal reflection belongs to the subject. The truth of God is deposited in *a Book;* and that Book is deposited in *every form among us.* Benevolence, both public and private, has spread the Bible of God amidst our people: oh, may that benevolence, generous to all others, be not found cruel to itself alone. May those who spurn as an abomination the thought of denying the Bible to the poor, beware how they deny it to *themselves!* Whatever be the ultimate purpose of God as respects the heathen, one thing is certain,—every man to whom the providence of God has sent the Scriptures or its preachers, is, in that very act, offered salvation, and amenable, if he reject it, to all the guilt of *deliberate* rejection. It is terrible to think what is the responsibility of entering a Christian Church! By that single act the complexion of an eternity is altered. The savage of the Pacific may plead ignorance before the bar of God, and a God of mercy may perhaps not consider the plea *wholly* inadmissible. But from him who has ever heard the offer of the Gospel, all excuse is from that hour cut off. I know not, if at this moment such a being may be in this assembly. *I* cannot read your hearts. Perhaps, even as I speak, there may be one, two, three, whose hearts are newly touched with a conviction of the terrible importance of the eternal world; one or two, from whose souls the shroud that hides infinity is withdrawn,—to whose spirit the gloomy abyss of everlasting ruin is unfolded! Perhaps to such the Lord has even now come near, and, in the unutterable language of His Spirit, warned them of the wrath to come. Before God, I know not whether I should wish it! I know not whether the ministers of Christ ought to wish always for success. " Woe is unto me if I preach not the Gospel!" but woe is also unto those who hear and will not heed, who are called and will not come, whom the Spirit of God is assailing with terrors and inducements, and who, after a moment's passing compunction, return to the world the children of a deeper ruin, the heirs of a more aggravated condemnation! Alas, our Lord said of the hypocrites of His day, that they made converts who were more thoroughly the children of hell for their conversion! is it not terrible that in *our* day the consequences of exercising the Christian ministry should often be as awful? I repeat it; by being this evening within this house of God, there is not one among us who has not come under an obligation, or *strengthened* an obligation, that cannot be cancelled for eternity. The *mere opportunity* is a new "talent," of which our Master will demand the use. The man who has once heard the Word stands for evermore on a new level. He has incurred new duties and new responsibilities. The very offer is his unutterable and eternal happiness, or a ruin such as no words can speak, or, thanks to Heaven, no mind (as yet) conceive by its earthly experience! "This day is salvation come to this house," said Christ when He became a guest in the house of Zaccheus; we have houses in which the offer of salvation is daily made, and in which Christ is evermore ready to be a spiritual guest; but where are the Zaccheuses that are willing to entertain Him?

Such, brethren, is the "Word of God;" such the heavy responsibility imposed upon those who, out of the millions of mankind, are permitted to be its hearers. The text tells you, that the people "*pressed*" to listen to the gracious words of Christ. It tells us little of their motives. But we may easily conjecture them. Admiration at the wonderful Teacher, amazement at His miracles, curiosity as to the end and object of His discourse,—all these feelings must have attached them to the speaker. Those who now take up the gospel story have little but the last to count on. It is not unlikely, however, that better principles were not wanting to this Galilean audience, if we may judge from the readiness with which Jesus yielded to their wishes; when, sitting in Simon's boat, majestically humble, He taught the crowd from that lowly pulpit. Neither the discourse which He delivered on this occasion, nor the result of it, is preserved. Whether new subjects were gathered to the kingdom of heaven, or additional guilt heaped on its despisers, we know not, any more than the ministers of the Gospel can know, when they imitate their Lord in discharging a similar office. But the God incarnate was not without an attentive audience. Doubtless, the Angels of heaven were gathered round to listen to those words which men neglected; and the choir of heaven was stilled, to hear those truths whose repetition many men can barely be brought to tolerate for an hour in each successive week!

Yet, my brethren, those of our time, too, can "*press* to hear the Word of God." If crowded churches were a certain test of thriving Christianity, our age might claim a high place in religious history. If earnest conversation and constant activity were the true and only development of the gospel spirit, the golden visions of prophecy would no longer be visions; our Millennium would even now be at hand! .... These things, brethren, have their value; but beware how they absorb you! It is no new device of Satan to make religion itself withdraw men from God. Of diffusive religion we have abundance; a concentrative Christianity is what we require. And, believe it, to "commune with our own hearts, and be still," is the finest preparative for external usefulness. He who would spring far, retreats first. There is a deep purport in that expression of St. James—" the fruit of righteousness is sown in peace."

We were lastly, brethren, to consider *the* "*people*" that press to hear; that is, *the characters* of those, who, in our time, are the readers and hearers of Scripture truth. This, indeed, is a topic which, it is evident, must necessarily mingle with every part of the subject; nor have I attempted to regard it altogether *apart from* the rest. Nevertheless, I *have* reserved its *more particular* consideration to a special space; because I am anxious, before we separate, to bring before you, in their respective colours, and with direct reference to their religious attainments as to personal spiritual happiness, the two great classes that practise the perusal of the "Word of God."

I beg of you, then, to remember, that there are two ways in which the revelation of the will of God through Christ may be presented to our minds. We may know it as a mass of doctrines and commands offered to our acceptance as beings possessed of reasonable faculties, and demanding from our understandings a simple assent to their truth; and we may know it in such a sense and degree, as that it becomes the pervading principle of all our actions, and the presiding director of our inmost thoughts; the soul of our souls; the fountain of our moral being; the central force of the whole system of life and conduct. We may know the religion of Christ just as we know the cotemporary history of the time in which He appeared, (a schoolboy-lesson whose principal facts we take care to master, that we may not appear ignorant of that which all men have learned;) that is, we may know Christ exactly as we know Pilate who crucified Him, or Tiberius in whose reign the event took place, with as little love for Christ, as little of confidence in Christ, as little of brotherly charity generated by the Spirit of Christ, as we have of love, of faith, or of charity, in contemplating the history of His enemies and murderers. We may read that New Testament which contains the account of a virtue, the bare conception of which no human intellect ever attained, or could attain, before the appearance of its divine Hero; and we may read that well-known volume of cotemporary annals which, in tracing the lineaments of Tiberius, draws a portrait of vice and misery, such as no human record antecedent to its publication, it is thought, can parallel; and we may lay down both volumes, presenting as they do an account of the Glory of all ages and the disgrace of his own, with equal fulness of intellectual assent, with equal (though opposite) degrees of languid moral emotion, and with equal, that is, with entire, absence of all resulting influence whatever upon our present daily course of life. Brethren, I appeal to your own experience, do I overstate the fact? and if it be (as is most certain) the truth of the case in innumerable instances, what shall I say, but that the existence of such inconceivable obduracy in so many cases, where every opportunity has been offered by Providence for kindling this dead inoperative acquaintance with Scripture into a real, vital, spiritual, practical knowledge and appreciation of God, stands as an appalling proof of the mystic depths of human corruption, and of the overwhelming necessity which exists of some extra-human aid which may counterwork this corruption by an operation as mysteriously profound, and pervading, and perpetual, as its own.

I pray God that I may be experimentally understood by many here present, when I reverse the picture, and declare, that if there be truth in the Scriptures of God, or in the history of His Church's saintly champions in every age, there is a knowledge of Christ as different from this miserable burthening of memory with names and dates and disputations, as the spring and spirit in the motions of a living body are from the shaking of the bones of a skeleton. The "new man which after God is created in righteousness and true holiness," obtains his newness of life by another process. Knowledge, indeed, he must possess; knowledge of the facts of the Christian story and the doctrines of its teachers—these are the bones and framework upon which the animated body of his holiness is based and built; and he who would contemn the most laborious exercise of our natural faculties in the pursuit of accuracy in the knowledge of the sacred record, forgets that our nature is made to reason and to know, as well as to feel and to aspire. But yet the feelings and the hopes are the noble portion—the portion prophetic of the future; and it is to these, accordingly, that Christianity mainly ministers.

He, then, who has found in his Bible the material for conversation, and the topic for discussion, and the field for criticism and controversy, but who has not found in it the unfathomable fountain of peace undisturbed, the solace for every earthly suffering, the silent but faithful friend, the glory that so dazzles the eyes with the brightness of the coming world, that, when they are turned from the page, they cannot *see* the misfortunes of this one,—he who has not found, in short, " righteousness, and peace, and joy in the Holy Ghost," ever inviting him within that volume,—though he may know the lore and the languages of antiquity, has yet to learn in the school of the Spirit. "The things of God knoweth no man, but the Spirit of God."

Now, brethren, to which of these classes does your acquaintance with the Word of God belong? No country on earth is more favoured than ours with opportunities of religious advancement. *It may not be long so. Few* men can dare to conjecture what may be its future destinies; *no* man can assure it a security in the continuance of its religious advantages,—unless, indeed, in those melancholy advantages which adversity may bring, when the God who will never forsake His Church may yet see fit to try it with persecution. The "refiner's fire" may be needed to purify it. I repeat, then, are you *even now* availing yourselves of the means which a pure scriptural Church affords you of scriptural enlightenment? Are you acting up to the position in which God has placed you in His Christian Church; and by which, from the pages of the Gospel, He will hereafter try you? Or are you poorly content with the cold ceremonial of Sabbath observances,—the religion of demure looks, and bended knees, and frigid regularity in services that have no life in them? Do you bring yourselves outwardly and visibly to these churches, but leave your hearts behind you as you enter; giving to God the weekly service of the lip, to man and man's devices the constant adoration of the soul? Think you that God made you to be religious *automatons?* Oh, brethren, beware (and by earnest prayer for God's Holy Spirit alone can you escape it)—beware of the Christianity of the *formalist!* The man who reads or hears this Word of God, unanimated by prayer, and untaught by the Spirit, is one who stands at the door of a temple he cannot enter; he holds the key of a treasury which he cannot unlock; he stands weak and thirsting beside a glorious and abounding torrent, which he cannot stoop to drink; or, like that infirm man who tarried so long by the pool of Bethesda, and had no one "to put him into the pool," on the very edge of which he lay diseased or dying. Oh, if any such be at this hour here present, may the Saviour Himself, looking upon *him* as He did upon that infirm one, say to him, "Rise, take up thy bed, and walk!" May he who thus lives in the midst of opportunities—in the very garden of the Holy Ghost's graces—be led once more to his Bible, and find the words that of old glided before his eye without leaving a trace on his spirit, impregnated now with a divinity better than that of school, or sect, or party,—the supernatural fervour and force which makes the "Word of God quick and powerful, and sharper than any two-edged sword!"

SERMON XXI.

THE CLAIMS OF SPIRITUAL DESTITUTION.

(Preached at St. Patrick's, Nov. 23, 1844, for the Additional Curates' Fund.)

2 CORINTHIANS X. 15, 16.

... Having hope, when your faith is increased, that we shall be enlarged by you, according to our rule abundantly, to preach the Gospel in the regions beyond you, and not to boast in another man's line of things, made ready to our hand.

IN all that concerns the diffusion of the Gospel, and the conduct of the ministerial office, one naturally turns, in the first instance, to the history of St. Paul; and still more to those wonderful letters of his, in which the high principles of the minister and the tender feelings of the man are so beautifully blended together, and portrayed with so subduing a power and impressiveness. Some of the excellences of these writings we may indeed owe, in no small degree, to the very fact that they *are* letters, and not—as some have vainly desired in their stead—grave didactic treatises on theological truths. There is a most observable wisdom in that arrangement of the revelation of God to man, by which so large and important a portion of its contents is conveyed in the peculiar form of Epistles—of Epistles, which, being the exact medium between the familiar flow of ordinary discourse and the methodical precision of the essay, may be said to unite all the characteristic advantages, and avoid the peculiar deficiences, of both. Christianity, eminently a practical institute, is taught by practical models; its blessed Founder's precepts live and move embodied in His life; His Apostles, like Himself, are not more the deliverers of doctrine than the earnest leaders of action. And, just that we may for ever know them as such, we have them with us, not merely in the historical portrait of a contemporary, nor yet in elaborate treatises of their own, where the distinctive personality of the writer might be almost wholly absorbed in his subject, but in letters, that spring out of action, and breathe its earnest spirit,—in letters, where the soul spontaneously paints its own glowing picture,—in letters the vivid, unconscious transcripts of the inmost heart.

Letters, too, will naturally enter upon *details*, to which systematic discourses can rarely descend. And though our blessed Lord's discourses were certainly not *systematic* expositions of truth, from them, also, the Apostolic Epistles—and eminently those of St. Paul—are in this respect remarkably distinguished. There is, in this point of view, a distinctive appropriateness in the styles of the Master and His disciples, which of itself forms no small internal evidence of the genuineness of both. The Lord usually delivers broad and comprehensive principles, and truths of universal application,—the profound parable, the pithy and almost proverbial maxim,—such as became the Founder and Legislator; the Apostles teach in more particular and special detail, as suited the practical appliers of His precepts. They explain, or direct, or predict detached instances, as those who are instructed by another; He proclaims from the beginning, in His comprehensive formulas, the whole operation of the Christian principles, as befitted the Author and Mechanist of the entire system: *they* are mainly busied with facts—He, with laws and relations; a difference so pervading at once and so refined, and corresponding so exactly to the respective capacity and dignity of the persons, as, I venture to say, no possible supposition but that of genuineness and reality can satisfy.

This close and intricate involution of the principles of Christian duty in the *facts* that embody them, may sometimes make it a matter of some difficulty to extract the whole amount of permanent instruction contained in a chapter or a passage of St. Paul; but, on the other hand, it makes the research always interesting, and it certainly often justifies applications and deductions which, at the first hasty glance, might seem not so much inferred as extorted from the text. The inspired Word of God bears the same relation to the happiest of human compositions, that His natural creations—His flowers of the field, His insects of the air—bear to our most exquisite mechanical textures; the increasing powers of the microscope but discover increasing beauties in the one, they but expose yet more and more the hidden defects and blemishes of the other.

It is not, however, any very forced or remote connexion, after all, that applies the passage before us, viewed together with some other notices that speedily follow it, of the Apostle's relation to the Corinthian Church, to the case of the Society whose interests have drawn us together this day. We are met to review, and to aid, the operations of an Association, whose object is to teach the various districts of the Church how to sympathise with each other's wants,—to make the preachers of Christ's Gospel, in the remotest regions of our land, the willing and happy debtors to Christian benevolence here. Now, the Apostle Paul was himself supported, during the period of his stay at Corinth, by the resources of a *distant* Church, as he is reluctantly obliged to remind the Corinthians in the next chapter, and the chapter following it,—a circumstance which, indeed, is latently present in the former of the verses under our consideration; for those who have studied the perfect courtesy of the Apostle's style, can scarcely doubt that he designs, in some measure, to compensate for this severe reflection on their liberality, when he there speaks of a support yet more precious and potent than their silver and gold,—of the increase of their "faith," as "abundantly enlarging" his powers of prosecuting the work of the Gospel; if not—as, indeed, it ought always to do—by direct contribution, (an application I might fairly make of the clause,) yet at least by spreading the influence, and facilitating the reception, of the truth. Again, his professed purpose in the second of these verses is, " to preach the Gospel in the regions *beyond* them ;" to carry the message of eternal life which he was commissioned to deliver, not merely to their city,—central, and wealthy, and politically important, like our own,—but to outlying districts, yet unvisited by the grace of God, but equally included in the ample terms of the apostolic mission. While, once more, in the next clause (as in the preceding context for two or three verses) is involved the important principle which directs the course of that preaching which Christian charity sustained; he had just said, that the range of his ministry was to be " enlarged " strictly according to his prescribed " canon," or definite district; he here adds, that he was resolute not " to boast in another man's," that is to say, he limited, not indeed the compass of his Christian love, but the exercise of his ministerial function, to a stated measure, " the measure," as he calls it a little before (ver. 13), " of the rule which God hath distributed to us ;" a principle in whose application Paul was guided by inspiration, we by settled ecclesiastical authority,—he as a missionary into new regions, we as helpers in the old; but which—except that, indeed, the latter consideration heightens the obligation—in itself is obviously unchanged from his day to ours, and the recognition of which forms one of the characteristic merits of the Society whose constitution and progress engage us on this occasion.

So that the passage—at least, when viewed under the light reflected from its context and the circumstances of its inspired writer—seems clearly enough to express, or to suggest, these three important principles: the great general duty of extending and maintaining the ministry of the Gospel *beyond* the more central, and prominent, and favoured districts of its domain; the blessedness of that charity which voluntarily supports a distant ministry, even while maintaining its own;

and the propriety of prosecuting the work in strict adherence to a settled distribution of ministerial labour, under prescribed authority, and especially—for on this the Apostle eminently insists—with a careful recognition of the rights of the ministry previously located in each district of the Church.

I. On the first of these great principles of divine guidance it can scarcely be necessary that I should very urgently insist. The spiritual claims of poor and remote districts are not only compatible with the acknowledgment of our own mercies, but they *grow* with it. As we are led more and more to appreciate the excellence of the truth that has brought light and joy and peace to ourselves, we *must* become proportionably alive to the misery of the want; so necessarily, indeed, that the one becomes the test and measure of the other; and we can as little imagine the consciousness of height without any conception of depth, as imagine the earnest reception of elevating truths in the heart and understanding of man without a corresponding sense of the deep and mournful destitution of those who are still sunk in the wretchedness of unenlightened, or almost unenlightened, nature. God, in His ordinary providence, has committed the fortunes of His truth in the world to the working of this diffusive principle. Commanding us to " preach the Gospel to every creature," He has provided that, in proportion as the preacher is by personal holiness qualified for his work, he should feel constrained to achieve it; that the duty should appear to grow in obligation exactly as the man grew in special fitness for discharging its requirements. But, beyond this principle, proceeding from the simple appreciation of the infinite value of the truth, we are to reflect, how—the progress and the triumph of the Gospel in the hearts of men standing, above all things, in the growth and the perfection of the principle of love—it becomes essential to its *thorough* reception, that its *universal* reception should be the object of desire; to observe and admire how the kingdom of Christ is thus maintained and diffused by the operation of the very principle it is itself constituted to maintain and to diffuse; how the Gospel thus possesses a self-supporting vitality, and the Church grows and gathers new elements into itself, like a living creature, by the natural and necessary working of the animating spirit that is within it. It is true that these principles apply to *all* missionary labour; souls are all equally capable of receiving the seed of immortal life; near or remote, as regards us, they are all equally near to the throne and to the heart of that God who fills the amplitude of immensity. But, undoubtedly, they also leave untouched that scale of comparative obligation, which, while it commends our own families, kindred, dependents, neighbours, to our first care, does also, by the very same principle, invest the spiritual poverty of the destitute districts of our own Church and country with a more urgent claim than any beyond their limits can plead. In *this* country it is indeed remarkable, that its most distant shores have of late been the very scenes of its highest religious interest; and we may, perhaps, venture to accept it as an indication that the spiritual life of our Church is still unimpaired when we find that its energies, far from needing to rally to the heart, are in full and vigorous action at its remotest extremities.

II. I pass to the second consideration presented in the text. I have spoken of the claims of poor and distant districts; I must now speak of the prompt beneficence that relieves them.

The Christians of Macedonia, like all other Churches of the time, were under a direct obligation to support their own ministry; that "deep poverty" which in this Epistle St. Paul expressly records, rendered this a task sufficiently onerous; but the sympathies of at least one principal society among them embraced the most distant of their Apostle's labours— he could not travel beyond the compass of their affection, nor the remoteness of the Churches to which he ministered, forfeit their claim on the beneficence of those their humble fellow-

Christians. Philippi is in one respect not the least remarkable spot in Europe; whatever amount of European conversions may have preceded the vision of the "man of Macedonia," Philippi was the scene on which the great teacher of the Gentiles first solemnly delivered the Gospel to that continent which has since been, with its adjacent islands, the grand theatre of the Church's history, and whose various races, gifted beyond all the tribes of mankind, have been manifestly designed by Providence to act as His chief instruments in evangelizing the whole earth. And the pre-eminence of its charity seems to have corresponded to the precedency of its faith; these poor and persecuted Philippians willingly constituted themselves the Apostle's treasurers; and whether he were in the course of travel, as at Corinth, or in prison, as at Rome, their beneficence found means to reach him. This was their liberality—often and earnestly acknowledged—to Paul himself. But when you remember that these same Churches of Macedon were likewise distinguished (in which indeed our Corinthians had also honourable share) for the promptitude of their ordinary charity to distant brethren; and that, of all the forms of charity, that would, in the estimate of men so devoted, rank the highest, which provides for famishing spirits the bread of eternal life,—you can scarcely doubt, that in this affectionate support of St. Paul himself, there was mingled a solicitude for the objects of his mission; that they helped him not merely as a beloved friend, but as that commissioned teacher from God, on whose maintenance in health, and energy, and resources, the immortal destinies of thousands were suspended. In supporting this distant minister, then, they knew themselves to be upholding the cause of the thousands to whom he ministered; in adding their voluntary taxation for the spiritual welfare of remote Churches to the maintenance of their own ordinary ministry, they become the appropriate example that directs, and that justifies, the operations of a Society such as yours. Into this particular branch of the subject I shall not further enter; as I learn that the force of this great and striking example has been already applied for your instruction; I doubt not, with a happiness of thought and clearness of expression, which I should probably do my own address to you little service by recalling to your remembrance. This, however, ought to be noted; that the cases are rare in which the Philippian example does not far transcend our copy. Obvious as the truth is, men require to be reminded that no one among us really contributes to the support of the ministry of his own parish, except as the channel through which an ancient endowment passes. The case, however, though rare, is not impossible. It must be remembered that it *is* competent for donors to this Society to dedicate their charity to their own district, *as well as* to the purposes of the general fund; and thus, to enable our opulent Christianity to present some adequate counterpart to the liberality of the poor Christians of Macedonia.

To demands like these men are often satisfied—for what sophistry cannot satisfy the reasoner who is willing to be deceived?—to allege the general plea, that the establishment of the Church in this country supersedes all fair claims on private charity for the support of additional clergy. They strangely forget that the establishment of the Church is just the reason why the demand may fairly be made; the reason— if it be fair to ask those at last to contribute, who have never yet been voluntarily, or even compulsorily, taxed for the support of the Gospel in the land,—for such is the meaning, and the operation, of an establishment;—the reason—if a great work begun and blessed with success becomes a fair argument for its own continuance; for what else is our establishment but the fruit of that same principle of voluntary charity which this Society is intended to elicit, and direct, and organize? The great mass of Church property is itself the product of charity, the permanent result of the love of souls and the love of God. Cathedrals, hospitals, educational institutions, parochial endowments are but visible memorials of ancient liberality; the established is, in a great measure, only the voluntary fixed and protected by law. Surely it would be difficult to match the perversity, which not only forgets the beauty and power of the example, but actually converts it into an argument against itself; nay, which not only thus erects the very monuments of ancient charity into the fortresses of modern avarice, but actually deludes men into imagining that they are themselves the contributors of the wealth which was inalienably conferred by a charity older than the oldest of their title-deeds.

There is, then, no reason why the principle of charitable establishment, of endowment for the ministers of religion, should be arrested in its course at *this* period any more than in its earlier ages; unless all the wants have been supplied which it was designed to meet, or unless we are miserably resolute to show that a pure religion cannot do what was done in days of scantier light. Religious establishments may tend, as they accumulate, to suspend the impulses of charity to men's souls, as a poor law may tend to supersede, and by disuse to paralyse, the impulses of charity to their bodies; both are tendencies which require, in those who will train their hearts in the loving spirit of heaven, to be vigilantly guarded against; and the wants and the calls of a Society like this may afford an useful supplemental discipline in one of these departments for those who would escape the peril.

Still, men are so powerfully impressed with the conviction of the enormous and superfluous wealth of this establishment of *ours*, that they are strongly disposed to maintain their principle as at least specifically applicable to us, however fallacious it may be in the abstract. We cannot, indeed, wonder at the extent of this illusion, when we remember the perseverance of falsehood with which it has been sustained; and when we reflect how much more the majority of mankind are led by repeated assertion than by any one distinct or definable evidence,—even as reiterated strokes from light and worthless substances, so they be but tough and durable, may at last effect an impression as deep as the single collision of a weighty mass. This is not the time, nor this pulpit perhaps the place, for any minute or extended statement of matters of ecclesiastical finance; but a fact or two may be commended to your consideration;—and those will judge, whether the wealth of the Church establishment of Ireland places it wholly beyond the need of voluntary aids, who are informed, or reminded, that nearly one-third of the benefices of our Church are under —many much under—one hundred and fifty pounds per annum; that much more than half of the entire fall below three hundred pounds per annum; that the average income of an Irish beneficiary, the income to provide for the wants of a household, the pressing demands of charity, the necessary expenses of a prominent local position to even the most economical, is just two hundred and twenty-five pounds, or, including assistant clergymen, the average for each member of our profession, one hundred and seventy pounds a year. In times when the warfare against Church property often only disguises a real hostility to the settled establishment of property of all kinds, it may be no material step in the argument to state, that the annual income of a single great proprietor, in the sister country, is estimated at a sum little, if at all, below the entire annual revenue of all the beneficed clergy of Ireland.

But it is still urged, that, even conceding the fact of this humble average provision for our parish ministers, the wealthy laity of our land are not called upon to supply the wants of its crowded, or its destitute, parishes, because that the property is *ill-distributed;* and that by a careful and judicious redistribution it might be so apportioned, in the ratio of population, as to relieve them of the intrusive claims of those isolated and unprovided congregations which you are endeavouring to supply. Of course, this form of objection totally discards the claims of our Church to be in truth and in God's high estimate,—and in our hope, which, however faint, we dare not wholly resign,—the rightful Church of the entire nation; a question of deep interest, on which I have, however, no time now to enter, and which, perhaps, it will be vain even to expect to impress upon the public mind, until the arm of our God shall raise up among us *men* who will, in the earnest spirit of missionaries, endeavour to verify it. But, meeting the objection on lower ground, it ought to be observed, in the first place, that it proceeds upon a very inaccurate estimate of the relative amount of labour required in our parishes, which, in a scattered Church population, is never in the exact ratio of numbers. This, however, it will be said, may be adjusted and allowed for. But how can men speak of a change like this, interfering, both through patronage and even through actual impropriate possession, with the rights and property of individuals, through all the upper classes of society, as of a matter in which practice can be made rapidly, or in any assignable period, to follow upon the calculations of theory? or how could any property be held secure in the operation, and in the certain influences, of such a revolution? Even supposing it feasible, it is quite evident that it must (on the principles confessed by even those most ardent in favour of such alterations of the property of corporate institutions) be *gradual*, and dependent on the successive deaths of existing incumbents. But, in the *meanwhile*, have the souls of men no claim upon the hearts of brother-men? are the enterprises of charity to pause before the vague possibilities of some future arrangement of parochial endowments? will nature suspend her curse, and man cease to die into ruin or into glory, until a theory is realized? The present alone is ours, the moral "evil" of our own "day" is a "sufficient" allotment for itself, and, God, He knows! a sufficient burden of responsibility for us who have to meet and to resist it! But observe, once more, how unsatisfactory, because how perpetually recurrent, is this pretext for delay. Population is liable to perpetual change; the past will repeat itself in the future; the variations of commerce, the irregular tide of emigration, will again alter the territorial distribution of our people; and the plea of disproportionate endowment, that now soothes the willing conscience of the Church layman, is likely to be plausible enough for that purpose, for ever.

III. So far for the claims of the distant and the spiritually destitute to the charity of their more favoured brethren; so far, too, for the objections one sometimes hears to the attempt of your Society to relieve them. I would I had more time than I can now venture to demand, for the other topic on which St. Paul so earnestly insists; the prosecution of this work of the ministry in adherence to the settled distribution of districts, and with careful recognition of the claims of his predecessors in each field of labour. It is certain that he regarded this matter as of high importance. "We will not," saith he, "boast of things without our measure, but according to the measure of the rule which God hath distributed to us." "We stretch not ourselves beyond our measure." "Not boasting of things without our measure, that is, of other men's labours." "Not to boast in another man's line of things made ready to our hand." Or, as he expresses it elsewhere, (Rom. xv. 20,) avoiding to "build on another man's foundation." It is impossible not to admit this to be of real consequence, when we perceive how anxiously and repeatedly he impressed it. Inspiration and experience combined to press its importance on St. Paul; nor are we wise if we hesitate to hear and obey his judgment. Your Society, by placing its ministers at the disposal of the Church, and, more especially, in subordination to the appointed pastors of each parochial district, has fully acknowledged the Apostle's principle of missions and ministry. You have thereby avoided what, doubtless, he sought to avoid; the possible interruption of harmony between ministers and people; the interruption, scarcely less pernicious, of the habitual convictions of the people themselves; evils, which greater evils may sometimes possibly justify, but which it is surely better to avoid, wherever the great object of all our ministrations can be otherwise as efficiently, nay, *more* efficiently obtained. For nothing *can* equal the value of the permanent ministry, as the Apostles themselves everywhere acknowledged by rapidly constituting it in all the Churches they created; the *acquaintance* it alone gives with the heart and habits of each of the people, and, what is perhaps still more important, the sense of a definite *responsibility* which the *fixed and settled* charge of souls alone can ever fully impress on him who is appointed to tend them. Transitory visits have their occasional use; God, I doubt not, has often blessed them to glorious results; they may awaken interest, and at times startle the worldly dreamer from his visions; but *he* knows little of the nature of man who can imagine that it is thus souls are really saved for heaven; that anything but care and patience, quiet and unremitting watchfulness, will ever be adequate; and oh, how little can we count on the adequacy of even this, to keep the wayward hearts of men steady on the path to life eternal!

St. Paul was guided by inspired communications to that " canon " which defined his movements; we, in this, as in all other matters of the kind, have the ordinary constitution of the Church to control us, instead of the extraordinary guidance of the Spirit; permanent *canons*, to adopt the Apostle's term, instead of occasional suggestions; but both, in their respective ways, rightfully demanding our obedient acquiescence. This Society gladly blends itself with the constitution, and the action, and the fortunes of the Church to which it ministers; and I should do little justice to either its claims or my own convictions, if I did not impress upon you the importance of thus, as it exemplifies, incorporating all the religious institutions of a country with the fixed pre-existing system of the Church itself; making them, as far as may be, sharers in its vitality, and coheritors of its blessing. Take the matter on the lowest statement, and shall we not fairly affirm, that, in whatever degree that system is beyond others, accordant with the mind of Christ, in the same degree may those supplemental institutions which are grafted into its stock expect to meet His special acceptance? they are not venturously aspiring after new favours, but humble candidates for old and established blessings; they have an implicit promise of vigour and permanence in being made sharers of a system which is, in its essential elements, by God's own promise, immortal. And thus ought *all* those institutions whose object is the eternal welfare of man,—institutions educational for the young, or (as this) educational for the adult too,—as far as may be possible to gather into and under the great central Institute of Christ Himself; they should stand, to borrow an image from the scene around me, something as those minor chapels and oratories that cluster round our great cathedrals, sheltered beneath the same roof, resting on the same consecrated ground, and partaking of the sanctity of the whole structure. In each department of its agency, the faithful and earnest development of the system, will, I doubt not, attest its divine constitution by its success; for I can discover no period in which it has not already done so. Wherever there has been failure in the operations of the Church, the failure is easily traceable to some ambitious human substitution for its primitive simplicity; whether in the direction of that formalism which oppresses the animating spirit, or of that spiritualism which despises the organizing form. Of this period of our Church history, a period so critically interesting in every respect, so charged with mysterious, with fearful, uncertainty in some, it is at least the unquestionable praise, that it has recognised this principle in one important field of labour and of duty. After two hundred years of total neglect, or desultory and irregular activity, Christian England has at length proceeded to evangelize her colonies as Paul and John would have done; the home Church has sent its Timothies and Tituses to be the angels of Churches abroad, and to gather, with the awful yet tender voice of authority and love, the stray sheep of those wild pastures into the fold of Jesus Christ. In no other spirit, I would fain hope and believe, does your Society desire to conduct its operations; the higher authorities are sent to the destitute Churches abroad, the inferior ministers are supplied by you to districts not less destitute at home; but both in their places ministering as parts of one common system of disciplined activity; and both, as I pray and beseech the most High God to grant, partakers of one blessing.

SERMON XXII.

THE BLESSEDNESS OF SUBMISSION.

(Preached at the Magdalen Asylum. May 28, 1837.)

MATTHEW XI. 30.

For my yoke is easy, and my burden is light.

You are well aware that these words, these few, but most impressive words, which I have just read, my brethren, are the words of Christ, and are spoken by Him as a character of the religion which He came on earth to found, and which you solemnly profess to believe. They are (when taken in connexion with the exhortation which immediately precedes them) to be considered as a declaration, invested with all conceivable authority, of the purpose and the qualities of that great final communication of the will of God to man which consummated all former revelations, and to which all former revelations were as much preliminary as the inferior and preparatory parts of a plant are introductory in time, and subordinate in dignity, to its last perfection in the fruit or flower. This character of practical Christianity was delivered *early* in the ministry of the great Prophet and Priest of our faith; as if He was solicitous to publish from the first, in a form simple and condensed, and universally intelligible, the true design and principles of His work on earth. Since the day when that sentence was spoken by Him who is Truth itself, it has been, perhaps, beyond any other passage of the Holy Volume, the strength and consolation of thousands. If it were given us at this hour to behold in vision the multitudes in every age who have drank of the well of blessings which is continually springing from this inestimable declaration; if our Bibles could retain the pictured shadows of those hosts of sad and sorrowing faces, that in the long succession of centuries, and the wide variety of Christianized countries, have bowed over the page that speaks these words of refreshment, and risen renewed in hope and happiness,—truly we might have wherewith to silence the scoffer, a cloud of witnesses to testify that " the eye of the Lord is upon them that fear Him, upon them that hope in His mercy!" (Psalm xxxiii. 18.) But the true disciples of Christ—they who imbibe the balm of His consolation, and make His service their refuge from the world's heartless services—are a scattered band. Dispersed, as they are, over places and ages, we cannot collect them into groups and assemblies to impress our eyes with their number; their invaluable testimony is too often lost amid the din and bustle of a world that never loses the advantage of its own restless boastfulness. The offers that the world makes to mankind to assume *its* gilded yoke, are loud and urgent; they who adopt the yoke of Christ are, by the very tenure of their service, humble, and submissive, and resigned. And where it is God's high purpose that His people, in their gradual progress to purification should walk by faith and not by sight, some partial concealment of this kind is perhaps best suited to such a state. If the scattered examples of Christian holiness and happiness could be combined into a single radiant band, if the separated members of the Church of Christ could, by some secret attraction, meet and coalesce, I believe that such an exhibition of genuine dignity and deep contented satisfaction would result, that the disciples of the Lord could scarcely be said any longer to walk by faith merely, when the heaven to which their faith is directed was thus presented to their very senses. The few that, by profound experience, know the "yoke" of Christ to be "easy," are specks in the multitude of man; they are collected into no single aggregate that man can perceive. The sheepfold of Christ's flock is no material or visible inclosure; it is the circle of love which is traced in the eternal mind of the good Shepherd Himself, and whose compass is known to Him alone. And if we are told that "the sheep hear His voice," yet we know that it is by the Spirit they hear; and if we are told that "He calleth His own sheep by name, and leadeth them out," yet we know that it is by the Spirit He addresses them, and by the Spirit He guides His little flock to the "pastures" and the "still waters." (Psalm xxiii. 2.) We know that the history of the people of Christ is a history not written in any earthly volume; there are no statistics of this holy nation; no record that can be numbered and understood by every cursory inquirer. The Father, "who seeth in secret," will "reward openly;" but this life is not the season of that reward.

I say, then, that we are not to be deprived of the valuable testimony of those who, in deep retirement of spirit, have learned to feel how easy is the yoke of Christ, and how light is His burden. If their very humility prevents some from making widely known the secrets of their joy, if a natural timidity prevents others, if habits of grave caution against self-reliance prevent a third class, if the loneliness of a way of life sequestered from the world prevent a fourth, or the absence of learned education and the want of suitable language hinder a fifth,— let not the general world count truth by multitude, or idly imagine that happiness does not exist because not made the topic of public report or busy boast. It is worldly happiness that seeks these accessories, because it is worldly happiness that alone *requires them!* And nothing can more strikingly evince the very hollowness of that restless dream which constitutes the pleasure of this life, than the very necessity which it involves of this perpetual recourse to others. Its happiness is, to be thought happy. It cannot stand the test of solitude. It is the creature of times, and places, and circumstances. When it does seek solitude, it is only such a solitude as the insanity of the miser or the grossness of sensual indulgence;

it ceases to be dependent on the fellow-mortal only to become equally dependent on the inanimate creation, the very fruits, nay, the very clay of the earth! But that scattered people of Christ, of whom I have spoken, know that there is a peace which asks no witness, though it loves a friend; a peace which can abide an earthly solitude, or contemn an earthly fame; because its solitude is peopled by angels, and its fame is bright in the records of heaven!

I do not speak now of the multitude of witnesses to the reality of the Christian promises of happiness, who have left their evidence on record; for my object has rather been to resist a prejudice than to establish a truth. But, brethren, if I were to open this page of the argument, with what facility might the fact be manifested! From the earliest Christian century even to our own day, the chain of linked piety may be said never to have been utterly broken, though often indeed attenuated; and so watchful and perpetual has been the providence of our gracious Master, that even in the midst of seasons the most discouraging, those blessings have never been absolutely extinct. We forget the internal nature of the Christian blessedness when we suppose that even in the worst of times "God left Himself without witness, in that *He did good.*" (Acts xiv. 17.) When Paul is asserting this point, he is speaking of those "times past" of heathenism, in which the "good" bestowed by God consisted in "rain from heaven, and fruitful seasons, filling our hearts with food and gladness." If such blessings as these were bestowed for a testimony in the dark days of idolatry, shall we believe that the dark days of the Church's history, after that "grace and truth had come by Jesus Christ," were not also (secretly, it might often be) refreshed with the spiritual "rain from heaven," the spiritual fruitfulness, and the spiritual gladness? It is, indeed, such a perpetuity of blessedness that constitutes (if such a thing exist at all) the true perpetuity of the Church of Christ. Trace in your minds the stages of that Church's annals. Persecution first fostered it, and the grace of Christ was found like the oak, that is said to strengthen in the storm. Prosperity next assailed it, but, even under this far more fatal trial, God still reserved to Himself many who had learned how to " use this world as not abusing it." And when the most subtle artifice of him who, for mysterious purposes, is suffered to hold principality over this world, had taken effect,—when the kingdom that was " not of this world" had indeed become the kingdom of this world,—when the mystic monarchy of Christ had been usurped by a mortal, and the incommunicable attributes of the Omniscient God had been invaded by assemblies great only in the magnitude of their presumption,—when that Spirit of Truth, of whom it was expressly said that the world cannot receive Him, was claimed by an hierarchy which itself represented and ruled a submissive world,—even then (as their remaining writings fully attest) there did exist, even in the centre of these delusions, many a saintly spirit whose graces vanquished the infelicity of his position. It is not until the last great day of account that it will be fully known what accessions each century of the Church has contributed to the witnesses of Christian happiness on earth, or to the eternal kingdom of Christ in glory. We are apt to trust confidently, that our own generation will occupy an honourable place in the great enrolment. Yet, let us be careful! Many may come from the east and the west, while the children of the kingdom are cast out into outer darkness. And I have often thought (nor to those who love the Christian heart, under whatever garment it beat, is the thought unconsoling) that from the monastic seclusions of the usurping Church of Rome will on that day be seen to issue numbers who, triumphant by God's free grace over the ignorance within and around them, have, in spite of the disasters of their outward calling, become " vessels unto honour, sanctified and meet for the Master's use, prepared unto every good work," (2 Tim. ii. 21,)—men and women who, in the midst of the Egyptian darkness, have had light in their houses of cloistered solitude,—and who will put to shame many of those who, living in a country of nominal illumination, have themselves walked in darkness and in the shadow of death! Alas, "if the light that is in *us* be darkness, how great is *that* darkness!"

We have now, brethren, summoned—or, rather, we have invited your own examination of—the witnesses to the truth of the promise of exclusive Christian happiness. We beseech you, by every principle of reason and truth; we beseech you, as you value the destinies of immortality, to weigh well the nature and force of the argument. Unless you can believe that, from the hour when (as we are told) " the disciples were filled *with joy* in the Holy Ghost"—nay, from the hour when the precursor of Christ leaped *for joy* in the womb of his mother—to this hour (for even now we are, thanks to Divine mercy! compassed about with a cloud of witnesses) the long line of the saints and martyrs of the Church united to deceive the world; unless you can believe that they who endured such persecutions as our ancestors in the faith endured, had no compensative satisfactions; unless you can distrust all the inferences of history, and all the direct testimony of express language; there is a happiness attainable by the service of Christ which it would be absolute insanity to ascribe to any earthly pursuit. I only ask you to exercise your reason on this greatest of all questions as you would exercise it on the pettiest question of worldly profit; and to choose for yourselves the solution, —Are all the records of devotional literature a lie, or, is the promise of the Lord capable of fulfilment? It has been esteemed a convincing argument in arguing the Christian evidences, that pain and persecution were undergone by those who bore the testimony; and it has been irrefragably concluded that such evidence under such circumstances evinced that the witnesses *had* seen and heard what, in the flames and among the lions, they persisted to declare they had seen and heard: but this scope of the argument is unreasonably limited if we forsake it when we have left the primitive age of persecution. If the convictions of sense, the sight and the hearing, were necessary to account for the fortitude of Peter and Paul and the rest, what shall we say of the followers of these early martyrs, who in every age have trodden the difficult paths of similar persecutions? What shall we say of the martyrs of Pagan Rome, or of the sanguinary triumphs of its Papal successor? What shall we say of the tens of thousands of "them that were beheaded for the witness of Jesus, and for the Word of God, and which had not worshipped the beast, neither his image, neither had received his mark upon their foreheads?" Nay, that I may pass the Ridleys and the Latimers, let me come to the day we live in; and ask you, what inference will you draw from the instances of more secret but not less real persecution that encompass the Christian course at this very hour? Have our martyrdoms ceased? Or are you not sadly conscious that, in *this* age, no less than in the age of him who wrote the words (in his very last Epistle, and as if a dying bequest of truth)—" all that will live godly in Christ Jesus shall suffer persecution?" We may weep with sincerity when we read of the rack and the stake; we may thrill with the triumph and the pathos of the history of such cases as that of the aged saint who declared that at the end of eighty years he would not desert the Christ who for eighty years had never deserted him, and turning round, bade them uncage the lions; but, I protest, I know not if we ought to be less deeply and sincerely moved, when we reflect on the numbers of those who at this present time are exposed to a more civilized, but scarcely a more lenient persecution. I am convinced I do not pass beyond the experience of many here when I speak of that cup of domestic bitterness, that alienation of friends, that solitude in the world and inexpressible loneliness of heart, which so **often** become the lot **of them who give up** father and mother for Christ. If this **inevitable connexion of worldly** sorrow with Christian joy were not destined by God Himself, what means the whole history of Him who, having the thrones of all the earth at His disposal, yet preferred to be a man of sorrows, and sanctified grief by eternally blending it with His own divine story? Was not the crown of the King of kings a crown of *thorns?* And yet, says the Apostle to the Hebrews, " we see Jesus crowned with glory and honour." Even so, in truth, it is;— the anguish of the Redeemer was His glory, His honour to fulfil, in His sacrificial afflictions, the will of His Father. If we would resemble Him in the eternal Paradise, we must first pass an hour with Him in the garden of Gethsemane.

But what I would insist on is this. If man be made to act by motives, if he possess the dignity of even a machine, and (like it) act continuously only from some one continuous *principle* of action,—I ask you, what principle will you introduce to account for the Christian's endurance of affliction? You admit that the first witnesses must have had visible proofs; how then do you account for the story of their successors? Christians! they " endured as seeing Him who is invisible." Believe me, the burden of their worldly agonies could not have been borne by human hearts, if Christ had not gradually replaced it by His " light burden." They, too, had their sensible proofs,—the felt happiness of their internal convictions. When Paul declares that " the godly suffer persecution," he also declares, that out of all his persecutions " the Lord delivered him." I argue, then, that the happiness promised by Christ to His servants is demonstrated from their contempt of worldly afflictions. Even in the very extreme of their woe, when all the earth seems arrayed against them, and Satan, at the rear of his host, urges on his ministers of persecution, to try the novice in the faith,—even then their struggling cries are hushed, and the feebleness of human nature is supported by the conscious presence of the Spirit of God. And then, " behold, a new heaven, and a new earth!" The things of this world gradually faint off into shadows, and the magnificent realities of eternity present themselves in bolder relief and prominence. The new believer (not always indeed, —for while " in this tabernacle, we groan being burdened,"— but *oftentimes* in his earthly experience) is introduced " to the heavenly Jerusalem, and to the innumerable company of angels," and to the rest of that bright assemblage,—all ending, however, with " Jesus, the Mediator of the New Covenant," with Him, who is the beginning and end of the believer's hope. It is at such hours—hours which we might all possess, if we but laboured by prayer and meditation, and separation from the world to attain them—that the child of God feels indeed that " the yoke is easy, and the burden light:" or, so to speak, that all which, in one sense of the term, can be called " *a burden*" has passed away, and wings are given to the spirit to bear it for ever nearer and nearer to the Divine Presence, till at length, passing through the gate of death, it finds itself in the ineffable enjoyment of infinite perfection.

And is such happiness as this the fiction of our hopes; is it only an illusive exaggeration? If you will not believe my words or my arguments, if you will not credit the exulting confessions of the saints of God in all times and countries, credit the declarations of Jesus Himself. Is it not said of Him, that " He is to guide our feet into the way of peace?" (Luke i. 79;) while the burden of the song with which the heavenly host greeted His advent on earth was, " on earth, peace!" And the declaration which I have selected for our meditation this evening does not stand alone in the discourses of our Divine Friend. " My peace I leave with you, my peace I give you," was, as you well know, His final bequest to His disciples; while also, He declares in words, that in a small compass contain all which I have been saying, " that in Me ye might have peace. In the world ye shall have tribulation." He casts no disguise over the roughness of the path we are to tread; He warns us of the hostility, but He promises also the victory. " Be of good cheer; I have overcome the world."

When Jesus passed away, the Apostles took up the same song of peace. "To be spiritually-minded," says St. Paul, "is life and peace." But higher gifts than even this *calmness of spirit* are promised to the believing Christian. Joy, surpassing and abounding joy, is made his inheritance. And Christ Himself is our surety. "These things," says He, "have I spoken to you that *My joy* might remain in you, and that your joy might be full." "Your heart shall rejoice, and your joy no man taketh from you." And the gift of joy is made the whole object of this revelation of beneficence; "These things I speak in the world, that they might have My joy fulfilled in themselves." After such testimonies from the fountain of all truth, it is unnecessary to have recourse to those streams that issued from His Spirit. If St. Paul prays, he tells us that he "makes request with joy:" if he purposes to tarry with his dear disciples at Philippi, he tells them that it is for their furtherance and "*joy* of faith." And, finally, when he would in one sentence sum up the characteristics of that state of being where God is set upon the throne of the heart, he tells us that "the kingdom of God is righteousness, and peace, *and joy* in the Holy Ghost."

Now, brethren, upon all these scriptural testimonies, this bright heap of divine promises and intimations, I will ask you but one simple question. Can you believe that any state which the nominal Christianity of our day attains to, can be considered to realize such descriptions as these? Suppose an inhabitant of another world, some one of those angelic essences, if such there be, whose knowledge has not yet reached the history of our earth, were to descend among us, and anxious to find here below some society that might remind him of, or compensate him for, the glorious company of his brother spirits, were to take up the Scriptures of Christ in order to make it his guide-book in the search of such a community. Would he discover the object of his inquiries? Does there exist a group of believers among us which could stand as the original of that picture? Where is the ardent faith, and the relying hope, and the all-grasping charity? Where is the " peace and joy in believing,"—the conviction expressed by every word and action that the " yoke" of Christ is indeed "easy," and His " burden light?" Christians! if we could not stand such an examination from even an angel, from a *brother* in creation, how shall we stand before Him whom " the angels of God worship?" May His divine mercy befriend us in the terrible day of His judgment! May He be the friend of those who are their own worst enemies!

SERMON XXIII.

THE HOLY TRINITY.

(Trinity Sunday, May 21, 1837.)

John I. 1.

And the Word was God.

In calling your attention to the great doctrine of this day, my brethren, I have selected, from among the host of passages which either directly or by necessary implication assert the proper Godhead of Christ, this peculiar and well-known affirmation, because it seems to me to be distinguished from them all by one especial character, which confers upon it an incalculable force in fortifying and consolidating our belief in the doctrine which it is by the universal Church adduced to uphold. I do not so much refer to the fact (though that is important) that it has been singularly preserved from the assaults of rash verbal criticism, scarcely any of those sectarian commentators who are most interested to impugn its genuineness,—and who assuredly have shown no indisposition to tamper with the parallel texts,—having ventured to question *its* reality as a portion of Divine revelation; and the attempts of those who have ventured to do so, being now almost wholly rejected by even their own party. I do not refer to this distinction so happily characterising this passage, because to fully establish it as a distinction would require a sort and extent of discussion not calculated for the present occasion, and because the other peculiarity to which I allude is, as I conceive, even more persuasive to the minds of candid and rational thinkers. That peculiarity is, that the form in which these words are couched is a form which, above all others, precludes every possibility of explaining them away by any resources of metaphorical or symbolical language. They are part of *a creed*—a creed uttered by the Spirit of God through the lips of the greatest of evangelists. It is impossible for any impartial man, opening up on this part of the New Testament, not at once to feel how enormous is the force derived from the place, the occasion, and the manner in which these words are spoken. By this I mean to say, that whereas in any part of the Scriptures they would, indeed, have been words of weight, and adequate to prove the point they involve, in this particular position and form they become absolutely insuperable. The opening verses of the Gospel of St. John are (as I have intimated) nothing less than *a creed;* that is to say, they are a series of doctrinal propositions altogether detached from any historical or circumstantial connexion, resting upon the authority of the proposer, and to be received with the measure of faith (whatever it be) due to that authority. Of such a composition, straightforward simplicity is the first and most essential attribute. Figurative language and the colourings of imagery have here no place. Nor can its expressions be explained away by references to contexts and connexions: other passages derive their force from their context; this derives its force from having *no* context. It is a naked, unmitigated, unqualified statement; it condescends to no parley with our petty and restricted human conceptions; it sternly calls for obedience, and, simply declaiming *the fact*, leaves us to dispute *the manner*. Had Christ, in any of His casual discourses, let fall such a declaration as this, we might, however unreasonably, have ventured upon glosses and qualifications to escape its astounding import. We might have said that He spoke *a parable*, that He was furnishing a partial knowledge to His disciples, which the spiritual Enlightener was afterwards to enlarge and complete, that He addressed Himself (as we know was His wont) to the passing occasion, and used words stronger than His meaning, in order to strengthen the meaning He intended: all this might have been said, and though it would have been said without truth, would at least have been said with plausibility. But here there is no room for evasions like these. The words stand alone; and if it be beyond our imagination to give them a higher than their literal meaning, it is against our reason to give them a lower. When St. John was writing these momentous syllables, he had no business to speak in parables. Parables are for infants in this truth, plain speech for men. " The time cometh," says our Lord in His last discourse, " when I shall no more speak unto you in *in proverbs*, but I shall show unto you *plainly* of the Father." And if ever there was a time when this plainness of speech was required in the first legislators of the Church, it was pre-eminently at the period when St. John wrote these words. He sat down to close the whole canon of Scripture; to terminate, in a full display of the abundant glories of the great " Sun of righteousness," that long pathway of light which, beginning with Moses, had extended for so many years—growing in glory as it approached its source —across the dark waters of this world's history. Was this the period for concealment or enigma? or shall we ascribe to St. John the *Evangelist* the obscurity which his mysterious subject obliges us to ascribe to St. John the *Prophet?* Was this the time when the Spirit of God would perplex the Church with a double sense, and bequeath it, as its formulary of faith, a mass of metaphors and uncertainties? But more than this: at the time when the pen of the great Evangelist was imprinting this mighty inscription upon the forehead of the rising Church, he arose to discharge the office in the very midst of unbelief. Inspiration arose to counteract and condemn actual and active *heresy*. When St. John, then, wrote these deep and awful words, he wrote them as the last inspired revealer of God's truth on earth; he wrote them as a watchword for the Church he loved, a formal depository of its final belief; he wrote them in the midst of an audacious heresy that questioned his authority and doubted his doctrine upon this individual topic; he wrote them, it may well be supposed, with a clear perception (for to him beyond all other of the followers of our Lord was it given to know the future) that they were to be for ages the source and spring of the Church's hope; under these circumstances he composed his creed, under these circumstances he wrote that "*the Word was God*." Can you, then, disbelieve the Deity of the Word, and not disbelieve St. John? Can you disbelieve St. John, and believe the Christ that he described, or the Spirit that inspired him? Without simulating a conviction which I do not feel, or exaggerating to suit a purpose, I may sincerely say that if not another passage in the sacred Revelations confessed the Divine essence of our blessed Saviour,—if by no implication or inference it were elsewhere involved or concluded,—I would feel myself bound, if once satisfied that the Spirit spoke *these words*, to bow before the cloud that covers the mercy-seat of God in His earthly manifestations, to acknowledge that these things were too hard for me to analyse as matter of science, but not too hard to believe as matter of faith,—and to admit that, while at best we know not what God *is*, but what He *does*, and while we know that Christ has *done* all that might beseem an incarnate God, we may fully believe that He *was* indeed the God He resembled; that, comparing the God whose goodness was manifested in Christ, with Christ Himself, we detect a similarity that may well be *identity*.

And now, as I hope it would be very unnecessary for me, in addressing my present hearers, to prolong to any minute detail, the direct scriptural arguments for this cardinal doctrine of our belief, I will beg of you to accompany me into a few brief reflections upon the nature of the prejudice that exists against it. I waive all more particular objections, and allude to that which, in truth, lies at the bottom of them all, the prejudice against the Trinity as *an incomprehensible mystery*, or, what is *nearly* as deplorable, the reception of it as a dogma which violates every principle of reason, and can only be accepted by a blind, unreasoning faith. It is the more necessary to resist this unfortunate prepossession, because (as I am persuaded, and as I know, indeed, by experience) there are many fair-minded thinkers who sometimes find themselves equally unable to refuse the scriptural attestations and to accept the doctrine attested. That the difficulty arises solely from a total misconception of *the manner in which the doctrine should be apprehended by the mind*, I have no doubt; and if there be a single person present—and I have known few large assemblies of Christians in which such mistakes have not been more or less afloat—who has ever felt the access of these perplexities, and has honestly wished to bring his mind to a more perfect coincidence with what he saw to be the true scriptural revelation, by liberating it from these vexatious incursions of unbelief, I beseech his attention for a very short discussion of the true attitude in which the mind should place itself to receive duly the doctrine, that " there are three that bear record in heaven, the Father, the Word, and the Holy Ghost;" and that " these three are One." The prejudice which I am regarding is countenanced by an error to which I have just now alluded, not at all uncommon in our own Church; and it is this latter which I am chiefly solicitous to resist, because it presents itself not in the garb of determined infidelity, but in the more seductive guise of superlative humility and all-absorbing devotion.

It is often said, then, that this great doctrine of the Trinity in Unity, which our Church maintains in common with a vast majority of the Church of Christ in all ages, is as a mystery set forth by the God of revelation in opposition to our reason, —in such a sense as that a violence of some kind or other must be done to the reason by the recipient of the doctrine;

and that the true victory of faith is perfected in this conquest which it thus effects over the prejudices which our corrupted human nature is constantly generating in opposition to it. The glory of the believing man is thus made to consist in the prostration of the reasoning man; and the highest triumph of the principle of faith to be accomplished in the lowest humiliation of the principle of reason. As I believe this view of our Christian mysteries (which you will find to have been held, unfortunately, by some men of the highest and purest minds) to be founded upon a most melancholy misunderstanding of the whole constitution of our nature, and as nothing is more frequently circulated (in a form, to be sure, more or less definite) in religious society, you will not, I think, misspend a few minutes in obviating it, and placing in your own minds our high and noble belief in the Trinitarian theology upon its proper basis.

The simplest way of contravening the error is to state the truth which its upholders imperfectly saw, and the distorted image of which is the error they taught and teach. The doctrine of a Trinity in Unity does not in any sense, or in any degree whatever, propose itself in opposition to our reason, or require its renunciation; but it does oppose all the possible exercises of the *imagination*, and does require the total renunciation of all impressions derivable from *that* faculty. It is the confusion of these very distinct parts of our nature in which the error of these reasoners consists: they perceive plainly enough that sense or imagination, wholly conversant as they are with our limited compass of ideas, are completely inadequate to *reconcile* the Unity with the Trinity of God,— that is, to *represent to themselves* a God that shall at once possess both these characters; and they hastily apply to the reason what is solely applicable to the imagination, forgetting that the Unity of the Divine nature is just as little capable of this sensible representation as its Trinity in Unity; and that, in fact, the only mode in which such an essence could at all approach itself to the imagination or senses, was by precisely such an incarnation as the orthodox theology maintains. But as to *the reason*, we defy the acutest adversary of the Trinitarian doctrine, or the most mystical of those theologians of our own Church who countenance views so unworthy of rational Christianity, to show cause why the structures of our reason must necessarily be thrown down in order to enthrone this mystery upon their ruins. Instead of being "opposed to our reason," or, as some more cautiously express it, "demanding the submission of our reason," it might be truly shown that the doctrine of an incarnate Deity is directly addressed to our moral reason, and fitted for the appreciation of our entire reason in such a degree as that it might in some sort be presumed even antecedently to any direct revelation on the subject. I say this advisedly, because I think that though the obscurity of this vast subject requires indeed much caution, the caution need not wholly prevent a real and perceptible progress. And as to the extension of the fact of incarnation, that the Deity involves that triplicity of being which we call a "triplicity of persons," it is unquestionably as little adverse to the conclusions of reason as His Unitarian attribute of *single personality*. If we believe that the principle of Deity is an *intelligent* principle, we cannot escape believing it *personal;* and if we can attain to the belief that such a principle can be personal at all, we must have the power of believing (that is, our reason must present no difficulty to our believing on proper evidence) that it develops itself in three persons, or in four persons, or in forty persons. In supposition there is no contrariety to reason; for there is truly no more difficulty in supposing a thousand persons in the Godhead (ignorant as we are of its essence) than in supposing a single person. And hence it is that so many who set out with the vaunted rationality of Unitarianism end in the lifeless vacancy of Atheism; they begin by denying the triple personality as unreasonable, and they end by finding (what indeed is perfectly true) that the single personality is just *as* unreasonable. In truth it is neither *more* nor *less* opposed to reason; both doctrines are equally possible, both equally probable, antecedent to all revelation of the will and nature of God. . . . It is plain that this assumption of the impossibility of the existence of personal division in a single spiritual essence arose from the comparison of our own nature, in which such a division seems inconceivable; as if our nature, though formed, indeed, after God's image, were adequate to represent the totality of the nature of God. Our nature, in its spirituality and intelligence, reflects, indeed, that of the Being we adore; but it reflects only one side of a figure whose sides are infinite. And even thus, it is not unworthy of our consideration, whether something of a divisibility of persons is not observable in our own system; for there are parts of our nature that sometimes act, and even seem to act voluntarily, without the consciousness or participation of the rest of the mental principle. Let us not be misled in making such a comparison. We should employ them merely as feeble illustrations of the possible compatibility with experience of a truth which is beyond our experience. Such a comparison, if unfounded, will only serve to establish, more and more firmly, the great principle which I am maintaining, —the danger, namely, of depending on imagination or human experience for our cordial reception of a doctrine which was never addressed to imagination or experience; which was addressed immediately to faith, and indirectly to the reason on which our faith is built; and which itself, tried by the severest test of reason, can never be shown to contradict any one of its conclusions.

I fear, my dear friends, that this kind of abstruse discussion may have exhausted the patience of some of you who are less accustomed to such investigations. Yet pause to consider— would you refuse to expend the labour which it might require to search into these things upon any one of the ordinary pursuits of your daily life? And is it only in the pursuit of clear and solid principles of belief in the things that are to give a colour to your immortality that your patience begins to flag? Is the acuteness that detects every turn of the chances in a bargain of worldly gain at fault—dulled and incapable—when the great question of profit and loss is proposed; a question whose slightest concerns ought surely to outweigh in your estimate the wealth of empires? Believe me, we have, most of us, understanding enough for these matters if we had will to employ it; the engine is given us to work by the Great Mechanist, but we are often too indolent to supply the moving-power, and the noble machinery is thrown aside like useless lumber.

But it is, indeed, true that the melioration of the heart is still the great and leading object to which all others are subordinate; and I could be well satisfied that such reasonings as these were never to occupy your intellects, if their practical consequences occupied your feelings. It is the fervent ardours of the heart that best illuminate the mind. " What profits it," says a very great saint in treating of the very subject of our thoughts this day, " what profits it that we should discourse with subtlety about the Trinity if we live so as to displease the Trinity?" A double measure of vengeance is reserved for him who knows his Master's will and performs it not.

And surely, brethren, to awake every feeling that can animate human breasts with piety, it is unnecessary to go beyond this mighty doctrine, which encompasses all Christianity, and bears within it the whole field of devotional contemplation and spiritual affections. In meditating upon the Three Glorious Personages who are the agents in the management of our salvation, we contemplate the whole magnificent work which they, of their sovereign goodness and wisdom and power, have agreed to accomplish. We behold with the eye of reason that unveiled paternal Godhead, whom with the corporeal eye "no man hath seen at any time," willing the wondrous sacrifice which was to purify us in His pure sight; we behold and hear the Eternal Son, who rose from the bosom of His Father to declare, "Lo, I come (in the volume of the book it is written of me) to do thy will, O God;" and we recognise, by His omnipresent efficacy, that blessed Spirit who superintended and animated the entire machinery of redemption. So that God, descending thus to man, becomes no longer an inoperative abstraction, but the living and felt companion of our souls. Till then the Godhead was like that imperceptible heat which animates the universe, an agent energetic indeed and all-pervading, but unseen. In the Son He assumes a direct and, as it were, a tangible form—the heat condenses into fire. And in the Holy Spirit the same Divine Essence issues forth in Light, a Light consummate, which cheers our spiritual sense, but which still is inseparable from the flame it accompanies. All are united, and all distinct. Such is the comprehensive doctrine you are this day summoned to consider. We have no day appropriated in our calendar to the Father of heaven—our year, nay, our life, is *His* day! We have days appointed to the distinctive commemoration of the achievements of the Son in our behalf; not, indeed, that we should not perpetually consecrate ourselves to Him also, that is, to the Father through Him, but because it assists the feeble grasp of our nature to apportion times and seasons, and His varied history on earth admits of such partial and detached contemplation. And we have a day which we devote to gratitude to that Holy Spirit who gave Himself liberally to the first establishers of our faith, and still is present to those who ask Him. But on THIS day all are blended into one mysterious harmony; on this day the separate holinesses of the year combine into one transcendent union; the dispersed sanctities of the seasons meet and mingle to-day. May the God who in the highest heavens unites in His own ineffable nature the paternal, filial, and spiritual characters, unite us also to Himself in like manner! May that Essence which is at once the Father, the Son, and the Holy Ghost, fulfil upon us the prayer which the Divine Jesus, the incarnate Son, when a pilgrim upon earth, uttered in our behalf to His Father,—" That they all may be one; as thou, Father, art in me, and I in thee, that they also may be one in us . . that they may be one, even as we are one; I in them, and thou in me, that they may be made *perfect in one!*"

SERMON XXIV.

WATCHMAN, WHAT OF THE NIGHT?

(College Chapel, Friday, May 31, 1839.)

ISAIAH XXI. 11, 12.

He calleth to me out of Seir, Watchman, what of the night? Watchman, what of the night? The watchman said, The morning cometh, and also the night: if ye will inquire, inquire ye; return, come.

THIS singular passage has, in its primary purpose and application, furnished material for very important and interesting investigation. To this, however, as scarcely appropriate to the present occasion, I will not now undertake to direct your attention; preferring rather to invite you to contemplate the wider moral significancy which is contained in the words. This wider significancy was probably intended by the prophet himself, or by the Spirit which spoke through his instrumentality; it is this very doubleness of application which renders these writings so invaluable, not only as *evidences* of our faith, but as lessons to our hearts; it is this pregnancy of meaning which makes them calculated not only for "correction and reproof" of the gainsayer of our hope in Christ, but for "instruction in righteousness" to ourselves who profess it!

Let us, then, speak first briefly of this inward or secondary meaning of the Word of prophecy in general; and afterwards offer a few hints towards a practical application of this inward meaning in the peculiar passage before us.

The whole Bible—both the Old Covenant, with its histories, its hymns, and its prophecies, and the New, with its narratives, its epistles of apostolic instruction, and its single momentous book of prophecy—has, as its common and pervading argument, one mighty subject, which, appearing under a thousand different forms, is substantially the same in every page of the sacred volume. That subject is, the salvation appointed for the chosen of mankind, and the ruin decreed for those who reject the offer. But this great revelation of happiness and misery is differently made according to the difference of times and seasons. The *Personage who makes it*, who in each dispensation comes in contact with man, however He may subsequently commit the subordinate functions of teaching to His servants, is no other than *God Himself;* a strong presumption, I may observe, for the Divinity of the Prophet and Legislator of the New Testament. In the earliest age of the world the Revelation was given *by God in person*, speaking to man without the intervention of any prophetical emissary, under some undescribed visible appearance. After the Fall it was probably left to the safe *keeping of tradition*, which, considering the longevity of mankind in these times, was, doubtless, a sufficiently secure depository. When, at and after the deluge, God was willing once more to save or to collect a people from the general mass of corruption, He again revealed His will, and the *Lord*, or the "*Angel of the Lord*"— no other than God—manifested Himself to the patriarchs, and, though obscurely, promised a wondrous future;—and not only a temporal but an eternal and invisible future,—for "the fathers looked not for transitory promises." ... In due time, the third series of revelation was delivered by one who declared of Himself, "I am the Lord thy God," and who constantly uttered His own high will personally to the people of Israel under the title of *The Lord*. ... And when "the ends of the world," the last section of the Divine dispensations, had arrived, the *fourth* series of revelation was opened, prosecuted, and concluded by the same Divine Being in the person of Christ Jesus, in whom God (according to the analogy of His preceding manifestations, and, as might be expected, in a way more perfect than any of them) once more exhibited Himself to man, leaving His Apostles, as He had before left His Prophets, to expand and enforce His personal teaching.

Thus was the revealer of God's will ever the same,—ever God Himself. The substance of the Revelation was also (since the Fall) unchanged; but its form and character were perpetually varied. The former was stable as the purpose of God; the latter suited to, and dependent on, the circumstances of man. It is even as the sun himself (so often made the emblem of God) is ever one and the same; but the effects He produces vary with *our* varying position, being at one time morning, at another noon, at another eve. The God of the patriarchs, of Moses, of the Gospel, is one immutable essence,—His purpose unalterable; but He varies in the revealings of His light, because we ourselves vary in our relative positions and capacities for receiving it. . . . Hence we may expect the ultimate object to be never forgotten in the temporary one; and though the Master may instruct and threaten by occasional examples, yet that these very examples of His direct agency, being guided by the same principles of government, adjusted after the same laws, and pointed with similar views, as His master counsels, should present, as it were, a *miniature* of them, and serve to instruct us, on the little stage of this world, in the far-reaching degrees of eternity. Unless God be at variance with Himself, we can reasonably anticipate no other result than that His temporal judgments and temporal pardons should be a *picture-language* expressive of His eternal: the *scale*, indeed, widely different, but the *proportions* the same.

And, therefore, when the prophetic Scriptures publish to us promises of peace and denunciations of woe, let us never deem that the Divine Spirit had no *ulterior* purpose in these predictions. Let us never cast aside the volume and cry,—

That we are not Edom, or Egypt, or Babylon, or Tyre; and that, therefore, we have nothing to do either with their crimes or their punishment. Let us not vainly dream that the mighty machinery of the prophetic messages was put into play merely to call down curses on a few of the temporary dynasties of this perishable world! "All Scripture was written for *our* use," and these "springing and germinant prophecies" (as they have been called) have a significancy beyond the revolutions of petty kingdoms. They represent in majestic order, and manifest type, the great truths of eternal salvation and eternal ruin; they exhibit, in the sensible language of exterior imagery, what the great Teacher of aftertimes gave in the higher language of spiritual truth. If the laws of God be uniform and unchangeable, we are justified in reading by this light from *heaven* the prophetic declarations of the course and the principles of His *earthly* providences.

With such views as these elevating our thoughts beyond the details of perished empires into the mightier truths of the eternal empire of our God, let us reflect briefly upon the words before us. Their precise purport has been controverted. Without entering on minute discussions, I shall adopt that which seems to me the most probable.

The prophet appears to introduce himself as addressed in scorn by the people of the land which he is commissioned to warn. "Watchman, what of the night?" What new report of woe hast thou to unrol, thou who hast placed thyself as an authorized observer and censurer of our doings? But the prophetical watchman—the calm commissioner of heaven—replies, adopting their own language,—"Yes, the morning (the true morning of hope and peace) cometh, and also the night (the real and terrible night of God's vengeance); if ye will (if ye are in genuine earnest to inquire) inquire! Return, come." Obtain the knowledge you seek, the knowledge of the way of life; and, acting on this knowledge, repent and return to the Lord your God.

Regard, then, the guilty Edom that is warned; and the office and answer of the watchman who warns it.

I cannot now command the time which would be necessary in order to sketch the vastness and variety of the lost Edom of this rebellious world, extending as it does through all ranks and divisions of men; from the beginnings of sin to the last abandonment of the desperately profligate. I am not now to undertake to count over the array of those who address the spiritual watchmen of the Church of Christ in tones of derision, and mock their ministry. Yet, if we reflect a moment, we may perhaps without difficulty call to mind a few of the more prominent of the many classes who thus (directly or indirectly) offer to the watchman of their souls the language of contempt, or fear, or indifference; and ask of him,—" What of the night?" disregarding, or despising, or dreading, his answer.

Some there are who ask the report of "the night" with utter *carelessness* as to the reply. These are they who haunt our churches from the indolence of habit, who smilingly confess themselves " sinners" without once remembering the tremendous purport of the words they employ; who echo the thrilling penitence of our liturgy in the same tone that inquires the news of the day; who are Christians because their fathers were, and would, without a murmur, be heathens for the same reason.

Some again there are, who ask the question not in carelessness but in *contempt*. Like the children of old, they come forth out of the city " to mock the prophet of the Lord." These are the disciples of fashionable infidelity, who find it easier to despise than to argue; who cannot endure to be of the same religion with the needy and the illiterate; and who coldly pronounce that a God who is not announced as governing the world on the principles of *their* experience (a point of space and a moment of time) cannot possibly be the God of reason and of truth. It is terrible to think, that, in His awful retribution, God can assume a spirit of derision like their own— " Because ye have set at nought all my counsel, and would none of my reproof, I also will *laugh* at your calamity, I will *mock* when your fear cometh. When your fear cometh as desolation, and your destruction cometh as a whirlwind, ... then shall they call upon me, but I will not answer; they shall seek me early, but they shall not find me!"

Some, again, ask the watchman,—" What of the night?" in a spirit very different from these, and perhaps yet more terrible. They ask it in *horror and anguish of heart*. The agonies of remorse have seized their spirit; they can see beyond this world no vista but an eternity of pain; conscience suggests their reward, and Revelation confirms it. Filled with fear of the terrible hour of woe, they ask and ask again, —" What of the night?" How speeds this gloomy time of darkness? How long have we yet to breathe before the gloomier dawn of everlasting vengeance begins?

And many more could we particularize; but even if time allowed, what would it profit? Every hearer's experience can too forcibly remind him of the number and the variety of these diversifications of evil. In every shade of wickedness they surround us; in every tone they ask advice of the watchman of their souls, and in every form they reject it!

But what is still the duty of him who holds the momentous position of watchman in the city of God? " O son of man," saith the Lord to His servant Ezekiel, " I have set thee a watchman unto the house of Israel; therefore thou shalt hear the word at my mouth, and warn them from me!" (Ezek. xxxiii. 7.) And in the same spirit and language the Apostle,—" Obey them that rule over you. ... for they *watch* for your souls." (Heb. xiii. 17.) On the occasion before us, remark—1st, He did not turn away from the question, in whatever spirit it was asked. 2d, He uttered with equal assurance a threat and a promise. 3d, He pressed the necessity of care in the study, and earnest inquiry after the nature, of the truth; and, in the last place, he summed up all by an anxious, a cordial, and a reiterated invitation to repentance and reconciliation with an offended but pardoning God. Thus, the single verse might be regarded as an abstract of the duties of the ministerial office. May God grant to His ministers a genuine anxiety to fulfil that office, to His people an equal anxiety to receive its labours!

Of the young whom I now address I know not but, few as they are, more than one may be destined for this high function of turning the disobedient to the wisdom of the Just. O my friends, if this be so, lose no time in commencing that discipline of heart and soul which alone can fitly qualify you for the mightiest office that man can hold on this side of the grave! It is an office whose responsibilities an archangel unsupported could not meet, but which the humblest of the Spirit-taught children of God may by Him be made able to bear in joy and triumph. From your earliest days accustom yourselves to feel devoted and dedicated to the service; be Christ's ministers in heart and practice from the first, and your commission, when you receive it, will find you strengthened for your calling, and old in the knowledge, though new to the ministerial service, of God!

But whether such be your purpose or not, in *one* character I am sure to meet you. You are immortal and accountable beings. Believe it, you cannot too soon enter upon the one business of life, the preparation to meet the living God; and that every seductive companion who would blind your eyes to this awful fact, is but the active minister of Satan in the work of deceiving souls. Every day gives its complexion to the day that follows it,—every year to the succeeding year,—every stage of life to that which follows *it*,—life itself is often wholly determined by *youth*, and life determines eternity! If this be so, the feelings, the resolves, of this week, this day, this hour, may yet make themselves felt through endless ages; the firm purpose to learn the faith and love of a

Christian, that rises in any one heart here at this instant, may be the earthly germ of heavenly and immortal glory. May God awake such purposes within you, and strengthen them when awakened; giving you power to overcome the force of evil example, and the tyranny of evil habit, and the dread of standing alone in the narrow path that leadeth to eternal life!

SERMON XXV.

THE PRINCIPLES OF THE FINAL JUDGMENT.

(Preached in behalf of the Association for the Relief of Distressed Protestants, St. Peter's Church, Dublin, Sunday, June 13, 1841.)

MATTHEW XXV. 40.

And the King shall answer, and say unto them, Verily I say unto you, Inasmuch as ye have done it unto one of the least of these my brethren, ye have done it unto me.

IT is Christ who speaks these solemn words from the throne of the final judgment. Listen to them with awe. Hear them as if in these accents you caught mysterious echoes from the very depths of eternity. Within the shadow of that throne of judgment we all live; and the shadow deepens fast; for every hour of our dream-like existence is bringing us nearer and nearer to the awful reality. With a view to that terrible scene of trial, the whole world exists; all the laws of nature—the succession of day and night, of seasons and years—are but ministers to that hour, speeding its coming, and preparing, whether unto weal or woe, every soul among us, for its irrevocable award. Not death itself is more inevitable; for death is but the commissioned officer of this tribunal; he exists only that he may lead us to its footstool. Not heaven's promised happiness is more assured; for this is the sole portal of heaven to man. Nay, the very being of our God is scarcely a more fixed truth; for even His being is not more certain than His justice, and His justice demands the judgment. Whatever is uncertain, or undecided, or controverted, this remains unquestionable; God shall "come to be glorified in His saints;" He shall be "revealed in flaming fire, taking vengeance on them that know Him not." To this all gathers, in this all is consummated.

And thus, in some respects, this mighty doctrine stands alone among the prophetic announcements of Scripture. Men may question as to exact significance of other predictions; they may question whether other predictions have any direct relation to themselves; and in this combination of uncertainties we know how the force of prophecy is too often blunted and enfeebled. But here there is no room for doubt or disputation. The judgment must be; and it must be personal to every child of Adam. The prophecies that proclaim it are for the most part referable, not to detached nations or tribes of men, but to man as such; to have been born into this world is the sole condition for being the subject of this tremendous dispensation. In the very being (the rational and moral being) that God has given us, He has inwoven the future judgment; He has constructed our nature so that it demands this award as its necessary completion. Our daily life is one long prophecy of that day. In the gloomy recollections of age, in the man of crime who struggles in vain to crush a rebuking conscience, in the youth who weeps the bitter fruits of passion, in the very child who runs to hide his conscious fault, in all alike is foreshadowed the terrible decree of universal judgment. For judgment we are born, for judgment we flourish, grow old, and die; Nature herself dares not deny the certainty of retribution; the Gospel but confirms her conviction; for even in regions where the Gospel has never sounded, HER voice, speaking in all nations, languages, and times, has proclaimed from pole to pole, that God shall judge His creature. But Revelation alone could tell the circumstances and accessories of this great event; and Revelation has abundantly done so. The Judge Himself has undrawn the curtain of Eternity; He has shown us His own everlasting throne, and the procedures of His court, and the test He shall demand, and the verdict He shall deliver.

It is a strange thing thus to read the story of our own hereafter; to hear delivered with all the minuteness of some history of past events, a scene in which each of us individually must perform his own special part, and that part the most awful and decisive in all eternity. Strange, to see one single point in the clouded future thus flashing out amid the impenetrable obscurity of all the rest; and that one, the point on which all the rest is ultimately to depend. Strange, indeed; yet stranger still, that it can be contemplated with so little emotion; that men can live admitting its certainty, yet never remembering its approach; that, when once granted to be true, it should not be found to occupy every thought, and to make the great directive principle of existence. Great God! to think that thus we shall each of us stand, bare to Thine eye and to assembled Heaven; all that we hide from our very selves made visible to the universe; no one shred left to shelter our secret corruptions, every fold of hypocrisy untwisted, every artifice of self-deceit exposed and spurned; to think that this is certain as that we are this day assembled in this house of prayer; and that, with such a decree thundered in our ears from every page of the Book of Truth, we should live as we do, indolent expectants of some imaginary mercies, of which we know neither the ground nor the condition; and scarcely alive, the most of us, to any real claims of duty to God beyond the formalities of exterior worship; of duty to ourselves beyond the suggestions of worldly calculation; of duty to our brethren beyond the accidental benevolence of party spirit, or pride, or caprice!

At such an hour as that noted in the passage before us, when Jesus Christ Himself proclaims the grounds of His judgment; when He tells us, in a form of unequalled solemnity, how He will personally decide the question of man's eternal destination; we may surely expect that those grounds alone, or chiefly, should be put forward which, in His own divine counsels, are regarded as of highest importance. I do not here enter into any discussion as to the special SUBJECTS of the awful decision announced in this memorable passage. Whether the scope of the words be universal as our race, or (as some have thought) more limited, I cannot now pause to canvass; my purpose this day confines me to the principle of the whole. It does so, because that principle is elsewhere so abundantly universalized, as fully to warrant any practical conclusion that can be drawn from supposing it universal here. And it does so, because it is on that principle, as understanding and recognising that principle, you are called upon to accomplish the office of charity to which I have now to invite you. By no sanction less than that of the final judgment do I bind you to this office; no voice less potent than that of Christ Himself shall plead for these poor brethren of His and yours. I supplicate for destitute members of His body; and I will not stoop to any argument but that with which He has Himself furnished me. From His own eternal throne He shall preach to you His demands and your duties.

What, then, are the principles involved in the awful verdict of the text? They are these:

That Christ is identified with His people, and especially His poor; and—

That they who love, for His sake, His people, do implicitly manifest their love to Him, and in that implication shall be rewarded.

1. Now, Christ is one with all mankind in the sameness of a common NATURE; He is one with His sanctified people in the sameness of a common SPIRIT; He is one with His poorer members in the sameness of a common EARTHLY LIFE. Let us follow these steps of union that lead us closer and closer to our incarnate God. Let us trace Him, though absent, by these His images, in the world and the Church. The nature He assumed, the grace He gives, the poverty He borrowed; these are the deputies of Christ in this life; these are commissioned to show Him forth "until He come."

He is one with our race in NATURE: and for this wonderful truth there are, doubtless, abundant reasons hidden in the counsels of God, and of which therefore we can know but little, and can scarcely dare to conjecture. This reason, however, is clearly enough intimated in Scripture; the expiation He accomplished could be fittingly made only in the nature whose guilt was to be expiated; if the immortal Friend of mankind was indeed to take upon Him the heavy penalty of our sins, it could only be by suffering as man for what man had done. Hence this great fact of Christ's unity of nature with the world He redeemed, is prominently and perpetually recorded in the statements of His sacrificial work; this is firmly fixed as the base and bulwark of the whole; and, indeed, in the texture of the Gospels, it is obviously His MANHOOD which is emphatically insisted on, as being truly the miracle, and not His superior nature, which is continually assumed indirectly, or referred to by the Divine Teacher, with that calm and lofty familiarity which marks it an ancient and inherent dignity. In truth, the constant careful ascriptions of manhood—the very phrase, "the Son of Man," chosen as an exclusive title—are themselves the most unequivocal proof that He who bore them was more than man; for otherwise, where were the force or pertinency of a designation equally applicable to every child of Adam? He must have been more than man ever was or could be, by whom "the Son of Man" was selected, or confirmed, as a special, appropriate, and distinctive title. Mightier than man, He has become man; by voluntary assumption He is one with us in nature; as such, He suffered for all; as such, He can sympathise with all; and as such, He will judge all.

He is one with us in GRACE, a deeper, and yet more blessed truth. What Christ's nature has done for our justification, Christ's Spirit has done—is doing—for our progressive renewal to His unclouded image. We have, as it were, given Him of our nature the material of our redemption; He has given us of His celestial nature the properties that are to qualify for the heaven He has won. In entering into the inner courts of heaven by His ascension, He has (they are but two corresponding forms of the same wondrous act) mysteriously entered into the Church, which is heaven upon earth; and thus, abiding in our hearts, becomes the perpetual source of that new and transcendent nature which alone, He has told us, is meet for the kingdom He has founded. Of this unimaginable mystery Christ is the substance, but the Spirit the agent; we receive Him, not in the deadness of a corporeal contact, but in and by His Spirit; we "eat of His body, and drink of His blood," but, in all this, "it is the Spirit that quickeneth, the flesh profiteth nothing." And thus we are, in a manner, incorporated into the mystic bond of the Trinity itself by the indwelling of the sanctifying Spirit of Christ; a relation to which our Lord Himself seemed to intimate some allusion, when He prayed that "they all may be one, as Thou, Father, art in Me and I in Thee, that they also may be one in Us;" where, in the very omission of the *third* person, we seem to recognise the intention of the Saviour, that the *inhabitation* of the Spirit should unite His followers, almost as closely with the Father and the Son, as the Spirit Himself is with them mysteriously united. Christ, then, one with His Spirit-guided people, beholds His own body in them, and loves in them His second self; "for no man ever yet hated his own flesh; but nourisheth and cherisheth it, *even as the Lord the Church.*" (Eph. v. 29.)

But I have said yet more than this. He is with one class of His disciples identified not in nature only, nor in grace only, but in CONDITION also. He has left holiness in the world as His inward representative; He has left poverty as His outward portraiture. For this assumption also the reason is furnished. "Perfected through sufferings," He was to become a consummate 'Leader of Salvation" to all who through the same path were to follow Him to the same glory.

" Though rich, He became poor;" that as a man of sorrows He might feel for sorrow; that the full and flowing tide of brotherly affection might fill at once His own Divine heart and the heart of His afflicted people; that no one temptation might assail a trusting servant which He should not be able to match out of His own treasuries of woe,—even that trial to Him beyond all trials,—the agonizing dread of a Divine desertion; and that thus, " having been tempted, He might be able to succour them that are tempted." For this cause the King of heaven despised the glories of earth; for this cause He selected, and has for ever consecrated, that state of suffering indigence for which I plead this day.

Such, then, is the threefold connexion of Christ with this world, in nature, in grace, in affliction. Let no man say that such a ground of appeal is obscure, or uncertain, or fantastic; never surely was there a description more solemnly and simply serious than this of the final judgment; yet HERE this mysterious incorporation is the very principle of the decisions of the tremendous Judge. In His poor disciples He sees His own earthly witnesses, and the affections that cling to them He regards as directed to Himself. At a moment when, above all others, clearness and simplicity might fairly be expected; and when, beyond all doubt, He does exhibit to us the simplest form, and the simplest ground, of His requirements; at such a moment it is that He tells us, that *He* is in the world wherever there is destitution, that *He* is relieved by our charity, that *He* is rejected by our avarice.

II. So much for the identity of Christ with sanctified and suffering man. Now, a word upon the nature of the corresponding duty of attachment to these representatives of our absent Saviour.

As, then, there is a threefold degree of *union*, so **in exact proportion to the closeness of this union is** the strength of the *claim* which the Christian heart is bound to acknowledge. The love to God made manifest in Christ Jesus, being the principle of the whole spiritual life, everything will be seen by the light which the blessed object of that affection sheds, and endeared in proportion as it approaches that centre and final standard of perfection. There is no bigoted exclusiveness, there is no irrational and arbitrary partiality (as men insinuate), in this way of distributing our affections; it is in strict accordance with that great eternal rule of reason which bids us love as men deserve our love; and it only presumes that they who are nearest the heart of God, and most richly visited by His graces, will best meet and answer the attachment of each other. In the same degree, then, that men are near to Christ, we are commanded that they be near to us. All humanity claims our affectionate sympathy, for He has assumed the nature of a man; every regenerate believer in Christ Jesus claims yet higher and more peculiar affection, for with him Christ is one, not in body alone, but in Spirit also. And if among these believers, thus one with Christ and with us in Christ, there be some who stand in the world as the very copies and images of the departed Master; some who present Him to us not only in mystical communion, but in outward form and lineament, showing forth His mournful life, and clad in the same uniform of woe; if there be some who hunger as He hungered, and like Him have not where to lay their heads; —who shall say that there is not a bond of special tenderness that draws such a people as this nearer to the Christian heart; who shall say that such as these are not to be loved for their very sorrow's sake—for that sorrow which mirrors the humiliation and the agonies of a Saviour, absent to our eyes, but present to our hearts in them?

Here, then, is the scale of Christian love; it does not supersede that of nature, but it adds new and peculiar motives to the promptings of the natural affections. " I love" (may the Christian disciple say) "everything that has life, because the Lord of glory gave that life; I love yet more every human being, because the same Lord has adopted and redeemed our universal nature; I love, with an affection yet more intense, the regenerate people of God, for Christ dwelleth in them; and of these His people, with the deepest sympathy of all, I love His poor, because they are what He *was*, bearing His image and superscription, bequeathed to us as living and abiding memorials of His poverty for ever. My affections are in His disposal; let Him expend them as He will; what most is He, that most I cherish; everything that I love below shall be but the reflection of the light I adore above." This is the Christian's canon of the affections; thus, in every earthly attachment, he is but training in the school of Christ, and loving Him in His. The Lord Jesus undergoes a kind of everlasting incarnation in His Church; and in our loving the gracious fruits of His indwelling in His people He is not Himself defrauded of our affections; it is still, in a manner, " God manifest in the flesh," whom we cherish and revere.

The affections, then, that cling to Christ in heaven, do yet embrace all His earthly manifestations; and chiefly those in which we behold His sanctifying graces and the image of His afflictions. This presence of Himself in His disciples is to be to us the ground of every tender office to the brethren; we are but loyal to Him in loving them. And, above all, in sorrow, in pain, in poverty, He is among us; *there* is the chosen sanctuary of His perpetuated presence; there is the temple of His shrouded glory. I have heard of a wild Italian legend which tells us that the Lord is still a tenant of our earth; and, with His beloved disciple, annually arrives an unknown wanderer, among the mendicants at the gates of Rome. Brethren, there is a meaning in the fable. It *is* among the poor ye must seek these divine features; it *is* beneath the garments of poverty ye must learn to recognise and venerate the Lord of life.

Oh, beloved in Jesus Christ! we feel not how divine a thing is sorrow, when we forget who it was that once voluntarily chose it as His own. A man of moderately pious sensibility would surely feel a strange pleasure, and a kind of natural dedication to holiness, if he could be ascertained that, by some happy caprice of nature, his outward face and form were accurately moulded to the image of those of Jesus of Nazareth; the Christian mourner wears the dress—the chosen dress, and form, and feature—of that Divine Redeemer's soul! "The poor ye have always with you, but Me ye have not always." Nay, Lord, in the poor we have Thee—Thee in Thine humble image. The poor man dwells in the same moral climate his Saviour inhabited; breathes the air his Saviour breathed: is there not something altogether sublime in sorrow, thus for ever brightened, glorified, transfigured by Him who rejected every other state to wear it?

Transcendent mystery! A GOD was to come among us. The heavenly portals open wide that He may issue forth, and millions of adoring angels accompany Him as He leaves the skies. They dare not—they cannot—look upon that awful face; they know it only by the light it sheds, as with timid eyes they watch its far-off radiance, and hang upon the skirts of its glory. He touches the verge of earth, and they retire to their celestial home; but, ere they vanished back, their song was heard that night by the waking shepherds of Bethlehem! And now He is among us! Arise and welcome Him, O earth! bring forth all that thou hast of precious and wonderful to lay at His feet; crowns, and sceptres, and regal purple; the glory of the throne, and the camp, and the senate; temples of incense, illuminated cities, and the shout of kneeling thousands. They are here; He has but to put forth His hands, and all is His; but one majestic miracle, and the world is paralysed to subjection. Let "the thunder of His power" be but heard, and every nation and tongue shall do Him homage; East and West, the haughty Roman and the soft son of Asia; Scythian and African, yea, the far undiscovered lands, burst open by the flashing of His presence—all will struggle who shall be the deepest slave. But how is this?

the offering is untouched, unheeded. The gorgeous vision slowly fades away. In its place arise a few bare hills, dotted here and there with the mean abodes of penury; in the foreground, a poor man, more destitute than even they; He is weak and wayworn, exhausted with weariness and watchings, with hunger and thirst, with cold and nakedness; He pauses at one of those miserable dwellings, and some few faint words are heard; and then the sullen repulse; and the Wanderer turns away with a groan, lifts His eyes to mark the gathering storm, and sighs as He resumes His path of pain, "The fowls of the air have nests, but the Son of Man hath not where to lay His head." Mighty Lord, who wast thus rejected that we might live, teach us, teach us to understand and feel this mystery of woe, teach us to love what Thou hast made Thine own; to honour the misery which Thou hast selected; to look with respect and awe upon the Christian poverty whose sorrows whisper us of Thine!

It is such poverty—the poverty of Christ present and embodied in His people—for which I have this day to plead; it is the poverty of gospel-taught brethren and sisters in the truth; of those who are the same with you in faith, who share a common hope, who are yours—as in faith and in hope, so, I trust in a merciful God this day may prove—in the bonds also of a common charity! It is for sorrows such as these, on which the very signet of Christ has stamped his own divine character, that I have to speak to you on this most solemn occasion; and you must forgive me if, in the justifiable freedom of my office, I speak to you in a tone of censure, painful, believe me, not less to him who speaks than to you who hear it. This Association for the relief of Protestant distress comes before you itself in the character of distress and difficulty: that it may relieve other suppliants it has itself to become a suppliant. You have not maintained it as it deserves. It is, brethren, it *is* a shame to your liberality, that this excellent institution should exhibit its melancholy defalcation; that, with increasing demands, it should be still forced to narrow its circle of blessings. You know well that this is no common charity; that its claims are far beyond the ordinary claims of special and local institutions; that it is the great means afforded in your city for rescuing the poorer members of the faith from degradation and famine; that it is almost the sole resource of voluntary benevolence applicable to cases not provided for by our few occasional and local aids; that in its comprehensive plan it is, in a manner, all charities spiritual and temporal in one. And yet, with all this well understood, the melancholy fact is equally certain, that the subscriptions in aid of this invaluable organ of public Protestant benevolence, have, in the last year fallen, by nearly four hundred pounds, below those of the preceding. What can account for this, or what can excuse it? Are our brethren in Christ less destitute, or are they less our brethren? with an increasing population, are there fewer to be fed? with increasing temptations for honest poverty, are there fewer to be rescued, and consoled, and fortified? The bonds that tie us to these poor people are woven by Christ Himself; but even were His will undeclared, ask your own sympathies as men and citizens, is this a time to desert the poor protectorless witnesses of His truth among those who cannot understand, and will not love, and dare not help them?

Let me not be told that the application of this charity is too *exclusive*. All applications of charity must be exclusive, in some sense, to be available. The special purpose of every charity confines it to that purpose; and what is this but to exclude all to whom that purpose will not apply? In any lower sense of degrading religious bigotry, the charge is notoriously unfounded: the subscription books of every public charity in this city sufficiently prove whether Protestantism can be *catholic* in at least the universality of its sympathies with human suffering; whether the professor of the pure faith of the Bible requires any evidence beyond the lineaments of a common humanity to determine the objects of his benevolence. Long may it continue so; it is the noblest way to confute the cavils of controversialists against the moral power of your faith; it is worth a thousand theological arguments. For all the general purposes of charity, the Gospel, we may be assured, was never sent to contract our purse-strings; it would be melancholy, indeed, if we were to read our Bibles only to learn whom *not* to relieve. Still, the same Bible fixes some nearer your heart than others. I scruple not to say, because I am sure you will not misunderstand or exaggerate my meaning,— that we have carried our habits of undistinguishing charity almost (if that be possible) to an excess; and that if the alleged exclusiveness of this Institution offend some of its censurers, it is only because we have so long forgotten that charity, to be just, ought to apportion its aids according to the equity of demands, the comparative closeness of connexion, and the immediate pressure of circumstances. The Gospel rule is simple. Love all; aid whom you can; but aid those most whom God has specially allocated to your bounty.

If, then, we must sometimes restrict and appropriate our charity, I remind you again, (for I descend to no other argument,) that, on the ground of the community in the truth of Christ that obtains between us and the poorest of these our brethren, we are bound to identify our interests with theirs, to regard them as members of our own spiritual constitution, to compassionate, and help, and cherish them as such. But doubly are we on religious grounds bound to this office, if in their poverty we have reason to see their extreme religious danger. If there be reason to fear that these poor people are encompassed with temptations to desert the faith of the Gospel; if they are known to be but a few scattered among thousands; if their number prevents mutual support, and combination, and countenance; if their comparative feebleness expose them to mockery and contempt; if they are surrounded by a population, every member of which deems it the highest conceivable merit before God to snatch His creature from the eternal perdition of unrepented heresy, and can scarcely deem any measure unwarrantable that promises to secure such a result; if in the prosecution of this supposed duty that population is urged and encouraged by a priesthood, perhaps through the world unparalleled in their zeal for nominal conversions; if frequent personal visitation, and seductive plausibilities addressed to the ear, and pompous processions addressed to the eye, and the influence of almost universal example addressed to both, surround and tempt the solitary Protestant; if these motives press, hour after hour, upon the lonely unprotected man, and the chief safeguard against their power, the regular attendance of church services, and the strengthening presence of his brother worshippers, — his wretched poverty forbids; what, I ask you, can be the result, but too often those wretched apostasies that vex and harass the guardians of Christ's little flock, and swell the triumph of their busy antagonists? Brethren, you must blunt the force of these temptations; you must shield the indigent Protestant from these perilous assaults upon the honesty of his heart and the strength of his convictions; "converted" yourselves, you must "strengthen your brethren;" it is for you to rescue these poor victims from being the perpetual objects of a warfare of petty cunning, and insinuation, and falsehood, by enabling them to *live* without leaving your communion, and to enjoy the invigorating services of religion in the same holy temples as yourselves, without the shame of entering those temples in the miserable livery of pauperism.

But men perpetually object, "Why paint us *now* these pictures of unreclaimed destitution? Public legislation has now superseded the necessity of private charity; a fiat has gone forth from the high places of the land that forbids any Irishman to starve; we contribute to this fund of statutory charity, and our consciences are satisfied." Brethren, this is a subject in which the pulpit should not be silent. For those who sincerely and conscientiously desire to do the will of God, there are probably few more important points of practical instruction at the present crisis. In this conviction I must plainly tell you, that your consciences ought *not* to be satisfied with any consideration that supersedes liberal voluntary charity; that in doing so you forget the law of Christ in the law of the land; and idly imagine that you are bearing the easy yoke and light burden of the Saviour, when you are really working in the harness of compulsory civil enactments. What? are all those texts of our Book that make the life of the Christian one incessant outbreathing of benevolence, that (as you heard this day)* declare God Himself to be Love, and Love the fulfilling of God's whole law—are all these to be obliterated because we pay so many pence in the pound to the district collector? Are we to *commute* with Christ, and refer Him for His high exclusive claims to the books of the parish officer, where we are debtors to the law, and pay because we cannot help it? Are these to be the agents of our gentle Christian charity, the men who enforce (and justly) our tribute money with the stern sanction in the rear of legal processes and penal inflictions? No, brethren, you must not confound these things. What you pay to the public collector for our poor, pay with cheerfulness, with hope, with prayer that a blessing may rest upon its distribution; but never forget that in doing so you are "rendering unto Cæsar the things which are Cæsar's," not rendering "unto God the things that are God's." I repeat it, on your peril confound not these obligations! The Church's charity to her poor rests on a ground altogether transcending the enactments of earthly policy, a basis eternal as the mind of God Himself, which no legal interferences can either strengthen or enfeeble. The Church's charity is God's own divine poor-law, with its spring deep in the regenerate human heart, and its diffusion

* First Sunday after Trinity.

wide as the world. Alas! were *that* law as practically efficient as He meant it to be, no other need ever have entered our statute books; Christ's Spirit would have solved the question that so long perplexed our statesmen, and no poor rate need have existed but that which once drove destitution out of the Church of God, because "these Christians so loved one another." But as it is, and since these remedies must be, I warn you that you imagine not that your payments to the state are to release one fraction of your payments to the treasury of Christ. Poor-laws exist because selfish men would not save a brother from starvation without them; but poor-laws are nothing to the Christian disciple. "The love of Christ constraineth *him;*" "Commandments" which "are not grievous," which are only the more powerful the more his "heart is set at liberty," are his secret laws; the voice of the poor he hears as the voice of Christ, their miseries as the miseries of Christ; it is Christ who groans upon the fevered couch, it is Christ who cries in the despair of hunger, it is Christ who is naked and asks for clothing, who is sick and must be visited, who is in prison and must be "come unto." These are the bonds of Christ Jesus, which are His, which are yours—no matter what poor-law compels you to charity. Misery enough will still exist to make needful all, and more than all, you ever gave; and your Christian obligation to relieve it by voluntary aid, no earthly legislation can any wise affect. Thank God it *will* exist; for were it not in the world, our indurated hearts could never be disciplined for the eternal charities of heaven.

For look to this, beloved brethren; you are here *educating* for immortality; love is the main principle of the education, for "never-failing" love is to be the main characteristic of the immortality. The poor are forbid " to cease out of the land," that this preparatory love may never in this world cease to have its appropriate objects. The more you learn to love the brethren, the more you come to resemble the living God; for, once more to recal the memorable Epistle of the day, "God is love; and He that dwelleth in love dwelleth in God, and God in him." Every sacrifice for our fellows, every real heartfelt intention for their happiness, works our nature yet more and more into the bright similitude of God; and fits our spirits to be eventually the loving tenants of a land of love.

Cannot you, then, feel that no public compulsory enactment can for a moment suspend the necessity for carrying on this *discipline* of your own hearts? Need I ask you, how is any man's nature the better for giving what he cannot escape giving? how does he rise in the school of love who pays through fear? And though much may be done towards sanctifying a compulsory gift through resignation, and making that an act of the pure will which cannot, at all events, be evaded, I need not remind you how deceptive and uncertain is such a process as this; how little we can depend on it as an instance of genuine benevolence; how, in short, we can depend on nothing as a training in the love of man and the likeness of God, but constant habitual tenderness of heart; charities liberal, disinterested, unostentatious, unforced,— wrought through the deep feeling of the communion of all men in the same nature, of the communion of all saints in the same regeneration.

You see, then, how this too-prevalent objection to our Christian charities, drawn from the existence of a poor-law enactment, when viewed in the blessed light of divine truth, has no real force,—how it rests upon low and earthly, and unspiritual views of the real demands of brotherly charity. We have seen how the Christian's bond of love is one with which no State enactment has any connexion at all,—which depends on principles that cannot be, in the slightest degree, disturbed by any interferences of the policy of this world; turning, as it does, solely on the glorious fact that Christ is ours, and with Christ, every member of Christ's family. Then, again, have we not seen, that as we are in this world training by love for a world whose happiness is love, so our charity must essentially be a loving charity—a charity of the heart; and that nothing can be safely regarded as such but that to which no earthly power compels us, which is bestowed solely by the sweet compulsion of affection, and thus becomes a real evidence of the affection that prompts it?

But once more. This is in itself a narrow and degrading objection for any man to advance. What? have we discharged all our duties to the poor Protestant, when we have abandoned him to the alms-house? Is that the acme of our Christian sympathy? Is that the glorious evidence of our brotherhood in the faith? We are bound to him by immortal ties; he is with us a witness for Christ upon earth; he is with us involved in those dangers and difficulties of position that must ever belong, more or less, to the truth, when the truth is in a minority; in his own humble sphere he works with us to manifest the power of a pure Gospel faith, in general honesty of life and simplicity of deportment; his sorrows are reported to us; men—kind, laborious men—come to us with his story; they tell us that this poor brother is starving, that his family are dying one by one around him, that he is too often the subject of mockery, slander, and all the infinite varieties of petty persecution: and we think it enough to reply, that truly we discharge the parish rates; that, thank God, no man can say we are in his books; and that, doubtless, this poor object, whoever he may be, can share the public charity with the rest of its dependents. Admirable! you have discharged your duty when you have raised your brother in the Gospel to the dignity of a parish pauper! The man, who once knew the content of honest industry, would gladly again enter his career of quiet usefulness; he abhors, like any independent spirit, the painful position of a fixed pensioner on legal charity; he asks you to save him from the degradation—a loan, a small loan, may do it; for when the heart is resolute how little may be the germ of prosperity! and your answer is—blush every

Christian who could conceive such an answer this day!—your answer is, that the workhouse is open for paupers, and among its rank and file of misery the forsaken Protestantism of your country may take its place! I tell you, the gospel-taught Protestant will not accept your answer, for he knows the validity of his Christian claim; I tell you, your teachers in Christ Jesus will not accept your answer, for it is a different lesson they have taught you; I tell you, that an authority mightier than your earthly brother or father in Christ Jesus will not accept your answer—the eternal Judge, who at this hour knows your hearts, and knows also the wants and the claims of every poor member of His mystical body; I tell you HE will not accept the plea that sends His poverty-stricken people from being the active, industrious examples of a neighbourhood, to pine and wither in the gloomy retreats of heartless, hopeless destitution. Surely this is a most important consideration, this public benefit of Protestant *example*, found to be, as we may confidently pronounce it, alike in this city and in the nation at large, a magnificent attestation of the practical excellence of the faith that produces it. Your duty is not to make the poor-house the stated refuge for the indigence of our people, but to rescue from the necessity of recurring to the poor-house; your duty is to interpose between your famishing brother and that sad home of paralysed poverty, to meet him on the way, to cherish his infirm purpose, and restore him, if possible, to the useful activities of social life. It is not that they may fade away in the silence of such asylums, that the providence of Christ has scattered His believing people through this unhappy land; it is not that they may decay and fester in nerveless inactivity, that He has set these watchmen of the Gospel faith in the midst of a superstitious population. He has meant that every professor of His truth, however lowly, should be a seed and germ of the truth to all around him, that these lights, dispersed through the darkness, should be the beacon-lights of temporal contentment and eternal happiness to whole circles of deceived and ignorant worshippers,—that the poor Protestant should be a living exemplification, and in his own humble way a perpetual apostle, of that "faith once delivered to the saints," to which Christ in His mercy has called him. No, no; you have *not* done your duty to your brother in Christ Jesus when you have sent him to pace the gloomy cloisters of the mendicant's last home; you have not fulfilled the purposes of the Church's Almighty Head, when you have withdrawn him from the office of standing for the truth in the broad daylight of the world, and thus making his existence known and felt, to bury him in the common heap of misery that stagnates behind the walls of a poor-house.

Moreover, this too must be remembered. If the public tax for our poor has secured from extreme cases of destitution, it has only altered the level on which the exertions of such an Association as this must operate. Suppose it certain that henceforth no Protestant in this city need die of starvation, are our charities really to be limited to securing our fellow-believers from the last agonies of famine?—is our benevolence satisfied when we have ascertained that men and women shall not die of hunger on the steps of our mansions? The truth is, that there is a class of cases infinitely more interesting and important that open to this Association, when its hands are relaxed from doling out shillings to the starving mechanic. If you want really to see and understand the blessedness of charity, you must sometimes travel a step higher. You must enter the parlour of the decent and reputable tradesman, to whom beggary would be pollution, and the poor-house little better; you must see him, by the casualties of his trade, reduced to a state of heart-broken poverty, which he is himself ashamed to acknowledge; you must discover—for often he will shudder to tell—how from step to step he has sunk till first his few superfluities, and then the common comforts, and then the last necessaries of life, had to be surrendered; you must watch the lip quiver, and the wasted cheek flush, as he murmurs his wretched admission, and still strives to disguise it, that before you speak of comfort to his soul, it is needful you should help the fainting body; for of a truth, my richer brethren, one meal in some six-and-thirty hours is scarcely sufficient to uphold our human frame. He is found, it may be, in bed: you inquire his ailment; you promise to procure medical aid: he murmurs his thanks, but declines your proffer; and the miserable secret slowly discloses itself—you know not whether to rejoice or grieve as you learn—that the sickness itself is counterfeit, a wretched artifice of poverty; that bed must be his only home, for he lacks common clothing, not merely to leave his own door, but even to sit beside his own hearth! Cases like these are, above all others, the cases in which this Institution may be a blessed means of invaluable relief. To restore a man of this station to his path of honest exertion,—to enable him once more to set the example of social usefulness,—this is to do charity in the happiest spirit; it is not to make its object a dependent, but to enable him to be no longer so; it is to benefit, not that immediate object alone, but a large section of society that is elevated and quickened by his recovered influence.

But I must cease; for I am aware I have detained your attention beyond the usual period. Pardon me, brethren; remember, that if I have addressed you at greater length than is common, it is no common cause for which I plead. The claims of *four hundred and eighty-five* families rejected during the past year for want of means; the voice of four hundred and eighty-five families supplicating to be saved from ruin, or the home-exile of a workhouse; a failure of nearly *four hundred pounds* in the amount of your contributions; proportionate difficulties and entanglements to the perplexed ministers of charity; these are the urgencies that have made me unwilling to leave this pulpit while one chance remained of awakening you to compassion. I ask for a large disbursement this day from those who are here; I ask, through them, for large and instant donations from those who are not. Be every one of you the echo of my voice through this city, that what is here said may be fully, and clearly, and widely known; for what is my voice but itself the echo of a thousand mourners, lingering in lanes and by-ways, in haunts where hunger tempts despairing poverty to crime, and piety itself has almost ceased to hope? Hear them, brethren, and help! Help them, and—not *I* will reward you; no mortal voice is that which promises your recompense; a mightier power than man's is pledged to remember your deeds this day. The minister gives way to the MASTER. "Behold, HE cometh!" A light not of earth is above us; the unsetting Sun of Eternity is risen! The walls of this earthly tabernacle made with hands vanish as we gaze; the everlasting temple of God and the Lamb expands around our ascended and glorified bodies; and amid the hosannas of ten thousand thousand that stand before Him, "the shout of the archangel and the trump of God," a VOICE is heard that pierces through them all—a voice soft as the breathings of infancy, yet awful too, as beseems the sceptred Monarch of eternity—"INASMUCH AS YE HAVE DONE IT UNTO ONE OF THE LEAST OF THESE MY BRETHREN, YE HAVE DONE IT UNTO ME."

SERMON XXVI.

ETERNAL PUNISHMENT.

(First Sunday after Trinity.)

St. Luke XVI. 26.

Between us and you there is a great gulf fixed: so that they which would pass *from* hence to you cannot; neither can they pass to us, that would come from thence.

It is well, my brethren, that the Church has taken care to set before us the awful topic of this day's gospel. One of the many obvious advantages of a fixed Liturgy is this,—that it maintains for the people the due proportion of divine truth; that it secures them (to a certain degree) from the arbitrary and exclusive selections of different schools of teachers, and thus preserves to them unimpaired their entire inheritance of Revelation. But in no department of divine truth is the evil thus partly remedied more lamentably prevalent than in the subject now before us. In this place, indeed, the very variety of your instructors—not to speak of the greater opportunities of sound and enlarged study—may probably help to correct the tendency to restrict the theology of the Holy Scriptures to a few selected tenets. But I appeal to all who have candidly observed the general current and complexion of Christian teaching in our days and Church, whether there be not a most undeniable comparative obscuration in that teaching, of a certain vast and weighty order of subjects, at least a lack of the directness and simplicity of Scripture enforcement with regard to them. You will readily apprehend that I allude to such great Scripture truths as the judgment of all men according to their works, and perhaps still more, its result in the awful everlasting doom of the wicked. Of course I do not for a moment mean to affirm that such doctrines are expressly denied; that men formally and verbally contradict the New Testament affirmations on the subject; but that they are not made to occupy *the place*, whether as to extent or importance, which they hold in the New Testament. One writer of great eloquence and power, who has exercised much influence on the general mind, thinks it necessary, whenever he approaches the subject of the rewards of righteousness, to soothe what he styles " the alarms of the orthodox." The orthodox! What must the " orthodoxy " be which starts with all the dread of anticipated heresy at the mere sound of a theme which, however it be explained, makes, directly or indirectly, the substance of a third of the Gospels!

The common disinclination to press, in the plain way of Scripture, these most awful subjects, arises from several sources. In the first place, it seems to be thought that these motives are of a low and earthly character, common to us with the morality of heathen philosophy, and hardly distinctive enough of the Christian gospel. Yet our blessed Lord ought to have understood His own divine system; and it will hardly be denied that *His* discourses at least abound with these statements of judgment and of retribution. And even supposing the general notion of retribution to be observable in much of the better human, as well as in the divine, ethics, one would think that this ought rather to impress the exceeding importance of a doctrine which God has deemed of such moment as never to have left mankind without some faint belief in it, while giving it, in the fulness of time, His own express confirmation. Still it may be granted, that fear of punishment is comparatively a low motive, in itself somewhat poor and slavish; and that it is less and less required as men rise in the scale of sanctification. Doubtless; but are our congregations ordinarily such men? It is the evil—the incalculable evil—of the partial and limited exhibition of divine truth I allude to, that it is almost wholly above the level of the real attainments of congregations, and thus inevitably tends to foster self-delusion as to their own state. Why address the decorous worldliness of fashionable religionism, as if it possessed motives it has never once realized? And while I am inclined to believe that a man cannot be ordinarily said to possess the faith that is accepted unto justification, who has as yet no true desire at all for *spiritual* enjoyments, I will nevertheless venture to affirm that a man who really feels *afraid* of God, who has a real belief of hell, and a real dread of it, has made *some* way. It is no small matter to realize the invisible in any of its regions. If a man believes a hell, he so far believes the Scriptures, and has generally some further knowledge of their contents: nor except in those dreadful cases of sudden remorse in the terror of death, and the like, or where the religious teaching has been miserably defective, is there commonly a real fear of hell without *some* attraction of the heart to holiness.

Another reason for this omission is probably to be found in a vague but powerful and influential notion, that these terrific disclosures of Scripture are so largely *metaphorical* as to be of little service for direct instruction. The everlasting is only a figure for lengthened duration; the fire of torment is not material, but symbolical of mental affliction—a mental affliction, observe, which, consisting mainly in the loss of God, the wicked cannot even conceive; the judgment itself is but a long process of gradual discrimination between different classes of character. By such qualifications as these the sharper and sterner features of the subject are smoothened away, and room is afforded for the fond, self-flattering visions of an indolence unwilling to be aroused or alarmed.

But in truth this welcome scepticism is carried much further. One would not without reluctance attribute it to any class of professional religious teachers in these islands: but

I fear *he* must have ill-observed the floating creed of general society, who is not aware how largely diffused is the positive disbelief of any outburst at all of divine anger in the world to come. Not merely the avowed rejecter of Christianity, but even men of some religious pretensions, seem strangely agreed to forget altogether the more awful side of the divine character; and with the majority of men of the world, the doctrine of an eternal doom of condemnation seems, when they think at all about it, monstrous, disproportioned, impossible.

Certainly, under these circumstances, it is well that the Church, as on this day, will not suffer us to overlook these tremendous declarations of Holy Scripture; where the same God who promises heaven, threatens hell, and the same scepticism which trifles with the one must reject both.

And, oh, my brethren, of a truth it is no marvel that such things as these should be bitter and unwelcome to man; that they should naturally tend to fade and disappear from our thoughts, like all else we dread and dislike! Strange, indeed, were such a doctrine or its preaching popular! Who that knows aught of our customary weaknesses can anticipate but that prepossessions, not to be overborne except by the most resolute perseverance of the watchmen of Christ, shall arise against a truth which, were it conceived in its full proportions, (a task perhaps impossible to man,) would involve the whole face of nature in gloom, would hang the very heavens in black, and make all their daily and nightly glories but the torchlights of a funeral chamber; a truth which loads every instant of life with a weight almost intolerable of responsibility, which contracting life to a short winter-day, stretches out beyond it the drear, the starless dark of a midnight on which no morrow shall ever dawn; which affrights us with horrible thought of a duration of woe counted not by years but by ages; which tells us—us who live by pity, social enjoyment, mutual kindness, friendship real or supposed—that there can be, and for millions will be, a time when no pity shall exist in the whole wide universe for them, no mercy from God, no compassion from each other, no refuge, no hope; when that on-looking tendency which makes the best happiness of us all, shall shrink back upon itself withered and blasted, or exist only to press home to the heart more keenly the reality of eternal, immutable wretchedness. Shall we, indeed, wonder that this mystery of woe—for a mystery it surely is—should ever be an unwilling theme for man to listen to or man to speak?

It was, indeed, in a great measure (we may suppose) this natural reluctance which in all ages of Christianity has led to the various hypotheses by which the broad and unqualified statements of Scripture as to the two states, eternal and opposite, have been modified. Men felt a twofold perplexity in this matter. When the moral differences between man and man appeared to graduate through every shade from utter depravity to mature saintliness, it seemed difficult to provide for all by the mere supposition of two opposite retributory states. Again; the tremendous doom of eternal misery appeared disproportioned to any amount of criminality. The latter of these difficulties led to the bold assumption of Origen and his followers, that all punishment is temporary: a doctrine which, though revived by some philosophic writers of repute even within the Church of later days, is now, as a formal theological tenet, confined almost wholly to that great and wide-spread heresy, whose only real canon of interpretation is this, that in all things alike—whether the nature of God or the destination of man—Revelation must bow, not indeed to reason, but to those illusory prejudices of sense and time which arrogantly usurp its name. The former—the variety and seeming proximity of the moral states in which men leave this world—led, as we all know, to the more popular, but hardly more satisfactory, hypothesis of purgatory.

Circumstances are now making the controversy with Rome of special interest, and I may, therefore, succeed in interesting you with some general considerations on the latter of these solutions. I shall then attempt to offer some observations (equally general) on the other topic: the great doctrine itself of the eternity of punishment, and the difficulties, whether real or supposed, that attend it.

I. Without at all undertaking (for which we have now no time, nor can you possibly need it) to expose the well-known pretences of Scripture authority for the tenet of a state of future temporary punishment of sin, let me ask you to consider how far, even as an hypothesis, it really meets the difficulty it professes to relieve.

The difficulty is this; that between the lowest spirit that is saved and the best that is lost, the moral difference must be immeasurably smaller than the tremendous difference of doom—an eternity of happiness and an eternity of woe.

The Scripture account of the case is far, indeed, from removing all mystery, but it certainly tends to alleviate the difficulty. Scripture most plainly intimates that there are to be *degrees* both of reward and of punishment in the two spheres of future existence; so that, as regards the individual varieties in each of these two great classes, the difficulty altogether ceases. But it must be confessed that between the two classes themselves, and so, between the individuals at each side next the awful boundary-line that separates them, it leaves the distinction and the difficulty; " a great gulf is fixed." When Dr. Paley conjectures that the difference of condition in this case may be as slight as the differences of moral character,—if he mean the differences *apparent to us*, and if he would thus indefinitely *approximate* the states themselves, he surely forgets the plainest and most unequivocal declarations of that record from which alone we can learn anything at all with certainty on the subject.

But now, were we to grant the purgatorial scheme, (which has hardly any merit at all except as it helps us in this strait, and probably owed most of its original currency to its supposed utility for that purpose,) should we be really advanced? The question, we have seen, is not as to the differences that shall exist between individuals of the good and evil classes respectively, but altogether turns upon that tremendous point where the utterly lost and the saved are disjoined from each other. But this difficulty the hypothesis of a purgatory only disguises and postpones; for it must surely be manifest, that it applies with undiminished force to the boundary that divides the worst sufferers in purgatory from the incalculably more terrific doom of the least criminal, who is to endure the eternity of hell. Nay, it aggravates the difficulty, by the very attempt to establish a proportion where it is manifest no proportion can subsist; for assuredly no ingenuity can ever make commensurable an eternal separation from God in misery, and any punishment, however intense, that terminates before the judgment.

This doctrine, however, having been of late specially noted as one of the peculiar and incomparable advantages of the Roman theology, I am induced to offer a few further observations on its claims; still restricting myself to its merits as an hypothesis, and without any discussion of the special passages alleged as Scripture confirmations.

The object of this supposed state is twofold; punitive and purificatory. The former I despatch in a word. There is not the shadow of evidence in the Christian Revelation for the principle, that punishment is ever reserved after complete divine pardon. The very object of the atonement of Christ was just to prevent this necessity; to make punitive justice (temporal or eternal is incidental, not essential, to the idea) compatible with absolute love; and any theology which maintains that further **punishment** *as such* (ratione pœnæ) is demanded by God, unquestionably so far substitutes a personal atonement for the atonement of Christ. I suppose I need hardly observe that this has no concern with the very different question, how far a man may usefully adopt self-mortifying habits; or God in His mercy send a corrective and disciplinary evil, "chastening whom He loveth;" or God permit the natural results of moral evil to follow after forgiving sin—results which He could only suspend by miracle. The question is simply, whether He inflicts punishment on the forgiven in the *same sense* in which He inflicts hell on the damned, though less in intensity and duration. This is what we repudiate as inconsistent with the whole tenor of Revelation. He who bore any of the penalty of sin, bore it all.

The question becomes perhaps more interesting when we canvass the hypothesis on the other ground; for it might be alleged, that even supposing a true spiritual vitality possessed by a soul departing in a state of grace, yet pain may be required *for its perfection;* a pain not sufficiently experienced —as (suppose) in a case of a very late conversion—during its earthly course. Now, in the first place, I would remind you of the exceeding peril of constructing fundamental and necessary doctrine out of such mere speculation as this; speculation too in a region (the nature, attributes, occupations, opportunities, of departed spirits) where we are so utterly ignorant of the very elements out of which alone we could form any conclusive judgment. In the next place, that cases are by these theologians themselves maintained (baptism, martyrdom) where this supposed necessity is altogether abandoned; and the convert of a week or a day conceived to be translated instantaneously to the presence of God. But waiving this, let us examine the speculation itself. We admit that in good men affliction has its uses on earth; that it prevents attachment to the world, that it lowers pride, that it exercises faith, that it tries fidelity, that it refines from fleshly luxuries, that it habituates to resignation. Now which of these " uses of adversity" can clearly apply to the supposition of intermediate purification by pain,—can apply to it, I say, in preference to the exalting effects, which I presume will hardly be denied, of the society of the blessed, and the similar instrumentalities which may be assumed to operate on the supposition of the immediate translation of the saved to real or expected glory? To imagine that severe pain can be needful to a man who has died a sincere and accepted servant of Christ, and is now in the very world of holiness, in order to wean his desires from the miserable shadows he has left for ever; or again, in order to impress the guilt of sin, and lower the proud independence of one who has already believed on the sacrifice, and now beholds the sovereign glory, of Christ, or to exercise his faith, the faith of one who has now passed the sphere of faith, and stands in the very presence and contact of reality, or to put his fidelity to proof, while it is admitted he cannot fail, and knows he cannot; or to reduce the tyranny of the flesh in a *disembodied* spirit: all these are notions which seem incompatible at once with the state of grace in which the subject of them is presupposed to have died, and with the possible or probable operations of mere pain in the circumstances proper to a departed spirit. On the closest scrutiny, I can discover no result of benefit which such suffering could be reasonably expected to produce, except that it might, perhaps, confirm that practical habit of resignation to the will of God, which, as our great philosophic theologian has observed, may be useful in producing a temper suitable to the world of blessedness. But on this plea (should it be offered) I would observe, first, that it is most daring of us to assume that God cannot mature the conformity of a true and accepted believer's will to His own, except by a process of protracted suffering; it being in itself clearly attainable through the quickening efficacy of increased spiritual knowledge and holy joy. Next, that the sufferer is himself as far from "rejoicing in tribulation," that he is supposed to be earnestly longing and praying for his own release; for that which the Church is commanded to do on his behalf on earth, it must, of course, be legitimate for him to do personally in purgatory. Again, that the fact of knowing himself ultimately and unchangeably secure of heaven must greatly weaken the discipline of humiliation, which with us so largely depends on the possibility of failure, and the vigilance perpetually required to "make the calling and election sure." Nor, indeed, this alone, for he is certain of bearing the discipline itself well, as otherwise the purgatorial sin of insubordination would deserve that more terrible doom from which he is supposed to be absolutely safe,—a certainty both present and future, which must be admitted likely to enervate the efficacy of this purgatorial discipline of resignation. Pain, indeed, with an absolute certainty of salvation, and pain with an absolute despair of it, seem equally unfitted for purposes of discipline. I would add, that the moral efficacy of mere pain is, in itself, so doubtful, that it requires great grace from God to prevent its injuring instead of improving the temper of the sufferer; and surely the same expenditure of grace would be, at least, as competent to insure the same exalting results in the world of happiness. Suppose divine grace refused, and the man will grow worse rather than better among the horrors of purgatory; suppose it granted, and the perfection of his nature may as well be consummated under the energy of that grace, amid the joys and the sanctities of heaven.

So much, then, for the speculative or philosophical merits of the hypothesis of purgatory; an hypothesis which, originating no doubt in a strong sense of real difficulties, introduces more difficulties than it solves; which, above all, leaves wholly unremoved that great and awful difficulty already mentioned which no imaginary protraction of graduated pain can ever even partially lighten, as long as time in all the multitude of its ages remains still incommensurable with eternity. There is no comfort in those unsubstantial shadows which the impatient curiosity, or the secret terrors, of man have interposed between himself and the inevitable truth. They leave us unsheltered, unreprieved; naked and trembling before the terrible simplicity of Revelation, of those unambiguous oracles in which that God who is " a consuming fire" hath described Himself in the very volume of mercy as bidding " the cursed into everlasting fire," into a " fire that is not quenched," that is " unquenchable," whose " smoke ascendeth up for ever," whose " torment is day and night for ever and ever."

II. I have hinted already, and I repeat it, that were it possible for man's imagination to conceive the horrors of such a doom as this, all reasoning about it were at an end; it would scorch and wither all the powers of human thought. Human life were at a stand, could these things be really felt as they deserve. Even for him who can humbly trust himself, comparatively secure in faith and obedience, were the thin veil of this poor shadowy life suddenly undrawn, and those immortal agonies, that never-dying death, made known in the way of direct perception,—and those, it may be, that such a one, with the keen sympathies so characteristic of the Christian, loves and values, seen to be at last among the victims of that irreparable doom,—can we doubt that he would come forth with intellect blanched and idealess from a sight too terrible for any whose faculties are not on the scale of eternity itself? It is God's mercy that we can believe what adequately to conceive were death.

Let us take advantage of this merciful dispensation: let us dare to speak about these eternal miseries as matter to which reason may address itself; with awe indeed, but, as yet, without being utterly lost and consumed in the terrible truth it contemplates.

It is the peculiarity of the Christian mysteries, that, though they be separately impenetrable, there is a wondrous consistency among them all. Each member of the system is incomprehensible, but it is seen to be a *system* still. We can feel, even by the little we do see of their bearing, that there is some remote centre far away in infinity to which they all converge; some heliocentric point (so to speak) from which, could we gain it, the whole vast system would be seen to revolve in perfect simplicity. It is thus, that while on the one hand appalled and perplexed with the eternity of punishment, we can yet see it to be but the counterpart of that other mystery of the unspeakable malignity of sin, which itself is demonstrated by that third tremendous mystery of the Divine Atonement it required. Doubtless, then, the true ground of the equity of this most awful dispensation of punishment is to be found in the infinite criminality of sin—of the voluntary contradiction by any subordinate will of the supreme all-righteous Will of the Universe; which we may well conceive to involve in it something incomparably more fearful than our miserable familiarity with the fact ever allows us practically to realize. It may also be considered (as our great divine, Jackson, has forcibly reasoned, Book XI.) that the punishment in this case is not merely in proportion to sin, but in proportion to the parallel eternity of glory offered. It is the punishment of beings to whom eternal life has been tendered, and by whom it has been rejected, of beings who have had an option, and have taken their choice. "*This is the condemnation, that light is come into the world,* and men loved darkness rather than light." It must be obvious that against *any* enormously long and severe punishment (and hardly any interpreter can pretend that Scripture does not, at least, affirm that) similar difficulties, in point of mere human estimates of equity, would arise—a consideration plainly evincing that the guilt of sin is something vastly beyond our apprehensions; and this once fairly admitted, what proof have we that it is not in the fullest sense infinitely beyond them; that is to say, such that no finite punishment can exhaust its real deserts? And as the punishment deserved and atonement accepted are in all ordinary conceptions of even human justice strictly correspondent, I am sure I need not again remind you how the infinite dignity of the atonement our sin required does in the most awful and impressive manner corroborate this view; for the sin which deserved but temporal punishment a created nature might atone; a divine expiation infers a boundless guilt, and boundless demerit; so that, terrific as is the dreadful truth we preach, it is most manifest that the harmony of the revealed system is utterly lost without it. These are mysteries indeed, but mysteries mutually related, and that suppose and demand each other; these are depths, no doubt, but even so, "deep calleth unto deep."

Still, that an everlasting state should be made wholly to depend on so brief a period, the fortunes of an eternity to turn upon the little dreamlike moment of this preliminary existence—this, it may be said, seems only the more overwhelming, the more we attain to fitting conceptions of eternity itself. Mysterious it is, indeed, yet no wholly unparalleled mystery. The case stands thus: In the present state means are given for the formation of a variety of characters; the distinction of the future states is, that they admit of but one respectively, and that permanent, for everlasting. Now as far as anything temporal can shadow forth the eternal, common experience furnishes numberless instances of the very same principle, of short periods determining periods indefinitely long; the brief but trying stage of infancy once past, health becomes comparatively secure: nay, upon the briefer period antecedent to birth, (and which presents so many striking analogies to our entire present state on earth, as related to the future state,) how largely health, and life itself, depend. The same general principle really seems to operate through the whole organized creation; in the vegetable kingdom the seed which a worm might destroy while beneath the soil, once but a little above it, expands into a tree of ages, the parent, it may be, of a forest. In every "critical case" (as we term it), of whatever kind, we have the same phenomenon repeated; minute diligence for a short period settles things for an indefinite one, for a period which, if we take in all the indirect results of human action, may be styled literally endless. Indeed, that even upon the merest *trifles* immense results perpetually depend, is proverbial. Take one dozen great names —names of men whose birth was itself the merest contingency; blot those twelve names—those twelve accidents—from the annals of mankind—twelve out of countless millions; and you alter, perhaps reverse, the whole history of the world. Not, however, to press this, we cannot, on the whole, fail to see how the principle of brief exertion, determining immense results of happiness or misery, constantly applies to our own daily life. The soul, if it be indeed immortal, must be of *some* character and some destiny, both dependent on *some* determining cause; and no possible reason can be assigned why that character and that destiny may not be finally determined *now*, at least, as well as at any other period of its endless existence.

But there is a point of view from which the whole of this awful dispensation of punishment appears conceivable with comparative simplicity; in which its miseries may be seen to enter into the course of natural justice; and become directly proportional to the guilt they avenge. The view which I am about to present seems to me to cast a real, though a fearful light upon the horrors of this doom, making them at once more intelligible, and more terrific, than before.

It cannot, then, be doubted that the character of ungodliness with which the lost spirit leaves this world is perpetuated to the state of being that follows it.* But much more than this is too awfully probable. The aggravating effect of mutual association in vice, the corrupting example of matured and hardened wickedness, and, above all, the desolating influence of utter despair, are facts notorious in the present world, miserably notorious in our own prisons and penal settlements; but which must be exhibited on a gigantic scale, in the region of hopeless and abandoned depravity, of which, with fear and trembling, I now dare to speak. The total absence of all divine grace leaving every evil propensity to rank luxuriance, the presence of all the accursed stimulants to desperate impiety, must surely combine to make the sinner, the punished sinner of this life, progressively, unceasingly, the everlasting sinner

---

* See on this Aquin. Sentent. IV. Dist. 50 :—
"Si mali in inferno peccabunt."

of the life that succeeds it. In this way of conceiving them, the *punishments of hell* are but the perpetual vengeance that accompanies the *sins of hell*. An eternity of wickedness brings with it an eternity of woe. The sinner is to suffer for everlasting, but it is because the sin itself is as everlasting as the suffering.

It is manifest that this is but to prolong the very connexion (of moral and physical evil) we all believe to be realized here. Nor can any objection to its probability, or its justice, be alleged which would not equally apply to the punishments of time, indeed to the idea of punishment at all. The supposition on which it turns—the perpetuation of sin itself in the world of suffering—is so far from requiring proof, that proof would really be required to establish the contrary. They who start at the disproportion of an eternal punishment to a temporary sin, cannot deny the proportion when the sin and the punishment are alike eternal; when the surrender of the soul to the moral evil it has chosen (a principle universally recognised in Scripture) is made the direct punishment of its earthly choice, and all else follows in the way of exact and proportioned penalty: while, if it be urged—wildly urged—that the sufferer might be annihilated, and so the miserable bond of wickedness and woe dissolved for ever,—we reply, so too he *might* never have existed; at any moment you select in the countless ages to come, how should that wretched spirit cease to exist on any ground which will not be as applicable to any *other* period, or which will not equally show he ought never to have existed *at all?*

There are one or two reasons why this mode of conceiving the dreadful subject before us seems to me to be eminently impressive and practical; and with them I shall conclude.

In the first place, it strongly illustrates (what so often perplexes even good and pious men) the tremendous doom of the *merely worldly*—the special object of the awful narrative in the gospel of this day. For it must in this view be evident, that no high visible manifestation or development of earthly wickedness is at all needed to produce the terrible results I speak of, any more than it is necessary that, in any ordinary case, a man should *begin* with absolute depravity. It is quite enough that there be in him the unexpressed, but real and habitual, choice of this world and its common corruptions as his portion, the deadness to celestial motives, the mind that is after the flesh. Such a man has in substance made his election. He who dies with this predisposition of the inward moral state is plainly unfit for heaven. And if you hesitate (as perhaps we are all at times tempted to do) to pronounce him directly deserving of eternal suffering, you cannot surely fail to see that he has in him the deadly germ of an unrighteousness that, when all restraints are removed—hope, and fear, and reputation, and the rest,—and all the fostering influences of a climate of perpetual sin, present and active, will inevitably quicken into that full maturity of wickedness for which misery, as enduring as itself, is the appropriate doom. The voluptuary, in the parable, retained still some of the better natural elements of humanity: "I have five brethren," was the intercession of no unamiable compassion. How long he retained even that poor relic of the boasted social virtues of this life—the virtues whose imaginary excellency, perhaps, flattered him to his ruin,—they can conjecture who remember how the misery of utter despair (history, nay, our own observation, abounds with such revelations) can wither every natural affection, trample out the very rudiments of our humanity, and almost make us in this world the conscienceless demons whose nature and presence is the worst horror we can conceive in the world to come.

But again, and closely connected with this, the representation I have submitted is calculated to impress on us all the necessity of an infinitely severer scrutiny of the real bias of our question, as I have exhibited it, will not be what I am, but what I am formed to *become;* not, what gross evil, with all the weight of social restraints, (like that of the atmosphere, unfelt because universal,) pressing me on all sides, I actually escape, but *what*, were these removed and I alone with only my faith and fear of God to control me, I *would* overcome. In this view *sudden temptation* sometimes effects frightful disclosures. It is commonly said, that such temptations are eminently excusable, because temporary surprises, isolated facts, that have no influence on, and give little indication of, our average state. I doubt this position. More frequently are they disclosures of what has all along been our state, latent from lack of opportunity, but now suddenly starting into manifestation the instant the appropriate occasion is offered. It is this that justifies, I fear, to the full, those delineations of human corruption which are so often charged with exaggeration. The true test and estimate of man is not what he does, but what with his present principles he *would do.* The petty corruption you dismiss as venial is *so far* a preference of evil to good; the deadliest sin is no more. But take this petty corruption with you from the world; bring it, and all your self-forgiven weaknesses, when they shall have scope to prove their real nature; and even as by the contemplation of God (as His inspired servants tell us), the blessed "are changed into the same image from glory to glory," "like Him, because seeing Him as He is;" so, doubtless, by the presence, and the contact, and the fellowship of evil, the wretched, irresolute disciple, not wholly saved, and therefore wholly lost, rapidly in that dread abode darkens into the likeness he contemplates, loses each faint fading ray of good, assimilated at length, and absorbed into the hopeless, heartless misery that surrounds him for evermore.

And here let me close a theme which no man can approach without reluctance, or leave without relief. But those terrors which the Great Physician, amid all His tenderness, deemed needful for the treatment of our disease, let us, His ministers, beware how we disguise; let those who hear, with salutary awe receive. And as he who delivers these truths, is, after all, himself, quite as much as others, a bearer of his own message, so must he feel and acknowledge a deep peril lest, in the very act of investigating and methodising such truths, he become too familiar for reverence, and lose in the exercises of the understanding some degree of that holy fear which they who, without reasoning, retain, are happier far than mere reasoning could ever make them. And, therefore, whatever be the fate of human speculations on this tremendous topic, be it ours to cultivate the simplicity of faith which is independent of them. Even though in its vastness and mystery it continue to rebuke our feeble reason, let it stand in the naked simplicity of fact; a TRUTH great, and terrible, and certain; planted deep in the nature of God's attributes, and therefore unfathomable as all things are that are of Him; but withal, addressing itself to the simplest and strongest feelings of man, his dread of pain, his horror of shame and misery and death; meeting him at every turn to evil, and casting a fearful shadow across those pleasures that are not of God, and those glories where God's glory is forgotten; meeting *you*, my younger brethren, at the first fatal steps upon that course which ends in the abyss of woe it denounces, and warning you at once to flee the bondage of seductions which grow as they are obeyed, and strengthen with every victory; warning you, that all the temporal results of sin—the shame of detection, the loss of reputation, the ruin of prospects, the destruction of health, the early grave—all are but shadows of the overwhelming penalty it brings, when the mercy, which still restrains to these limits the fulness of divine vengeance, shall have ceased; and the sin and the punishment, which are now but temporary, passing together into the world of eternity, and still, as ever, bound in inseparable links, shall become themselves alike eternal!

LONDON: R. CLAY, SON, AND TAYLOR, PRINTERS,
BREAD STREET HILL.

www.ingramcontent.com/pod-product-compliance
Lightning Source LLC
Chambersburg PA
CBHW032034220426
43664CB00006B/468